A Textbook of Botany for Colleges and Universities, Part 1

A
TEXTBOOK OF BOTANY

FOR

COLLEGES AND UNIVERSITIES

BY MEMBERS OF THE BOTANICAL STAFF OF THE UNIVERSITY OF CHICAGO

JOHN MERLE COULTER, Ph.D.
PROFESSOR OF PLANT MORPHOLOGY

CHARLES REID BARNES, Ph.D.
LATE PROFESSOR OF PLANT PHYSIOLOGY

HENRY CHANDLER COWLES, Ph.D.
ASSISTANT PROFESSOR OF PLANT ECOLOGY

VOL. I., PART I. MORPHOLOGY

NEW YORK ∴ CINCINNATI ∴ CHICAGO
AMERICAN BOOK COMPANY

626121

COPYRIGHT, 1910, BY
AMERICAN BOOK COMPANY.

ENTERED AT STATIONERS' HALL, LONDON.

A TEXTBOOK OF BOTANY.

W. P. 2

PREFACE

The study of plants has assumed so many points of view that every laboratory has developed its own method of undergraduate instruction. No laboratory attempts to include all the phases of work that may be regarded as belonging to botany; and therefore each one selects the material and the point of view that seem to it to be the most appropriate for its own purpose. During the last ten years the Hull Botanical Laboratory at the University of Chicago has been developing its undergraduate instruction in botany to meet its own needs. Freed from the necessity of laying special stress upon the economic aspects of the subject, and compelled to prepare students for investigation, it seemed clear that its selection must be the fundamental facts and principles of the science. Its endeavor has been to help the student to build up a coherent and substantial body of knowledge, and to develop an attitude of mind that will enable him to grapple with any botanical situation, whether it be teaching or investigation. It has been thought useful to present this point of view in the present volume. The material of course is common to all laboratories, but its selection, its organization, and its presentation bear the marks of individual judgment.

The three parts of the book represent the three general divisions of the subject as organized at the Hull Botanical Laboratory. They are felt to be the fundamental divisions which should underlie the work of most subdivisions of botanical investigation. For example, a study of the very important subject of plant pathology must presuppose the fundamentals of morphology and physiology; paleobotany is, in part, the application of morphology and ecology to fossil plants; and scientific plant breeding rests upon the foundations laid by morphology, physiology, and ecology. In our selection for undergraduate instruction, therefore, we believe that there has been included the essential foundation for most of the varied work that is included to-day under botany.

We recognize that the presentation of the three great subjects here included is very compact, but the book is not intended for reading and recitation. The teacher is expected to use it for suggestive material and for its organization; the student is expected to use it in relating his observations to one another and to the general points of view that the book seeks to develop. There is a continuity of presentation in each part, so that random selection may miss the largest meaning. For example, in the part on morphology, the thread upon which the facts are strung is the evolution of the plant kingdom, and each plant introduced has its peculiar application in illustrating some phase of this evolution. When certain groups are selected for laboratory study, therefore, the intervening text should be read.

It is important to call attention to the fact that the book has been prepared for the use of undergraduate students. It does not represent our conception of graduate work, which should include much that is omitted here. For example, the graduate student should be introduced to the original sources of information, which would involve an extensive citation of literature far beyond the needs of the undergraduate. Still less has this book been written for our professional colleagues, who will notice what they may regard as glaring omissions. Such omissions must be taken to express a deliberate judgment as to what may be omitted with the least damage to the undergraduate student. The motive is to develop certain general conceptions that are felt to be fundamental, rather than to present an encyclopedic collection of facts. This purpose has demanded occasionally also a greater apparent rigidity of form in general statements than is absolutely consistent with all the facts; but it was a choice between a clear and important conception for one with no perspective and a contradiction of large truths by isolated facts, resulting in confusion. For the same reasons, the extensive terminology of the subject has been kept in the background as much as possible. Definitions usually are made an incident to the necessary introduction of terms. It is assumed that in so far as the definite application of a term may not seem clear, the student will find a compact definition in the current dictionaries.

PREFACE

For the benefit of the teacher and of our professional colleagues, it should be stated that much attention has been given to the avoidance of any phraseology that might involve a teleological implication. It has not been possible to avoid such phrases in all cases without introducing clumsiness of expression or breaking the continuity of some important series of structures or events. It should be kept in mind, therefore, that all teleological implications of language that remain are disavowed.

It seems hardly necessary to say that most of the material presented in the book has been worked over by classes repeatedly. Some new matter has been developed incidentally in all the parts in connection with ordinary laboratory and field work; and especially in Part III have many scattered observations and some new points of view been included. There has been no intention to include any formal contribution, but merely to present in general outline some of the material worked over by undergraduates, some of the results of investigation already published in contributions from the laboratory, and some observations and conclusions that hardly seemed to justify separate publication. Provision has been made for students with more interest or more time than usual to get a somewhat larger view, by including in smaller type further details of structure, additional illustrative material, and suggestive theories. Most of the illustrations are original, in the sense that they have been prepared especially for this book or have appeared in our own contributions. Those that have been copied or adapted are credited; the former usually being indicated by "from," the latter by "after."

The three authors are individually responsible only for their own parts, and, while they had the advantage of mutual criticism, it could not be expected that they would agree absolutely at every point. This will explain any lack of harmony that may be discovered in the three parts. A morphologist, a physiologist, and an ecologist look at the same material from different angles, and lay emphasis upon different features; but all their points of view should be included in any general consideration of plants. It is for this reason, also, that the parts contain a certain amount of repetition, which is absolutely necessary when the same structures or functions are being considered from different points of view.

The selection and preparation of the illustrations for Part I were under the efficient direction of Dr. W. J. G. LAND, and most of the original drawings of the book were made by Miss ANNA HAMILTON, an artist to whom great credit is due. We owe certain original illustrations to the cooperation of our colleagues, who are named in connection with the figures; and also some of the drawings in Part III to Miss ANNA M. STARR. In addition to the mutual criticism of the authors, Dr. C. J. CHAMBERLAIN, Dr. WILLIAM CROCKER, and Mr. GEORGE D. FULLER made helpful suggestions in reading the proof. For such errors as remain, after all our efforts to eliminate them, the authors themselves assume full responsibility. In correcting them, we shall welcome the help of the wider circle of users to whom the book now goes.

JOHN M. COULTER.
CHARLES R. BARNES.
HENRY C. COWLES.

THE UNIVERSITY OF CHICAGO.

CONTENTS

VOL. I., PART I. MORPHOLOGY

CHAPTER	PAGE
I. Thallophytes	1
1. Myxomycetes	1
2. Schizophytes	4
(1) Cyanophyceae	4
(2) Schizomycetes	10
3. Algae	14
(1) Chlorophyceae	15
(a) Volvocales	15
(b) Protococcales	20
(c) Confervales	24
(d) Siphonales	33
(e) Conjugales	37
(f) Charales	41
(2) Phaeophyceae	44
(a) Phaeosporales	45
(b) Fucales	49
(3) Rhodophyceae	54
4. Fungi	61
(1) Phycomycetes	62
(a) Oomycetes	62
(b) Zygomycetes	67
(2) Ascomycetes	70
(a) Protoascales	70
(b) Protodiscales	71
(c) Helvellales	71
(d) Pezizales	71
(e) Tuberales	74
(f) Plectascales	74
(g) Pyrenomycetales	75
(h) Laboulbeniales	77
Lichens	78
(3) Basidiomycetes	80
(a) Ustilaginales	81
(b) Uredinales	82
(c) Auriculariales	86
(d) Tremellales	86
(e) Dacromycetales	86
(f) Exobasidiales	86
(g) Thelephorales	87
(h) Clavariales	87

CHAPTER	PAGE
(I) (i) Agaricales	87
(j) Hymenogastrales	90
(k) Sclerodermales	90
(l) Lycoperdales	90
(m) Nidulariales	90
(n) Phallales	90
Lichens	91
II. Bryophytes	92
1. Hepaticae	93
(1) Marchantiales	93
(2) Jungermanniales	101
(a) Anacrogynae	101
(b) Acrogynae	103
(3) Anthocerotales	106
2. Musci	110
(1) Sphagnales	110
(2) Andreaeales	114
(3) Bryales	115
III. Pteridophytes	122
(1) Lycopodiales	122
(2) Psilotales	142
(3) Sphenophyllales	143
(4) Equisetales	143
(5) Ophioglossales	149
(6) Filicales	155
(a) Filicineae	155
(b) Hydropteridineae	170
IV. Spermatophytes	180
A. Gymnosperms	181
(1) Cycadofilicales	181
(2) Bennettitales	185
(3) Cycadales	190
(4) Cordaitales	203
(5) Ginkgoales	207
(6) Coniferales	212
(a) Taxaceae	212
(b) Pinaceae	219
(7) Gnetales	228

CHAPTER	PAGE	CHAPTER	PAGE
(IV) B. Angiosperms	238	(IV) Classification	276
Stem	239	Monocotyledons	276
Root	247	Archichlamydeae	279
Leaf	250	Sympetalae	280
Flower	251	V. Organic Evolution	283
Stamen	256	Environment	284
Carpel	260	Use and disuse	284
Female gametophyte	264	Natural selection	285
Male gametophyte	267	Mutation	288
Fertilization	268	Orthogenesis	289
Endosperm	270	Weismannism	290
Embryo	271	Isolation	292
Parthenogenesis	275	Mendel's law	292
Polyembryony	275	Heredity	293

PART I — MORPHOLOGY

CHAPTER I — THALLOPHYTES

Introductory. — Thallophytes form the lowest great division of the plant kingdom, the name meaning "thallus plants." A thallus is a plant body in which there is little or no differentiation of vegetative organs. Among the higher plants differentiation results in such distinct vegetative organs as stems and leaves. A thallus body does not distinguish thallophytes absolutely, for some thallophytes have differentiated vegetative bodies, and thallus bodies are found in other groups of plants. However, the greatest display of thallus bodies is found among thallophytes, and the name is reasonably distinctive.

As the thallophytes include the lowest plants, the group is especially interesting as representing the living forms nearest to the beginnings of the plant kingdom. Among these plants the beginnings of structures are found that are observed to become modified in various ways in the higher groups. A fundamental conception of the plant kingdom is that it begins with simple forms and advances gradually to more complex forms, until the highest group of plants is reached. To appreciate this evolution of the plant kingdom it is necessary to study plants in this order, beginning with the thallophytes.

A natural classification of thallophytes, which means a classification based upon relationships, is impossible at present, and any presentation of them must be more or less artificial. Two groups stand out conspicuously, known as *Algae* and *Fungi*; but there are other groups of thallophytes whose relationships are puzzling. Sometimes the latter groups are distributed among algae and fungi, but this is far from satisfactory. In the following presentation the doubtful groups will be kept separate from the true algae and fungi.

1. MYXOMYCETES

General description. — These organisms are commonly known as slime molds or slime fungi. They combine characters of plants and of animals in such a way that opinions differ as to whether they should be regarded as plants or animals. Those who incline to the view that they are animals use the term *Mycetozoa* (fungus animals) for the group. It should not be surprising to find at the lower confines of the plant and animal kingdoms organisms which do not appear to belong to either.

The lowest slime molds are aquatic, but most of them are terrestrial, being common in forests on humous soil, decaying wood, fallen leaves, etc., and one of the largest occurs on spent tan bark. The body contains no chlorophyll, and this fact has induced many to regard slime molds as fungi. The absence of chlorophyll means inability to manufacture food, and hence a dependent habit, slime molds being for the most part saprophytes (see p. 61).

Plant body. — The characteristic body is called the *plasmodium*, which is a naked mass of protoplasm (the living substance) with a creeping motion, putting out and withdrawing regions of its body (*pseudopodia*) like a gigantic amoeba (see p. 444). This slimy body is for a time very sensitive to light, in the case of the slime mold of tan, for example, shrinking away from it into the crevices of its substratum. Within the body there are found embedded many nuclei (protoplasmic organs), and streaming movements in the cytoplasm (the general protoplasm) may be observed (fig. 1). The most unplantlike behavior of the plasmodium is its habit of engulfing solid food instead of admitting it in solution, and within the body may be seen engulfed bacteria and other minute organisms. Under certain conditions, the whole plasmodium or parts of it become encysted, the surface becoming hardened and often crusty and inclosing a mass of resting protoplasm of waxlike consistency. These hardened masses are called *sclerotia*, and are wonderfully resistant, being capable of renewing their activity after remaining dry for years.

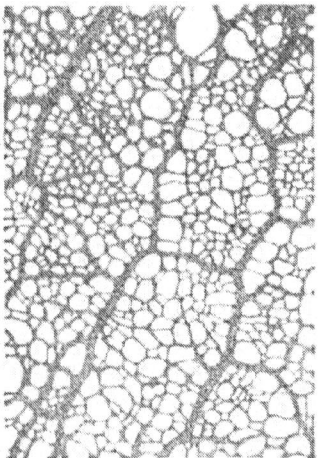

FIG. 1. — A small portion of the plasmodium of a slime mold (*Fuligo*), highly magnified; the cytoplasm is very vacuolate, so that it appears as a network of strands of varying width, in which numerous nuclei may be observed. — Adapted from LISTER.

THALLOPHYTES 3

Reproduction. — At the time of reproduction, the plasmodium comes to the surface of its substratum, sometimes climbing along various supports, and then locomotion ceases. The whole plasmodium then forms a single-stalked *sporangium* (spore case); or it organizes several regions, each of which produces a sporangium, the sporangia often forming a close cluster (fig. 2). In sporangium formation the pulsating advance of the protoplasm has been observed, forming the hollow stalk and finally the terminal spore case, whose wall hardens into a firm sheath. Nothing is left of the unused plasmodium except a network of tough strands. The spore case is exceedingly variable in form and general appearance, and often within it there is organized a network of tubes known as the *capillitium*. In the meshes of this network countless spores are formed, with cellulose walls, most characteristic reproductive cells of plants. The wall of the spore case dries and ruptures, and the hygroscopic capillitium expands, often carrying up and exposing the spores to dispersal.

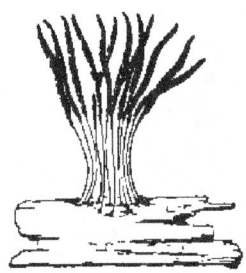

FIG. 2.— A group of sporangia of *Stemonitis*, arising from a plasmodium on a fragment of wood, showing the slender stalks and linear spore cases.

The structure of the sporangium is not always so complicated as the one described, for sometimes there is no capillitium, and sometimes there is no stalk. Even the spore case may be lacking, the spores being cut off from branches sent out from the stalk. A still greater modification in spore formation is exhibited in such forms as the common flowers of tan (*Fuligo*), in which no distinct sporangia are seen, but the whole plasmodium and sometimes several blended plasmodia become transformed into a cushion-like or cakelike mass, known as the *aethalium*. Within the aethalium the spores are found in irregular chambers, which may be taken to represent a confused mass of indefinite and blended sporangia.

Life history. — In following the life history from spore to plasmodium great variations are encountered, for at every stage there is exhibited extreme sensitiveness to external conditions. A representative series of stages is as follows: From the spore wall the amoeboid protoplast escapes and soon develops a single cilium or flagellum, by means of which it moves very actively. This ciliated cell has quite the appearance of certain low animals in structure as well as in movements, and it multiplies freely by division. Eventually the cilium disappears and the cell becomes amoeba-like again, and in this condition it may multiply indefinitely by division. Finally these amoeboid cells begin to coalesce and a plasmodium is gradually built up (fig. 3). The individual amoeba-like cells that enter into the structure of the plasmodium may lose their identity or not, but their nuclei do not fuse. A plasmodium, therefore, is a mass of coalesced naked cells, each represented in the complex body at least by its nucleus. It would be confusing to indicate the variations that may occur in this life history. It is sufficient to say that the flagellum stage is regularly absent in certain forms, and that the flagellum stage and amoeba stage may encyst repeatedly before the formation of a plasmodium.

FIG. 3.—A small group of amoeboid cells, each containing a distinct nucleus, beginning to coalesce in the formation of a plasmodium.—Adapted from SACHS.

In general it may be said that the structure and behavior of the nutritive body of these organisms would seem to relate them to animals; but that the reproductive structures are just as distinctly those of plants.

2. SCHIZOPHYTES

The name of the group means "fission plants," referring to the fact that the characteristic cell divisions occur in rapid succession and represent the only method of reproduction. The two divisions of schizophytes are distinguished in general by the presence and absence of chlorophyll, which means that one group comprises independent, food-manufacturing plants, and that the other comprises parasites and saprophytes (see p. 61).

(1) CYANOPHYCEAE

General description.—These are the blue-green algae, as indicated by the name, and very commonly they are presented as one of the groups of algae. This association is made chiefly because of the presence of chlorophyll, but the differences from the true algae are so important that the ability to manufacture food should not outweigh them. A consistent name for the group is *Schizophyceae* (fission algae), but we have retained the name which is in far more common use, and which refers to the most conspicuous feature of the group, namely, the usual presence of a blue pigment (phycocyanin) in addition to the green. This association of chlorophyll (?) and phycocyanin gives to the plants, at least in mass, a characteristic bluish green color, quite distinct from the yellow-green color of the green algae.[1]

The Cyanophyceae are found everywhere in fresh and salt water; and also on damp soil, rocks, bark, etc. A conspicuous free-floating form gives the characteristic hue to the Red Sea, a fact which indicates that "blue-green" algae may be red. They occur also in the water of hot springs, thriving in a temperature that most other plants could not endure. The sinter deposits which give character and attraction to the craters of the hot springs and geysers of the Yellowstone National Park, for example, are associated in some way with the presence of Cyanophyceae. Many of the group are also endophytic in habit; that is, they live within cavities of other plants, as in *Anthoceros*, *Azolla*, roots of cycads, etc.; and still others enter into the structure of those composite organisms known as lichens.

A general conception of the group may be obtained by examining a few common forms.

Gloeocapsa.[2] — The adult individual is a single spherical cell (fig. 4), and therefore the body is as simple as it can be, if cells are to be regarded as the units of the gross structure of plants. This single cell consists of a protoplast invested by a wall, and among Cyanophyceae in general the protoplast has no such obvious organization as among the true algae. In general it may be differentiated into two regions: a peripheral zone, colored throughout by the green and blue pigments; and a central region (central body), containing no pigment, and now concluded to be a nucleus. In both regions small granules appear. This differentiation of a pigment region from the rest of the protoplast is not apparent among all the blue-green algae, for in some (as *Gloeocapsa*) the pigments seem to be diffused throughout the protoplast, but in others (as *Oscillatoria*, fig. 6) it is quite

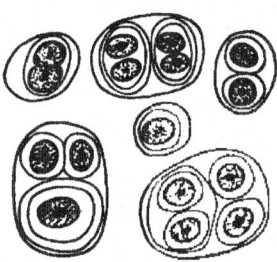

FIG. 4. — *Gloeothece*: a single plant in the center, showing the protoplast surrounded by the swollen wall and a layer of mucilage; the other figures show various stages of cell-multiplication, the cells being embedded in the gelatinous matrix produced by their walls.

---

[1] The precise nature and relations of the pigment or pigments of this group are uncertain. It is possible that there is a single pigment which splits into blue and green constituents.

[2] *Gloeothece* is a form closely related to *Gloeocapsa*, from which it differs chiefly in its somewhat elongated cells.

MORPHOLOGY

evident, and represents all the organization that has been found in this group. This apparently simple structure of the protoplast is in striking contrast with that found in the true algae and in all higher plants.

The division of the cell is of equal simplicity, for it takes place by the development of a ringlike wall which grows inward and cuts the protoplast in two, the central body (or nucleus) also playing a part. This process of cell-division is the only method of reproduction among the Cyanophyceae, a method known as vegetative multiplication, and meaning that an ordinary working cell (individual) divides and forms two new individuals.

In *Gloeocapsa* the cells may be observed in various stages of division, but the multiplying cells (individuals) are held together mechanically in a gradually accumulating gelatinous matrix (fig. 4), this swelling mucilaginous material being derived from the cell walls, which are being renewed constantly from within by the protoplast. This formation of mucilage by the walls and the imbedding of cells is characteristic of the Cyanophyceae. These groups of cells held together mechanically are spoken of as colonies. In *Gloeocapsa* the colonies are irregular and indefinite, but among other Cyanophyceae they will be observed to assume very definite forms.

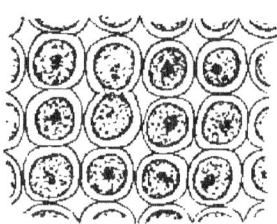

FIG. 5.—*Merismopedia*: a portion of a colony, showing the one-celled plants in rectangular arrangement, and all held together by the gelatinous matrix; in one case cell-division has not been completed.

Merismopedia.— In this form, very common in ponds, the cells are arranged so as to produce a remarkably regular rectangular colony (fig. 5). It is evident that this rectangular form is determined by a series of perfectly regular and simultaneous divisions in two directions.

Oscillatoria. — In this well-known form the colony has become a simple filament, and the mucilage sheath is so thin as to be visible only in specially prepared sections (fig. 6). In the related *Lyngbya* the sheath is quite evident. In these forms a filament is built up because the successive cell-divisions are all in the same direction. Each cell of the *Oscillatoria* filament, excepting the end ones, has the form of a short cylinder, indicating that the ends of each cell have been flattened by the pressure of the contiguous cells. At the end of the filament the free surface of the end cell is seen to be convex; and where some cell in the filament has become destroyed, as mentioned below, the adjacent walls of the two neighboring cells are observed to bulge out. The filament does not grow indefinitely in length, but breaks up now and then by the disorganization of one or more cells, and each fragment begins to construct another colony. This process of fragmentation results in the multiplication of colonies, which may be called colonization.

The protoplast of *Oscillatoria* exhibits the two regions described under *Gloeocapsa* for Cyanophyceae in general; in fact, this differentiation is probably more evident in *Oscillatoria* than in any other common form. The most striking feature of the plant, however, is the characteristic swaying and revolving movement of the filaments, a movement which suggested the name. If a mass of filaments be placed on a solid substratum, the filaments begin a creeping movement and become spread out radiately in a film. It is evident that this movement is possible only as the cells of a filament work together, and this introduces into a colony of cells the idea of an individual composed of many cells. In fact, the many-celled colony merges so gradually into the many-celled individual that there is no boundary between the two.

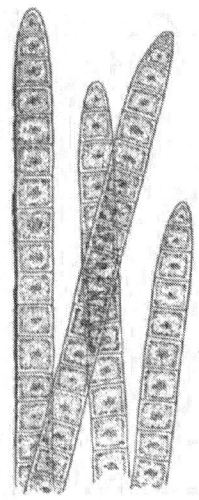

FIG. 6.—*Oscillatoria:* the cells of the simple filaments show the differentiation of the protoplast into the peripheral pigment region and the central region; in the center of the latter there appears an irregular aggregation of dark material (*chromatin*) characteristic of a nucleus.

Nostoc.—In this form the colony is also a filament, but when the cells divide, they so nearly separate and round off that they become tangent to one another, resulting in a filament resembling a string of beads. Each filament has its own mucilaginous sheath, as in *Lyngbya*, but there is an extraordinary development of mucilage in connection with groups of filaments. As a consequence, *Nostoc* appears in nature as lumps of jelly, in which numerous filaments are found embedded (figs. 7, 8).

The most noticeable fact in reference to these filaments is that the cells are not all alike. At intervals cells appear which differ in contents and usually in size from the ordinary working cells. They are derived from ordinary working cells, which usually enlarge, lose their contents, and become thick-walled. The loss of pigments makes these cells stand out very distinctly in the filament. They are called *heterocysts*, but this means only "other cells," and suggests nothing as to their behavior. By means of the heterocysts, therefore, the working cells of a filament

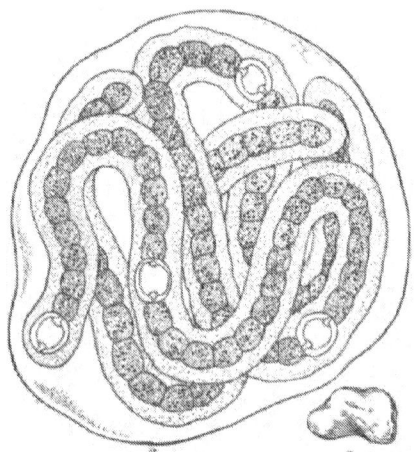

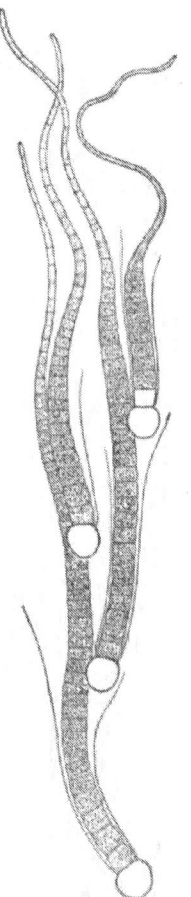

FIGS. 7, 8.—*Nostoc:* 7, the jelly-like mass in which the filaments are embedded; 8, filamentous colonies coiled within the gelatinous matrix; four heterocysts shown, dividing the filaments into hormogonia.

are separated into distinct sections, and these sections are called *hormogonia*. It has been observed that when colonization occurs, the heterocysts anchor the filament, and that the hormogonia break loose from them and wriggle out through the jelly-like matrix and establish new colonies. So far as observed, therefore, this differentiation of heterocysts seems to be associated with the fragmentation of the filament.

Nostoc illustrates well an ordinary plant method of enduring an unfavorable season, as winter. At the inception of the period of danger, certain cells of the filament enlarge, accumulate reserve food, and become thick-

FIG. 9.—*Rivularia:* the filaments show the basal heterocysts and the whip-like extension of the apex.

walled. These cells are able to endure cold or drought; and upon the return of favorable conditions, the heavy wall is broken through and a beginning filament emerges. These resting vegetative cells are

THALLOPHYTES 9

often called *arthrospores*, but they are not spores in the same sense as are those which characterize higher plants. In its life history, therefore, *Nostoc* displays three kinds of cells: vegetative cells, heterocysts, and resting cells.

A common form very closely related to *Nostoc* is *Anabaena*, whose name ought to be familiar, but whose separation from *Nostoc* need not be attempted by the elementary student.

Rivularia. — This form may be taken to represent the extreme differentiation of a colony. It is a compact, filamentous plant, like *Oscillatoria;* but the basal cell of the filament is a heterocyst, and the apex of the filament tapers into a very slender, whiplike extension (fig. 9). In this case the filament has a distinct base and apex.

Tolypothrix. — This plant serves to illustrate what is called false branching. It is a filament with distributed heterocysts, and, therefore, composed of several

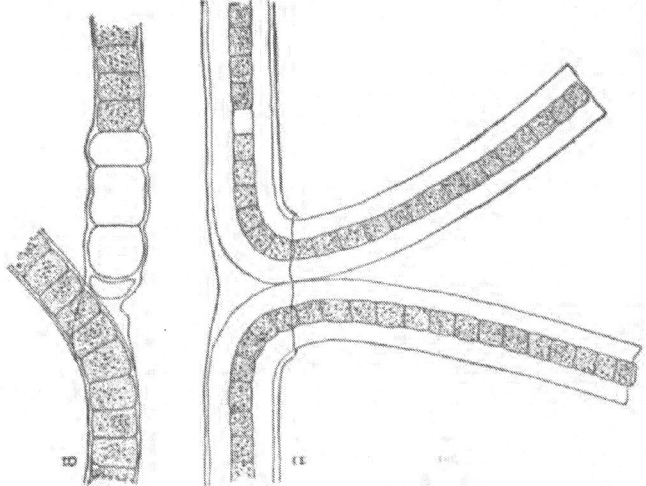

FIGS. 10, 11. — False branching: 10, *Tolypothrix*, showing false branching by a hormogonium pushing past a heterocyst; 11, *Scytonema*, showing false branching by the pushing outward of two abutting cells of a hormogonium, each of which continues division.

hormogonia. In some cases the end of a hormogonium pushes past a heterocyst and continues division, giving the appearance of a lateral branch (fig. 10). In other cases, as in *Scytonema*, a hormogonium may continue to increase in length without breaking away from the heterocysts, and the pressure results in pushing some two abutting cells outward, each of these two cells then being free to continue the development of a filament (fig. 11).

Stigonema. — In some Cyanophyceae, however, true branching occurs, and this is illustrated by such forms as *Stigonema*, in which branches are started by lateral outgrowths from individual cells of the filament rather than by mechanically freeing some of the cells (fig. 12).

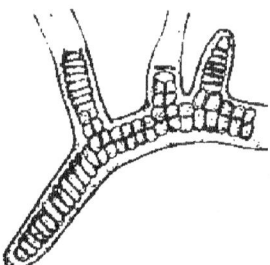

FIG. 12.—*Stigonema:* showing true branching.—After BORZI.

Conclusions. — A brief summary of the important features of the Cyanophyceae may be stated as follows: —

(1) The plant body is a single cell, and the general tendency is to organize a colony of cells into the form of a simple filament.

(2) There is a characteristic mucilaginous swelling of the walls, which favors colony formation by imbedding the individual cells.

(3) The protoplast is apparently simple in organization, giving no evidence of distinct chloroplasts, and with a nucleus ordinarily not sharply limited by a membrane, both of which features are in contrast with the protoplasts of true algae.

(4) There is some differentiation of cells, notably in the formation of heterocysts; and differentiation reaches its extreme expression in such forms as *Rivularia*, with base and apex.

(5) The power of locomotion is evident in the group, notably in *Oscillatoria*, and also in connection with colonization by means of hormogonia.

(6) The only method of reproduction known is vegetative multiplication, and the cell divides by an ingrowing wall plate.

(7) Protection against unfavorable conditions is provided for by the transformation of ordinary vegetative cells into resting cells, the chief changes being enlargement, accumulation of reserve food, and a heavy wall.

(2) SCHIZOMYCETES

General description. — The name means fission fungi, and corresponds in form to Schizophyceae (fission algae), a name often applied to the blue-green algae. However, they are best known as *bacteria*. The group has many characters in common with the Cyanophyceae, such as the one-celled body which often forms filaments (colonies), a protoplast of simple structure, the tendency in certain conditions to produce a mucilaginous matrix that embeds the cells, the power of locomotion, and reproduction only by vegetative multiplication, the cell-divisions being simple but in remarkably rapid succession. However, in most forms there is no chlorophyll, so that bacteria in the main are parasites and saprophytes.

The immense economic importance of bacteria has stimulated their investigation to such an extent that bacteriology has become a distinct field of research, with its special technique. An outline of plant morphology can only indicate the existence of this great region of research, for to enter it would demand a course in bacteriology; but bacteria are plants, and their general place among other plants must be considered.

Bacteria include the smallest known organisms, cells having been measured that are only 0.0005 mm. in diameter. The cells are either solitary or they may form filaments, as among the Cyanophyceae. For general purposes, individual cells are often referred to three form groups: *coccus* forms, in which the cells are spherical; *bacterium* or *bacillus* forms, in which the cells are oblong or have the form of short rods; and *spirillum* forms, in which the cells are curved (figs. 13–20). When these various forms of cells enter into the structure of filaments, corresponding variations in the form of the filaments follow.

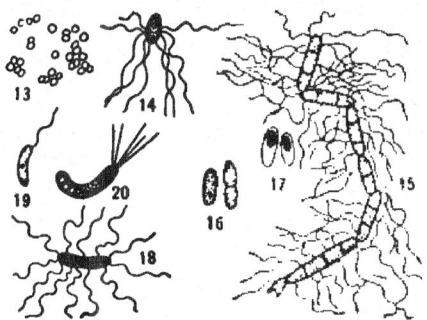

FIGS. 13–20. — *Bacteria:* 13, coccus form, from pus; 14–18, bacillus forms (14–17, hay bacillus); 14, motile cell; 15, filament of motile cells; 16, non-motile cells; 17, cells with "spores"; 18, typhoid-fever form (*Bacillus typhi*); 19, 20, spirillum forms; 19, cholera form (*Vibrio cholerae*); 20, *Spirillum undula*. — After A. FISCHER.

The occurrence of bacteria may be described as almost literally everywhere: in waters of every depth, in air, in soil, in all organic bodies, living or dead, etc. Their resistance to conditions impossible for other plants to endure is remarkable — a feature suggested by their associates, the Cyanophyceae. Extreme cold, high temperatures, and desiccation that would destroy ordinary plants are successfully withstood by bacteria.

Structure. — The structure of the bacterial cell appears to be extremely simple; in fact it may be said to be almost structureless. The protoplast is invested by a membrane, appears to be homogeneous, and usually contains a few granules. It seems not to have even such simple differentiation as occurs in the cells of certain Cyanophyceae; but in all such cases it must be kept in mind that we are dealing with very minute objects and that presently a technique may be developed that will reveal an amount of organization that we have no means of seeing at present.

Many of the bacteria are ciliated, the cilia being distributed over the body in various ways, and always extremely difficult to detect. These ciliated forms are very active, and their movements have suggested that bacteria are animals. Under certain conditions many bacteria pass into a quiescent stage and collect in colonies that are held together by a gelatinous matrix formed from the walls. These quiescent colonies, thus embedded, form characteristic pellicles on nutrient media, as on a decoction of hay, on bouillon, on stagnant water, and on various solid media. This quiescent, pellicle-forming stage is known as the *zoogloea* stage.

Multiplication. — The multiplication of cells by division is exceedingly rapid, the progeny of one cell in twenty-four hours often running into many millions. As already said, these newly formed cells either separate or hang together in filaments. When the nutritive supply fails, the protoplasm condenses in the middle or end of the cell and becomes invested by a heavy membrane. These are the so-called spores, but they are really resting cells such as are formed among the Cyanophyceae, except that they are formed within the old cell. These resting cells are even more resistant than the ordinary vegetative cells. In favorable conditions the protecting membrane bursts and the protoplast resumes active division.

Cultures. — It is very difficult and often impossible to recognize species of bacteria by the appearance of the individual cells, but in mass cultures the colonies are often very distinct in form, color, structure, and effect on nutrient media. These mass cultures are made in liquid media or upon solid media (gelatin, agar, potato, etc.). For purposes of investigation pure cultures are absolutely necessary, which means the separation of the form under investigation from every other form with which it may be associated, a process requiring a special technique.

Activities. — Many bacteria are peculiar in that they are able to live in the absence of free oxygen, which in other plants is associated with the fundamental process of respiration. Such bacteria are called *anaerobic*, the contrasting term for those bacteria that need free oxygen being *aerobic*. These are not names of groups, but of two modes of life that may be found in any group. The activities and effects of bacteria are remarkable, many of them holding a most important relation to human interests. A very brief statement of some of these activities must suffice, but it may serve to indicate the economic importance of the group.

Saprophytic bacteria. — These forms attack the dead bodies or the organic products of plants and animals, and bring about putrefaction and fermentation. When they are excluded from such organic material, it does not decay or ferment, and the process of canning, for example, is intended to effect this exclusion. When protein material is attacked and broken up, there is an escape of ill-smelling compounds, causing the offensive odor associated with putrefaction. In fermentation, complex carbohydrates are attacked, and simpler substances, such as alcohol, carbon dioxid, lactic acid, butyric acid, etc., are produced from them, according to the kind of bacteria at work.

Pathogenic bacteria. — These are the disease-producing forms, their activities being connected with living organisms. The disease is the result either of a direct attack upon the tissues, or of the excretion of a poison (toxin), or of both. Modern medicine and surgery are largely based upon excluding or destroying or neutralizing these forms. Such diseases as erysipelas, tetanus, diphtheria, tuberculosis, typhoid fever, pneumonia, cholera, pear blight, cabbage rot, etc., are known to be bacterial diseases. Besides the dangerous forms which occasionally attack human beings, there are numerous harmless forms constantly present throughout the alimentary tract.

Nitrogen bacteria. — These are certain bacteria of the soil that are able to utilize the free nitrogen that exists in such abundance in the air. Ordinary green plants can use nitrogen only in certain of its compounds, so that the power of these bacteria is both remarkable and important. They are best known in connection with the tubercles of certain Leguminosae (figs. 1101, 1102), as the clovers, which can be used, therefore, in the restoration of nitrogen compounds to impoverished soil (see p. 379).

Nitrifying bacteria. — These are also soil forms, and although they contain no chlorophyll, they can manufacture their own food. They can obtain carbon from carbon dioxid, without the presence of either chlorophyll or light; and their "nitrification" consists in taking ammonia (and other simple nitrogen compounds) and oxidizing it to nitrous acid so that nitrites are formed, when these in turn are oxidized to nitrates, which are nitrogen-containing compounds available for green plants.

Iron bacteria. — These forms live in iron-containing waters, and as a result of their activities iron oxid is deposited in the gelatinous matrix. This characteristic reddish slimy deposit is exceedingly common about iron springs and their outlets.

Sulphur bacteria. — These bacteria are able to oxidize sulphuretted hydrogen, storing free sulphur in their cells. Most conspicuous among them is a high-grade filamentous form (*Beggiatoa*) closely resembling the filamentous Cyanophyceae.

These statements illustrate the remarkable powers found among bacteria, and when they are grouped together, the list is a striking one. A group which is remarkably resistant to external conditions that destroy other plants, which can manufacture carbohydrate food without chlorophyll or light, which can use free nitrogen, which can live without oxygen, is suggestive of the possibilities of plant life under conditions that would forbid all existing vegetation.

Myxobacteriaceae. — This group of organisms has been recognized recently, and is evidently related to the bacteria, as the name suggests; but it is distinguished from them by a remarkably complex colony organization. The individual cells resemble those of the bacteria, but they are combined in structures of definite and often elaborate form. For example, one colony resembles a stalk bearing a group of sporangia at its summit. The life histories of the individual cells are like those of the bacteria, and resting cells (so-called spores) are formed in the same way, from which rodlike cells escape and assemble to organize the complex colony. The name suggests a combination of the characters of slime molds and bacteria, the individual cells resembling the latter, and the cells coming together to form a complex body, as the plasmodium of the slime molds is formed. The group is included here because of its resemblance to the bacteria, but it must not be inferred that it belongs to the schizomycetes or even to the schizophytes. It must remain at present as one of the thallophyte groups of uncertain position.

3. ALGAE

These make up the great chlorophyll-bearing assemblage of thallophytes, capable of manufacturing food (see p. 363), and representing the forms from which the higher groups of plants have probably been derived. The three groups of algae are named from their characteristic pigments, as follows: *Chlorophyceae* (green algae), *Phaeophyceae* (brown algae), and *Rhodophyceae* (red algae). These differences in pigments are associated with important differences in structure, which will appear as the forms are discussed.

(1) CHLOROPHYCEAE

General character. — The green algae usually contain no pigment in addition to the chlorophyll, and their appearance justifies the name. They include the simplest algae, and are generally supposed to be the forms from which the higher groups of plants have been derived. On this account green algae may be regarded as the beginning of our present vegetation. The protoplast always has a distinct nucleus and one or more chloroplasts, and this mode of organization is continued throughout all the higher green plants. As presented here, the Chlorophyceae contain six distinct groups, as follows: *Volvocales, Protococcales, Confervales, Siphonales, Conjugales,* and *Charales*. It is recognized that some of these groups are very artificial, and that some of them perhaps should be set apart from the Chlorophyceae; but in this elementary presentation of the forms, it is more convenient and less confusing to use this grouping. The doubtful situations will be indicated in connection with the different groups.

(a) Volvocales

General character. — These aquatic forms are distinguished from other green algae by the fact that the vegetative cells have cilia and therefore are motile. They are sometimes regarded as animals, for they grade plainly into the Flagellates, a group of organisms of mixed plant and animal affinities (see p. 20). A few representative forms will indicate the structure and tendencies of the group.

Chlamydomonas and Sphaerella. — *Chlamydomonas* consists of a single cell bearing two cilia, the protoplast being closely invested by a thin membrane (fig. 21). The structure of *Sphaerella* is in general the same except that the cell has a loose membrane, which is connected with the protoplast by strands and is pierced by the two cilia (fig. 22).

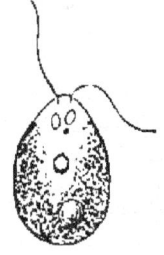

FIG. 21. — *Chlamydomonas*: showing the large cuplike chloroplast, the embedded pyrenoid, the centrally placed nucleus, the two contractile vacuoles, the red pigment spot, and the two cilia. — After WEST.

FIG. 22. — *Sphaerella*: showing the protoplast invested by a loose membrane, which is pierced by the two cilia. — After WEST.

Structure. — The structure of the protoplast of *Chlamydomonas* (fig. 21) may be taken as representative of the whole group. There is usually a single, large, cup-shaped chloroplast at the larger end of the protoplast, in which is embedded a large protein body (*pyrenoid*). In the cup of the chloroplast the nucleus is found; near the base of the cilia are two contractile vacuoles; at the forward end a red pigment spot ("eye spot") is observed; and two long apical cilia complete the equipment. The cells are very active and their motion is influenced by light, to which the "eye spot" is supposed (without adequate ground) to be very sensitive. In some forms a red pigment appears so abundantly as to give a reddish hue, giving rise to the accounts of "red pools" and "red snow." Under certain conditions the cell may drop its cilia and become quiescent, and this temporary loss of motility in the vegetative cells of Volvocales becomes the permanent condition in higher forms.

Reproduction. — In this quiescent stage, the protoplast may divide into several new cells, which escape as new and active individuals. These daughter cells, formed within the old mother cell, are called *zoospores* (swimming spores, swarm spores), but they are also the adult form of the plant. Therefore, the ordinary vegetative cells of Volvocales are like the zoospores of the higher forms, in which the vegetative cells and zoospores are quite distinct.

Certain cells form more numerous and smaller zoospore-like cells, which escape, swim freely, and fuse in pairs to form new cells (figs. 24-27). This is a sexual process, and therefore these pairing cells are called *gametes* (sexual cells). Since the pairing gametes are alike, the condition is called *isogamy*, and the plants are said to be *isogamous*. It is evident that the gametes are related to the zoospores, and it is thought that they are only modified zoospores. The origin of gametes is the origin of sex, and isogamy is the simplest form of sexuality. This fusion of two gametes to form a single cell is the act of fertilization, but to distinguish it from the higher forms of fertilization it has become customary to call the fusion of similar gametes *conjugation*. The cell resulting from conjugation is a *zygospore* (or *zygote*), spore being the general name of a cell set apart for reproduction, and the prefix in this case indicating that the spore has been formed by conjugation. In isogamous plants, therefore, the gametes conjugate and produce a zygospore. In general the zygospore is a resting cell, being formed at the inception of unfavorable conditions, having a heavy wall, and starting new generations upon the return of favorable conditions. In the case of *Sphaerella*, when the zygospore germinates, the protoplast divides, forming two or four cells, which escape as free-swimming cells.

It should be remarked that reproduction by zoospores (an asexual method) results in multiplying plants during the growing season; while reproduction by zygospores (the sexual method) is connected with the formation of a protected cell which endures unfavorable conditions.

Pandorina. — Among Volvocales, as among the previously described groups, there is a prevailing tendency to colony formation, which finally reaches an extreme expression. *Pandorina* illustrates a simple colony, which is composed usually of sixteen similar cells held together by a gelatinous matrix (fig. 23). The protoplast of any cell of the colony may divide into sixteen daughter cells, which form a new colony that escapes from the mother cell and from the mother colony. There is also sexual reproduction as described above, the gametes being produced just as are the daughter colonies. The pairing gametes are similar, and therefore *Pandorina* is isogamous and the sexually formed spore is a zygospore (figs. 24–27).

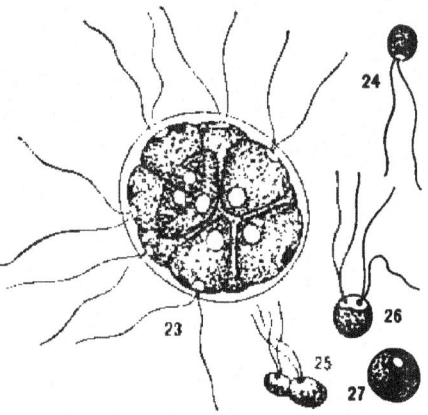

FIGS. 23–27. — *Pandorina*: 23, the free-swimming colony; 24, a gamete; 25, two gametes beginning to fuse; 26, fusion of gametes almost complete; 27, the zygospore. — After PRINGSHEIM.

Eudorina. — In this form there is a larger colony or cell family. New families are formed as described for *Pandorina*, but sexual reproduction is different (fig. 28). Certain cells of the colony, not much different from the vegetative cells, assume the function of *eggs*. Other cells divide to form groups of *sperms*, which hang together in a plate, but finally break up and fuse with the eggs. In this case the pairing gametes (egg and sperm) have become very dissimilar, and hence the condition is called *heterogamy*, the plant being *heterogamous*. The larger gamete, often called the *oosphere*, is better called the egg; and the smaller one, often called *antherozoid* or *spermatozoid*, is better called the sperm. The process of fusion in this case is called *fertilization*, and the product is an *oospore* (fertilized egg).

It is evident that in passing from isogamy to heterogamy there is a differentiation of sex, so that we recognize a male gamete and a female

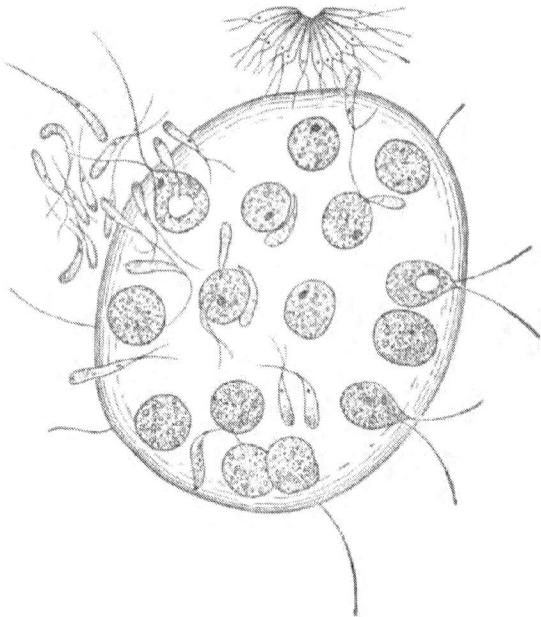

Fig. 28.—*Eudorina:* cells of the colony functioning as eggs, with which sperms are coming into contact; above the colony a group of sperms still hanging together may be seen.—After GOEBEL.

gamete. The female gamete has developed its nutritive supply, and hence its size, at the expense of activity, and finally becomes an entirely passive cell; while the male gamete retains its activity.

Volvox. — In this form the highest expression of colony formation is reached, the free-swimming colony being a hollow sphere composed often of thousands of ciliated cells (figs. 29, 30). These cells are connected by strands of cytoplasm, and therefore the structure may be regarded as a multicellular individual rather than as a colony. At first all cells of the colony are alike, but two kinds of cells may be observed in a mature colony: small vegetative cells which do not divide, and among the thousands of these smaller cells a few (rarely over ten or twelve) much larger ones which divide to form new colonies. These large colony-forming cells are derived from the smaller cells and have been called *gonidia*, a very inappropriate name.

The sexual reproduction is much as in *Eudorina*, but the eggs become much larger than the ordinary cells and lose their cilia. The sperms, produced by the division of certain cells, are elongated, yellow, and biciliate. Fertilization occurs in the cavity of the colony (fig. 31), and the

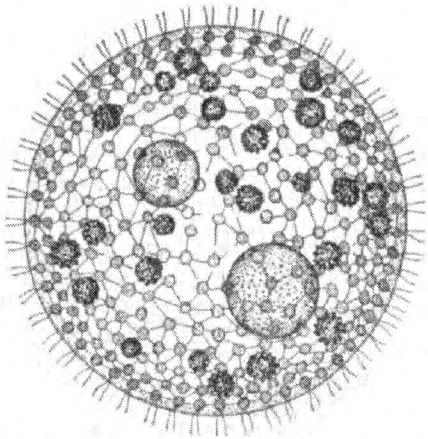

FIG. 29.—*Volvox:* the large globular colony composed of small vegetative cells connected by strands of cytoplasm, two large colony-forming cells, and numerous oospores with rough walls.

resulting oospore is a resting, protected cell (fig. 32). Upon germination the oospore produces a swarm of active cells (zoospores) that cling together and organize a new colony.

In this so-called *Volvox* colony differentiation has resulted in four distinct kinds of cells: ciliated vegetative cells, colony-forming cells, eggs, and sperms.

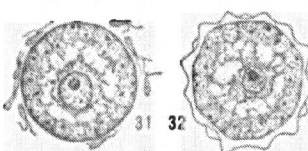

FIGS. 30–32.—*Volvox:* 30, peripheral cells of the colony (after WEST); 31, an egg surrounded by sperms; 32, an oospore with heavy wall.

Conclusions. — A summary of the features of the Volvocales may be stated as follows: The forms range from isolated cells to complex spherical colonies, all the ordinary cells being ciliate; a new colony is formed from the division of a single mother cell; sexual reproduction is present, advancing from isogamy to heterogamy, that is, from the origin of sex to the differentiation of sex. *Volvox* and its colony-forming allies are to be regarded as specialized forms, and

MORPHOLOGY

the connection with the next group of green algae is to be sought in such forms as *Chlamydomonas* and *Sphaerella*.

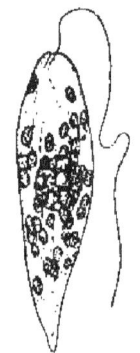

FIG. 33.—*Euglena:* showing a single cilium (flagellum), a large nucleus, and numerous chloroplasts.

Flagellates. — This problematical group of organisms is so suggestive of a relationship to Volvocales that it should be mentioned in this connection. They are one-celled, active, aquatic forms, with one or two (sometimes more) cilia (fig. 33). The cell is naked or with a distinct membrane, which rarely contains any cellulose. The protoplast shows contractile and amoeboid movements, and contains a nucleus, a pulsating vacuole, and in many forms distinct green or brown chromoplasts. Some of them are very animal-like in taking food, ingesting solid particles; and their usual multiplication by longitudinal splitting is not plantlike. No sexual reproduction is known, but the frequent formation of thick-walled "resting spores" is suggestive of plants. This combination of plant and animal characters has suggested that the flagellates may be regarded as the starting point for such one-celled thallophytes as the Volvocales on the one hand, and for Protozoa on the other. In fact, by some authors Volvocales are included among the flagellates.

(b) Protococcales

General character. — The group of forms included here under this name is probably a very heterogeneous assemblage, and it has been much broken up recently by the special students of algae, but it will serve our purpose. The plants occur mainly in fresh water, ranging from an extreme aquatic habit to occurrence in moist places, such as tree trunks, shaded earth, etc. Some are endophytic, living in the intercellular spaces of certain aquatic seed plants; others enter into the structure of lichens; while still others give the green color to certain animals, as fresh-water sponges, hydra, etc. The possible connection of the solitary (one-celled) forms with such solitary Volvocales as *Chlamydomonas* is apparent, the former being characterized by the absence of cilia on the vegetative cells; in other words, there is an occasional loss of motility by the vegetative cells of Volvocales, and this is the permanent condition of the vegetative cells of Protococcales.

Pleurococcus. — This is an exceedingly common green slime found on flower pots, damp bricks, tree trunks, etc., and it may be regarded as a representative one-celled green plant. If there is any connection between Protococcales and Volvocales, it is through such forms as

THALLOPHYTES

Pleurococcus (fig. 34). The globular cell has a definite wall, a central nucleus, and a large lobed chloroplast whose lobes suggest several chloroplasts. These cells multiply rapidly by division, and they may be seen clinging together in irregular groups. No other method of reproduction is known, so that the life history is exceedingly simple.

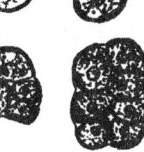

FIG. 34. — *Pleurococcus*: the single cell with its nucleus and large chloroplast, and cell-groups of various sizes.

The other forms selected as illustrations are colony formers, this tendency being as striking as among the Volvocales.

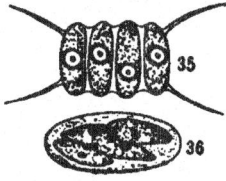

FIGS. 35, 36.—*Scenedesmus*: 35, colony of four cells; 36, cell forming a new colony.

Scenedesmus. — This form represents the simplest colony, consisting of two to eight cells lying side by side, the end cells often with more or less conspicuous appendages (fig. 35). Each cell divides internally to form a new colony (fig. 36), and no other method of reproduction is known.

Pediastrum. — The colony in this form is a floating or suspended, more or less star-shaped plate of polygonal cells, sometimes as many as sixty-four in number (fig. 37). Within any cell distinct zoospores are formed, which escape from the mother cell inclosed by a delicate membrane and then become arranged into a new colony (figs. 37–39). Sexual reproduction is also present in its simplest form, certain cells forming zoospore-like cells, smaller and more numerous than the zoospores, which function as gametes (figs. 40–44). *Pediastrum*, therefore, is isogamous, forming zygospores that are resting or protected cells.

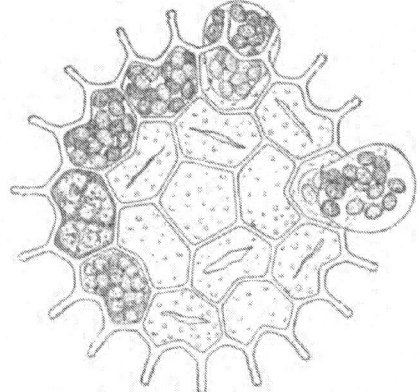

FIG. 37.—*Pediastrum*: a colony of polygonal cells, some of which are forming new colonies; two colonies escaping from the mother colony.

Hydrodictyon. — This is the well-known water net,

one of the most remarkable of plant colonies. This hollow net is freely floating, and sometimes attains a length of 25 to 30 cm. It is formed by an end-to-end union of long cylindrical cells in such a way as to form polygonal meshes, three or four cells abutting at each junction (fig. 45). The cytoplasm forms a thick layer inclosing a large central vacuole, and the chloroplast is an irregular plate that finally breaks up into many small chloroplasts.

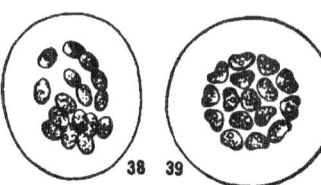

FIGS. 38, 39.—*Pediastrum:* cells with daughter colonies in different stages of formation.—After A. BRAUN.

When the cell reaches a certain size, the protoplast divides into very numerous (7000 to 20,000) biciliate zoospores, each with a nucleus and a small chloroplast (fig. 46). These zoospores do not escape, but swim about freely for a time within the large mother cell, come to rest, and gradually develop a small net within the mother cell (fig. 47). The wall of the mother cell finally softens and the young net is set free and grows to adult size without any cell division.

FIGS. 40-44.—*Pediastrum:* 40, zoospore; 41, gamete; 42, 43, gametes fusing; 44, zygospore.—After WEST.

The sexual reproduction is isogamous, certain cells producing a remarkable number of gametes (30,000 to 100,000), which escape from the mother cell at once and fuse in pairs, forming zygospores (figs. 48-50). Experiments upon *Hydrodictyon* have succeeded in securing at will the production of zoospores (forming young nets)

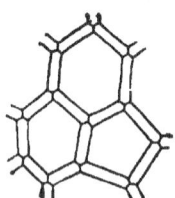

FIG. 45.—*Hydrodictyon:* arrangement of cells in forming the net.—After WEST.

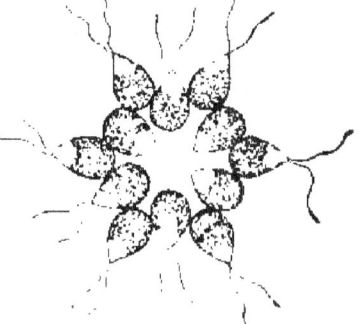

FIG. 46.—*Hydrodictyon:* zoospores within a mother cell beginning to form a net.—After KLEBS.

or of gametes, by using various nutrient media. The zygospore is a heavy-walled resting cell that settles to the bottom of the water and resembles a *Pleurococcus* cell. After a more or less prolonged resting period, the zygospore produces two or four large biciliate zoospores, which escape into the water (figs.

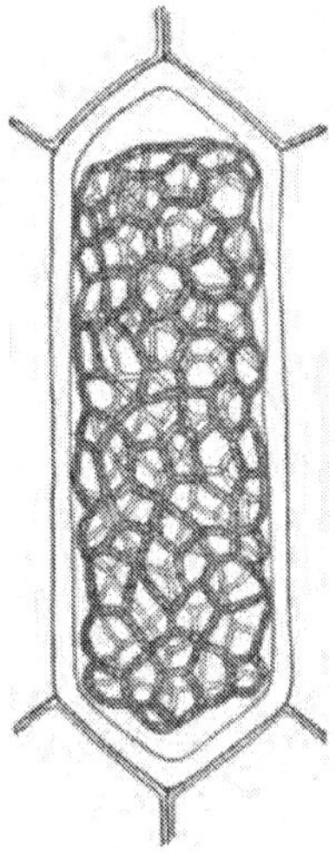

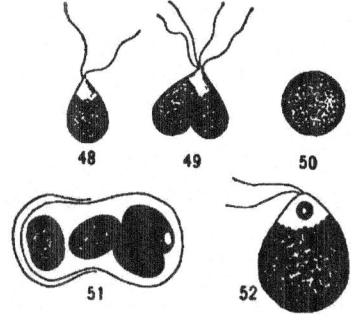

FIG. 47.—*Hydrodictyon:* a completed young net within its mother cell.—After KLEBS.

FIGS. 48–52.—*Hydrodictyon:* 48, gamete; 49, gametes fusing; 50, zygospore; 51, four zoospores developed by the zygospore; 52, zoospore escaped from zygospore.—48–50, after KLEBS; 51, 52, after PRINGSHEIM.

51, 52) and develop into large, irregular, many-angled, thick-walled cells (polyhedra), which persist through the winter (fig. 53). Upon the

FIGS. 53, 54.—*Hydrodictyon:* 53, polyhedron formed by a zoospore; 54, young net forming within a polyhedron.—After PRINGSHEIM.

return of favorable conditions, each of these polyhedra (resting cells) forms internally a small net of 200 to 300 cells (fig. 54), which escapes, and the multiplication of nets is begun. It is a noteworthy fact that the zygospore does not produce a net directly, but gives rise to other cells which do.

Conclusions. — Taking the whole assemblage of forms included here under Protococcales, the range of form is from a solitary cell to a complex colony, *Hydrodictyon* holding the same highly specialized position in this series that *Volvox* does among the Volvocales. A marked feature of difference, however, is that the vegetative cells are not motile. Colony reproduction occurs as among the Volvocales, the zoospores produced by a mother cell being held together or retained until they are organized into a new colony. The lowest forms of Protococcales exhibit no sexual reproduction, but among the higher forms isogamy is attained; while among Volvocales heterogamy is reached.

(c) Confervales

General character. — Under this name what may be regarded as the representative green algae are assembled. The assemblage is a very artificial one, and it has been broken up and scattered by the special students of algae, but for our purpose it is convenient to consider these forms together. They are nearly all aquatic, usually filamentous, and always septate (with cross walls). Under certain conditions these filamentous bodies may break up into isolated cells and remain in this condition for a time, resembling the forms of Protococcales with isolated cells, as *Pleurococcus*. All of them produce zoospores, and it is probable that all of them have some form of sexual reproduction. In considering certain representative forms, two categories are convenient; namely, the isogamous forms and the heterogamous forms.

(a) *Isogamous forms*

Ulothrix. — This very common alga may be taken to stand for a representative isogamous conferva form. It is a simple filament, whose basal cell is modified to form a holdfast that anchors the body and permits a permanent position in moving water (fig. 55). The ordinary vegetative cells are short, and each one contains a nucleus and a large chloroplast which is peripherally placed and has the form of a thick hollow cylinder. Any of the cells may produce zoospores, which may range in number from one to thirty-two even in the same filament (fig. 56), the size of the zoospore depending upon the number of divisions. A large zoospore bears four cilia (fig. 59), and resembles a vegetative cell of the Volvocales, even to the "eye spot" and contractile vacuoles. The spores escape through an opening in the wall of the mother cell, swim about, come to rest, settle upon some support, ciliate end foremost, develop a holdfast, begin cell division, and new filaments are started (fig. 57). This differentiation between zoospores and ordinary vegetative cells, and the behavior of the zoospores in escaping individually from the mother cell and starting independent individuals, are features in contrast with the ordinary situation among the Volvocales and Protococcales. In any event, it should be kept in mind that the zoospore type of cell is probably to be regarded as the most primitive type among the green algae.

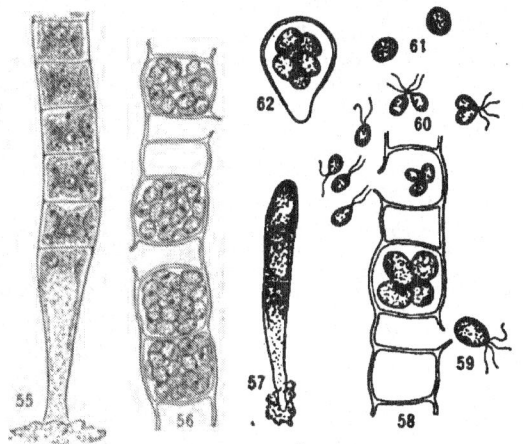

FIGS. 55-62.—*Ulothrix:* 55, base of filament with holdfast; 56, filament producing zoospores or gametes; 57, young filament developed from zoospore; 58, filament discharging zoospores and gametes; 59, an escaped zoospore; 60, escaped and pairing gametes; 61, zygospores; 62, zygospore producing zoospores.—55-61, after COULTER; 62, after DODEL-PORT.

The sexual reproduction is isogamous, the gametes being produced just as are the zoospores, but differing in usually being smaller, and of course more numerous, and in being biciliate (fig. 60). The freed gametes conjugate in pairs and form zygospores (fig. 61), which after the resting period do not give rise to new filaments directly, but produce several zoospores (fig. 62) that give rise to filaments. This intercalation of zoospores in the life history between the zygospores and the new filaments is an important fact to note.

Ulothrix is very often used to illustrate the origin of sex among the green algae. In many forms the vegetative cells are found producing swimming cells of all sizes, varying from the large zoospores to the small gametes, so that it is often impossible to distinguish between zoospores and gametes by their appearance. Some of the swimming cells

26 MORPHOLOGY

that are smaller than zoospores and larger than gametes, and which have two or four cilia, germinate slowly in producing filaments, but are evidently zoospores in behavior. Under certain conditions, also, some of the smaller swimming cells that ordinarily function as gametes produce small filaments, thus functioning as zoospores. These facts have suggested that gametes are derived from zoospores; that is, that the sexual cells are simply very small zoospores, which fuse in pairs before germination.

Ulva. — This is the well-known sea lettuce, a marine form, with a membranous flat thallus, like a leaf in appearance but not at all in structure. It is interesting in being a flat sheet of cells rather than a filament, but it shows the same reproductive level as *Ulothrix*, the zoospores and gametes being of the same general kind. The zygospore, however, instead of giving rise to zoospores, as in *Ulothrix*, produces a new thallus directly.

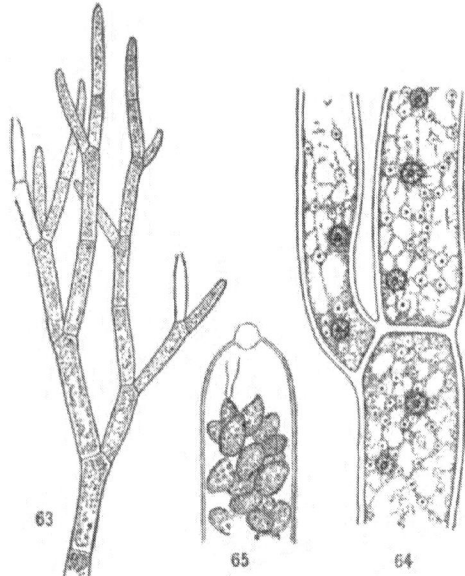

Chaetophora. — This form illustrates a freely branching · filamentous body, in this case the branches bearing hairlike terminations, a character indicated by the name. The zoospores and gametes are as in *Ulothrix* and *Ulva*.

Stigeoclonium. — The body of this form is of the same general type as that of *Chaetophora*, and with the same methods of reproduction. It displays in a striking way a feature more or less characteristic of all filamentous Confervales, being remarkable for passing long periods as a one-celled plant. Under certain conditions the cells of a filament, when they divide, round off and separate, this one-celled stage being called the *palmella* form.[1] Under different conditions the filamentous form is resumed (figs. 858–860).

FIGS. 63–65. — *Cladophora*: 63, portion of branching filament; 64, enlarged cells, showing several nuclei in each cell and numerous pyrenoids (after CHAMBERLAIN); 65, portion of tip cell forming biciliate zoospores (after STRASBURGER).

---

[1] The name *Palmella* was given to the one-celled form before its relation to *Stigeoclonium* and other Confervales was known. It is now retained to indicate the one-celled stage.

These changes from the filamentous to the palmella form and back again have been brought under experimental control (see Part III).

Cladophora. — This is one of the most common of the green algae, being a profusely branching and anchored filamentous form, the branches arising from the upper ends of the elongated cells (fig. 63). The cells are remarkable in containing many nuclei, such multinucleate cells being called *coenocytes* (fig. 64). A filament composed of a series of coenocytic cells suggests a structure on the way towards a completely coenocytic body, such as characterizes the Siphonales (see p. 33). In addition to the nuclei, the *Cladophora* cell contains many chloroplasts in the peripheral layer of cytoplasm, and numerous pyrenoids in the plastids. The cell division in this case is by means of a plate that begins as a ring at the cell wall and growing centripetally cleaves the protoplast. In enlarged apical cells (usually) a very large number of biciliate zoospores are formed (fig. 65), and biciliate gametes may be formed in any cell. The zygospore in germination develops a new filament directly.

(b) *Heterogamous forms*

Sphaeroplea. — This form is a simple filament, with multinucleate (coenocytic) cells, as in *Cladophora*, and there is the same abundant development of zoospores. In sexual reproduction, however, two kinds of gametes are produced; one being the usual biciliate, zoospore-like cell (the sperm); the other being a larger cell, with no cilia (the oosphere or egg). The cell producing the numerous sperms is an *antheridium* (fig. 66), and the cell producing the several eggs is an *oogonium* (fig. 67); but in this case antheridia and oogonia are vegetative cells, unchanged in form. In the same way, the cells producing zoospores may be called *sporangia*, but it is not usual to apply these names until these cells become distinct in appearance from the vegetative cells. The sperms find entrance into the oogonium and fertilize the eggs, the resulting oospores being protected cells (figs. 67–70). In germination the oospore produces a number of zoospores (figs. 71, 72), which in turn give rise to new filaments (fig. 73).

Oedogonium. — This very common alga is a simple anchored filament of uninucleate cells containing a single peripheral chloroplast. Certain of the vegetative cells produce zoospores, which are large, usually solitary, and with a crown of cilia (figs. 74–76). Other cells of the filament become enlarged and very conspicuous, forming the oogonia,

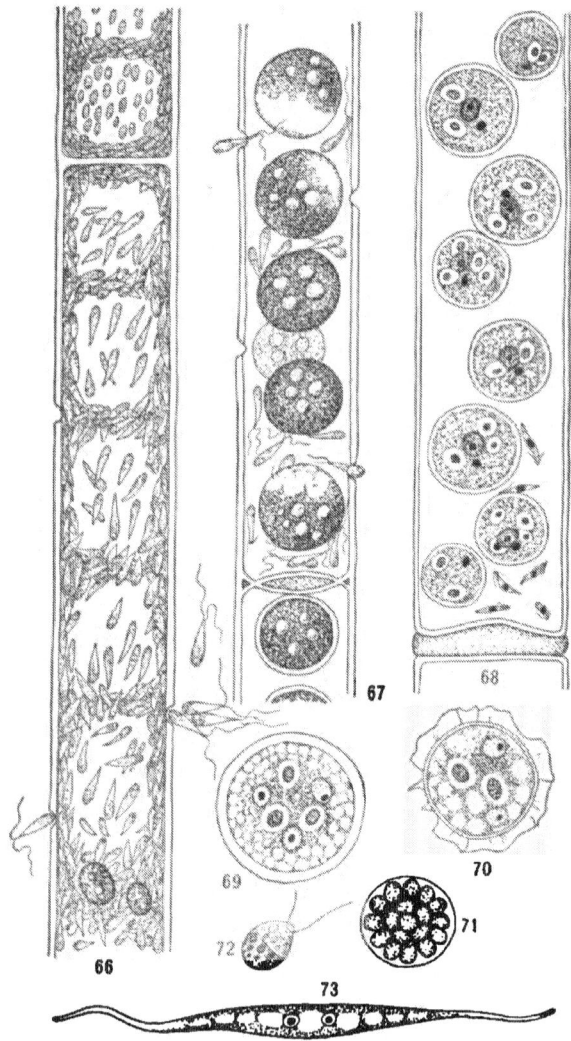

FIGS. 66–73. — *Sphaeroplea*: 66, cells producing sperms; 67, cells producing eggs, which are surrounded by sperms; 68, eggs immediately after fertilization, each with one nucleus; 69, fertilized egg (oospore) further advanced, with several nuclei; 70, oospore with heavy wall; 71, zoospores formed by oospore; 72, escaped zoospore; 73, young filament produced by zoospore. — 66, 67, 71, after COHN; 68–70, after KLEBAHN; 72, 73, after HEINRICHER.

THALLOPHYTES

each one of which produces a single very large egg, conspicuously filled with reserve food, and develops a perforation which the sperms enter. Still other cells of the filament divide, the daughter cells not elongating, thus producing a short row of small cells, the antheridia, within each one of which one or two sperms are developed (fig. 77). The sperms are much smaller than the zoospores, but they have the same crown of cilia, and this evident relationship between spore and sperm is constantly

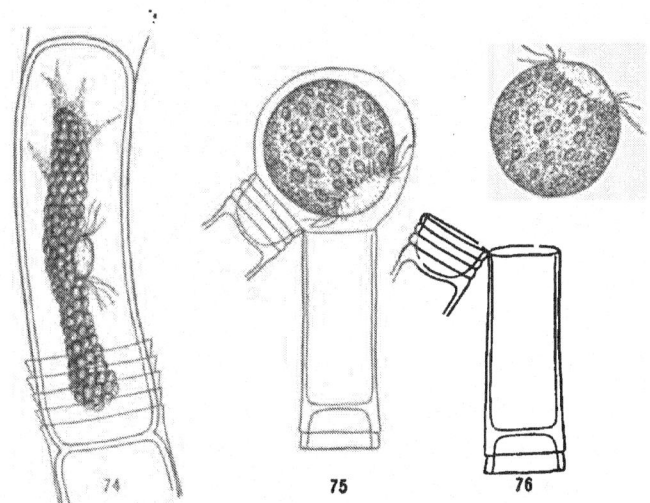

FIGS. 74–76.—*Oedogonium:* 74, large zoospore forming within the cell, including all the contents; 75, zoospore escaping from cell; 76, zoospore freed from its membrane. — 74, after PRINGSHEIM; 75, 76, after HIRN.

appearing. In this case the oogonia and antheridia are distinct from the vegetative cells, but still they are transformed vegetative cells. The sperms escape from the antheridia, swarm about the oogonia, enter them through the perforation, and fertilize the eggs. Although several sperms may enter an oogonium, only one is concerned in the act of fertilization, the essential feature of which seems to be the fusion of the two nuclei. The oospore is a heavy-walled cell, which upon germination produces four zoospores, each one of which gives rise to a new filament (figs. 80–82).

In the form of *Oedogonium* just described, the oogonia and antheridia occur in the same filament, but in certain species they occur on different

MORPHOLOGY

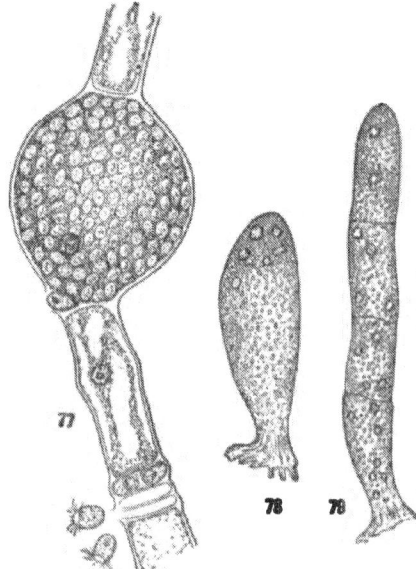

FIGS. 77-79. — *Oedogonium:* 77, portion of a filament showing the large oogonium, which contains an egg filled with food reserve and a single nucleus; at the base of the oogonium a sperm is seen entering; also three antheridia, from two of which sperms have escaped; 78, 79, young filaments developing from a zoospore. — After COULTER.

filaments, which may then be spoken of as male and female filaments. This separation of the sexes in different individuals is a condition called *dioecism*. Among these *dioecious* forms an interesting modification may arise, the male filaments being very much dwarfed. These dwarf filaments are produced by special small zoospores, which are larger than the sperms but smaller than the regular zoospores, and are called *androspores* from their male product. These androspores swarm for a time and finally settle down upon female filaments or even upon oogonia, where they become anchored and each produces a filament of a few cells, whose small terminal cells (antheridia) develop sperms that are set free by the opening of the caplike lid (fig. 83).

Bulbochaete.—This well-known form has the same general life history as that described for *Oedogonium*, but it is a branching filamentous form.

Coleochaete.—This is a most interesting and a very much discussed

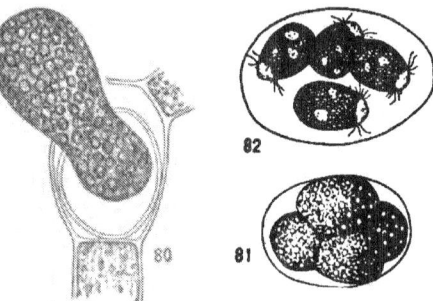

FIGS. 80-82. — *Oedogonium:* 80, contents of oospore escaping from the heavy wall in germination; 81, four zoospores forming in oospore; 82, the four zoospores completed. — After JURANYI.

THALLOPHYTES

form. It belongs to the fresh waters and is found attached to the leaves and stems of various aquatics, as water lilies, etc. The body is a flat thallus, being either a complete disk composed of radiating rows of cells (fig. 84) or a cushion with free branches. The zoospores are solitary, biciliate, and may be produced by any vegetative cell (fig. 89). In the discoid species the antheridia are formed by the division of a vegetative cell into four cells, each one of which produces a biciliate sperm (figs. 85, 86). In the branched forms, the antheridia appear as special club-shaped cells at the ends of branches. In the discoid forms the oogonia are near the ends of the radiating rows of vegetative cells, differing from them chiefly in size (figs. 84, 87). In the branched forms, the oogonia are free at the ends of branches, each developing a long tubular prolongation through which the sperm enters.

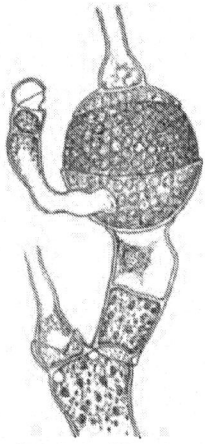

FIG. 83.—*Bulbochaete:* showing a dwarf male filament, with its terminal antheridium, attached to an oogonium.—After PRINGSHEIM.

Fertilization results not only in a thick-walled oospore, but in the branched forms contiguous cells of the thallus send out branches which invest it in a cellular case, making a sort of spore case (sporocarp), which is the resting stage of the plant. In germination the oospore gives rise to a several-celled body, each cell of which produces a zoospore that escapes and develops a new thallus (fig. 88).

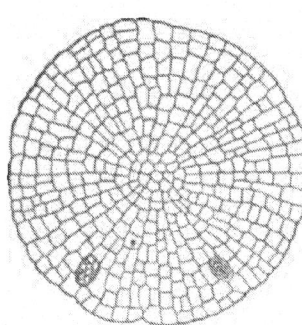

FIG. 84.—*Coleochaete scutata:* discoid form; the two larger and shaded cells are developing as oogonia.

Alternation.—Two noteworthy facts in this life history are the formation of a case of sterile cells about the oospore as a result of fertilization, and the multicellular body produced by the oospore. This last fact has been taken to represent the *alternation of generations* which is established as a constant feature of the higher plants. This phenomenon consists of the alternation of a sexual and a sexless generation in a life cycle, each generation giving rise to the other. In *Coleochaete* it was supposed that the sexual generation (*gametophyte*) is represented by the ordinary gamete-producing plant, and the sexless generation (*sporophyte*) by the spore-producing body developed by the oospore. In subjecting this life history to what is regarded as a critical test of the two generations, it has been discovered that this special spore-producing body is not a sporophyte. The test has to do with the number of chromosomes in the nucleus, a number which is definite for each plant species. The chromo-

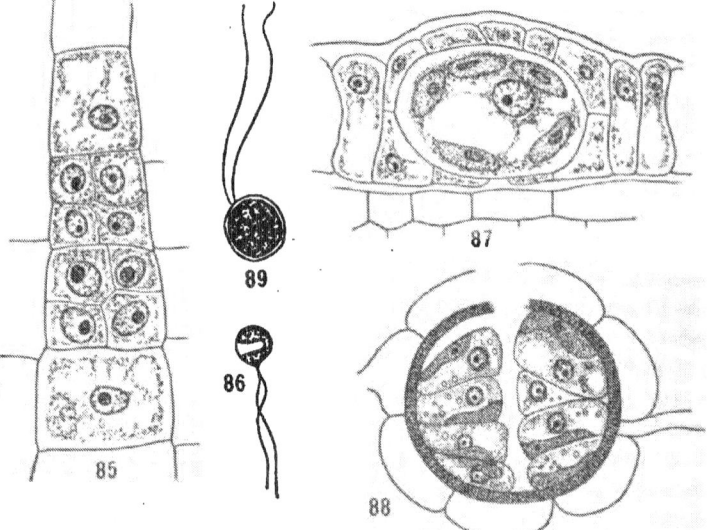

FIGS. 85-89.—*Coleochaete:* 85, development of antheridia, by the division of a vegetative cell into four cells; 86, a sperm (after PRINGSHEIM); 87, an oogonium, containing an egg showing nucleus and chloroplasts; 88, the heavy-walled oospore, invested by a jacket of sterile cells, and producing a multicellular body each of whose cells produces a zoospore (after OLTMANNS); 89, a zoospore (after PRINGSHEIM).

somes are doubled in number by the fusion of the sperm and egg to form the oospore; and this means that at some other point in the life cycle the number must be reduced again. Accordingly the sporophyte, which arises from the oospore, is characterized by the double or $2x$ number of chromosomes in its nuclei; and the gametophyte, which gives rise to the gametes, is characterized by the reduced or x number of chromosomes. Upon applying this test to *Coleochaete*, it was discovered that the special spore-forming body produced by the oospore contains the reduced number of chromosomes and is therefore not a sporophyte. In fact, in this case, the doubling of chromosomes in the formation of the oospore is followed immediately by their reduction during the divisions of the oospore.

Conclusions. — Upon considering the assemblage of green algae here brought together under Confervales, the following general statements may be made: The body is a simple filament, a branching filament, or a flat thallus, and is either completely septate or partially coenocytic. Zoospores are produced abundantly, and are generally biciliate, *Oedogonium* being a notable exception. The sexual reproduction ranges from isogamy to a stage of heterogamy in which distinct oogonia and antheridia are developed. The zygospores may give rise directly to new plants or may produce zoospores; but the oospores always develop zoospores, a process which culminates in *Coleochaete* in a specially organized zoospore-producing body.

(d) Siphonales

General character. — This is a very well-defined group, comprising mostly marine forms. The distinguishing character, suggested by the name, is that the plant body has no cross walls, being one continuous multinucleate protoplast enclosed by the peripheral wall, a kind of body called coenocytic. In this case the body is completely coenocytic, as distinguished from such partially coenocytic bodies as those of *Cladophora* and *Sphaeroplea*. The bodies are more or less diffusely branching, and in some of the marine forms the differentiation of the body is remarkable, as in *Bryopsis*, *Caulerpa*, *Acetabularia*, etc. The two prominent fresh-water forms are as follows.

Botrydium. — This interesting plant develops in damp places, such as the mud of drying-up ponds, wet plowed ground, boggy fields, and especially on flood plains. It appears as groups of little green, balloon-shaped bladders, about the size of a pin's head, which grip the substratum by means of colorless, rhizoidal branches (fig. 90). Numerous small nuclei are embedded in the thin wall layer of cytoplasm, and in the aerial part there are numerous chloroplasts.

The asexual methods of reproduction are various, dependent upon varying conditions. A new bladder may bud out from the aerial part, send rhizoidal branches into the substratum, and then become separated from the parent by a wall. If covered with water, the whole inflated aerial portion may be converted into a sporangium producing a multitude of uniciliate zoospores (figs. 91, 92). These zoospores germinate immediately upon damp earth, but if under water, they form a double wall and become resting spores. When the aerial portion of the plant is exposed to drought, the contents retreat into the protected rhizoidal branches and round off into a large number of non-motile spores (*aplanospores*), which rest until the return of favorable conditions and then initiate new plants (fig. 93). The development of aplanospores is common among algae, being a method used by the protoplast of bridging over unfavorable conditions, in which connection it appears more as a method of self-preservation than of reproduction. The aplanospores in germination give rise to new plants directly or to zoospores.

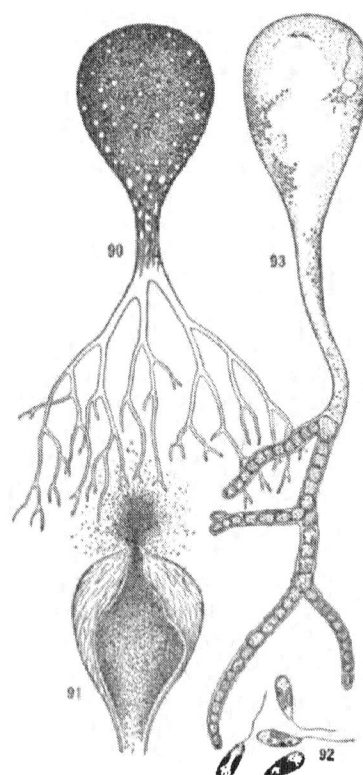

FIGS. 90–93. — *Botrydium:* 90, the ordinary vegetative form, showing the aerial green portion and the subterranean rhizoidal portion of the coenocytic body; 91, aerial portion of the body converted into a sporangium; 92, zoospores; 93, the formation of aplanospores in the rhizoidal region. — After ROSTAFINSKI and WORONIN.

The testimony in reference to the sexual reproduction of *Botrydium* is conflicting. It has been stated that the aplanospores give rise to numerous small biciliate gametes that conjugate, but it is claimed that the gametes observed are those of *Protosiphon*, a form which grows with *Botrydium* and closely resembles it. In any event, the presence of gametes among these simpler Siphonales is the important point for our purpose, and it is of interest to note that they either conjugate or germinate as small zoospores.

Vaucheria. — This is the very common green felt, which occurs in coarse feltlike masses of branching filaments on damp soil and in fresh or brackish water (fig. 94). As in all coenocytic bodies, the nuclei and chloroplasts are numerous, and in this form oil-globules are abundant.

Zoospore. — The asexual reproduction is modified in an interesting way by the coenocytic habit. At the tip of a branch a very large zoospore is formed by the protoplast, and is cut off from the general body by a wall (fig. 95). It is discharged through an opening at the end of the branch and moves actively by means of cilia that are distributed over its whole surface (fig. 96). The zoospore is multinucleate, containing the nuclei that were in the end of the branch at the time of its formation, and in connection with each nucleus a pair of cilia is formed. This large zoospore, therefore, may be regarded as a compound zoospore, corresponding to a number of biciliate zoospores.

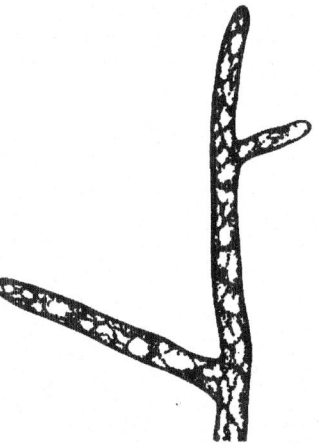

FIG. 94. — *Vaucheria*: a small portion of the filamentous, branching, coenocytic body.

It germinates directly, producing a new filament (fig. 97).

Sexual reproduction. — The structures connected with sexual reproduction are more highly developed than any previously mentioned, for not only is *Vaucheria* heterogamous, but it produces special sex organs which are not transformed vegetative cells, but are specifically for gamete-production from the beginning. In one of the species, for example (fig. 99), a special branch is put out from the side of the filament, and a terminal cell is cut off by a wall and enlarges into a more or less globular oogonium, in which a single large egg (oosphere) is formed. This egg at first is multinucleate, but

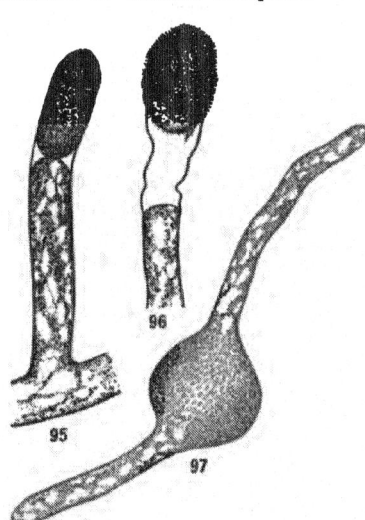

FIGS. 95-97. — *Vaucheria*: showing formation (95), escape (96), and germination (97) of zoospore. — After COULTER.

after the partition wall is formed, it becomes uninucleate by the degeneration of the other nuclei. In the wall of the oogonium a more or less beaked opening is formed by which the sperms enter. The antheridial branch is similar in origin, but is longer, the antheridium being cut off at the curved tip by a wall as a small cell. In other species a single sexual branch bears both oogonia and antheridia (fig. 98), a common arrangement of the cluster being a terminal antheridium and a group of laterally developed oogonia. In each

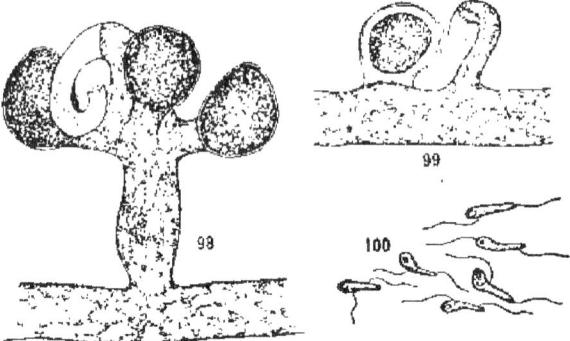

FIGS. 98–100. — *Vaucheria:* 98, 99, two methods of forming oogonia and antheridia; in both cases the terminal antheridium has discharged its sperms (100). — 100, after WORONIN.

antheridium numerous sperms are formed (fig. 100), which are discharged, enter through the beaked openings of the oogonia, and fertilize the eggs. The heavy-walled oospore is the protected stage of the plant and germinates directly into a new filament.

Experiments. — The experiments upon *Vaucheria* are of great interest, since by varying the character of the medium, the nature of the nutrition, the light, etc., there may be produced at will sterile plants, zoospore-producing plants, or gamete-producing plants. *Vaucheria* also has great power of resisting unfavorable conditions, in the presence of which the filament becomes chambered by the formation of thick cross walls, and the contents of each compartment round up as an aplanospore. In favorable conditions each aplanospore either forms a new filament directly, or discharges an amoeba-like protoplast, which rounds off as a green sphere, covers itself with a wall, and either forms a filament directly or enters again into a period of rest. This ability to respond promptly to varying conditions and to change the program at almost any period in the life history is very marked among the lower plants.

THALLOPHYTES

Conclusions.—The body of Siphonales is coenocytic and usually complexly branched and differentiated. Zoospores are formed, which sometimes take on the character of the coenocytic body and may be regarded as compound zoospores, as in *Vaucheria*. Sexual reproduction ranges from isogamy to heterogamy, in the latter condition extending to the formation of special branches bearing the sex organs. Aplanospores or non-motile protected cells are produced under conditions unfavorable for vegetative activity, and from all spores or resting cells there is a direct development of new filaments. A possible connection of Siphonales with Confervales is suggested by such partially coenocytic forms as *Cladophora* and *Sphaeroplea*, but in any event it is to be regarded as a highly specialized group.

(e) Conjugales

General character.—This is also a very distinct group, which is separated by some writers from Chlorophyceae on account of its peculiar features. It is a fresh-water group, the bodies being single cells or simple filaments, and characterized by remarkable chloroplasts, by the absence of asexual spores, and by a peculiar method of sexual reproduction. The absence of all ciliated cells, including both spores and gametes, in an aquatic group is remarkable. The following families may be used to illustrate the group.

Desmidiaceae.—The desmids are one-celled plants that exhibit the greatest possible variety of form and are often extremely beautiful. The cell is peculiar in being organized into two symmetrical halves, often separated by a deep constriction which makes the *isthmus*. In each half there is a large, irregular, often complex chloroplast and several pyrenoids, while in the isthmus connecting the two halves the single nucleus is placed. Many of the desmids can move about, and they are very sensitive to light, taking a position determined by the incident rays.

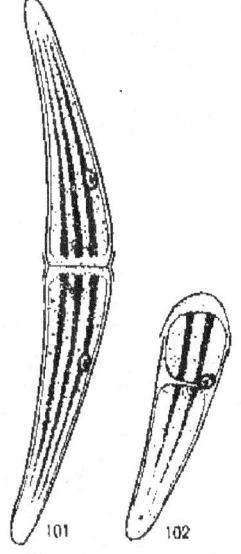

FIGS. 101, 102.— *Closterium*: 101, cell dividing, the two nuclei and the wall having been formed; 102, the plastid in an old "half cell" having divided, and the nucleus becoming placed between the two plastids.— After A. FISCHER.

Individuals are multiplied by cell-division. The nucleus divides and a wall is formed across the isthmus (fig. 101). The division thus results in two new cells, each consisting of one half of the old cell and a portion of the isthmus, which enlarges into a new half, when the two cells separate. During this process the plastid in each half divides, so that the new cell contains the usual two plastids (fig. 102).

In sexual reproduction the cells pair, the walls are ruptured at the isthmus, the protoplasts escape and fuse, and a zygospore is formed (figs. 103–105). In some species a little tubular projection puts out from

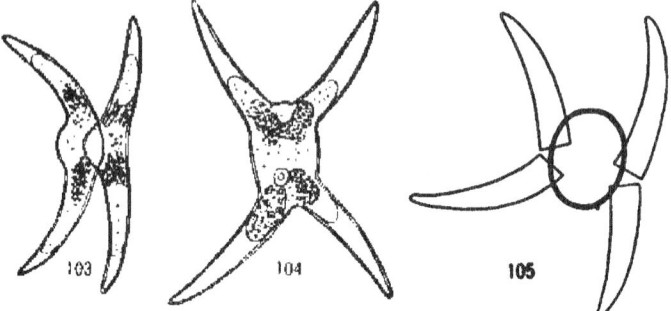

FIGS. 103–105. — *Closterium:* 103, two cells pairing for conjugation; 104, the two protoplasts fusing; 105, the zygospore formed. — 103, 104, after DE BARY; 105, after WEST.

each cell at the isthmus, and the two projections meet to form a short tube in which the protoplasts meet and fuse. The sexual fusion in desmids is true conjugation, in which two vegetative protoplasts fuse without the organization of distinct gametes. In the germination of the zygospore the heavy wall is ruptured, the protoplast escapes, and four nuclei are formed, only two of which usually persist in the development of new desmids.

Mesocarpaceae. — In this family the body is a filament of similar elongated cells, in each of which there is an axial platelike chloroplast. Cell division is accomplished by nuclear division and a centripetally growing wall. Sexual reproduction occurs between adjacent filaments, whose cells pair and come in contact by kneelike bends or by short tubes, and the two abutting walls becoming perforated at their contact, permit the two similar protoplasts to come in contact for fusion. The zygospore upon germination forms a new filament directly.

Zygnemaceae. — These are pond scums, and are among the most common of the green algae. The characteristic genera are *Zygnema*

THALLOPHYTES

and *Spirogyra*, the latter being especially abundant and long used for laboratory study. They are both filamentous plants with elongated cells, and differ from one another in the form of the conspicuous chloroplasts, which in *Zygnema* are two radiate or starlike bodies in each cell

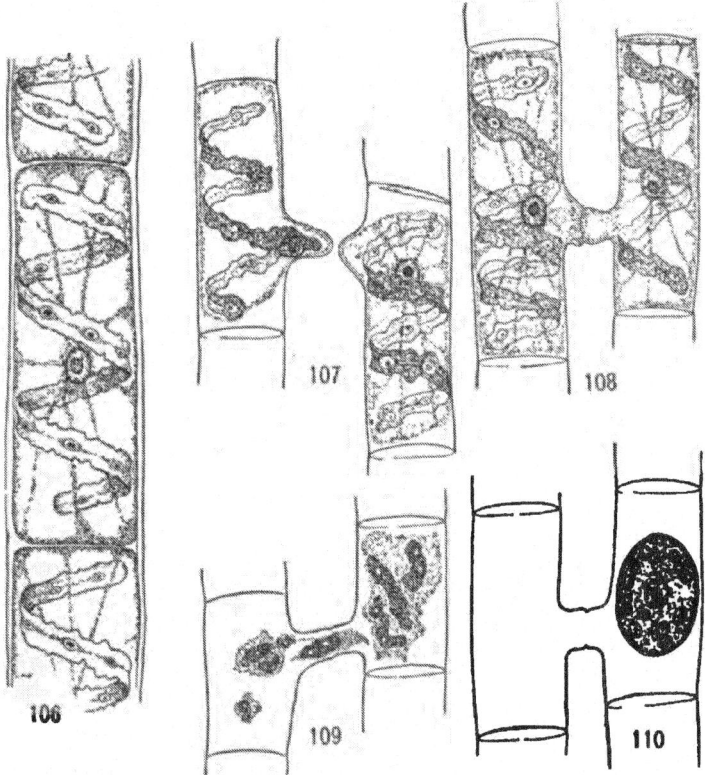

FIGS. 106–110.—*Spirogyra:* 106, cell showing the spiral bandlike chloroplast containing pyrenoids, and the centrally swung nucleus; 107, cells developing a conjugating tube; 108, conjugating tube complete; 109, passage of one protoplast through the tube; 110, the zygospore. — After COULTER.

(fig. 111), and in *Spirogyra*, one or more bands that extend spirally from one end of a cell to the other (fig. 106). *Spirogyra* may be selected to represent the family. The conspicuous green, spiral, bandlike chloroplasts lie peripherally in the cell and contain conspicuous, nodule-like pyrenoids, which are often surrounded by a starch jacket. The nucleus is swung in the center of the vacuolate cell by strands of cytoplasm that connect the sheath of cytoplasm about the nucleus with the peripheral layer of cytoplasm. The cell division is as described for the Mesocarpaceae.

Sexual reproduction. — Sexual reproduction is most characteristic (figs. 107-110, and fig. 112). Conjugating tubes put out from the cells of adjacent filaments and fuse, until the two filaments connected by conjugating tubes resemble a ladder. The protoplast of one cell passes through the conjugating tube into the connected cell, and the two protoplasts fuse, forming a large, heavy-walled zygospore. The conjugating protoplasts in this case differ in behavior, one being passive and the other relatively active, so that there is apparent a distinction of sex, although the two protoplasts are similar in appearance. This distinction often extends to the filaments, one filament emptying all of its protoplasts into the cells of the connected filament; in which case the former filament can be regarded as male and the latter one as female. It is very common to see a filament, all of whose cells are empty, connected with another filament, each of whose cells contains a zygospore. On the other hand, the same filament may give and receive protoplasts; and in some species conjugating tubes connect adjacent cells of the same filament. Occasionally, also, bodies which resemble zygospores are found within cells that have established no connections, and so they have been formed without fusion, a phenomenon called *parthenogenesis* (fig. 112). Great variations in the establishment of connections for conjugation may be found in almost every collection of zygospore-forming material. The zygospore is the winter condition of the plant, and upon germination gives rise directly to a new filament.

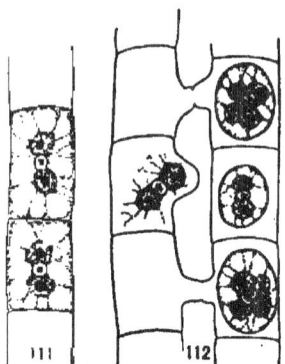

FIGS. 111, 112. — *Zygnema:* 111, cells showing the two radiating chloroplasts, between which is the nucleus; 112, conjugation, showing two zygospores (each with two nuclei and four chloroplasts) formed by the fusion of two protoplasts, and a third zygospore-like cell not formed by fusion (illustration of parthenogenesis).

Conclusions. — The body of the Conjugales consists of a single cell or a simple filament, and in its vegetative phase is distinguished by large and characteristically shaped chloroplasts. There is no asexual reproduction by spores, and no motile cells of any kind are formed. Sexual reproduction is effected by the conjugation of protoplasts brought together usually through conjugating tubes, and while in a general way only isogamy is attained, there is evident in some forms an incipient heterogamy shown by the different behavior of the pairing protoplasts. The group as a whole seems to stand stiffly apart from all those previously considered, and must be regarded as very highly specialized.

(f) Charales

General character. — The stoneworts, as these forms are called, constitute a very isolated group among thallophytes, which seems to hold no definite relation to any other group. If they are algae, they must be included among the green algae; but they are considered by many to be quite separate from algae; and some would even remove them from thallophytes. Until something more is known of their relationships, however, it is convenient to consider them in connection with the green algae. They are found in fresh and brackish waters, attached to the bottom and covering large areas with a dense mass of vegetation. Some of the bodies are incrusted by such an abundant deposit of calcium carbonate that it makes them rough and brittle, and suggested the name stoneworts. The common genera are *Chara* and *Nitella*, and the general structure is very uniform.

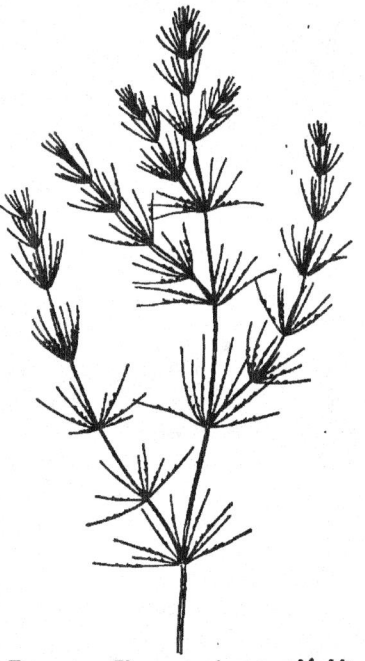

FIG. 113. — *Chara:* showing general habit of body.

Vegetative body. — The vegetative body consists of a cylindric stem or main axis which branches profusely (fig. 113). All of the axes are differentiated into short *nodes* and long *internodes*, and from the nodes the whorls of branches arise. These branches are of two kinds: (1) those of limited growth, the so-called "leaves"; (2) those that resemble the parent axis in indefinite growth. The branches of limited growth form the whorl or rosette of branches at each node; while usually in the axil of one of them the branch of indefinite growth appears. The axillary position of the main branch suggested that the smaller subtending branches are leaves.

The main and lateral axes elongate by means of an apical cell (fig. 114), which by successive transverse walls cuts off a longitudinal series of cells (segments). Each segment divides transversely into two cells, the lower one of which enlarges, forming the long internodal cell (sometimes 10 cm. or more long), the upper one giving rise by successive divisions to the plate of nodal cells, which develop the branches. In *Nitella* the long internodal cells remain uncovered; but in *Chara* they become covered by a sheath of cells developed from the basal cells of the short branches, so that a cross section of an axis shows a central cell of large caliber sheathed by a ring of small cells (cortical cells). The protoplast of the internodal cell consists of a thick peripheral layer of cytoplasm surrounding a large central vacuole and embedding numerous nuclei and oval chloroplasts. In a young internodal cell there is a single large nucleus, but in connection with the great enlargement of the cell the nucleus gives rise to numerous nuclei by fragmentation. The internodal cells of *Nitella* are noteworthy for exhibiting streaming movements of protoplasm with remarkable distinctness.

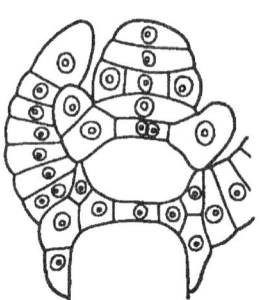

FIG. 114. — *Chara*: apical cell cutting off segments to form nodes and internodes; the nodal cells forming branches. — After SACHS.

Reproduction. — No asexual spores are produced, but vegetative multiplication is secured by tuberlike outgrowths, special branches, etc., from the nodes. The structures connected with sexual reproduction, however, afford the most distinguishing feature of the group. The antheridia and oogonia, instead of being single cells, as in the groups previously described, are highly complex structures. They are borne at the nodes of the short branches and are visible to the naked eye, the mature antheridia being deep orange to red (fig. 115).

Antheridium. — The antheridium is globular, the wall being com-

THALLOPHYTES

posed of eight triangular, platelike cells known as *shields* (fig. 115). Projecting centripetally from the center of each shield is an elongated cell (*manubrium*), which bears a terminal cell (*head cell*). These head cells give rise to a varying number of similar cells, and each ultimate cell produces a pair of long filaments, each consisting of approximately 200 cells, each cell producing a single sperm (figs. 117, 118). The interior of the antheridium, therefore, is a tangle of filaments, and the

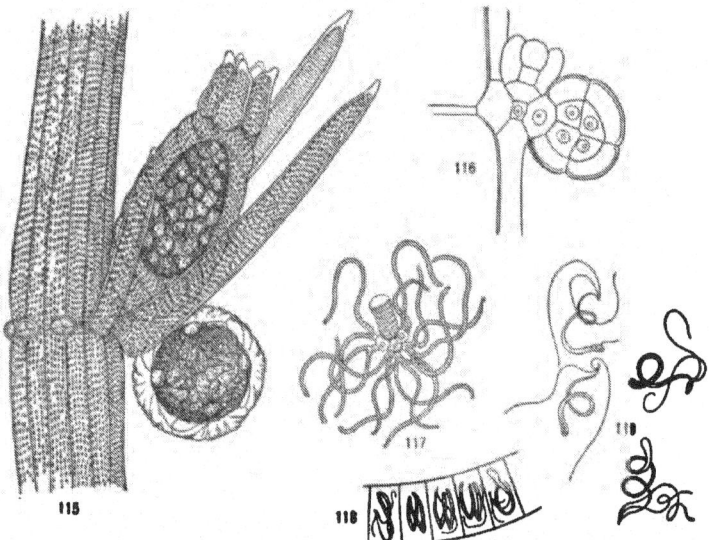

FIGS. 115-119.—*Chara:* 115, branch bearing oogonium (showing its sterile jacket and crown) and antheridium (showing its interlocking, shieldlike wall cells); 116, young oogonium (stalked and not yet completely invested by the jacket) and antheridium; 117, manubrium bearing head cells and sperm-containing filaments; 118, detail of cells of filament showing contained sperms; 119, sperms (spirally coiled and biciliate).—After SACHS.

sperm output of a single antheridium may range between 20,000 and 50,000. The sperm is a more specialized structure than is the zoospore-like sperm of the ordinary algae, and more resembles the sperms of higher plants. The nucleus with its sheath of cytoplasm forms the *body*; the cytoplasm extends to form an elongated more or less spirally coiled *beak*, and from its tip two long cilia are produced (fig. 119).

Oogonium.—The oogonium, which replaces a secondary branch, is an enlarged apical cell, and produces a single large egg filled with starch grains and oil drops. The complexity arises from the fact that the oogonium is closely invested by spirally wound elongated cells that arise from the cell beneath. Above the oogonium each investing cell cuts off a tip cell, the cluster of tip cells forming the so-called *crown* (figs. 115, 116). In fertilization the crown cells spread apart at the base, leaving five small slits, through which the sperms pass. Upon the formation of the oospore, the walls of the envelope cells thicken and harden, forming a nutlike spore case, which is the resting stage. Upon germination, the oospore sends out a simple filament and an elongated rhizoidal cell, a structure called the *proembryo*, and from the proembryo the adult shoot arises as a lateral branch. The adult plants, therefore, arise as lateral branches from a very different body.

Conclusions. — It is evident that the Charales cannot be related to the other green algae, since they differ strikingly in vegetative body, sex organs, sperms, and life history — in all of which particulars the resemblances are rather with the higher plants. They should at least be isolated as a distinct group of Thallophytes, or preferably should constitute a group between Thallophytes and Bryophytes.

(2) PHAEOPHYCEAE

General character. — The brown algae are almost all marine. They occur on all seacoasts, but are more abundant and conspicuous in the cooler waters. The forms exposed to tidal action have tough, leathery, and firmly anchored bodies, which sometimes reach such dimensions as hundreds of feet in length. They are also often highly differentiated, both as to form and tissues. The nature of the characteristic pigment or pigments is in doubt. The green constituent may or may not be chlorophyll, but in any event there are also present certain brown or yellow constituents which give the characteristic color to the plants, referred to in the name of the group. It must not be supposed that all brown algae are necessarily brown, for there are gradations in the hue of the bodies from brown to olive green, but the characteristic brown or yellow constituents are always present. Two of these constituents have been separated and named *phycoxanthin* and *phycophaein*. Another general character of brown algae is that all the motile cells (zoospores and sperms) are laterally biciliate, in sharp contrast with the apically ciliate cells of most algae.

The group is regarded as a highly specialized one, giving little or no indication of its origin. There is certainly no indication that it has

THALLOPHYTES

been derived from the Chlorophyceae, and it has possibly developed independently from such organisms as gave rise to the green algae. None of the true brown algae are one-celled, the simplest being a simple conferva-like filament, and the group also includes forms with very complex bodies. Sexual reproduction is probably present in all the forms, having been discovered recently in *Laminaria*, and is chiefly represented by isogamy, but a small group has attained heterogamy.

The two orders of brown algae are distinguished by their methods of reproduction: *Phaeosporales*, characterized by the formation of zoospores and by prevailing isogamy; *Fucales*, characterized by the absence of zoospores and by well-developed heterogamy.

(a) Phaeosporales

General character. — This group includes the large majority of brown algae and also the most bulky. The zoospores and gametes are alike, and are produced in special organs — the *sporangium* and the *gametangium*. It will not be possible or profitable to give an account of the numerous families, but the general features of the group may be indicated by the following illustrations:

Ectocarpus. — This form occurs as tufts of branching, many-celled filaments. The filament may consist of a single row of cells, in which case the body is called *monosiphonous;* or it may consist of several parallel rows of cells, in which case the body is *polysiphonous*.

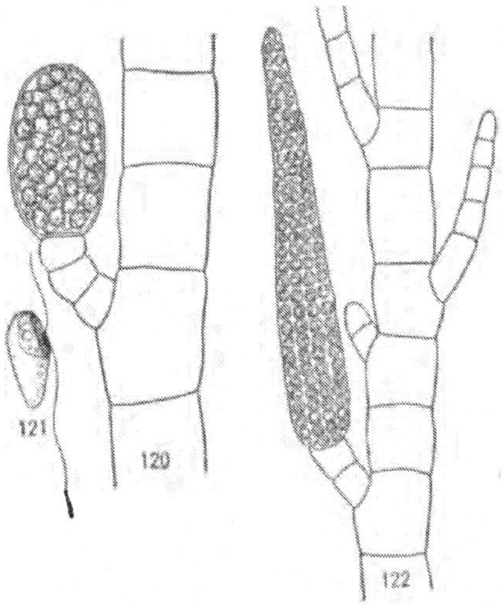

Sporangium. — The sporangium is a single cell, which in some forms is a cell of

FIGS. 120-122. — *Ectocarpus:* 120, monosiphonous filament bearing a sporangium on a short lateral branch; 121, a zoospore, showing the laterally biciliate character (after KUCKUCK); 122, filament bearing a gametangium ("plurilocular sporangium").

the filament changed in function and usually in size; and in other forms is developed at the end of a special short lateral branch (fig. 120).

46 MORPHOLOGY

In either case the zoospores produced are laterally biciliate (fig. 121) and develop new filaments directly.

Gametangium. — The gametangium is a many-celled structure, and, like the sporangium, is developed either from ordinary cells of the filament or at the end of a short lateral branch (fig. 122). The small cells composing it are cubical, being packed together closely, and each one produces a biciliate, zoospore-like gamete. Upon escaping, the gametes pair and fuse, and a zygospore is formed. This gametangium is of great interest on account of the variations that occur, leading sometimes to uncertainty as to whether the structure should be called a gametangium or a sporangium; in fact, it is often called a *plurilocular sporangium*, in distinction from the true *unilocular sporangium*. In some cases the gametangium is reported to produce both zoospores and gametes, judged by their behavior. The question might be raised whether the so-called zoospores in this case are not parthenogenetic gametes (see p. 40). Other cases are reported in which the gametangium is said to produce motile cells of three sizes, the medium-sized ones germinating directly, and the largest and smallest ones pairing. In this case, we should have not only zoospores, but also dissimilar gametes. In another case it is reported that the larger gamete comes to rest and is fertilized in this quiescent condition; in which case heterogamy would be very apparent. In the same genus, therefore, there occur both zygospore and oospore formation, and more or less confusion of gametes and zoospores. The group would seem to be an unusually favorable one for observing both sex origin and sex differentiation.

Fig. 123. — *Laminaria;* showing bladelike body, stipe, and holdfast.

Sphacelaria. — In general structure and reproductive habits this form resembles *Ectocarpus*, but it may be used to illustrate the appearance and powers of an *apical*

THALLOPHYTES 47

cell. In such filamentous bodies as were met among the green algae, the filament is elongated by the division of all the cells; in other words, the power of cell-division is distributed throughout the filament. In *Ectocarpus* this power of cell-division to elongate the filament is more restricted, often being specially present in a region behind the tip, where the divisions occur in unusually rapid succession. In *Sphacelaria* this special power has become restricted to the apical cell, which

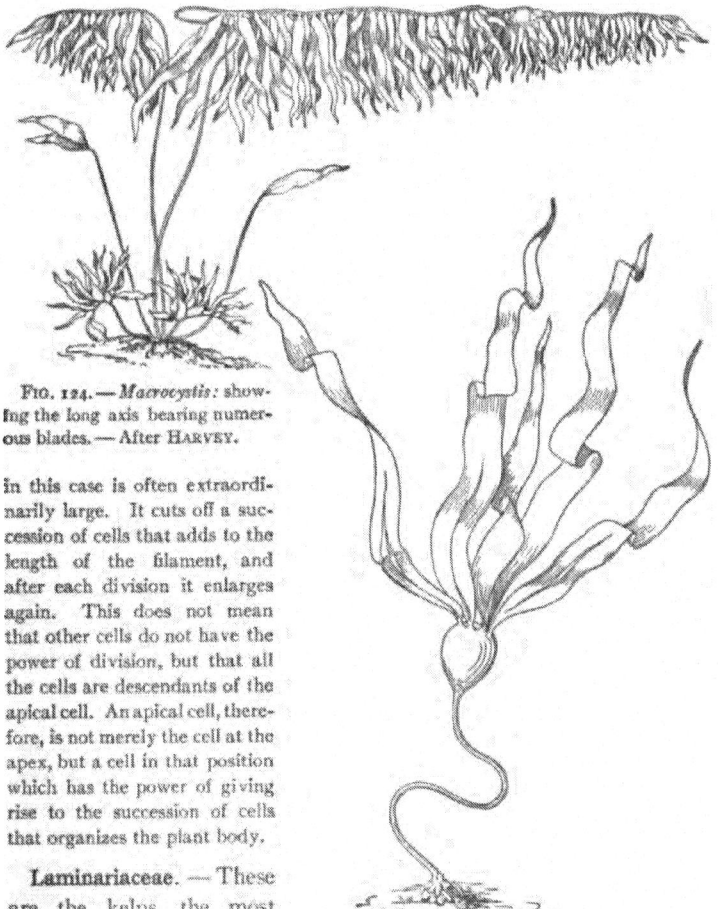

FIG. 124.—*Macrocystis*: showing the long axis bearing numerous blades.—After HARVEY.

in this case is often extraordinarily large. It cuts off a succession of cells that adds to the length of the filament, and after each division it enlarges again. This does not mean that other cells do not have the power of division, but that all the cells are descendants of the apical cell. An apical cell, therefore, is not merely the cell at the apex, but a cell in that position which has the power of giving rise to the succession of cells that organizes the plant body.

Laminariaceae. — These are the kelps, the most common and the largest of the brown algae. They are common on rocky coasts,

FIG. 125.—*Nereocystis*: showing the blades arising from the bladder-like expansion of the tip of the stipe.

being most abundant in northern latitudes. In the North Atlantic the large forms are chiefly species of the *Laminaria* type, the body resembling a huge leathery and stalked leaf blade sometimes 9 to 10 m. long, anchored by a rootlike holdfast (fig. 123). The most remarkable forms, with variously arranged blades, occur on the Pacific coast, among them being *Macrocystis* (giant kelp), whose huge bulk sometimes extends 200 to 275 m. (fig. 124); *Nereocystis* (bladder kelp), with long flexible stem (reaching 60 m.) that swells at the end into a large globular float to which are attached large blades (fig. 125); *Lessonia*, with a dichotomously branching stem like a tree trunk; and *Postelsia* or sea palm, whose name suggests its habit (fig. 126).

FIG. 126. — *Postelsia* (sea palm); showing numerous blades from the massive stipe, and the system of holdfasts.

The bodies are differentiated into blade, stipe (sometimes extremely long), and holdfast. The holdfast often takes the appearance of an excessively branching and very tough root system, but it should not be confused with roots in either structure or function. There is also often a marked differentiation of the cells into distinct tissues. For example, a section of the stipe of *Nereocystis* shows an outer pigment-bearing zone (cortex), a zone of storage cells, and a pith region (medulla) of loosely woven elongated cells. Although often very large and complex in form and tissues, the kelps, so far as known, are very simple in their reproductive methods. The gametangia occur in dense masses on certain portions of the ordinary

THALLOPHYTES

blades or on special blades, and the gametes which they produce were formerly mistaken for zoospores. It seems probable that zoospores have been eliminated from the life history of the kelps, as in the Fucales, and that the only spores are zygospores.

Cutleriaceae. — The body in this family is a broad, flat, forking thallus, and zoospores are formed as in other Phaeosporales; but there is a differentiation of gametes that deserves attention. Gametangia of two kinds are produced, similar in appearance, but dissimilar in gametes. One kind of gametangium produces fewer and larger gametes, the other more numerous and smaller gametes, and both kinds are ciliated and set free. In such a case, the two kinds of gametangia may be regarded as multicellular oogonia and antheridia, the fusion as fertilization, and the product as an oospore. Cutleriaceae, therefore, may be taken to represent a transition from Phaeosporales to Fucales.

(b) Fucales

General character. — This relatively small and specialized group of brown algae is characterized by the absence of zoospores and the presence of well-developed heterogamy. The common representatives are *Fucus* (rockweed) and *Sargassum* (gulfweed).

Fucus. — The body of these exceedingly common forms is a flat thallus which forks repeatedly (fig. 127), a type of branching called *dichotomous*. It grows by means of an apical cell, which soon becomes placed at the bottom of a notch by the more rapid growth of the two branches. The body is attached to its support by a basal disk, and is made buoyant by air bladders or floats that are inflated intercellular spaces. There is also a distinct differentiation of tissues into the more compact cortex and the looser medulla. The absence of zoospores in an aquatic form or of asexual spores of any kind is hard to understand.

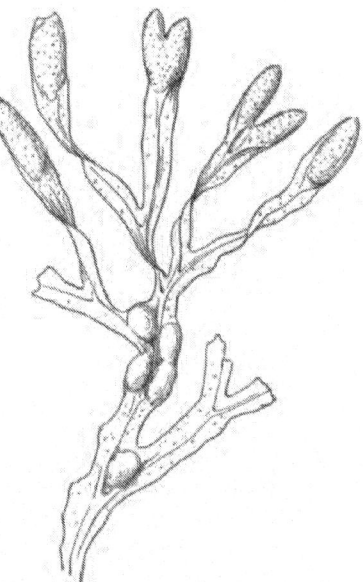

FIG. 127. — *Fucus:* showing the dichotomous thallus, the region of sex organs at the branch tips, and the air bladders.

MORPHOLOGY

Sex organs. — In the thallus body, often at the tips of special branches, there occur the *conceptacles*, which are chambers, each of which opens to the surface by a small porelike opening. Within these conceptacles the antheridia and oogonia are produced, the two organs appearing in the same conceptacle or in different ones (figs. 128, 129). The conceptacles contain also numerous branching filaments (*paraphyses*), which

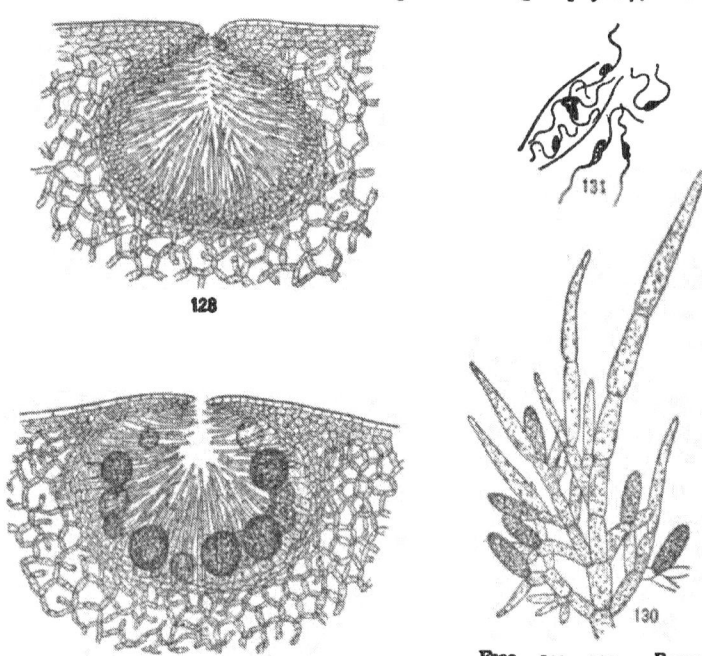

FIGS. 128, 129.—*Fucus:* 128, an antheridial conceptacle; 129, an oogonial conceptacle.—After THURET.

FIGS. 130, 131.—*Fucus:* 130, the oval antheridia borne on a branching paraphysis; 131, the laterally biciliate sperms.—After THURET.

arise from the cells bounding them. The antheridia are borne as lateral branches of these paraphyses and are produced in great profusion (figs. 130, 131). They are oval cells that produce numerous small laterally biciliate sperms. The oogonium is a large, globular, stalked cell and commonly produces eight eggs (oospheres) (figs. 132–136). There are related genera whose oogonia produce four or two eggs, and often only one; but in all of them eight nuclei appear. Such evidence suggests

THALLOPHYTES 51

that the forms with one, two, or four eggs have been derived from those with eight, some of the eggs not developing, but all eight represented by nuclei. Both sperms and eggs are discharged and escape from the conceptacle. *Fucus* is remarkable, therefore, not only in the production of eight eggs by the oogonium, but also in the fact that they are discharged before fertilization. The eggs float and are surrounded by

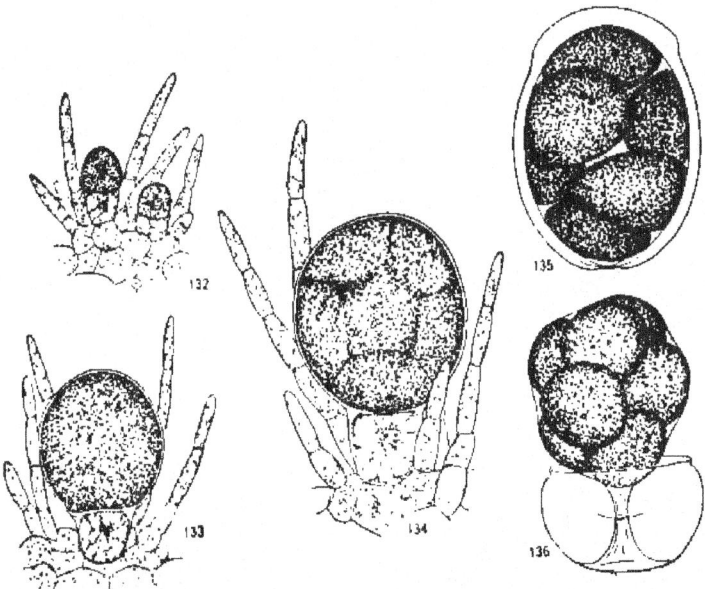

FIGS. 132–136. — *Fucus:* 132, young oogonia among the paraphyses; 133, an older oogonium; 134, oogonium beginning to develop the eight eggs; 135, the eggs rounded off; 136, the eggs escaping from the oogonium. — After THURET.

swarms of sperms, which have been observed to set them rotating (figs. 137, 138). The functioning sperm enters the egg, comes in contact with its nucleus, and the two nuclei lying in contact gradually fuse. Apparently the oospore is not a resting cell, but develops a new plant at once (figs. 139, 140).

In following the life history of *Fucus* it has been found that the number of chromosomes, which is doubled by the fusion of the male and female nuclei, is not reduced until the gametes appear. Therefore, using the number of chromosomes as a test, the whole vegetative plant is the sporophyte generation (the one with $2x$ chromosomes), and the gametophyte (the x generation) is represented only by the gametes.

Sargassum. — The gulfweeds are well known on account of their connection with the so-called Sargasso Sea. In that great ocean eddy, these gulfweeds accumulate in vast quantities, and the impression has been that they have been torn from the coast and swept out to sea. In any event, they continue growing, and perhaps pass through their whole life history in this floating condition. They are remarkable for the differentiation of the body into regions which may well be called leaves and branching stems, and they also produce short branches that develop the bladder-like floats which resemble small berries (fig. 141). So far as is known, the reproduction resembles that of *Fucus*.

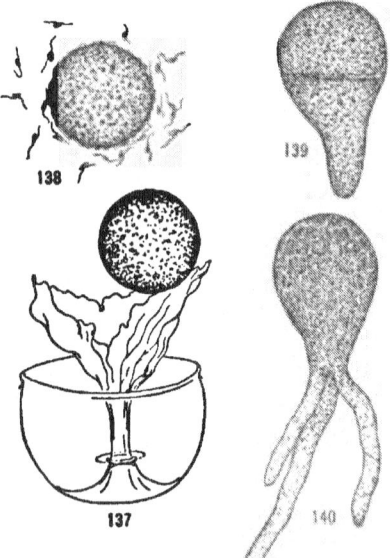

FIGS. 137-140. — *Fucus:* 137, an egg freed from the oogonium; 138, an egg surrounded by a swarm of sperms; 139, a fertilized egg beginning to germinate; 140, a young plant. — After THURET.

In connection with the brown algae, it is convenient to consider two groups of thallophytes whose connections are entirely uncertain. It must be understood that they are not presented as brown algae, or as algae at all.

Diatoms. — This is a vast assemblage of one-celled plants that occur in profusion in fresh and salt water and damp soil. They exist in such tremendous numbers in the ocean as to form a large part of the floating *plankton*, that free-swimming and free-floating world of minute organisms. Many diatoms occur as fossils, forming large deposits, as the so-called siliceous earths, etc. They are solitary and free-swimming forms, or are attached by gelatinous stalks excreted by the cells, the stalks often profusely branching. The forms of the cells are too numerous for description, a common free-swimming form being boat-shape (*Navicula*), but there are rods, wedges, disks, etc. (figs. 142-145).

Cell wall. — The cell wall is a special feature, for it consists of two siliceous valves, one overlapping the other, like the two parts of a pill box. The wall is so impregnated with silica that it forms a complete and resistant siliceous **skeleton**.

In many cases the valves are sculptured with fine transverse lines (really rows of dots), the markings being so regular and minute as to serve as a test of the definition of lenses. There is also a longitudinal line (*raphe*), which represents a cleft or a series of openings through which pseudopodia are thrust for locomotion. There are two distinct aspects of such cells: that showing the relation of the valves being the *girdle* side and that showing the face of a valve being the *valve* side.

Structure. — The protoplast consists of usually peripheral cytoplasm, a central nucleus swung in a bridge of cytoplasm, and two large or numerous smaller brownish yellow chromoplasts, often called *endochrome plates*. Their color is due to the

FIG. 141. — *Sargassum:* showing the appearance of stem and leaves, and the berry-like floats.

chlorophyll (at least a green constituent) and a characteristic golden brown constituent called *diatomin*.[1]

Cell-division and auxospores. — In cell-division the growth of the protoplast separates the valves, and division occurring in the plane of the valves, each new protoplast possesses one of the old valves and forms a new valve on the naked side. It is evident that one of the two cells thus produced has the same size as the parent cell; while the other cell is smaller, for the smaller valve of the parent cell becomes the larger (overlapping) valve of the daughter cell. This means that among the progeny cells there are series of individuals of diminishing size. When this diminution in size has reached a minimum, the *auxospores* are formed, the name indicating "enlarging spores." Auxospores may be produced in a variety of ways, the simplest being the separation of the valves and the escape of the protoplast, which in this free condition grows to the maximum size and develops new valves. In this case the auxospore is simply the escaped protoplast. In other

[1] The precise relation of these pigments is not certainly known.

cases the protoplast divides into two daughter protoplasts that escape and function as auxospores, the process suggesting real spore formation. Both of these methods are also associated with sexual reproduction: in the one case the escaped protoplasts of two contiguous cells conjugate to form the auxospore; and in the other case the four daughter protoplasts from two contiguous cells pair and conjugate. An auxospore, therefore, may be a naked protoplast, an asexual spore, or a zygospore, the feature in common being that there is a restoration of size before valve formation.

Relationships. — Such characters do not suggest any evident relationships for the diatoms, and they seem to stand apart from other groups of thallophytes, excepting perhaps the Peridineae (see below), and such a connection would not help the problem much. In certain particulars the cell structure suggests that of the desmids, and by some the diatoms are associated with them under Chlorophyceae (Conjugales). The brown pigment associated with the green suggests Phaeophyceae, and hence in some texts diatoms are found among the brown algae. It is perhaps best at present to keep the group apart from others, as one of the several unrelated groups of thallophytes.

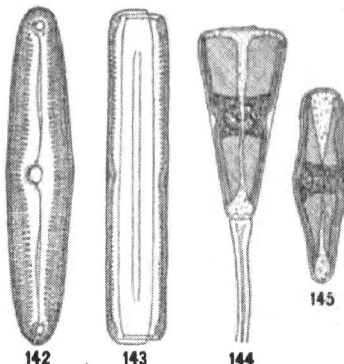

FIGS. 142–145. — *Diatoms:* 142, free-swimming form, valve side; 143, same form, girdle side, showing the relation of the valves; 144, 145, girdle and valve views of a stalked form. — 142, 143, after PFITZER; 144, 145, after ENGLER and PRANTL.

Peridineae. — These organisms are mostly marine and are associated with diatoms in forming much of the plankton of the ocean. They consist usually of single cells which are naked or have a cellulose wall, which is often sculptured. The naked forms are laterally biciliate, thus resembling the zoospores of the brown algae. The nucleus is distinct; there is a complex system of vacuoles; and there may be green, yellow, or brown chromoplasts, or none at all; meaning that some forms have the food-manufacturing power of algae and others have not. Many of the forms multiply freely by ordinary cell-division, and sometimes there are regularly formed zoospores. No gametes are recorded, but it seems very probable that the free "zoospores" may sometimes conjugate. The characters given indicate a low synthetic group; for the ciliated vegetative cells suggest the simpler Volvocales; the sculptured walls, chromoplasts, and other features suggest diatoms; the laterally biciliate motile cells and yellow or brown chromoplasts suggest brown algae; and the forms without chromoplasts do not suggest algae at all.

(3) RHODOPHYCEAE

General character. — This great group, containing only a few freshwater forms, includes the majority of the marine algae. They are by no means so bulky as many of the brown algae, but they are much more diversified in form. In the simplest forms the body is a simple or branching filament, which is monosiphonous or polysiphonous (see p. 45), or it may be flat and filmy, or ribbon-like. The more complex forms show an extreme differentiation of the body into branching stems, leaves, and holdfasts. The species of *Corallina* resemble branching coral on account of the abundant deposit of calcium carbonate in their cell walls. The general hue of the plants is red or violet, sometimes dark purple or reddish brown, the color being due to the presence of a red pigment (*phycoerythrin*) that may be separated from the green (which may or may not be chlorophyll). In addition to the presence of phycoerythrin, one of the chief peculiarities of the group is the absence of any ciliated cells, either swimming spores or gametes, which is a surprising feature in so extensive an aquatic group. Another conspicuous peculiarity is the method of sexual reproduction, which often results in a very complicated life history.

The Rhodophyceae seem to form an independent group, with no evident connections, and are certainly the most specialized of algae. The Florideae so nearly include all of the red algae that the name is often used as synonymous with Rhodophyceae. It is impossible to present adequately the maze of forms, and three of the best known are selected as illustrations, two representing the simpler forms and simpler sexual reproduction, the third representing the more complex forms and complex sexual reproduction.

Before presenting these types, mention may be made of a small group that combines certain characters of brown and red algae.

Dictyotales. — This is a small group of marine forms, of uncertain affinities, but interesting on account of the combination of characters. They are sometimes included among the brown algae, and sometimes among the red algae, so that they may well be mentioned between these two groups. The body is a narrow, repeatedly dichotomous thallus, whose pigment contains a brown constituent suggesting that characteristic of the brown algae. Sporangia are developed on the surface of the thallus, and each sporangium produces four non-motile spores (*tetraspores*), a conspicuous character of the red algae. The antheridia occur in clusters on the surface of the thallus, and produce sperms with a single terminal spiral cilium, a character that belongs neither to brown algae nor to red algae. The oogonia also are clusters of superficial cells, each one discharging a single egg, a character suggesting the egg-discharging habit of *Fucus*. In such a case, the comparative value of characters must be estimated, and perhaps tetraspore formation is to be regarded as the most important among those given. If this be true, the Dictyotales are to be considered as an aberrant group of red algae.

Nemalion.—This marine form will serve to illustrate the simpler red algae. It is a branching filament, and probably produces no tetraspores.

Antheridia.—The antheridia occur in clusters at the ends of short branches (fig. 146), each antheridium being a single cell, which at first contains a single nucleus. This nucleus divides, so that the protoplast of the mature antheridium contains two male nuclei. Physiologically, therefore, the antheridium contains two sperms, but they are not organized as morphologically distinct sperms. This binucleate protoplast is discharged from the antheridium, and not being ciliate it is carried by water currents to the female organ. This non-motile sperm, or sperm complex, is usually called a *spermatium*, but there is no special advantage in multiplying the names of a male cell. The special name was felt to be necessary when motile sperms were called *spermatozoids* or *antherozoids*, but the general term *sperm* can be applied to non-motile as well as to motile male cells.

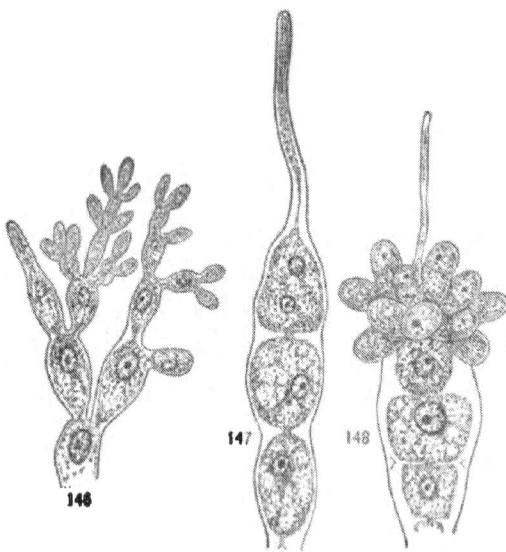

FIGS. 146–148.—*Nemalion:* 146, branch showing antheridia forming at the tips; 147, the procarp, consisting of trichogyne and carpogonium (in the latter the male and female nuclei are observed, the former having passed in from the trichogyne); also showing two other cells with the broad cytoplasmic connections; 148, a cystocarp, showing the carpospores being cut off at the tips of short branches, which have arisen from the fertilized carpogonium.

Female sex organ.—The female sex organ of *Nemalion* illustrates, perhaps in its simplest form, this remarkable structure among the red algae, which usually consists of several cells and is called the *procarp*. In *Nemalion* the procarp consists of what may be regarded as two cells

THALLOPHYTES

at the end of a branch; the *carpogonium*, a cell which is the equivalent of the oogonium of other algae in that it contains the female nucleus, although no definite egg is organized; and the *trichogyne*, an elongated, hairlike cell terminating the carpogonium, which acts as the receptive cell with which the sperms come in contact (fig. 147). At first the trichogyne contains its own nucleus, but soon this nucleus disappears, and the two cells appear as a single one, with a bulbous base and a hairlike extension.

In fertilization the floating sperm comes in contact with the trichogyne, the two walls in contact become resorbed, and through the perforation one or both of the male nuclei are discharged. More than one sperm may come in contact with the trichogyne, and several male nuclei may be discharged into it; but only one passes on into the carpogonium and fuses with the female nucleus (fig. 147).

Cystocarp. — As a result of this act of fertilization, numerous short filaments are developed by the carpogonium, and at the tip of each one a spore is formed (rounded off), called the *carpospore* (fig. 148). This whole structure — carpospores, filaments, and central carpogonium — is the *cystocarp*, but it is not a cystocarp representative of this organ among the red algae, as will be seen in the other illustrations. The carpospores upon germination give rise to the sexual plants, thus completing the life history.

In such a life history, the sexual plants may be multiplied directly by tetraspores (when they occur); but the sexual act results in the formation of a cystocarp, a structure producing carpospores, which in turn reproduce the sexual plants.

Batrachospermum. — This fresh-water form is related to *Nemalion*, and will serve to illustrate other features of the simpler red algae. The life history is very much like that of *Nemalion;* but while the carpospores are forming, loose filaments appear as outgrowths from cells at the base of the carpogonium, representing the case of the true cystocarp of other groups, the envelope or case having suggested the name. This encasing outgrowth from adjacent sterile cells is a very common accompaniment of the act of fertilization not only among the red algae, but also in other groups. It will be remembered that a similar envelope is developed by *Coleochaete* and by the Charales, but in the latter case it appears before fertilization.

Germination. — When the carpospore of *Batrachospermum* germinates, it gives rise to a filamentous body very different from that of the sexual *Batrachospermum*, and once believed to be an independent plant it was named *Chantransia*. These *chantransia* forms multiply by spores (not tetraspores); but sooner or later one of the lateral branches develops as the sexual *Batrachospermum* filament. The *chantransia* form, therefore, is only one phase in the life history of *Batrachospermum*, giving rise to sexual branches of very different kind, which once were thought to be independent plants. It should be noted that both these phases constitute one vegetative body, the product of the carpospore. This striking variation in form, where one structure gives rise directly to a very different structure, is found in the life history of many plants, and it has been referred to in connection with the life history of Charales.

Polysiphonia. — This form is selected to illustrate the more complex and the more numerous red algae. This more complex majority includes in the life history the formation of the characteristic tetraspores, which are non-motile, naked, asexual spores, a group of four being produced by each one-celled sporangium. In the maturing sporangium there are two successive nuclear divisions, and in connection with these four nuclei the spores are organized. This definiteness in the number of nuclear divisions indicates some definite process, which will be considered later. The sporangia of red algae occur in various situations, either at the tips of short lateral branches or embedded in the thallus, in the latter case being either scattered or in special receptacles.

Polysiphonia has received its name because the complex branching filament is polysiphonous (figs. 149–151), consisting of a central row of elongated cells (axial siphon), surrounded by peripheral cells (cortical cells). Ordinarily there are three kinds of individuals: (1) male plants, bearing antheridia; (2) female plants, bearing procarps; and (3) sexless plants, bearing sporangia that produce tetraspores.

Male plant. — The antheridia occur in clusters on special branches (fig. 149). The structure of an antheridial branch is as follows: From the cells of the axial siphon large numbers of small cells arise laterally, each of which gives rise in turn to a terminal cell. An oblique division of this terminal cell cuts off a cell which is the antheridium (fig. 152). The antheridium does not discharge its protoplast as a sperm, as in *Nemalion*, but is cast off bodily, in this case the so-called "spermatium" being an antheridium that functions directly as a sperm. Its nucleus does not divide, as in *Nemalion*, so that the antheridium contains only one male nucleus. A second or even a third antheridium may be cut off successively by the same parent cell.

THALLOPHYTES 59

Female plant. — In *Polysiphonia* the procarp includes several cells in addition to the carpogonium and trichogyne. The carpogonium arises from a large cell of the axis, called the *pericentral cell*, and around

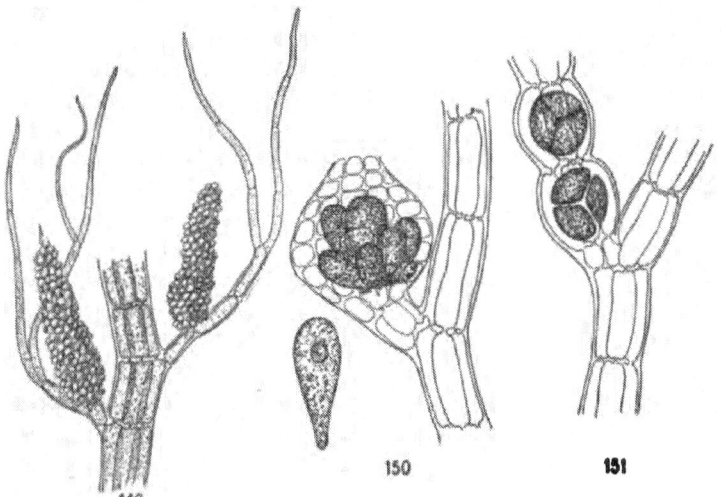

FIGS. 149-151. — *Polysiphonia:* 149, showing the polysiphonous bodies bearing two clusters of antheridia; 150, cystocarp, showing the sterile jacket investing the group of carpospores, and also an isolated carpospore; 151, two mother cells forming tetraspores.

this cell a group of *auxiliary cells* is formed, one of which crowds between the pericentral cell and the carpogonium. This whole complex structure — trichogyne, carpogonium, pericentral cell, and auxiliary cells — is the procarp (fig. 153).

Fertilization occurs as in *Nemalion*, the floating sperm (antheridium) coming in contact with the trichogyne and discharging into it its contents. The male nucleus passes to the carpogonium and there fuses with the female nucleus. The fusion nucleus divides within the carpogonium, and then what are called cell fusions begin. A passageway is opened from the carpogonium, through the intervening auxiliary cell, and into the pericentral cell, and by this means the two daughter nuclei of the fusion nucleus are free to migrate into the pericentral cell. At the same time, the auxiliary cells begin to fuse with one another and with the pericentral cell, until a large, irregular, multinucleate cell or chamber is formed. In this irregular chamber the two nuclei from the carpogonium begin a series of successive divisions, which result in a large number of nuclei that have descended from the fusion nucleus. The irregular fusion chamber puts out lobes, into each one of which a nucleus passes and divides. At the tip of each lobe a spore is developed by a sort of budding, and into it one of the two lobe nuclei passes. In this way sixty or more carpospores are formed in a single cystocarp. The usual envelope of sterile cells, in this case an urn-shaped envelope, is developed about the whole carpospore-bearing structure from the adjacent cells (fig. 150).

Tetrasporic plant. — Upon germination the carpospores give rise to plants that produce tetraspores, but no sex organs. The sporangia arise laterally from the axial siphon, each sporangium standing on a stalk cell and finally pushing through the covering of cortical cells (fig. 151). Upon germination the tetraspores give rise to plants that bear sex organs (antheridia and procarps).

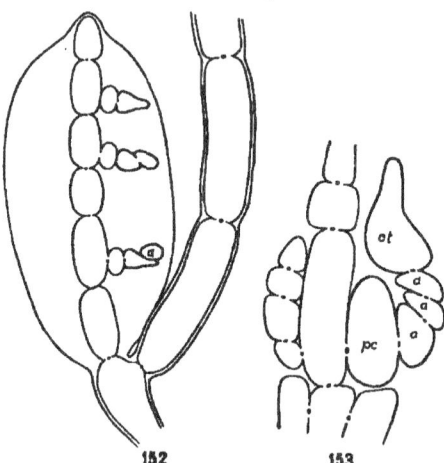

FIGS. 152, 153. — *Polysiphonia*: 152, diagram showing formation of antheridia (*a*); 153, diagram showing structure of procarp (*pc*, pericentral; *d*, carpogonium and trichogyne; *a*, some of the auxiliary cells, one of which crowds in between the carpogonium and the pericentral). — After YAMANOUCHI.

Alternation of generations. — This remarkable life history introduces us to the alternation of generations, a type of life history that is invariable in the great plant groups above thallophytes. It is an alternation of sexual and sexless individuals, each producing spores that give rise to the other. The cytological test of alternation, referred to under *Coleochaete*, has been applied to *Polysiphonia*, and the fact of a real alternation has thus been established. It will be remembered that in such an alternation the number of chromosomes characteristic of the nuclei is doubled by the act of fertilization; therefore, the nuclei of the sexless individuals (sporophytes), which are products of fertilization, contain the double number ($2x$) of chromosomes; while the nuclei of the sexual individuals (gametophytes) contain the half number (x). This means that in passing from sporophyte to gametophyte, $2x$ must be reduced to x. In *Polysiphonia*, the sexual individuals (gametophytes) show twenty chromosomes in their nuclear divisions, and of course this number characterizes the male and female nuclei which they produce. At fertilization the fusion nucleus receives forty chromosomes, and this number persists through the cystocarp, the carpospores, and the tetrasporic plants. This indicates that the tetrasporic plants are true sporophytes, and it is in the sporangium, in the nuclear divisions concerned in the formation of the tetraspores, that the reduction in the number of chromosomes occurs. These nuclear divisions are called *reduction divisions*, and they represent one of the two important epochs in the life history, the other being the act of fertilization. On account of the reduction division, each tetraspore contains the half number of chromosomes, and this number is continued through the sexual plant which it produces. In *Polysiphonia*, therefore, the male and female plants are gametophytes, and the tetrasporic plant is a sporophyte, the cystocarp also being sporophytic in the series of nuclei that extends from fusion nucleus to carpospore.

4. FUNGI

General character.—This enormous assemblage of thallophytes is characterized by the absence of chlorophyll, resulting in a lack of power to manufacture carbohydrate food. As a consequence, they are either *parasites*, dependent upon living plants or animals as *hosts;* or *saprophytes*, dependent upon organic débris or products from plants or animals. These are not terms of classification, for some fungi are able to live either as parasites or as saprophytes, and such are called *facultative* forms; while those restricted to either the parasitic or the saprophytic habit are *obligate* forms. The possible range of parasitism is quite different in different forms, some parasites attacking miscellaneous hosts, others being restricted to closely related hosts, others to a single kind of host, and still others attacking only certain organs (see p. 381).

The vegetative body of a fungus is the *mycelium*, composed of interwoven filaments called *hyphae*. The mycelium may he very open and delicate, or it may be feltlike, or even form a compact body (as in lichens). The mycelium establishes absorbing connections with its food supply (the *substratum*), and when these connections are definite and more or less specialized, they are called *haustoria* (suckers). In the case of a parasite, the substratum is either the surface or the internal tissues of the host (internal or external parasites), and in such cases the haustoria are very distinct structures (figs. 1079, 1080).

Under appropriate conditions the mycelium also produces vertical branches (*sporophores*), which in a variety of ways give rise to spores. In the case of internal parasites, the sporophores reach the surface of the host, the spores thus being formed in surroundings that favor dispersal. Fungi are notable for the vast number of spores produced, and in most cases their dispersal is aerial, so that mycelia are multiplied with great rapidity and over wide areas. The sexual reproduction of fungi is exceedingly varied: in some cases the sex organs are as evident as are those of algae; in other cases the sexual act is so obscure as to raise the question whether in some life histories it has not been eliminated entirely.

Usually three great groups of fungi are recognized: (1) *Phycomycetes* (algal fungi), (2) *Ascomycetes* (sac fungi), and (3) *Basidiomycetes* (basidial fungi). The Phycomycetes differ so much from the other two groups that the latter are often spoken of together as the *Eumycetes*, or true fungi, and they contain the large majority of fungi.

(1) PHYCOMYCETES

General character. — This comparatively small group of fungi resembles the green algae in many features, a fact which has suggested the name. It is not hard to imagine that the Phycomycetes are green algae which have lost their chlorophyll and have developed the dependent habit. Such a claim cannot be made for the Eumycetes, which have so little resemblance to the algae that any connection with them is too obscure to consider. The mycelium of Phycomycetes is composed of coenocytic hyphae, suggesting a connection with Siphonales; and this connection with green algae is further emphasized by the sex organs, which are equally prominent and of the same structure. In fact, the two groups of Phycomycetes are distinguished by their sexual apparatus: (a) *Oomycetes*, which are heterogamous, and (b) *Zygomycetes*, which are isogamous.

(a) Oomycetes

General character. — These heterogamous forms are regarded as more primitive than the isogamous Zygomycetes because they are more closely related to the algae. They are mostly aquatic and produce zoospores, in these features differing from the Zygomycetes, in which the aerial habit is established and no motile reproductive cells are produced. However, the two groups cannot be separated rigidly upon this basis, for the aquatic habit with zoospores gradually merges into the aerial habit without zoospores. If this order of succession is true, it is an interesting illustration of the derivation of isogamy from heterogamy, which would mean a line of degeneracy so far as the apparent sexual apparatus is concerned. Illustrations of Phycomycetes may be selected from three important groups.

Chytridiales. — These are regarded as the simplest of the Phycomycetes, many of them being aquatic and parasitic on algae, and others attacking seed plants. Two of the prominent genera are as follows:

Chytridium. — A species of this genus which attacks *Oedogonium* may be used as an illustration. The zoospore has one cilium, and settling upon an oogonium sends a tube through to the egg on which it feeds. The external region of the parasite grows bulbous and functions as a sporangium, discharging zoospores which attack other plants (fig. 154). When the oospore of *Oedogonium* is formed, the fungus develops within it thick-walled resting cells; and upon the germination of the oospore, these resting cells put out tubes that produce terminal sporangia, and the infection of the oogonia of *Oedogonium* begins again. These resting cells of *Chytridium* are very commonly seen in the sexually formed spores of *Oedogonium, Spirogyra, Cladophora,* etc. In some species of *Chytridium* these resting cells are said to be formed sexually; and in another genus of Chytridiales there are antheridia and oogonia, which fuse and form the resting cell, which in that case is an oospore.

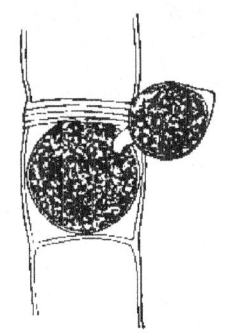

FIG. 154.—*Chytridium:* attacking the oogonium of *Oedogonium.* — After CAMPBELL.

Synchytrium. — This parasite attacks the epidermal cells of many seed plants, the uniciliate zoospores moving over the surface of young epidermis and entering the cells. In the young epidermal cell the zoospore grows as a naked protoplast, inciting the host cell to an unusual growth until it forms a blister-like pustule, distorting the adjacent tissue. Finally the protoplast develops a wall and becomes a resting cell, which in the next season sends out a swarm of zoospores. No gametes are known.

Saprolegniales. — The water molds are the most important family (*Saprolegniaceae*) of the group, being aquatics whose body resembles a colorless *Vaucheria*. The representative genus *Saprolegnia* contains saprophytic species found on dead bodies of crustaceans, water insects, etc., and also parasitic species attacking fishes, frogs, etc. One species that attacks the eggs and young of fishes is very destructive in hatcheries.

The asexual reproduction resembles that of *Cladophora*, sporangia developing as terminal cells and producing vast numbers of biciliate zoospores, which escape through a terminal pore (figs. 155, 156). The oogonium is a spherical cell, borne terminally or laterally, and contains one to several eggs. The antheridium is tubular in form, arising from another hypha or from the same one, and grows up in contact with the oogonium in various ways, sometimes curving about it. A small fertilizing tube sent out by the antheridium pierces the wall of the oogonium, reaches an egg, and through it the contents of the antheridium are discharged (fig. 157). Fertilization results in heavy-walled oospores, which upon germination form new hyphae directly.

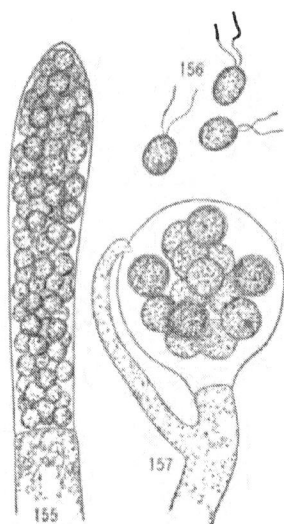

FIGS. 155–157. — *Saprolegnia:* 155, terminal cell producing zoospores; 156, free zoospores; 157, fertilization, showing oogonium containing several eggs, and antheridial tube piercing the oogonial wall.

Parthenogenesis. — *Saprolegnia* is notable for the frequent and perhaps usual occurrence of parthenogenesis. All stages of abortion of the male apparatus have been observed: as, for example, the antheridial tube reaching the egg but remaining closed; the tube piercing the wall of the oogonium but not reaching the egg; the suppression of an antheridial tube; or even the suppression of the antheridium. In all these cases the eggs develop as if fertilized, and produce new plants.

Experiments. — The culture of *Saprolegnia* under experimental control has succeeded in determining the conditions that favor vegetative activity, zoospore formation, and gamete formation. If well nourished, the plant vegetates indefinitely; if it is starved, as by removal to pure water, zoospore formation is induced; if the temperature is lowered, or if the plant is transferred to a solid substratum, conditions forbidding swarm spores, oogonia are formed.

Monoblepharis. — This is a form similar to *Saprolegnia* in many respects, being an aquatic saprophyte on decaying plants; but it is chiefly interesting as the only fungus that has retained swimming sperms. These sperms are uniciliate, as are the zoospores, a fact which suggested the generic name.

Peronosporales. — These are the downy mildews, and they include many destructive parasites that live within the tissues of the host, the hyphae branching through the intercellular spaces, crowding between the cells, and sending haustoria into them. This internal mycelium sends sporophores to the surface of the host, and spores are formed by rounding off the tips of the sporophores or their branches. This process of cutting off spores is called *abstriction*, and such spores are called *conidia*. Oogonia and antheridia are formed upon the internal mycelium, and fertilization is effected through a fertilizing tube.

This is the one group of Oomycetes with distinctly aerial habit, as in the Zygomycetes; but the forms are heterogamous, and in the life history of many of them zoospores appear. The prominent genera are as follows:

Albugo. — *A. candida* is the white rust which attacks members of the mustard family, causing distortions, especially in the flower clusters. The mycelium traverses the intercellular spaces of the host, the haustoria sent into the host cells being slender branches which enlarge at the ends into little knobs. The sporophores arise in clusters and press up the epidermis, which then appears like a white blister (fig. 158). Finally the epidermis is broken and the sporophores are exposed, each ending in a chain of spores (conidia), which have been formed by successive abstrictions of the sporophore. The conidia are multinucleate, and

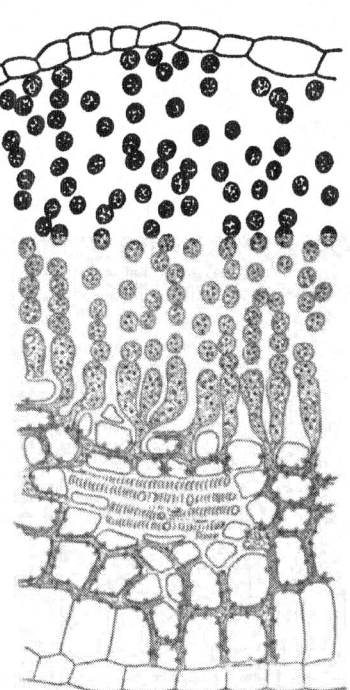

FIG. 158. — *Albugo candida* (white rust): showing mycelium crowding among host cells and sending into them small button-like haustoria, sporophores arising under epidermis and abstricting multinucleate conidia (spores), and the detached and dying epidermis. — After CHAMBERLAIN.

upon germination produce numerous laterally biciliate zoospores. The zoospores germinate promptly, each one sending out a tube that penetrates the seedling host and starts a new internal mycelium.

The sex organs of this genus are formed on the deep mycelium, the oogonia and antheridia appearing on separate hyphae. The oogonium is a globular, multinucleate cell. In the organization of the egg, the protoplast is differentiated into a peripheral zone of cytoplasm (*periplasm*), which contains all the nuclei except one, and a central mass of cytoplasm (*ooplasm*) containing a solitary nucleus for fertilization (fig. 159). The antheridium is also a multinucleate cell (fig. 160), which sends out a fertilizing tube that reaches the egg, and through this the male nuclei are discharged. One male nucleus fuses with the solitary nucleus of the ooplasm, and a heavy-walled oospore is formed. The oospore is liberated by the decay of the surrounding host tissue, and on germination either produces zoospores or develops a mycelium directly.

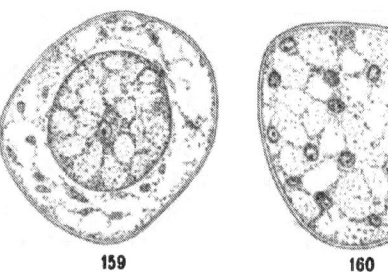

FIGS. 159, 160.—*Albugo:* 159, oogonium showing differentiation of protoplast into periplasm (containing numerous nuclei) and ooplasm (containing one nucleus); 160, oogonium showing no such differentiation of protoplast, resulting in multinucleate fusion during fertilization; also the multinucleate antheridium in contact.

In certain other species (*A. Bliti* and *A. Portulacae*), the numerous nuclei of the egg remain distributed throughout its mass (fig. 160), and when the male nuclei are discharged, there is multinucleate fusion, many nuclei pairing and fusing.

Phytophthora. — *P. infestans* is the fungus producing potato rot, a disease of great economic importance. The mycelium vegetates in the green parts of the plant, causing wilting and withering of leaves and stem. The sporophores are sent to the surface in immense numbers through stomata, and branch, bearing solitary conidia on the branches. Damp, windy weather is said to spread the disease like wildfire. The mycelium winters in the tubers.

Plasmopara. — *P. viticola* is the grape mildew, the groups of branching sporophores appearing like downy spots upon the surface of the host (conspicuous on the leaves.) The conidia upon germination develop a mycelium directly, instead

THALLOPHYTES 67

of zoospores, a feature which distinguishes the genus from *Peronospora*, under which the grape mildew was placed formerly. In the life history of *Plasmopara*, therefore, zoospores, characteristic of Oomycetes, have been eliminated. This disease is of American origin and was unknown in Europe until American grape stocks were introduced as a protection against the destructive phylloxera.

Peronospora. — These forms are very common parasites on ordinary vegetables, as peas, beans, spinach, etc., and differ from *Plasmopara* in the production of laterally biciliate zoospores by the conidia, as in *Albugo*.

(b) Zygomycetes

General character. — This group of Phycomycetes is distinguished from the Oomycetes in general by the establishment of the aerial habit; by the elimination of zoospores; by so-called isogamy, so far as the sexual reproduction is known; and perhaps by the sexual differentiation of individuals, although there is no distinct development of gametes.

Mucorales. — These are the black molds, which are mostly saprophytes. The characteristic cobwebby, fleecy-white mycelium, com-

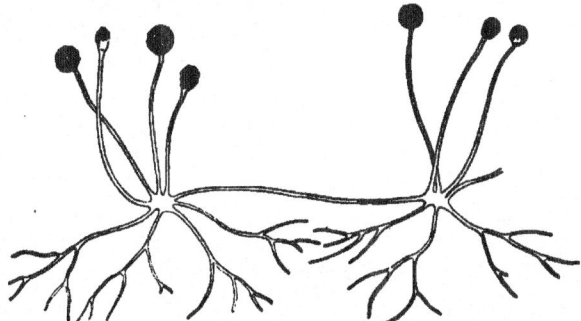

FIG. 161. — *Mucor*: diagram showing mycelium and sporophores.

posed of large, often glistening, profusely branching hyphae, is very common on decaying material, stale bread (kept moist and warm), fruits and fruit juices, etc. The ordinary form on dung is *Mucor Mucedo*, while the common bread mold is *Rhizopus nigricans* (fig. 161).

Sporangia. — The stout sporophores bear globular sporangia, the spores and stalk being dark or even black, suggesting the name black mold. After the terminal sporangium cell is cut off, the separating wall bulges into the sporangium cavity, forming the so-called *columella* (fig. 162). The sporangium wall finally becomes mucilaginous and the spores are set free and dispersed, forming new mycelia directly.

Sexual reproduction. — Sexual reproduction occurs under special conditions, when suitable individuals are brought together. The two kinds of individuals are called *strains*, and have been distinguished as (+) and (−) strains, which apparently correspond to female and male individuals. In general, the two strains are not recognizable by sight, but are known to be sexually different by their behavior. Fertile branches (*suspensors*) are developed by pairing individuals, come into contact (fig. 163), and a terminal cell (gametangium) is cut off by each (fig. 164). These two abutting gametangia are multinucleate, a perforation is developed at the contact, and the two protoplasts fuse, a very large and heavy-walled zygospore being formed (figs. 165, 166), from which a new mycelium is developed (fig. 167). In many cases the pairing suspensors and gametangia differ decidedly in size, in which case a differentiation into male and female individuals becomes visible (figs. 164-166). It has also been observed that the larger gametangia and suspensors arise from more robust mycelia, and these in turn from larger sporangia than do the smaller gametangia and suspensors. It seems possible to arrange a series of pairing gametangia, ranging from such inequality in size that the pair may be regarded as an oogonium and an antheridium (as in *Albugo*), to absolute equality. Such a series suggests a line of degenerating sexual organs, in which distinct heterogamy passes into isogamy; but of course it might be read in the opposite direction.

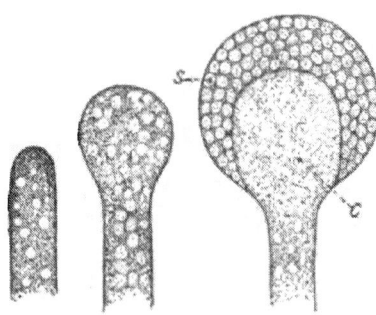

FIG. 162. — *Mucor:* showing the development of a sporangium at the end of a sporophore; in the last member of the series the spores (*s*) and columella (*c*) are evident.

Pilobolus. — This mold is abundant on stable manure, and resembles *Mucor*, but it is remarkable for the method of dehiscence of its sporangium. The sporophore becomes very turgid and swollen just beneath the sporangium and finally bursts, hurling the sporangium with considerable force. This curious habit has given to the plant the name squirting fungus. If a bell jar is placed over the plants, the inner surface becomes dotted with discharged sporangia.

Entomophthorales. — These are parasites fatal to insects, the common house fly often being destroyed by them. The spore (conidium) in germination sends out a tube that penetrates between the body segments or through the breathing pores of the insect. The mycelium finally kills it, filling the body in its vegetative growth. At this stage reproduction begins, the mycelium sending out numerous short branches, from which eventually sporophores arise, reaching the surface of the body and each abstricting a single conidium, which is squirted off much as is the sporangium in *Pilobolus*, the dead body of a fly adhering to a window pane often being surrounded by a "halo of spores."

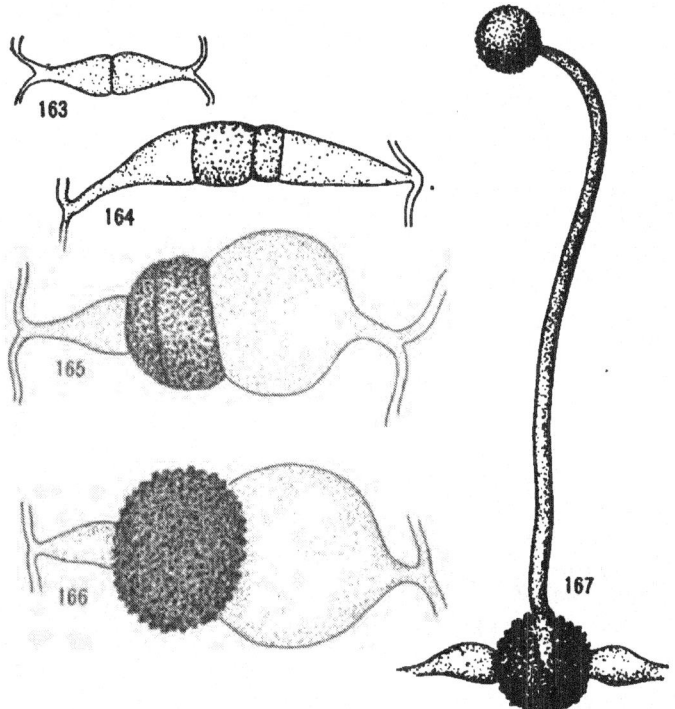

FIGS. 163-167. — *Mucor:* 163, fertile branches (suspensors) in contact; 164, gametangia (unequal) cut off; 165, 166, formation of zygospore by two very unequal suspensors; 167, zygospore producing a mycelium, which has already produced a sporangium (after BREFELD).

Conclusions. — The Phycomycetes strongly suggest relationship with the green algae, their coenocytic bodies resembling those of the Siphonales. They also show a transition from an aquatic (Oomycetes) to an aerial (Zygomycetes) habit, accompanied by a transition from zoospores to aerial spores. There is also an apparent reduction of the sexual apparatus, from heterogamous alga-like forms to isogamous forms. At the same time, although the sex organs lose their dissimilarity in appearance, there is retained, at least in some forms, a physiological differentiation which extends to individual mycelia.

(2) Ascomycetes

General character. —The sac fungi include the majority of fungi, and their connection with the algae is very vague. In contrast with the Phycomycetes, the mycelium is composed of septate filaments, and the sex organs are much reduced and even suppressed. The common character of this great assemblage of forms is the appearance of an *ascus* (sac) in the life history, in which the *ascospores* are formed. The ascus is a special cell, usually club-shaped or elongated, which at first contains two nuclei. These nuclei fuse, and the fusion nucleus begins a series of three successive divisions, resulting in eight nuclei. About each nucleus a wall is formed, cutting out some cytoplasm, producing eight ascospores (fig. 176). These definitely three successive nuclear divisions, resulting always in eight ascospores, are found to be reduction divisions, resulting in reducing the number of chromosomes, and therefore the ascus holds the same important place in the life history of an ascomycete as does a spore mother cell in the higher plants (see p. 95). In the majority of forms, a spore case is developed in connection with the asci, more or less investing them with a protective jacket. This investing structure is the *ascocarp*, and it holds the same relation to the asci as does the cystocarp of red algae to the carpospores.

The group is so extensive and varied that no representative forms can be selected. A few illustrations from the eight usually recognized orders are as follows:

(a) Protoascales

The yeasts (*Saccharomycetes*) are the most familiar forms, but their position here is very doubtful, for it is felt that their whole life history is probably not known. They are solitary, oval cells,

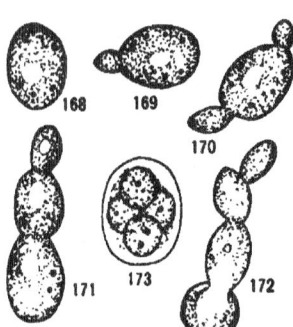

FIGS. 168–173. — *Yeast:* 168, yeast cell; 169, 170, cells budding; 171, 172, sprout chains; 173, cell containing four spores. — 168–171, after COULTER; 173, after REES.

THALLOPHYTES

which reproduce by rapid budding, forming *sprout chains* (figs. 168–172). When cultivated under certain conditions, four internal spores are formed, and this is the only ascomycete connection (fig. 173). If the connection is a true one, the yeast cell under certain conditions becomes an ascus. The great economic importance of the group in alcoholic fermentation is well known (see Part II, p. 409).

The group Protoascales, however, is based upon a few forms with a true mycelium, which are otherwise about as simple as yeasts.

(b) Protodiscales

This is a small group parasitic on seed plants, especially trees. A characteristic genus is *Exoascus*, *E. deformans* causing the disease known as peach curl, which results in a characteristic crinkling and deformity of the leaf. The mycelium sends to the surface patches of asci, each ascus discharging eight ascospores. The form is simple in the absence of ascocarp formation, the layer of asci, called the *hymenium* or *hymenial layer*, arising from the mycelium with no accompanying sterile structure. *E. pruni* forms the so-called plum pockets, in which the young fruit becomes of abnormal size and shrivels, the asci appearing in the wrinkles. Other species of *Exoascus* form brushlike deformities on certain trees, as wild cherry, hornbeam, etc., known as witch brooms. The best-known witch brooms, however, are formed by a very different group of fungi.

(c) Helvellales

The mycelium of these forms is usually subterranean, being saprophytic on decaying organic matter, and is common in the humous soil of forests. The ascocarp is a remarkable fleshy structure, rising above the surface like a mushroom, the hymenium occurring as a superficial layer variously distributed. The best-known form is the edible morel (*Morchella*), the surface of the cap region of the ascocarp being reticulated with irregular pitlike depressions lined with hymenium (fig. 174). A section shows that the hymenium is a mixture of paraphyses (sterile filaments) and asci.

FIG. 174. — *Morchella* (morel): the fleshy ascocarp arising from the mycelium.

(d) Pezizales

General character. — The cup fungi form a very large group of saprophytes, characterized by a broadly open ascocarp lined with the hymenium. The ascocarp may take the form of a flat disk, a bowl, a cup, a funnel, and is usually called an *apothecium*, to distinguish it from other forms of ascocarp. The group is also often called the *Discomycetes*, on account of this characteristic apothecium. In some of the forms sex organs have been discovered, and the ascocarp follows from the sexual act; in others the ascocarp may perhaps arise vegetatively, or at least from no apparent sex organs. Some familiar forms of Pezizales are as follows:

FIG. 175.—*Peziza:* ascocarps (apothecia) arising from the mycelium, and lined with the hymenium.

Peziza.—This genus is conspicuous on account of the brightly lined cups (ascocarps) that arise from the mycelium in decaying wood, humous soil, etc., one of the most common forming a cup with scarlet lining (fig. 175). In the development of the ascocarp, fertile branches (*ascogenous hyphae*) arise from the mycelium and give rise to asci; sterile branches intermixed with these give rise to paraphyses (fig. 176); while other investing sterile branches form the cup. The probable relation of these structures to the act of fertilization is suggested by the following investigated forms:

Pyronema.—In this genus well-developed sex organs have been found (fig. 177). The female sexual apparatus superficially resembles the procarp of *Nemalion* (see p. 56) in consisting of a globular cell (oogonium) and an elongated, tubelike cell (trichogyne or conjugating tube). The antheridium is a terminal, more or less club-shaped cell which comes into contact with the tip of the conjugating tube and fuses with it. The contents of the antheridium pass into the conjugating tube, whose basal wall is then resorbed, and the antheridial material passes on into the oogonium (fig. 177). Both antheridia and oogonia are multinucleate, so that fertilization consists of multinucleate pairing (see under *Albugo*, p. 66). The fertilized oogonium is cut off from the conjugating tube again by a wall, and gives rise to branch-

FIG. 176.—*Peziza:* fragment of a section through the hymenium, showing three asci, each containing eight ascospores, and the hairlike paraphyses.—After CHAMBERLAIN.

ing filaments (ascogenous hyphae), whose ultimate branches form asci. This fertilized oogonium giving rise to ascogenous hyphae is usually called an *ascogonium*. From hyphae beneath the ascogonium branching filaments arise that produce the colored paraphyses, and still other sterile hyphae give rise to the ascocarp (fig. 178). Usually several ascogonia are involved in a single ascocarp.

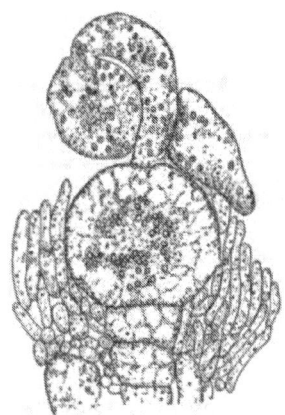

FIG. 177. — *Pyronema:* oogonium with its conjugating tube (or trichogyne); antheridium curved around the trichogyne (hence in section the latter appears as if piercing the former); trichogyne tip fused with antheridium and receiving nuclei; nuclei collecting in oogonium. — After HARPER.

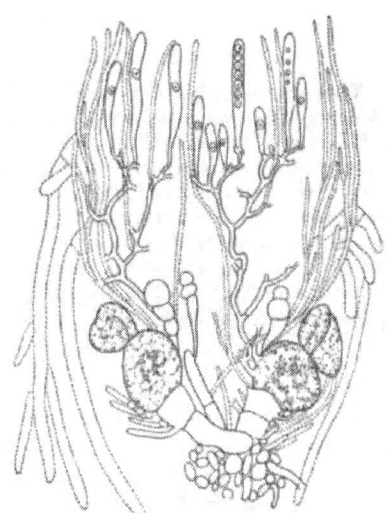

FIG. 178. — *Pyronema:* somewhat diagrammatic section of an ascocarp (involving two ascogonia), showing ascogenous hyphae arising from the fertilized oogonium (ascogonium) and producing asci. — After HARPER.

Ascobolus. — In this form structures resembling sex organs have been found, and may be interpreted with the help of the life history of *Pyronema*. From the mycelium there arises a large, bow-form, septate hypha (the "swollen hypha"), to which other slender branches become attached. No fusion has been observed, but the position of the slender branches suggests that their function may be that of antheridia. In any event, the septate swollen hypha becomes a single chamber by the disappearance of the cross walls, and then gives rise to ascogenous hyphae that bear the asci. The paraphyses and the ascocarp also arise in the way described for *Pyronema*. It seems safe to infer that the "swollen hypha" represents the female sex organ, which by fertilization or not becomes the ascogonium.

Applying these facts to *Peziza* and to the other Pezizales, it is probable that in them an ascogonium related to a sexual act is present either actually or historically; and that the nuclear fusion, which represents the essential feature of fertilization, is likely to have persisted in the life history even though apparent sex organs may have disappeared.

(e) Tuberales

These are the truffles, whose mycelium is entirely subterranean in humous soil. A remarkable subterranean, tuber-like, fleshy ascocarp is produced, which is the edible truffle. The ascocarp completely incloses the asci, and this closed type is often designated a *cleistothecium*, to distinguish it from the open ascocarps (apothecia). The cleistothecium of Tuberales consists of a fleshy cortex and a central ascus-forming region. In maturing, the interior sterile tissue and the asci disappear, leaving the ascospores free within the cortex. Very little is known of the life history of the Tuberales. It has been suggested that the mycelium may be that of some root fungus (*mycorhiza*), for in France and Italy, the chief market sources of the truffles of commerce, they are found constantly under oak trees.

(f) Plectascales

This group comprises saprophytes with an extensive mycelium, closed ascocarps (cleistothecia) of peculiar structure, and abundant production of conidia. The best-known representatives are the blue and green molds: *Aspergillus* (*Eurotium*), the herbarium mold, also on bread, preserves, etc.; and *Penicillium*, the common blue mold on bread, etc. From the mycelia the sporophores (conidiophores) arise in profusion, and their terminal branches by abstriction produce rows of conidia (fig. 179).

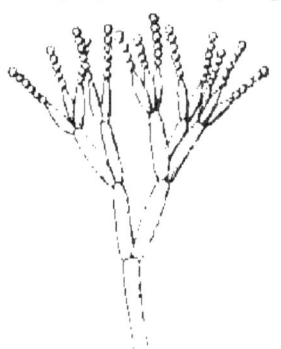

FIG. 179.—*Penicillium:* branches of a sporophore producing rows of conidia.

The sex organs are represented by two short, spirally intertwined filaments. Their fusion has not been recorded, but from one of them ascogenous hyphae arise and bear numerous small asci containing eight ascospores. At the same time, the usual investment of sterile filaments is developed and forms a compact, parenchyma-like tissue, through which the asci are scattered. There is thus no definite layer of asci (hymenium), as in other groups, a feature that characterizes the Plectascales.

(g) Pyrenomycetales

This is an enormous group of fungi, comprising thousands of species. There are two well-defined subgroups: the mildews and their allies (Perisporiales), and the black fungi (Pyrenomycetes proper). A representative or two from each subgroup will serve as illustrations.

Mildews. — These fungi form a family of Perisporiales known as the Erysiphaceae (often written Erysipheae). They are superficial parasites on the higher plants, the cobweb-like mycelium especially running over leaves, and sending out small haustoria into the epidermal cells (fig. 180). From the mycelium there arises a profusion of simple sporophores, each producing a terminal row of conidia, which multiply the parasite rapidly.

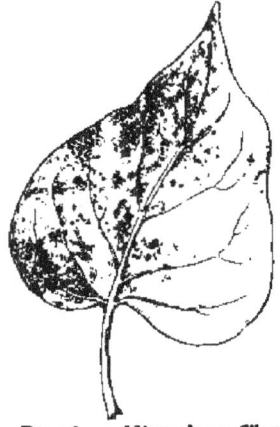

FIG. 180. — *Microsphaera* (lilac mildew): ascocarps (cleistothecia) appearing as black dots on the mycelium which spreads over the surface of the leaf.

When conidium production declines, the sex organs appear. The oogonium and antheridium are uninucleate cells at the tips of branches, develop in contact, and through the usual perforation developed in such cases the male nucleus enters the oogonium and fuses with the female nucleus. As a result of fertilization, the oogonium becomes a short filament, the ascogenous filament or ascogonium. In some of the mildews (as *Sphaerotheca*) the terminal cell of the ascogonium becomes the solitary ascus; in others (as *Microsphaera* and *Uncinula*) the terminal cell gives rise to ascogenous hyphae that produce several asci. From the cell beneath the oogonium (the stalk cell), the sterile hyphae arise that form the sheath of the closed ascocarp (cleistothecium), and from the sheath cells there arise the characteristic appendages in the form of simple hairs, dichotomously branching hairs, hairs with hooked tips, etc. (figs. 181, 182). The ascocarps appear on the mycelium as small black or brownish dots irregularly scattered (fig 180).

MORPHOLOGY

Black fungi. — This (Pyrenomycetes proper) is an exceedingly large and varied group, characterized by a flask-shaped ascocarp opening at the top (*perithecium*) and lined by the hymenial layer of asci and hair-like paraphyses (fig. 184). It includes parasites on various parts of plants, especially cortex and leaves; and also saprophytes on decaying wood, etc., often forming black spots, knots, etc., resembling charred places and suggesting both the technical and common names. The perithecia arise either singly on the mycelium (as in *Plowrightia*), appearing

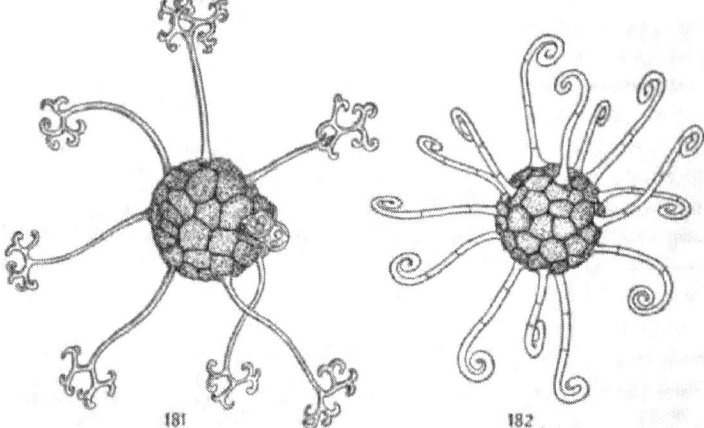

FIGS. 181, 182. — *Mildews:* 181, ascocarp of *Microsphaera*, showing the heavy case, dichotomous appendages, and asci crushed out of the case; 182, ascocarp of *Uncinula*, with hooked appendages.

as small black dots irregularly scattered, as in the mildews; or they occur in groups embedded in a variously shaped mass of compact (parenchyma-like) mycelium, the whole structure being known as the *stroma* (pl. *stromata*). A single illustration of each kind will be given.

Black knot (Plowrightia morbosa). — This is a destructive disease that attacks the plum and cherry (fig. 1100). In the spring the mycelium is under the bark; then it breaks through, beginning the knot, which may become quite large and solid, composed of the mycelium of the parasite and hypertrophied host tissue. Numerous sporophores arise from the mycelium, abstricting conidia; and in the autumn the perithecia appear over the surface of the knot as small papillae, open at the top and lined with a hymenial layer. In the following spring the ascospores escape and begin fresh infections.

THALLOPHYTES

Ergot fungus (Claviceps purpurea). — This is a common parasite on young ovaries of grasses, especially rye. The ascospores infect the ovaries in early summer, and on account of the growth of the mycelium the ovary becomes enlarged and deformed. The mycelium produces abundant sporophores, the conidia being abstricted in clusters, and also excretes copious honey dew, which is sought by insects, and in this way the embedded conidia are carried to other ovaries.

After the absorption of the tissues of the ovary, the mycelium becomes transformed into a compact, parenchyma-like mass, the *sclerotium* (fig. 1120). These elongated, dark violet, often curved sclerotia, replacing the ovaries and projecting from the spike, are the so-called *ergot*, the source of the astringent drug that bears the same name. The sclerotia fall to the ground and pass the winter. In the spring, when the rye is in flower, the sclerotia produce stellate bundles of hyphae, that in turn give rise to long-stalked, rose-colored, globular heads (stromata), in which are numerous sunken perithecia which communicate with the surface through porelike openings. The ascospores are remarkable in being very long and filiform, and are carried by the wind to the flowering spikes.

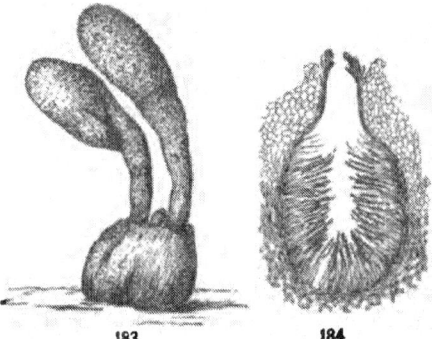

FIGS. 183, 184. — *Xylaria*: 183, club-shaped stromata arising from the sclerotium, the surface perforated by the porelike openings of the perithecia; 184, section through a perithecium, showing asci and paraphyses; the ascus wall is so delicate that the row of ascospores is the conspicuous feature.

Xylaria, which belongs here, is a very common saprophyte, forming conspicuous hard black masses on dead wood. From the sclerotium there arise club-shaped stromata (fig. 183), whose surfaces are perforated by the very numerous porelike openings of the perithecia (fig. 184).

(h) Laboulbeniales

This is a remarkable group of fungi parasitic on insects, especially aquatic forms. The sexual apparatus is much like that of the red algae, the procarp consisting of carpogonium, trichogyne, and auxiliary cells; and the antheridia producing sper-

MORPHOLOGY

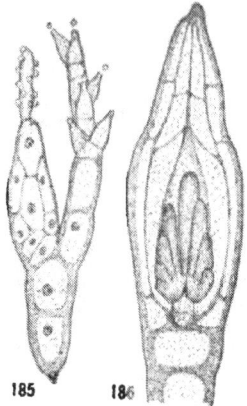

FIGS. 185, 186.—*Stigmatomyces:* 185, sex organs; right branch showing antheridia discharging spermatia; left branch being a procarp showing trichogyne (with attached spermatia), carpogonium, and auxiliary cells; 186, the formation of asci within the perithecium after fertilization.—After THAXTER.

matia that fuse with the trichogyne (fig. 185). Perithecia are formed, and the asci bud out from the auxiliary cells (fig. 186), the whole process suggesting the formation of cystocarps among the red algae.

Lichens

General character.—With a single exception (p. 91), lichens are Ascomycetes parasitic upon certain algae, the relation between the two organisms being so intimate as to result in a structure resembling a single organism. The dual nature of lichens was announced by Schwendener in 1868, but it was many years before the proof of it became convincing. In 1889 Bonnier began to synthesize lichens; that is, to bring together "wild algae" and lichen fungi and thus produce artificial lichens. The parasitism is peculiar in that the algae do not seem to be harmed in most cases, the cells being rarely penetrated by the fungus. The algae concerned in lichen formation are for the most part Cyanophyceae and Protococcales. As would be expected, the algae thrive without the fungus, just as do the wild species; but the lichen fungus soon perishes if it does not come into contact with the appropriate algae. (See p. 91 and fig. 1117.)

Body.—The lichen fungus usually forms a thallus body much more definite and differentiated than do other mycelia, the thallus often resembling in form that of certain liverworts. In structure, there is a distinct compact cortical region and a central looser region, in either of which the algae may occur (fig. 190). Two structural types of thallus body are recognized, dependent upon the distribution of the algae: (1) *homoiomerous*, in which the algae are scattered; and (2) *heteromerous*, in which the algae occur in layers.

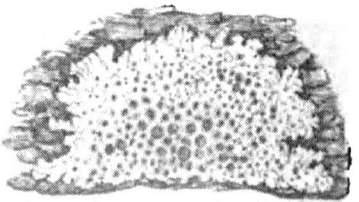

FIG. 187.—*Physcia:* a flat foliose lichen on bark, showing numerous shallow apothecia.—After COULTER.

THALLOPHYTES

On the basis of habit, three types are recognized: (1) crustose lichens, with an undefined mycelium often penetrating the substratum; (2) foliose lichens, with a definite liverwort-like thallus, which has marginal growth and rhizoids (as *Physcia*, fig. 187, and *Parmelia*, fig. 188); and (3) fruticose lichens, which are erect and often branching (as *Cladonia*, the reindeer moss), or pendent and branching (*Usnea*, fig. 189).

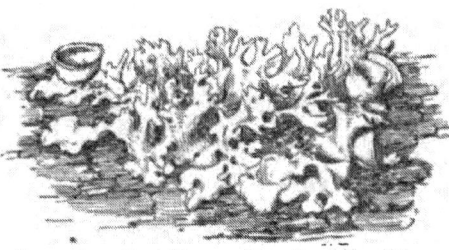

FIG. 188. — *Parmelia:* an almost free foliose lichen on bark, showing cuplike apothecia.

Vegetative multiplication is secured by *soredia*, which are scalelike or globular bodies, composed of a little tangle of mycelium with some algal cells (figs. 1114–1116). The ascocarps are very conspicuous structures, usually being apothecia (disklike forms), but some are perithecia. The hymenium is the usual mixture of asci and paraphyses, and the ascus produces the usual eight ascospores.

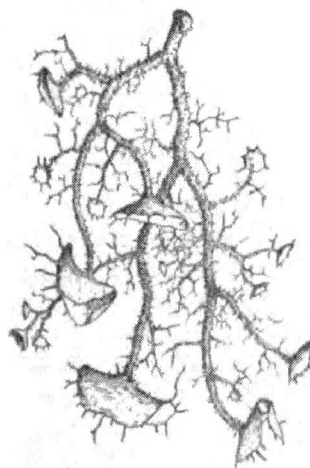

FIG. 189. — *Usnea:* a pendent and branching fruticose lichen, bearing conspicuously flaring apothecia.

Sex organs. — The sex organs of the lichen fungus are evident in some cases. The antheridia occur on branching hyphae within a conceptacle-like chamber called the *spermogonium*. They are very small cells that bud out and become abstricted, suggesting conidia, as they have often been considered. These antheridia are cast off and function directly as sperms, as is true of certain of the red algae, and they are also called spermatia.

The female sex organ also suggests that of the red algae. It is a multicellular filament spirally coiled and terminating in a filamentous extension to the surface of the thallus. The spirally coiled region has been called the *archicarp*, and the filamentous extension to the surface the *trichogyne*. The spermatia have been found attached to the exposed tip of the trichogyne, with their nuclei gone; so that discharge and nuclear fusion seem to be safe inferences. The archicarp then enlarges and divides, becoming transformed into the ascogonium, from which arise the usual ascogenous hyphae. From hyphae beneath the ascogonium the sterile branches arise that produce the investing sterile tissue of the ascocarp, the whole structure finally breaking through the surface of the thallus, usually in the form of a disklike or saucer-like ascocarp (apothecium, fig. 190). One ascocarp may involve a single ascogonium or several, just as described under Pezizales (see p. 73).

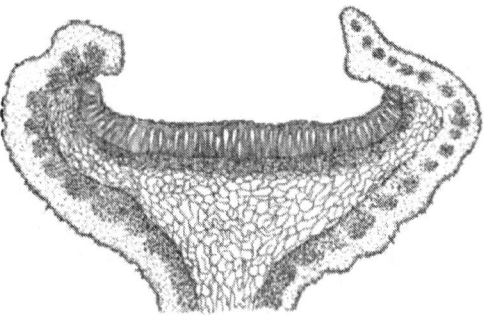

FIG. 190.—*Anaptychia*: section of an apothecium of a lichen, showing the hymenium made up of asci and paraphyses overlying the inner loose mycelium of the lichen body, and all invested by a thick cortical mycelium, within which are apparent groups of algae. — After SACHS.

(3) BASIDIOMYCETES

This great group of fungi is characterized by the occurrence of a *basidium* in the life history. A basidium is the swollen end of a hypha, and consists of four cells or one cell; but in either case it usually gives rise to four slender branches (*sterigmata*), and each sterigma cuts off at the tip a spore (*basidiospore*) (fig. 201). The basidium holds the same place in the life history of a basidiomycete that an ascus does in the life history of an ascomycete. The essential feature of a basidium is that it produces spores externally and that the theoretical number of spores is four. As in the history of the ascus, the young basidium contains two nuclei which fuse. Unlike the ascus, however, the fusion nucleus of the basidium, by two successive divisions, gives rise to four nuclei, and it is these four nuclei that are found in the four spores. In some cases four sterigmata are not produced and four spores are not formed, but four nuclei appear in the basidium.

THALLOPHYTES

Among the higher Basidiomycetes the basidia form a definite layer (hymenium), whose structure and position are important in classification. As yet, the classification of this great group is very uncertain, but for our purpose two great series may be recognized.

I. *Protobasidiomycetes*, in which the basidium is four-celled, each cell bearing a spore; and II. *Autobasidiomycetes*, in which the basidium is one-celled and bears four spores (or at least produces four nuclei).

I. PROTOBASIDIOMYCETES

(a) Ustilaginales

General character. — These are the smuts or brand fungi, destructive parasites that attack the floral and other organs, notably the ovaries of grasses, and are of course best known in connection with their ravages among cereals. *Ustilago Maydis*, the corn smut, may be taken as a representative.

Corn smut. — The mycelium ranges widely through the host, even in the roots, and becomes externally visible only upon flowering. At that time the ovary, for example, becomes packed with mycelium, which causes a distorted, swollen, tumor-like growth. These tumor-like swellings may be observed also in other parts of the plant, including the tassels. Later this mycelium forms additional cross walls; the short cells become rounded off and thick-walled, and the mycelium is thus transformed into a mass of black spores, which are the so-called brand spores, the whole mass being the so-called smut. This kind of heavy-walled spore, which is a transformed vegetative cell of a septate mycelium, is called a *chlamydospore*, the name referring to the heavy, protective wall. These spores fall to the ground and pass the winter. Upon germination in the spring, the spore develops a short filament of three or four cells. This filament is saprophytic and each cell buds out spores laterally and the end cell terminally, suggesting conidium-formation. If abundant food supply is available, spores continue to be abstricted in great numbers, and may be multiplied further by the yeastlike budding of the spores (see p. 70). This filament of three or four cells is thought to represent the basidium, but in this case the very indefinite number of spores produced obscures the resemblance. The spores produced, therefore, are probably basidiospores, and the brand spores hold the same place in the life history of smuts as that held by the teleutospores in the life history of rusts (see p. 82).

The basidiospore develops a mycelium that penetrates the young seedling of the host plant.

(b) Uredinales

General character.—These are the well-known rusts, all of them being destructive parasites, whose mycelia live in the intercellular spaces of higher plants, especially in the leaves. The best-known form is *Puccinia graminis*, one of the wheat rusts, and an outline of its life history will serve as an illustration of the group.

Wheat rust.—The mycelium traverses the tissues of the young wheat plant, and during the growth of the host it sends to the surface numerous sporophores, each bearing a single spore, the *uredospore* (fig. 191). The groups of uredospores (summer spores) on the surface of the host form reddish spots or lines, giving rise to the name rust or red rust. By means of the uredospores the disease spreads rapidly through the growing wheat, the spores falling on the surface of uninfected wheat plants and sending out germ tubes that penetrate the host and form new mycelia. As the wheat plants mature, the mycelium sends to the surface of the host another kind of spore, the *teleutospore*, which is two-celled and thick-walled (figs. 192, 193). The teleutospores (winter spores) are the winter stage of the parasite, germinating in the following spring.

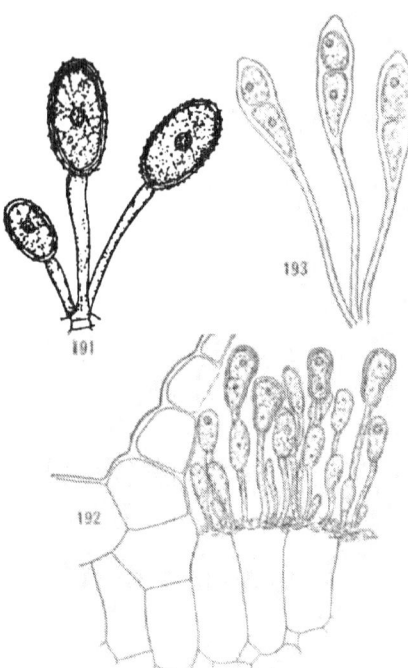

FIGS. 191-193.—*Wheat rust:* 191, uredospores (summer spores) (after COULTER); 192, group of young teleutospores (winter spores), among which there may be some uredospores (after CHAMBERLAIN); 193, mature teleutospores.

Basidium.—The germination of the teleutospore

results in a filament of four cells, each of which gives rise to a slender branch bearing a spore (fig. 194). This saprophytic filament has been called the *promycelium*, and its spores *sporidia;* but it represents a four-celled basidium bearing basidiospores, and is the structure that determines the position of rusts among Basidiomycetes.

Aecidium. — The basidiospores that fall upon young barberry leaves germinate, and an extensive mycelium is developed among the tissues of the new host. This mycelium develops very evident structures of two kinds. Opening usually upon the upper surface of the leaf, small, flask-shaped organs appear, known as *spermogonia*, within which there arise slender filaments that form by successive abstrictions numerous very small cells, the *spermatia* (fig. 195). The names spermogonium and spermatium indicate the belief that this structure is the male apparatus, to be compared with a male conceptacle in *Fucus* (see p. 50). However, this function has not been demonstrated, and some regard them as spore-producing structures, in which case they are spoken of as *pycnidia* producing *pycnidiospores*. If this is a sexual apparatus, it would seem to be a vestigial one.

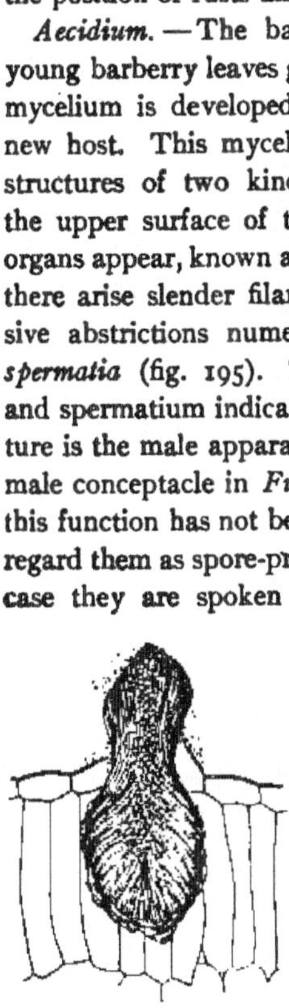

FIG. 194. — *Wheat rust:* teleutospore producing basidia ("promycelia") bearing basidiospores ("sporidia"). — After TULASNE.

The other structure produced by the mycelium in the barberry leaf is the *aecidium* or *clustercup*. The aecidia usually appear in groups on the lower leaf surface, each opening upon the surface as a cup containing numerous simple sporophores bearing rows of spores, the *aecidiospores* (fig. 196). The scattered aecidiospores that fall upon young wheat plants germinate, the host is penetrated, and the mycelium is produced that begins to form uredospores.

FIG. 195. — *Wheat rust:* a spermogonium (producing spermatia) arising from the mycelium of the barberry leaf. — After CHAMBERLAIN.

Polymorphism. — In this life history the fungus passes through three distinct phases (the parasitic mycelium bearing uredospores and teleutospores, the saprophytic promycelium or basidium bearing basidiospores, and the parasitic mycelium bearing aecidiospores), lives upon two unrelated hosts, and produces four (perhaps five) kinds of spores. It is natural that such a polymorphous plant should not have been understood at first, and that the different phases should have received different names. The mycelium bearing uredospores was named *Uredo;* that bearing teleutospores, not known at first to be the

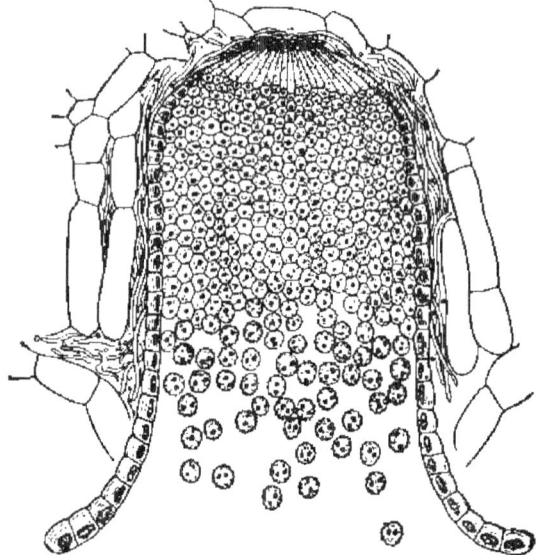

FIG. 196. — *Wheat rust:* an aecidium (clustercup) arising from the mycelium of the barberry leaf, and showing the rows of aecidiospores. — After CHAMBERLAIN.

same mycelium, was named *Puccinia;* and the form parasitic on the barberry was named *Aecidium.* Now the name *Puccinia* is retained for the plant, and the other names are used for convenience in designating the respective stages. Not all rusts include two hosts in their life history, and it is usual to distinguish rusts as *autoicous* (those having one host) and *heteroicous* (those having more than one host).

Alternation. — Recently the nuclear changes in the life history of wheat rust have been traced. In the aecidium, the cell which produces a row of aecidiospores contains two nuclei, the second nucleus having entered it from an adjacent cell of the mycelium. In the subsequent cell divisions the two nuclei divide independently, so that each aecidiospore contains two nuclei. This binucleate condition continues in the uredospore-producing mycelium, in the uredospore, and in the young teleutospore. In the maturing teleutospore, however, the nuclei fuse, so that the cells of the mature teleutospore are uninucleate. This uninucleate condition continues in the cells of the basidium (promycelium), in the basidiospores (sporidia), and in the mycelium on the barberry. Some investigators see in this nuclear history an alternation of generations, the double number of chromosomes ($2x$) being represented by the two nuclei, and the reduction division (resulting in the x number) occurring in the formation of the four cells of the basidium. If this view is correct, the mycelium on wheat is a sporophyte, and the mycelium on barberry is a gametophyte.

Other rusts. — Owing to its infrequency in those regions, it is evident that barberry cannot be a general host in the chief wheat-producing areas of North America. Much of the rust attacking the wheat in these fields is not *P. graminis*, but *P. coronata*, whose aecidium develops on buckthorn (*Rhamnus*), and *P. rubigo-vera*, whose aecidium develops on *Echium*. It has been discovered also that uredospores may retain their vitality throughout the winter and attack directly the young wheat in the spring, thus eliminating the need of an aecidium host. It is also found that the basidiospores may germinate upon very young wheat plants and infect them, eliminating the aecidium stage in another way.

The common species of wheat rust mentioned above have now been broken up into numerous species and varieties upon what are called physiological characters. This means that although they may be alike in their appearance, they can be distinguished by their behavior in the selection of hosts.

As might be expected, the complete life histories of comparatively few rusts having different hosts are known. The two hosts do not suggest one another, and therefore numerous rusts in their various stages are described as *Uredo*, *Puccinia*, and *Aecidium*, without any knowledge as to the forms that belong together in a single life history. Recently the work of linking these forms together has gone forward with considerable rapidity. The following list will serve as an illustration of a few of the results, showing also the unrelated character of hosts:

Uredo-Puccinia host	*Aecidium host*
Cereals	Barberry, buckthorn, etc.
Poa	Buttercup
Pea	Euphorbia
Senecio	Pine
Heaths	Spruce
Juniper	Apple, haw, etc.

(c) Auriculariales

These are the ear fungi, appearing as gelatinous, earlike growths on bark, board fences, etc., a very common form being seen on old stems of elder. When moist, the ear is gelatinous and brightly colored; when dry, it becomes hard and gray and wrinkled, and externally hairy. This ear is a complex sporophore arising from a mycelium, its internal surface being lined with a hymenium. A section of the hymenium shows basidia transversely divided into four cells, each cell giving rise to a slender branch (sterigma) which produces a basidiospore. This basidium so much resembles that of the Uredinales (the promycelium) that the ear fungi are sometimes grouped with them; but the complex sporophore is distinctly like that of the fleshy fungi.

(d) Tremellales

These fungi also appear as gelatinous growths on decaying wood and tree trunks, these growths being complex and more or less indefinite sporophores from a mycelium. When moist, they appear usually as thick, wavy, or folded coatings of quivering gelatinous consistency and indefinite form. The wavy ridges are coated with a hymenial layer, and the basidia are peculiar in being divided longitudinally into four cells, each cell terminating in a long, slender filament (sterigma) bearing a basidiospore.

II. AUTOBASIDIOMYCETES

These are the true Basidiomycetes, the basidium being one-celled, and they constitute the large assemblage of forms known as the fleshy fungi. Two great subgroups are recognized: (I) *Hymenomycetes*, in which the hymenium is exposed; and (II) *Gasteromycetes*, in which the hymenium is inclosed.

1. *Hymenomycetes*

(e) Dacromycetales

These forms are interesting on account of their evident relationship to the Tremellales, which they resemble in their gelatinous sporophores. The one-celled basidium forks into two long sterigmata, and hence produces two basidiospores. It has been discovered that the nuclear fusion in the basidium is followed by two successive divisions, resulting in four nuclei, as in all basidia. In spore formation two nuclei remain in the basidium, or the two nuclei may move in pairs into the sterigmata, one of each pair entering the terminal spore.

(f) Exobasidiales

This group of parasites attacks, among other hosts, members of the heath family, as huckleberries, cranberries, etc., the tips of the shoots, buds, flowers, or young ovaries of the host becoming enlarged and distorted into gall-like growths. These affected parts finally become covered with a whitish bloom, made by the basidia

THALLOPHYTES

coming to the surface, after having broken through the epidermis. These basidia, each bearing four spores, arise directly from the mycelium, without any complex sporophore formation, differing in this respect from the following groups.

(g) Thelephorales

The sporophores of these forms appear on tree trunks as flat and tough leathery incrustations, the hymenium spreading over the smooth upper surface; or as brackets raised above the substratum, the hymenium extending over the under surface; or as funnel-shaped bodies lined with the hymenium. The general character of the sporophore distinguishes this group from the next; and the indefinite extent of the hymenium over the sporophore distinguishes both groups from those which follow.

(h) Clavariales

These are the coral fungi, with fleshy sporophores that often simulate branching coral in form, the hymenium covering the whole surface of the branches. There are also unbranched, club-shaped sporophores; but all are characteristically fleshy and hymenium-covered.

(i) Agaricales

This is by far the greatest group of fleshy fungi, containing most of the so-called mushrooms and toadstools. The complex sporophore is

FIG. 197. — *Lepiota:* a common edible mushroom. — After COULTER.

usually definite in form, being differentiated into *stipe* and *pileus* (fig. 197), the latter having special surfaces for the hymenium. The principal families are as follows:

Hydnaceae. — These are the tooth fungi, so named because the hymenium covers toothlike or spinelike processes. In simpler forms the sporophore resembles an incrustation, in which case the teeth are on the upper surface. In other cases the teeth occur on the under surface of a bracket-like sporophore; while in *Hydnum* they are upon the under surface of the pileus of a mushroom-like sporophore.

Polyporaceae. — These are the pore fungi, so named because the hymenium lines tubes that terminate on the surface with porelike openings. The sporophores may be incrustations, with pores on the upper surface; or bracket forms (as *Polyporus*), with pores on the under surface; or mushroom-like forms (*Boletus*), with pores on the under surface of the pileus. The incrusting forms and the hard, gray, hoof-shaped bracket forms are very common on tree trunks, fallen logs, stumps, etc. Many are destructive to trees, the mycelium spreading extensively under the bark and through the wood.

Agaricaceae. — These are the gill fungi, being the common mushrooms and toadstools, and the largest family of fleshy fungi. There are bracket forms, but the prevailing type of sporophore is the mushroom, with stipe and pileus (figs. 198, 199); and in every case the hymenium covers bladelike plates, which are the *gills* (figs. 200, 201). Many of the Agaricaceae also are destructive parasites on trees, the mycelium penetrating the host extensively.

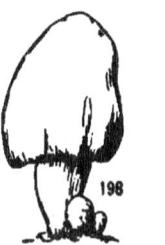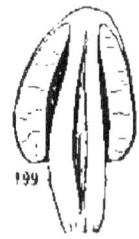

FIGS. 198, 199. — *Coprinus:* 198, habit, showing stipe and pileus, and young sporophores; 199, longitudinal section, showing relation of stipe and pileus.

The development of the characteristic sporophore is as follows. The small *buttons* consist of interwoven hyphae. Soon the rudiments of stalk and pileus appear inclosed in a loosely woven envelope (*volva*). The elongation of the stipe ruptures the volva, whose torn remnant may form a ring or sheath about the base of the stipe. In many cases a membrane (*velum*) of hyphal tissue extends in the young sporophore from the margin of the pileus to the stipe, covering the gills. When the velum is ruptured by the growth of the pileus, it may remain as a ring of tissue (*annulus*) about the stipe (fig. 197).

The presence of two nuclei in the young basidium, the nuclear fusion, the two successive divisions, the migration of the four nuclei into the four sterigmata and

THALLOPHYTES

so into the basidiospores, have all been observed in mushrooms. In the common field mushroom (*Agriacus campestris*) the basidium often produces only two sterigmata and spores, but in such cases four nuclei have been observed in the mature basidium. The vegetative mycelium has been observed to be binucleate, the condition found in the uredospore-teleutospore mycelium of rusts. With a uninucleate basidiospore and a binucleate mycelium, it is a matter of interest to determine where the binucleate condition originates. It is suggested that the basidiospore upon germination becomes binucleate. In that case, if the interpretation applied to the rusts (see p. 84) obtains among the mushrooms, the mycelium with its sporophore is the sporophyte, and the basidiospore represents the gametophyte.

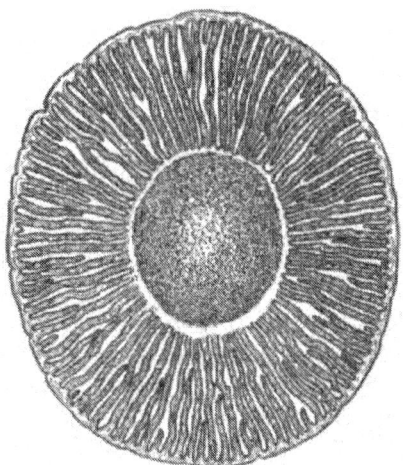

FIG. 200.—*Coprinus*: section of under side of pileus, showing section of the stipe in the center, and the radiating (sometimes branching) gills coated by the hymenium.

2. *Gasteromycetes*

These are the most highly organized of the fungi, the complexity appearing in the structure of the sporophore. The hymenium is inclosed within the sporophore,

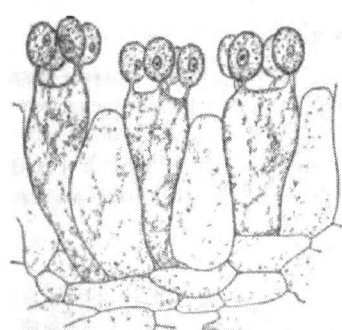

FIG. 201.—*Coprinus*: section of the hymenium, showing basidia bearing basidiospores; the curving of the basidia makes it impossible to show their actual connections in a section.

which opens only after the spores are mature. The sporophore is differentiated into an outer zone of cortical hyphae (*peridium*) and an inner mass of tissue (*gleba*) which contains the numerous basidium-bearing chambers. These chambers either are filled with loosely woven hyphae whose lateral branches terminate in basidia, or are lined by a definite hymenial layer. The gradually increasing complexity of the sporophore will be observed in the following groups:

(j) Hymenogastrales

This group contains the simplest Gasteromycetes, and the name suggests characters belonging to both Hymenomycetes and Gasteromycetes. The peridium is simple; that is, it does not develop in layers, and ruptures irregularly. The gleba is not chambered, the basidia simply terminating lateral branches of the glebal hyphae.

(k) Sclerodermales

In this group the nearly spherical sporophores have a thick leathery (light brown) peridium, which finally becomes cracked or ruptured at apex. The leathery peridium suggested the name of the group. The gleba is chambered, but the chambers are filled with interwoven hyphae whose lateral branches bear pear-shaped basidia, upon which appear four sessile spores, sterigmata not being formed.

(l) Lycoperdales

These are the true puffballs, with globular sporophores which sometimes reach 50 cm. in diameter. The peridium is distinctly two-layered and with definite dehiscence. In *Lycoperdon* the outer layer of the peridium gradually flakes off, and the inner layer bursts at the apex. In *Geaster* (earth star) the outer layer splits into stellate spreading segments, and the inner layer dehisces by a terminal pore (figs. 1123, 1124).

The gleba contains numerous distinct chambers lined with a hymenial layer and also containing a *capillitium*, which is a fibrous structure of interwoven branching hyphae arising from the wall of the chamber and aiding in the dispersal of the spores.

(m) Nidulariales

These are the nest fungi, as the name suggests. The separate chambers of the gleba become invested each by a membrane of interwoven hyphae, and at maturity become freed by the breaking down of the intervening tissue. When the peridium opens, forming a cuplike structure, the free, membrane-covered hymenial chambers are seen lying like eggs in a nest.

(n) Phallales

These are the stink horns, whose sporophore is more complex than that of any other fungi. The sporophore develops on the mycelium as a white, egg-shaped body. The peridium is two-layered, but the tissue within, which is all gleba in the other groups, is differentiated into a central hollow cylindrical axis and an investing dome-shaped and chambered gleba. At maturity the cylindrical axis elongates with great rapidity into a stout, hollow stalk, bursts through the peridium, and carries up on its summit the caplike and chambered gleba, the whole structure suggesting a stipe and pileus. The gleba thus exposed deliquesces into a slimy, dripping mass with the odor of carrion, which attracts carrion flies, by whose agency the embedded spores are dispersed.

Lichens

The Ascomycetes, with a single exception, are the lichen formers (see p. 78), and this exception is a basidiomycete. This lichen is the tropical *Cora pavonia*, of loose texture, whose mycelium produces basidia at the surface, instead of the ordinary ascocarp. The algal symbiont is *Chroococcus* or *Scytonema*.

CHAPTER II — BRYOPHYTES

Introductory. — This great division of plants comprises the liverworts (*Hepaticae*) and mosses (*Musci*). The conspicuous features of the group as contrasted with thallophytes are as follows:

1. The establishment of a definite *alternation of generations*. Distinct sexual and sexless individuals alternately produce each other, the gametophyte producing the sex organs (containing gametes), the sporophyte producing the asexual spores. The two generations are further distinguished by their chromosome numbers: the $2x$ number arises from the fusion of the sexual cells, and occurs in all the cells of the sporophyte; and the x number occurs in all the cells of the gametophyte, the reduction taking place in connection with the formation of the tetrad of spores by the mother cell.

2. The appearance of the *archegonium*. This female sex organ is very characteristic of the groups that possess it (bryophytes, pteridophytes, and gymnosperms). On this account they are often spoken of collectively as archegoniates, but the groups are too unrelated to deserve a collective name. The archegonium is a flask-shaped organ, consisting of a jacket of sterile cells (neck and venter) surrounding an axial row of cells (neck canal cells, ventral canal cell, and egg) (fig. 219). The cells of the axial row are doubtless to be regarded as potential eggs, only the innermost one maturing and functioning as an egg, the others breaking down and leaving an open canal to the egg.

3. The appearance of a *multicellular antheridium*. Multicellular sex organs and even multicellular antheridia appear among the algae, as in *Ectocarpus* (see p. 46) and Charales (see p. 42), but the antheridium of bryophytes is a very uniform and characteristic structure. It is more or less stalked, and consists of a single layer of sterile jacket cells investing a mass of small cubical sperm mother cells (fig. 210). The sperm is also of a definite kind, consisting of a small, more or less spirally curved body bearing a pair of long terminal cilia (fig. 211).

1. HEPATICAE

General character. — The liverworts are of great interest on account of their apparent relationship to the green algae on the one hand, and to the higher plants on the other. Through them the aerial habit of green plants seems to have been established. This change in habit involved more compact and better protected bodies, and the change from swimming spores to aerial spores; but it is important to note that the swimming habit was retained by the sperms. Three groups of liverworts are recognized, each having developed special features: (1) *Marchantiales*, (2) *Jungermanniales*, and (3) *Anthocerotales*.

(1) MARCHANTIALES

This group may be represented by its two prominent families, *Ricciaceae* and *Marchantiaceae;* the former representing the more primitive forms, the latter the highly specialized forms.

Ricciaceae. — The genus *Riccia* (including *Ricciocarpus*) contains aquatic as well as terrestrial species, so that this family belongs to both the water and the land.

Gametophyte. — The gametophyte is a flat, dorsiventral body and branches dichotomously (fig. 202). This dorsiventral habit results in a differentiation of the body into two distinct regions. The dorsal (upper)

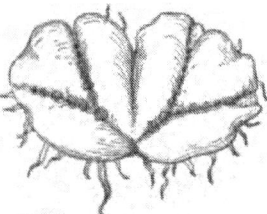

FIG. 202. — *Riccia:* showing the dorsiventral, dichotomously branching gametophyte, which puts out rhizoids and scales from its ventral surface; the rows of dark bodies in the bottom of the conspicuous grooves on the dorsal surface are sporophytes, which show also the position formerly occupied by the archegonia.

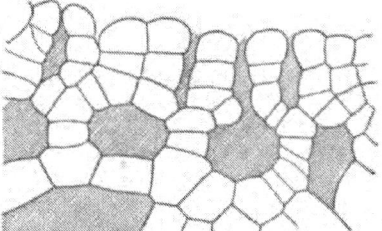

FIG. 203. — *Riccia:* section through dorsal region of thallus, showing the intercellular clefts, often enlarging into chambers, by means of which the cells containing chloroplasts are bathed by an internal atmosphere. — After BARNES and LAND.

region is composed of green tissue, the intercellular spaces developing as numerous deep and narrow clefts, which in some cases broaden into chambers (fig. 203), so that all the green cells are bathed by an internal atmosphere. The superficial cells (*epidermis*) of the dorsal region, discontinuous on account of the numerous clefts, may or may not contain chloroplasts. The cells of the ventral region, against the substratum, do not contain chloroplasts, and the superficial cells often give rise to simple, hairlike rhizoids that serve as holdfasts.

Antheridium. — The antheridia occur in discoid areas slightly raised above the general surface of the thallus, each antheridium standing at the bottom of a deep pit formed by the overgrowth of the surrounding tissues (fig. 204). The antheridium develops from a single superficial cell (antheridium initial), and consists of a superficial layer (wall) of sterile cells investing a compact mass of sperm mother cells (fig. 210).

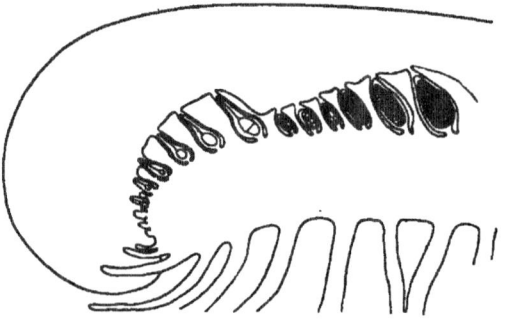

FIG. 204. — *Riccia*: section through the thallus along one of the dorsal grooves, showing the tissue at the bottom of the groove bearing antheridia (to the right) and archegonia (to the left); the rhizoids are shown arising from the lower surface of the thallus.

The antheridium initial develops a papillate protrusion, which is cut off by a transverse wall as a projecting cell. A series of transverse divisions transforms this projecting cell into a row of cells. Then vertical (*periclinal*) walls cut off central cells, which by successive divisions produce the mass of sperm mother cells (figs. 205–210). In each mother cell two sperms are formed, the oblique spindles for which are shown in two regions of fig. 210.

Archegonium. — The archegonia are sunk in deep pits or furrows of the thallus by the overgrowth of the surrounding tissues. The archegonium develops just as the antheridium as far as the projecting cell. This cell, however, divides by three vertical walls that surround an inner cell on all sides. A transverse division of this cell then completes the investment of a central cell. This central cell, by transverse divisions, develops the axial row, consisting of four neck canal cells, a ventral canal cell, and the egg. The investing sterile cells develop the venter and neck, the latter consisting of six vertical rows of cells (figs. 212–219).

Sporophyte.—The fertilized egg (fig. 220) produces the sporophyte (called *sporogonium* in the bryophytes), which when mature is a spherical body, consisting of a wall layer of sterile cells investing a mass of sporogenous cells (figs. 221–226). In producing this body the egg by successive divisions usually first becomes a sphere of eight cells (octants). Then periclinal (parallel with the surface) walls cut off an outer layer of cells (*amphithecium*) that forms the wall of the sporophyte. The group of inner cells is the *endothecium*, which by successive divisions produces a mass of sporogenous tissue. The cells produced by the last divisions of the sporogenous tissue are the spore mother cells, each of which produces a tetrad of spores (fig. 226), during which process the reduction in the number of chromosomes occurs. The mature sporophyte, therefore, is simply a spore case. The venter of the archegonium grows also, forming a special investing structure, the *calyptra* (fig. 225). Finally the wall layer of the sporophyte and the layers of the calyptra become disorganized, and the spores are free in the archegonial chamber. The spores upon germination produce the gametophyte body.

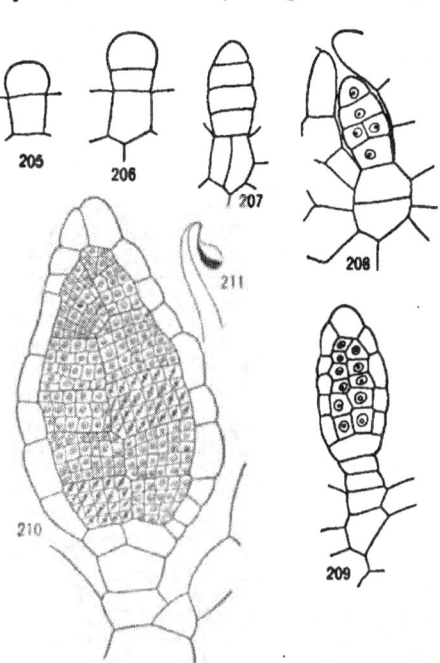

FIGS. 205–211.—*Riccia:* development of the antheridium; 205, first division of the superficial initial cell, the protruding cell to give rise to the antheridium; 206, first transverse division of the antheridial cell; 207, further transverse divisions; 208, the beginning of vertical walls; 209, completion of periclinal walls separating the wall of the antheridium from the spermatogenous cells; 210, an almost mature antheridium, showing the short stalk, the wall, and the mass of cubical spermatogenous cells in conspicuous blocks; 211, a sperm, showing the biciliate bryophytic type (body of sperm black; adjacent light mass is cytoplasm dragged out of the mother cell).

MORPHOLOGY

Conclusions. — The life history of the Ricciaceae suggests certain important conclusions. The sporophyte is the simplest known among

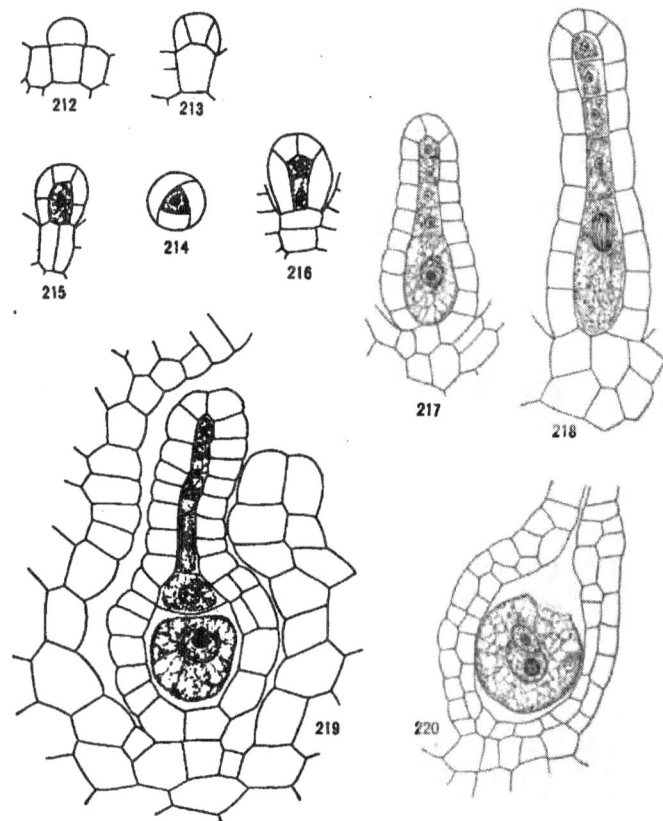

FIGS. 212-220. — *Riccia:* development of the archegonium; 212, first division of the superficial initial cell, the protruding cell to give rise to the archegonium; 213, the three vertical walls (two seen in section) investing an inner cell, the relation between the three walls being shown in the cross section, 214; 215, further development of jacket cells, completely investing a central cell (first cell of axial row); 216, first division of central cell into primary neck canal cell (upper one) and primary ventral cell; 217, further development of the jacket and axial row, the latter showing the four neck canal cells and the ventral cell (lowest and largest); 218, division of the ventral cell to produce the ventral canal cell and the egg; 219, a completed archegonium, showing neck and venter, and the axial row, consisting of four neck canal cells, a ventral canal cell, and an egg; 220, fertilization, showing male and female nuclei fusing in the egg.

BRYOPHYTES

liverworts, being only a spore case, and from such a structure many suppose that sporophytes of the higher plants have developed. This primitive sporophyte is dependent in a large measure upon the gametophyte for its nutrition, so that it appears simply as a spore case developed by the gametophyte.

The gametophyte, on the other hand, is far from being the simplest gametophyte known among liverworts, being quite complex in structure. The simplest liverworts should combine the simplest gametophyte with

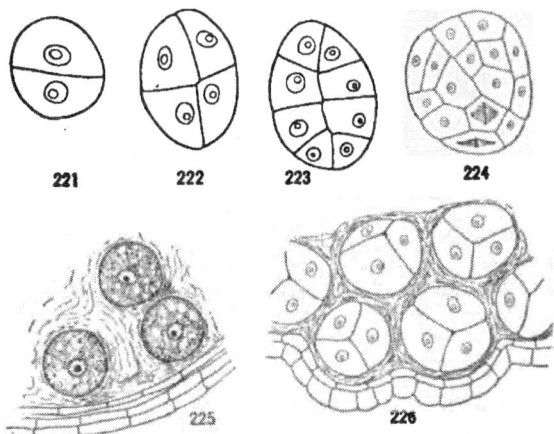

FIGS. 221-226.—*Riccia*: development of the sporophyte (sporogonium); 221, first division of the fertilized egg (oospore), transverse to the long axis of the archegonium; 222, quadrant or octant stage; 223, still later stage; 224, the coming in of periclinal walls that separate the amphithecium (outer layer of cells) from the endothecium (after GARBER); 225, portion of sporophyte showing three of the numerous free mother cells produced, and the investing calyptra (two layers of cells); 226, tetrads (of spores) produced by the mother cells.

the simplest sporophyte, but such a combination is not known, and perhaps it no longer exists. It follows that while the history of the liverwort sporophyte may well begin with the Ricciaceae, the history of the liverwort gametophyte must begin with other forms.

Marchantiaceae.—This family includes the most highly specialized of the Marchantiales. The familiar genus *Marchantia* may be used as an illustration.

Gametophyte.—The gametophyte body is a highly developed thallus, whose dorsal region contains a series of large air chambers domed by the epidermis and containing special chloroplast-containing cells (fig. 227).

These special cells are in short and more or less branching filaments that arise from the floor of the chamber and contain the chloroplasts, and are thus freely exposed to the internal atmosphere. This remarkable apparatus is one of the specialized features of the Marchantiaceae. In the center of the epidermal dome, roofing each air chamber, there is developed a chimney-like air pore. In the ventral region the tissue is composed of colorless cells, and the ventral epidermis

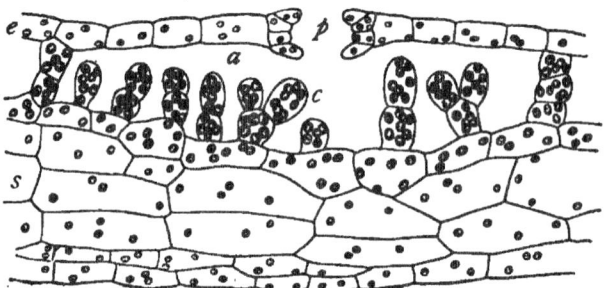

Fig. 227.—*Marchantia*: section through young air chamber (*a*), showing the special chloroplast-containing cells (*c*), the epidermal roof (*e*), and the air pore (*p*); the cells beneath the air chamber (*s*) also contain chloroplasts; the rhizoids and scales on the ventral surface are not shown.

develops two kinds of rhizoids and two longitudinal rows of scales. Upon the dorsal surface cuplike structures (*cupules*) are produced, which contain special reproductive bodies (*gemmae*), which can develop new gametophytes (figs. 228, 229). The gemma of *Marchantia* is a discoid body with two notches on opposite sides, the growing points being located at the bottom of the notches (figs. 1118, 1119).

In the development of the gametophyte body there are usually three distinct stages: (1) a filament of varying length; (2) the development in the terminal cell of an apical cell with two cutting faces,[1] by means of which the thallus begins to broaden; and (3) the development of an apical cell with three or four cutting faces, by means of which the thallus begins to thicken.

Sex organs. — The sex organs are not scattered over the dorsal surface, but are restricted to definite areas, these areas becoming disks of

[1] The current names for apical cells are somewhat confusing. For example, an apical cell with two cutting faces is called "two-sided"; one with three cutting faces a "three-sided apical cell," etc. It is evident that in each case the free surface of the cell forms another side, and that a "two-sided apical cell" is really three-sided; a "three-sided apical cell" is really four-sided, etc. That there may be no confusion, we have used the somewhat clumsy expression "an apical cell with two cutting faces," etc.

special structure (*receptacles*). In some cases the receptacles are sessile, but in *Marchantia* they become long-stalked, the archegonial and antheridial receptacles occurring on different gametophytes.

The receptacle borne by the antheridial branch is a disk with lobed margin, a growing point being at the tip of each lobe (fig. 228). Over the upper surface of this disk the antheridia occur in flask-shaped cavities formed by the overgrowth of the adjacent tissue. From the bottom of each cavity a single antheridium arises (rarely two), similar in structure to those described under Ricciaceae (figs. 205–210).

The receptacle borne by the archegonial branch is star-shaped (fig. 229), the archegonia occurring in the notches between the rays, in connection with the growing points. They arise from the upper surface

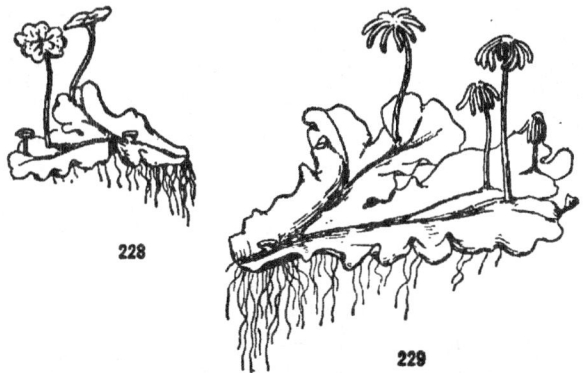

FIGS. 228, 229.—*Marchantia:* 228, thallus bearing antheridial branches and a cupule; 229, a larger thallus bearing archegonial branches and a cupule.

(morphologically) of the disk, but as this becomes the apparent lower surface by the overgrowth of the upper surface, they hang within the notches neck downward. They develop as in the Ricciaceae, but there are usually eight neck canal cells (figs. 212–219).

Sporophyte.—The sporophyte begins to develop as among the Ricciaceae, but not all of the cells of the endothecium produce sporogenous tissue. Approximately half of these cells give rise to the sporogenous tissue and spores. This means that the sporogenous tissue in the sporophyte of *Marchantia* is reduced as compared with that of the Ricciaceae. The remaining tissue of the endothecium, since it does not produce spores, is said to be *sterile*. This sterile tissue in *Marchantia*, which was sporogenous tissue in the Ricciaceae, forms a region of the sporophyte quite distinct from the spore-producing region, so that in the mature sporophyte three regions are recognized: (1) the capsule, containing the spores; (2) the seta, a short stalk beneath the capsule, which elongates rapidly as the capsule matures; and (3) the foot, a spreading structure in which the seta ends, and which anchors the sporophyte in the gametophyte and also acts as an absorbing organ (fig. 230).

FIG. 230.— *Marchantia*: sporophyte, showing capsule (containing spores and elaters), seta, and foot (embedded in tissue of gametophyte).

The spore production of *Marchantia* is further diminished by the fact that not all the potentially sporogenous cells produce spores. Some of them become converted into curious elongated, fiber-like cells with spiral thickening (*elaters*), which by their hygroscopic movements assist in loosening up the spore mass in connection with dehiscence and scattering. The usual calyptra is formed about the developing sporophyte by the venter of the archegonium, but at maturity the capsule breaks through this by the rapid elongation of the seta. After its escape from the calyptra the capsule breaks irregularly and discharges its spores.

Conclusions.—The Marchantiales are characterized by a distinct and strong differentiation of the tissues of the gametophyte, leading to the highly complex thallus of *Marchantia*, with its specialized mechanism for photosynthesis. There is observable in the group also a distinct tendency in the sporophyte toward the sterilization of the potentially sporogenous tissue into the sterile tissue developing the seta and foot. This means that seta and foot are derived historically from sporogenous tissue. The development of the seta, moreover, is associated with the dispersal of spores, its rapid elongation freeing the capsule from the calyptra. The further sterilization of potentially sporogenous tissue in the production of elaters is another feature of the group, and is also associated with spore dispersal. On the whole, the chief distinction of Marchantiales as compared with the other groups of liverworts is the differentiation of the tissues of the gametophyte, which has reached its extreme expression in *Marchantia*.

BRYOPHYTES

(2) JUNGERMANNIALES

General character. — This is by far the largest group of liverworts, its members living in all conditions of moisture from very wet to very dry. They are especially abundant in tropical forests, being very common on the bark of trees (*epiphytic*) and on leaves (*epiphyllous*), while some grow on the ground. Two great groups are recognized: (1) thallose forms, whose gametophyte body is a thallus resembling that of the Marchantiales in general outline (see fig. 777); (2) foliose forms, with leafy bodies (fig. 235). However, there is complete gradation from thallus bodies, through those whose thallus is more and more deeply lobed, to those in which the lobes have become distinct leaves.

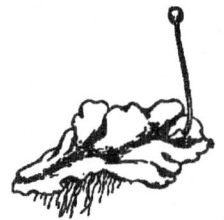

FIG. 231. — *Pellia*: thallus bearing a sporophyte with long seta (indicating also position of archegonium); the black dots on the older portion of the thallus indicate antheridia.

The most essential distinction between the two groups is based upon the position of the archegonia, which of course involves the position of the sporophytes. In the thallose forms the archegonia are on the dorsal surface of the thallus (figs. 231, 232); and on this account they are called the *Anacrogynae*, meaning archegonia not at the apex. In most foliose forms the apical cell becomes an archegonium initial; and on this account they are called *Acrogynae*, meaning archegonia at the apex (fig. 235). The acrogynous Jungermanniales are known commonly as the leafy liverworts, or sometimes as scale mosses.

FIG. 232. — *Symphyogyna*: thallus showing lobed margin and bearing two sporophytes on its dorsal surface.

In contrast with the Marchantiales, the Jungermanniales show very little differentiation of the *tissues* of the gametophyte; but they show very great differentiation in the *form* of the gametophyte.

(a) Anacrogynae

Gametophyte. — The gametophyte of the simplest Anacrogynae, such as *Aneura* and *Pellia*, are the simplest gametophytes known among liverworts (fig. 231). They consist of dichotomously branching plates of similar cells, all containing chloroplasts, and with no differentiation of tissues into dorsal and ventral regions.

In developing from the spore, only two stages are to be observed: (1) the filamentous stage, followed by (2) the stage of the apical cell with two cutting faces. Among the Marchantiales it was noted that these two stages are followed by another, which is accompanied by a distinct differentiation of tissues. The adult thallus of *Aneura* and *Pellia*, therefore, represents an embryonic stage of the thallus of Marchantiales.

If the sporophyte of *Riccia* were combined with the gametophyte of *Pellia* in a single life history, the result would be the simplest hypothetical liverwort. Among the more highly developed Anacrogynae (*Fossombronia, Blasia, Symphyogyna*, etc.) the gametophyte becomes more complex, beginning to lobe and to develop indistinct leaves (fig. 232), and in some cases the body becomes distinctly leafy. These leafy forms are classed among the Anacrogynae, however, because the archegonia are dorsal and not terminal.

The gametophytes may be multiplied vegetatively in various ways: (1) by the death of main axes, thus isolating branches; (2) by gemmae, which are many-celled bodies formed on the surface of the thallus or cut off from the margin; in *Aneura* two-celled gemmae were said to escape from cells of the thallus, but this statement has been disproved; (3) by tubers, which are special subterranean branches formed at the end of the growing season and which remain dormant until the return of favorable conditions.

Sex organs. — The sex organs occur singly or in groups on the dorsal surface of the thallus (figs. 231, 232) or of special branches. In *Aneura*, for example, the antheridia are sunk singly in pits or chambers formed by the overgrowth of the surrounding tissue (as in *Marchantia*).

The development of the antheridium is very different from that described for the Marchantiales. The projecting papillate cell, derived from the antheridium initial, divides transversely, the lower cell by successive divisions building up a stalk of varying length. The outer cell, which is to form the somewhat globular body of the antheridium, divides by a vertical wall, and this is followed by four other vertical and intersecting walls, so directed as to cut off four peripheral cells, which inclose two central cells. The peripheral cells form the wall of the antheridium, a single layer of cells in thickness; while the two central cells give rise to the sperm mother cells. The sperm has a more or less coiled body and the usual pair of long terminal cilia.

The archegonia are developed as among the Marchantiales, with three vertical intersecting walls, a cap cell, and a central cell which develops the axial row. In this case the neck canal cells are six to eight in number.

Sporophyte. — The sporophyte, even of *Aneura*, is more complex than that of *Marchantia*. Much more of the sporophyte is sterile tissue, the sporogenous tissue being still more restricted. The sterile tissue develops a foot and an elongated seta (fig. 231); and the spore output is still further reduced by the development of elaters and by the use of some of the sporogenous tissue in nourishing the functioning mother cells. In certain forms there occurs also a mass of sterile tissue projecting into the spore chamber from above (*Aneura*) or from below (*Pellia*), which, on account of its relation to the elaters that radiate from it, is called an *elaterophore*. As in *Marchantia*, the seta elongates with great rapidity when the capsule is mature. The capsule opens usually by the longitudinal splitting of the wall into four pieces (*valves*), which is a more definite and special mechanism for dehiscence than is developed among the Marchantiales.

Conclusions. — The anacrogynous Jungermanniales exhibit some of the simplest gametophytes known among liverworts. There is a tendency for the gametophyte to pass from the thallose state to the leafy state, thus changing in form, but without any marked differentiation of tissues. The sporophyte is more highly developed than among Marchantiales, in the sense that there is more sterilization, more organization of the sterile tissue, a stronger development of the seta, and a more specialized dehiscence. Apparently it is a group which has retained the primitive structure of the gametophyte for a long time, but in which the sporophyte has developed rapidly. In *Pellia* and *Aneura*, therefore, we find the simplest gametophyte associated with an advanced sporophyte, the converse being true of the Ricciaceae.

(b) Acrogynae

General character. — A good representative of the leafy liverworts is *Porella*. As has been said, the Acrogynae are characterized not only by being leafy forms, but chiefly by the fact that the apical cell of special branches becomes an archegonium initial. This apical position of the archegonium and hence of the sporophyte (fig. 235) is in sharp contrast with their dorsal position among the Anacrogynae.

Gametophyte. — In the development of the gametophyte there may be three stages: (1) the filamentous stage, (2) perhaps the stage of an apical cell with two cutting faces, and (3) the stage of the apical cell with three cutting faces. It should be noted that this is one more stage than shown by *Aneura* (see p. 102), but it is not absolutely certain that the second stage occurs, at least with any regularity. The apical cell of the last stage, cutting off three series of segments, gives rise to three rows of leaves — two dorsal and one ventral. The mature dorsiventral body consists of a distinct branching axis (stem) bearing two rows of dorsal leaves (figs. 233-235), which are usually two lobed; and one ventral row of very small leaves against the substratum (*amphigastria*), variable in form (fig. 233). The two lobes of the dorsal, chlorophyll-bearing leaves are equal or unequal; and in certain epiphytic forms the lower (ventral) lobe forms a small sac containing water.

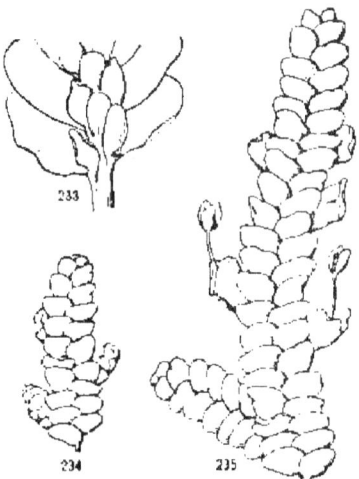

FIGS. 233-235. — *Porella*: 233, ventral view, showing two ventral leaves (amphigastria) in the middle line, and the dorsal leaves with their ventral lobes; 234, portion of gametophyte showing three antheridial branches; 235, gametophyte with two archegonial branches bearing terminal sporophytes (opening by four valves), and three other archegonial branches.

The kinds of vegetative multiplication are the same as given under Anacrogynae (see p. 102), but the gemmae are usually simpler, often consisting of only one or two cells separating from the leaf margins.

Sex organs. — The antheridia of *Porella* are on short lateral branches, which differ very much in appearance from the sterile branches (fig. 234). They are conspicuous on account of the closely imbricated leaves, in each of whose axils there is a single, long-stalked, and globular antheridium (fig. 236). The development of the antheridium is as described under Anacrogynae (see p. 102).

The archegonia also occur on short lateral branches (fig. 235), being found in a group at the apex. This group is usually surrounded by a rosette of modified (usually enlarged) leaves. The archegonia arise from segments of the apical cell, and finally the apical cell itself becomes an archegonium initial. The neck canal cells are six or eight in number, and the neck is almost as broad as the venter.

The two kinds of sex organs may occur upon the same plant (*monoecious*) or upon different plants (*dioecious*).

Sporophyte. — The sporophyte (sporogonium) is as described for the Anacrogynae (see p. 103), with a conspicuously elongated seta, the same reduction of sporogenous tissue, and the capsule dehiscing by four spreading valves (fig. 235).

Conclusions. — The essential contrasts between Jungermanniales and Marchantiales may be stated as follows: In Marchantiales there is (1) a differentiation of the tissues of the gametophyte, but no special differentiation of form, (2) less sterilization of potentially sporogenous tissue, (3) little or no development of the seta, and (4) irregular dehiscence of the capsule. In Jungermanniales there is (1) a differentiation of the gametophyte into axis and leaves, but little

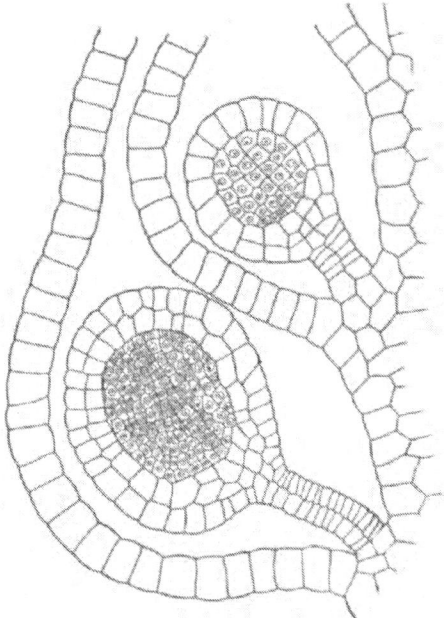

FIG. 236. — *Porella*: portion of antheridial branch showing two axillary antheridia.

or no differentiation of tissues; (2) greater sterilization of potentially sporogenous tissue; (3) strong development of the seta; and (4) a definite dehiscence of the capsule by four spreading valves. The two groups differ also in the method of development of the antheridium. In the main, the archegonia of the two groups are similar, the axial row including six or eight neck canal cells (the exceptions being *Riccia* with four and *Sphaerocarpus* with two). The archegonium is a very persistent ("conservative") structure, but the gradual disappearance of the neck canal cells is one of the conspicuous facts in its very slow evolution. It is this gradual disappearance that must be noted in connection with subsequent groups.

(3) ANTHOCEROTALES

General character. — This is a small group comprising four genera: *Anthoceros* and *Notothylas* of the temperate regions; *Dendroceros*, an epiphytic tropical genus; and *Megaceros*, a genus recently described from Java. Although few in numbers, the group is of great morphological interest on account of the claims made for it that it possibly represents the ancestral forms of pteridophytes. Its possible relation to the mosses also further emphasizes its important genetic position. It differs so much from the other liverworts as to have suggested its separation from them as a third great group of bryophytes, coordinate with liverworts and mosses. In Marchantiales and Jungermanniales there is extensive differentiation of the body of the gametophyte, either in structure or in form; but in Anthocerotales there is a simple gametophyte, while the sporophyte is the most complex among liverworts.

Gametophyte. — The body of the gametophyte is a simple thallus (figs. 239, 240), almost as simple as that of *Aneura*, and much simpler than that of *Marchantia*. The margin is often wavy, lobed, or crisped; and in *Dendroceros* the lobing in some cases suggests rudimentary leaves. The thallus matures by means of an apical cell with four cutting faces, the preceding stages appearing as usual. There are two marked peculiarities of the gametophyte body in most of the genera: (1) the usually single large chloroplast, generally in contact with or even more or less investing the nucleus; and (2) the mucilage cavities, which open by clefts on the ventral surface. In these cavities endophytic *Nostoc* colonies occur.

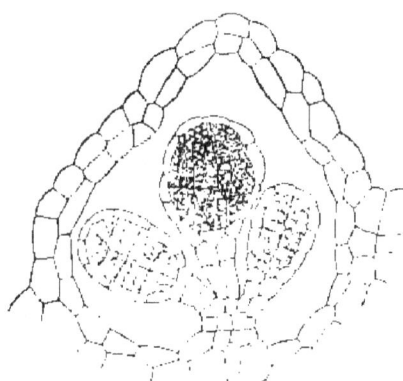

FIG. 237. — *Anthoceros:* an antheridial chamber containing three antheridia.

The sex organs are developed on the dorsal side of the thallus, but in certain features they differ strikingly from those of other bryophytes.

BRYOPHYTES 107

Antheridium. — The antheridia are embedded in the thallus and are therefore hard to detect (fig. 237). The antheridial initial is a superficial cell, but it does not develop a papillate protrusion as in the other liverworts. A transverse (periclinal) wall divides it into an outer and an inner cell. In the other groups the outer cell develops the antheridium, but in Anthocerotales the antheridium is developed from the inner cell. By a succession of anticlinal and periclinal divisions, the outer cell produces two layers of cells, which form an outer wall or roof to the antheridial chamber.

The inner cell develops one to several antheridia. The method of development of an antheridium, whether directly from the inner cell or from one of its daughter cells, is as follows: two vertical walls at right angles to each other result in four cells; transverse walls result in several tiers of four cells each; periclinal walls in the upper tiers cut off an outer wall layer and an inner group of spermatogenous cells; and the lower tiers (sometimes only the lowest) develop a more or less elongated stalk. The antheridium or group of antheridia thus produced lie in what may be called an antheridial chamber (fig. 237).

Archegonium. — The archegonia also are in the tissue of the thallus, in this respect resembling the archegonia of pteridophytes (fig. 238). In all other bryophytes they are entirely superficial structures. As a result of this relation to the thallus, there are no sterile jacket cells (neck and venter) very distinct from the adjacent cells of the thallus. The essential part of an archegonium, however, is the axial row, and in the Anthocerotales this is the only distinct structure.

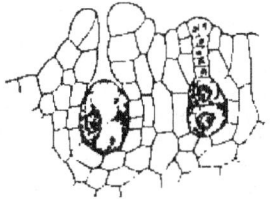

FIG. 238. — *Anthoceros:* archegonia, showing "embedded" character; in the archegonium to the right the complete axial row is shown (beginning below, the cells are the egg, ventral canal cell, and four neck canal cells) capped by the neck cells (two visible); in the archegonium to the left, the neck cells have been thrown off, the canal cells have disorganized, and there is a passageway open to the egg, which is ready for fertilization.

The general outline of development of this axial row is as follows: a superficial cell divides transversely, giving rise to outer and inner cells; the outer cell divides transversely, giving rise to the *cap cell* and the *primary neck canal cell;* the inner cell is the *primary ventral cell;* the primary neck canal cell, by two successive divisions, develops a row of four neck canal cells; the primary ventral cell, by a single transverse division, forms the ventral canal cell and the egg. At maturity the cap cells are thrown off, the neck and ventral canal cells break down, and a broad canal is open to the egg (fig. 238).

MORPHOLOGY

Sporophyte.—The sporophyte of Anthocerotales deserves special attention on account of its structure and on account of its degree of independence (figs. 239, 240). The outline of its development is as follows: the fertilized egg divides by a vertical wall (transverse in other bryophytes); subsequent transverse and vertical walls result in three tiers of four cells each; the three tiers produce foot, seta, and capsule. The innermost tier develops a foot which penetrates the thallus by rhizoid-like processes, and finally becomes a large bulbous structure (fig. 241). The middle tier, which also contributes somewhat to the foot, develops the so-called intermediate zone, corresponding in position to the seta of other groups. It is a region of active cell-division, continually adding to the capsule below, which thus becomes an elongated structure by basal growth (as distinct from apical growth). This growth may not continue long, resulting in a short capsule (*Notothylas*, fig. 240); or it may continue long enough to result in a much elongated linear capsule (*Anthoceros*, fig. 239). Where the sporophyte (sporogonium) emerges from the thallus, a tubular sheath is developed around its base by the tissue of the thallus.

FIGS. 239, 240.—*Anthocerotales*: 239, thallus of *Anthoceros* bearing sporophytes; the two sporophytes to the right show the dehiscence by two valves, leaving the columella exposed; 240, thallus of *Notothylas* bearing sporophytes.

Capsule.—The development of the outermost tier in capsule formation is especially noteworthy. By a series of transverse walls a number of tiers of cells is produced, and periclinal walls cut off a peripheral layer of cells (amphithecium) inclosing a group of central cells (endothecium). Among the Marchantiales and Jungermanniales there is the same setting apart of two regions, the amphithecium producing the capsule wall, and the endothecium developing the sporogenous tissue. Among the Anthocerotales, however, the two regions develop in a very different way. The endothecium does not develop sporogenous tissue, but forms a central axis of sterile tissue (*columella*), which in *Anthoceros* usually shows sixteen cells in cross section. By periclinal walls, the amphithecium becomes two-layered, and the inner layer is the sporogenous tissue, which thus caps the columella in a domelike layer;

later the sporogenous tissue becomes two layers of cells. The outer layer of the amphithecium develops a capsule wall of four or more layers, the outermost one being the epidermal layer, consisting of elongated narrow cells and containing stomata similar to those of vascular plants. The stomata are related to the fact that the wall layers beneath the epidermis are chlorophyll tissue, giving to the sporophyte the ability to manufacture food. The intermediate zone adds continuously new capsule regions below; therefore in a longitudinal section of a capsule the whole sporogenous series may be seen, from one-layered sporogenous tissue below, through two-layered sporogenous tissue, mother cells, and tetrads, to mature spores above (fig. 241). The capsule dehisces by splitting into two valves, which separate downwards as the spores mature, leaving the spores exposed upon the columella (fig. 239).

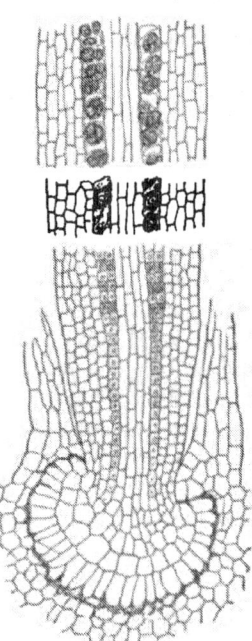

FIG. 241.—*Anthoceros:* longitudinal section through portions of a sporophyte, showing bulbous foot embedded in the gametophyte; above the foot is the zone of actively dividing cells elongating the sporophyte; the base of the capsule shows the peripheral chlorophyll tissue, the sporogenous tissue (at first one layer of cells, then dividing to form two layers), and the columella; section from middle region showing spore mother cells with sterile cells between; section from upper region showing tetrads and sterilized sporogenous cells.

In many cases some of the sporogenous cells do not form spores. These sterile groups of cells break up the continuous mass of sporogenous cells into more or less separated groups. This tendency to break up the sporogenous tissue into separate smaller masses by intervening sterile tissue is an important fact, which will be referred to later. These sterilized and somewhat modified sporogenous cells are called elaters, but they are different from those found among Marchantiales. This green sporophyte, with its sterile and elongating axis, and its sporogenous tissue broken up into smaller masses, is very suggestive of a possible relation to the completely independent sporophyte of the pteridophytes.

Conclusions.—Among the Anthocerotales there is a remarkable association of a primitive type of gametophyte with a highly developed sporophyte. In considering the sporophytes of liverworts in general, it is evident that from *Riccia* to *Anthoceros* there is a progressive sterilization of sporogenous tissue, the sterilized tissue forming the vegetative structures. Among the Anthocerotales three additional features of the sporophyte are noteworthy: (1) the beginning of independence by the development of green tissue; (2) the beginning of sporangia by the breaking up of a continuous sporogenous mass into separate smaller masses; (3) the establishment of a sterile axis by the transfer of the sporogenous tissue to the outer region of the capsule, which suggests the beginning of a region for the development of vascular tissues and the beginning of superficial sporangia.

It should be understood clearly just what is meant by such a statement as that the Anthocerotales have certain features suggestive of the pteridophytes. It does not mean that the pteridophytes have been derived from the Anthocerotales or from any of the bryophytes. It means simply that the sporophyte of the Anthocerotales represents a stage of progress like one through which the pteridophytes may have passed during their evolution. The plant groups as we know them now certainly did not give rise to one another, but they can be used to suggest general stages of progress, of whose real details and connections we know nothing.

2. MUSCI

General character. — This is the great group of bryophytes, both in numbers and in specialization. While the liverworts may be the more interesting from the standpoint of suggestions as to phylogeny, the mosses are the representative bryophytes in our present flora. For so great a group it is very well defined and consistent. Mosses are widely distributed, being found in all habitats except salt water, and are especially conspicuous in colder regions (alpine and arctic), where they form a prominent feature of the vegetation. They seem to have been derived from liverworts, and their sporophyte characters, at least, suggest a possible connection with Anthocerotales; while in certain features of the gametophyte the resemblance to Jungermanniales is more evident. Three groups are recognized: (1) *Sphagnales*, (2) *Andreaeales*, and (3) *Bryales*.

(1) SPHAGNALES

General character. — These are the bog mosses, all of which belong to the single genus *Sphagnum*. They are large, pale mosses, character-

BRYOPHYTES

istic of the swampy regions of higher latitudes, where they often fill up bogs and form peat, whence they are often called peat mosses.

Gametophyte. — The gametophyte begins as a filament (fig. 242), and then by means of an apical cell with two cutting faces develops as a simple flat thallus with rhizoids (fig. 243), just as in the simpler liverworts. The moss character appears in the development from this liverwort-like thallus of an upright leafy branch (fig. 243). This radial leafy branch, from a dorsiventral body, is called variously the adult shoot, the gametophore, or simply the leafy branch. The name gametophore is used because this branch

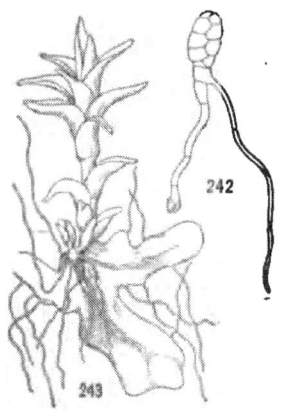

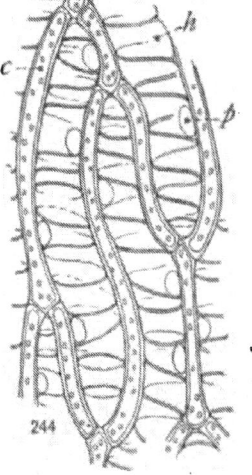

FIGS. 242, 243.—*Sphagnum:* 242, young gametophyte, showing the filament arising from the spore, a rhizoid, and the thallus beginning to develop by an apical cell; 243, mature thallus, with rhizoids, producing leafy branches.— After SCHIMPER.

FIGS. 244, 245.—*Sphagnum:* 244, surface view of cells of leaf, showing the narrow elongated cells (*c*) containing chloroplasts, and the less numerous hyaline cells (*h*) with pores (*p*); 245, portion of cross section showing same features.

bears the sex organs, just as in *Marchantia* the sex organs are borne on erect but leafless branches.

The leafy branch develops by means of an apical cell with three cutting faces, and hence there are three vertical rows of leaves. These branches are densely leafy and profusely branching, forming terminal tufts (fig. 246).

MORPHOLOGY

The leaves at first have similar cells, but later there is a striking differentiation, certain of the cells becoming enlarged, hyaline, and perforate (figs. 244, 245).

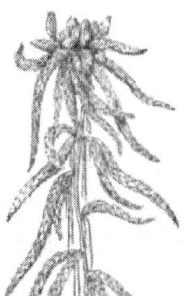

It is this abundance of hyaline cells and paucity of chlorophyll-containing cells that give a pallid look to the leaves.

The axis of the leafy branch is differentiated into three regions: (1) a cortex of empty and perforate cells, like the hyaline cells of the leaf; (2) a cylinder of elongated cells with thick walls and small caliber (*prosenchyma*); and (3) a pithlike axis.

There are no special structures for vegetative multiplication, but great masses of individuals are formed by the indefinite growth and branching above, accompanied by dying off below.

FIG. 246.—*Sphagnum*: terminal cluster of antheridial branches.

Antheridium.—The antheridia occur on special densely leafy branches resembling small catkins (fig. 246). The leaves also usually differ in color from the ordinary leaves, and in the axil of each there is a solitary globular and long-stalked antheridium (fig. 247), just as in *Porella* (see p. 104). These antheridia develop by means of an apical cell with two cutting faces, the lower segments forming the stalk, and the upper segments forming the capsule, which is initiated by a series of periclinal walls that cut off the peripheral wall layer from a central spermatogenous group of cells. The antheridium opens by irregular lobes and discharges the two or three-coiled biciliate sperms.

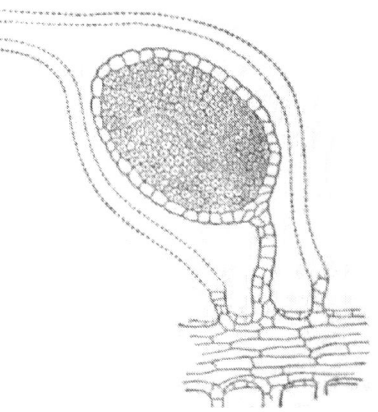

FIG. 247.—*Sphagnum*: an antheridium arising on branch between two leaves, showing the slender stalk and the globular head; the latter consisting of a wall (a single layer of cells) investing a mass of spermatogenous cells (in which blocking can be distinguished).

Archegonium.—The archegonia occur at the apex of short branches, at the top of the plant (figs. 248, 249). They are stalked and free, and develop as in the acrogynous Jungermanniales, the archegonium initials being segments of the apical cell, which itself finally becomes an initial. The mature archegonium is stalked, with a massive venter, a long and often twisted neck, and numerous neck canal cells (fig. 249).

Sporophyte.—The sporophyte (fig. 250) develops at first by a series of transverse walls until a short filament is formed, which later becomes massive by means of vertical walls. The upper tiers develop the capsule, which is organized as in *Anthoceros*, with the endothecium developed as the axial columella, with the sporogenous tissue cut off as an inner layer (becoming four layers) of the amphithecium and capping the columella like a dome, and with a wall of five to seven layers. These *Anthoceros*-like features are further emphasized by the large bulbous foot and the rudimentary seta, which is only a necklike connection between capsule and foot, and is often called the neck. Very important differences, however, are as follows: (1) there is no such development of chlorophyll tissue in the wall of the capsule as characterizes *Anthoceros*; (2) the neck is not a growing region, and hence the capsule does not elongate; and (3) the capsule dehisces by a definite lid (*operculum*), which is distinctly a moss character. As in all bryophytes, during the development of the sporophyte the venter of the archegonium develops the encasing calyptra, which in *Sphagnum* is ruptured by the growing capsule.

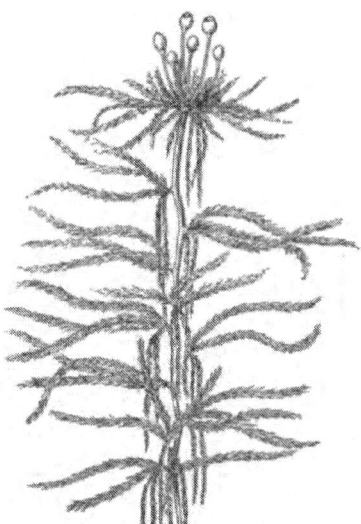

Fig. 248.—*Sphagnum*: stem bearing a terminal cluster of sporophytes, showing the position of archegonia.

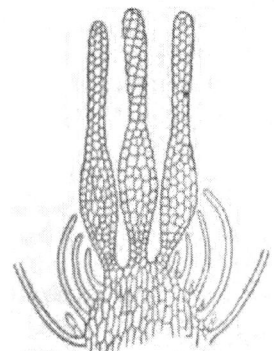

Fig. 249.—*Sphagnum*: surface view of three archegonia; the middle archegonium shows the spiral direction of the cell rows of the neck.—After SCHIMPER.

A peculiar feature of *Sphagnum* is the *pseudopodium*, which is a structure replacing in function the suppressed seta. It is formed by the elongation of the axis of the leafy branch beneath the sporophyte, and as it bears the capsule at its summit, it resembles an ordinary elongated seta (fig. 250). Of course the foot of the sporophyte is embedded in its tip.

Conclusions.—The Sphagnales present a remarkable mixture of liverwort and moss characters. The simple thallus body of the gametophyte resembles that of the anacrogynous Jungermanniales; the special leafy sex branches suggest the acrogynous Jungermanniales; while the sporophyte is organized as in the Anthocerotales. On the other hand, the erect leafy branches of the gametophyte and the operculum of the sporophyte are both distinctly moss characters. In addition to these characters in common with liverworts and true mosses, *Sphagnum* possesses other characters peculiar to itself.

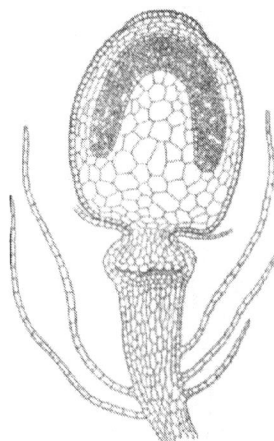

FIG. 250.—*Sphagnum*: sporophyte, showing the globular capsule with operculum (lid) and dome-shaped mass of sporogenous tissue (in tetrad stage), the very short necklike seta, the bulbous foot embedded in the apex of the leafy axis (gametophyte), which is extended beyond the leaves to form the stalklike (seta-like) pseudopodium.

It was remarked that the simplest conceivable liverwort would be produced by combining the gametophyte of *Pellia* with the sporophyte of *Riccia*. So in producing *Sphagnum*, one might imagine a combination of the gametophytes of the two groups of Jungermanniales with the sporophyte of *Anthoceros*.

The features of *Sphagnum* that distinguish it from true mosses in general are (1) the thallose gametophyte, (2) the axillary antheridia, (3) the dome-shaped sporogenous tissue derived from the amphithecium, and (4) the pseudopodium.

Such a form is often called a *transition* form, but better a *synthetic* form, for it combines the characters of several groups.

(2) ANDREAEALES

General character.—This group comprises a single genus (*Andreaea*) of siliceous rock mosses. *Sphagnum* is hydrophytic, but *Andreaea* is very xerophytic.

It is introduced here partly to illustrate the possible effect of changed conditions upon structure, but chiefly to illustrate another synthetic form.

Gametophyte. — The gametophyte develops first as a mass of cells (*primary tubercle*). From the superficial cells of the primary tubercle extensively branching filaments arise, which represent the *protonema* of the true mosses, as contrasted with the thallus of *Sphagnum* and the liverworts. The branches of the filament that enter the rock crevices are rhizoids; those that remain exposed to the light are green and may assume any one of three forms dependent upon conditions: (1) they may remain filamentous; (2) they may form flat plates; or (3) they may form cylindrical masses. The leafy branch may arise from any of these three forms. Arising from filaments, it resembles a true moss; arising from a plate of cells, it resembles *Sphagnum*.

Sex organs. — The antheridia occur at the apex of a special branch, involving the apical cell; this resembles true mosses and not *Sphagnum*. In form, however, the antheridium is globular and long-stalked, resembling *Sphagnum* and not the true mosses. The archegonia also occur at the apex of a special branch, this character being common to leafy liverworts, sphagnums, and true mosses.

Sporophyte. — The sporophyte presents the great peculiarities of the group. The sporogenous tissue is cut off from the endothecium as the outermost layer of cells, a feature resembling true mosses but not *Sphagnum*; but the sporogenous tissue caps the columella like a dome, a feature resembling *Sphagnum* but not true mosses. A pseudopodium develops instead of a seta, as in *Sphagnum*. The dehiscence of the capsule is very peculiar, for instead of the operculum of other mosses, there are four vertical slits that do not reach the apex, recalling the four valves of the capsule of Jungermanniales. In fact one of the Jungermanniales (*Symphyogyna*) has just this dehiscence by means of four vertical slits.

Conclusions. — The combination of characters may be summarized as follows: the gametophyte is either thallose, as in *Sphagnum*, or partly filamentous, as in true mosses; the antheridia are terminal, as in true mosses, but long-stalked and globular, as in *Sphagnum*; the sporogenous tissue is derived from the endothecium, as in true mosses, but caps the columella, as in *Sphagnum* and *Anthoceros*; the capsule dehisces by four slits or valves, as in Jungermanniales, and not by an operculum, as in other mosses; a pseudopodium is developed, which is a feature of *Sphagnum*, but not of true mosses.

(3) BRYALES

General character. — This is the great assemblage of mosses, distinguished from all others as true mosses. It includes the most highly organized bryophytes, and is their most representative group, but it seems to be a closed line; that is, it has given rise to no higher groups. Although a vast group, it is so uniform in general structure that a single account will suffice.

Gametophyte. — The gametophyte is a branching filament (*protonema*, fig. 251), which is the equivalent of the thallus of *Sphagnum* and the liverworts. In these groups the thallus in its development passes through two or three stages, the first one being filamentous; in the true mosses this earliest filamentous stage persists. This fact is associated with the development of the erect leafy branch (gametophore) characteristic of mosses. With green tissue displayed by erect branches the display of green tissue by the thallus body declines, and the thallus finally remains in an embryonic stage. Although the leafy branch is the conspicuous part of mosses, it should not be thought of as the gametophyte, but as a branch of the gametophyte (fig. 251). In certain mosses, known as reduced forms, this branch is not so prominent in its display of green tissue, only a few leaves appearing; in fact it may bear only a single scale leaf in addition to the sex organs.

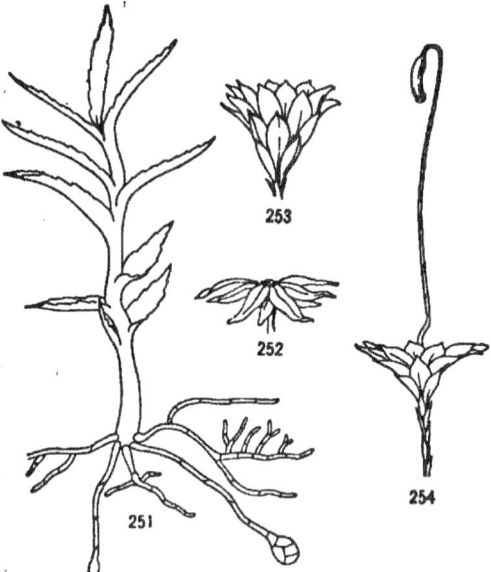

FIGS. 251–254.— *True moss:* 251, leafy branch arising from protonema and putting out rhizoids; a well-developed "resting bud" is shown; 252, terminal rosette containing sex organs; 253, rosette containing archegonia; 254, a sporophyte arising from a cluster of archegonia.

The leafy branch develops by means of an apical cell with three cutting faces. The segments are cut into outer and inner cells, the former, for the most part, developing the leaves; the latter the axis. The leaves usually consist of a single plate of green cells, often thickened in the middle so as to resemble a midrib.

Vegetative multiplication. — The power of vegetative multiplication is remarkably developed. The leafy branch bears the sex organs above the moist substratum, so that the conditions are not favorable for swimming sperms. As a consequence, fertilization in many mosses

BRYOPHYTES 117

is rare, and in some cases even sex organs are rare. Therefore, it is probable that reproduction is chiefly by vegetative multiplication, which may occur as follows: (1) the isolation of branches by the death of older axes; (2) the production of gemmae; (3) the production of resting buds on the protonema, which seem to be only arrested branch buds (fig. 251); and (4) under appropriate conditions, the development of a new protonema from any part of the leafy branch, or from fragments of leaves and axes. It follows that a gametophyte once started may propagate indefinitely.

Sex organs. — The sex organs are grouped at the end of the main stem or of its branches. Around this terminal cluster of sex organs the leaves usually become modified in form and sometimes in color, forming a sheath or a rosette (figs. 252, 253), the whole being the so-called moss "flower," a most inappropriate name. The antheridia and archegonia may occur together in the same cluster, or they may be in separate clusters, and sometimes they are intermixed with multicellular hairs (*paraphyses*).

In the true mosses the antheridia hold the same relation to the apical cell that the archegonia hold in the acrogynous Jungermanniales and in Sphagnales. The antheridium initials are segments of the apical cell, and the apical cell itself usually becomes an initial. The growth is by means of an apical cell with two cutting faces, and the form is usually club-shaped, with a stalk of variable length. In discharging the sperms, the cells at the apex separate, the mother cells are discharged *en masse*, and then the tip cells spring together again, so that empty but complete antheridia are often observed (fig. 255).

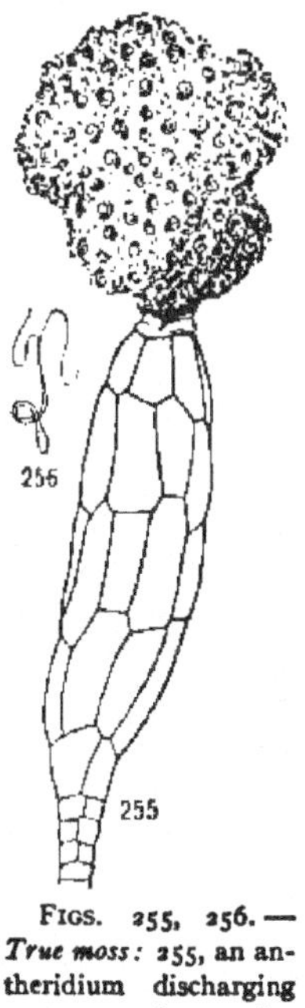

FIGS. 255, 256. — *True moss:* 255, an antheridium discharging sperm mother cells; 256, a single sperm. — After SACHS.

The archegonia differ from those of the liverworts in one important particular. The central cell (*primary oogenous cell*) does not form all of the axial row, which is added to by successive divisions of the cap cell. The mature archegonia of mosses are usually more conspicuously stalked than in the other groups, with more massive venter, and with smaller, more numerous, and more ephemeral canal cells (fig. 257).

MORPHOLOGY

Sporophyte. — The sporophyte is the most characteristic and complicated structure in true mosses (fig. 254). As it develops from the fertilized egg, the venter and stalk of the archegonium develop a remarkable calyptra, which enlarges very much, but is finally ruptured near the base by the growing sporophyte and is carried up as a cap or hood on the top of the capsule. The first division of the egg is transverse, and an apical cell with two cutting faces is developed in the outer cell or in some one of its early progeny. A variable number of segments is cut off (fig. 258), resulting usually in a much elongated embryo. In the upper end of the embryo the usual differentiation into amphithecium and endothecium occurs; the former develops into several layers, the latter into quite a mass of cells (figs. 259, 260). The sporogenous tissue is cut off late from the periphery of the endothecium, but does not cap the columella, which extends completely through the capsule as an axis (figs. 261, 262). The sporogenous tissue becomes two layers of cells, the mass not being dome-shaped, as in *Anthoceros* and *Sphagnum*, but barrel-shaped. Among bryophytes, the sporogenous tissue, therefore, reaches its greatest relative reduction in true mosses.

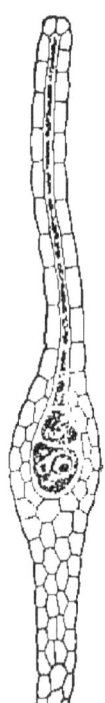

FIG. 257. — *True moss*: an archegonium, showing the conspicuous stalk, the long neck, and the axial row (composed of egg, ventral canal cell, and numerous disorganized neck canal cells).

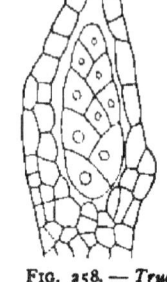

FIG. 258. — *True moss*: a young sporophyte, showing the work of the apical cell. — After BARNES and LAND, ined.

Capsule. — The final structure of the capsule is extremely complex, and a longitudinal section may be outlined as follows (fig. 263), beginning with the outside: (1) the epidermal layer, (2) several layers of wall cells, (3) a region of intercellular cavities traversed by threads of chlorophyll tissue, (4) a tapetal layer (see p. 126); these four regions belong to the amphithecium. The endothecium is differentiated as follows: (5) the two layers of sporogenous cells, (6) an inner tapetal layer, (7) a region of intercellular cavities traversed by threads of chlorophyll tissue, (8) the columella. The inner region of cavities (7) is present only in such peculiarly organized forms as *Polytrichum*. At the maturity of the capsule the water fails, all the tissues between the epidermal layers dry up, and the spores are free in the large cavity.

Operculum and peristome. — The development of the operculum is complicated (fig. 264). It is sometimes early differentiated from the capsule by a shallow depression where a narrow zone of cells forms a plane of cleavage. Above and below this cleavage plane the tissue grows more rapidly, resulting in two evident rings; the upper one is the *annulus*, the lower one the *rim*. The rim is the more or less thickened top of the urnlike capsule; but the annulus is a definite ring which often becomes detached. The sterile apex is at first solid, the center, occupied by endothecial tissue, being a continuation of the columella. The sporogenous tissue and the region of cavities end just opposite the cleavage plane, so that they are not represented at the apex. The amphithecial region of the apex develops in a peculiar way. The outer walls of one of the inner layers of cells (usually the innermost) become much thickened; this layer is anchored to the rim below by a plate of thick-walled cells. When the tissues of the capsule dry out, all the tissues within the operculum,

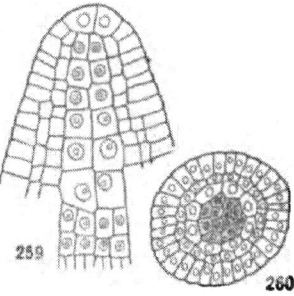

FIGS. 259, 260. — *True moss:* 259, longitudinal section of tip of young sporophyte, showing differentiation into amphithecium (three layers of cells below) and endothecium; 260, cross section of the same, the cells of the endothecium shaded. — After CHAMBERLAIN.

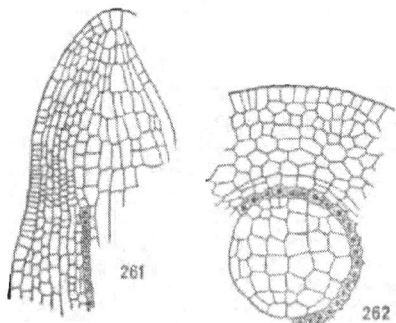

FIGS. 261, 262. — *True moss:* 261, longitudinal section of tip of sporophyte showing (below) the several wall layers (amphithecium), the sporogenous layer (shaded) cut off from the endothecium, and (above) the beginning of the operculum; 262, cross-section of same, showing (beginning at center) columella, single layer of sporogenous cells, and eight or nine wall layers developed from the amphithecium. — After CHAMBERLAIN.

except this heavy layer of walls, disappear, and the operculum slips off like a cap, leaving these heavy walls in a conical group of toothlike projections (*peristome*) anchored below to the rim. Sometimes there are two sets of peristome teeth, in which case both the inner and the outer walls of the peristome-forming cells become thickened. There are many variations in peristomes in detail of development and in pattern.

Apophysis. — The lower part of the capsule does not always develop sporogenous tissue; it is then characterized by a greater display of chlorophyll tissue and stomata (fig. 263). This principal chlorophyll-bearing region of the sporophyte (*apophysis*) often is conspicuous, and sometimes becomes remarkably expanded.

Seta. — The seta is highly organized, with a central strand of elongated cells (not vascular); in fact it is the most highly differentiated axial structure below vascular plants (see figs. 1013–1016).

The great groups. — The principal groups of so large an assemblage of forms as the true mosses should be indicated, but it should be understood that they are extremely unsatisfactory, because they are very

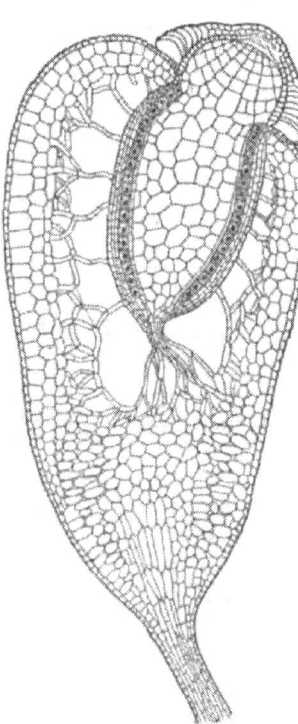

Fig. 263. — *True moss:* longitudinal section through a mature capsule, showing operculum, peristome, columella, sporogenous tissue, complex wall of the capsule (conspicuous in which is the air-chamber region), and the apophysis (the region between the seta and the bottom of the air-chamber region).

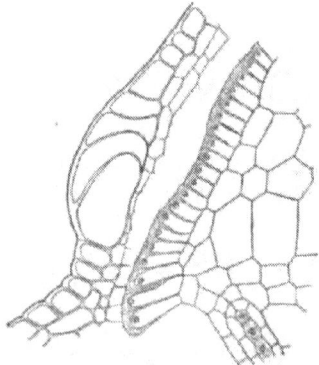

Fig. 264. — *True moss:* structure of the operculum in longitudinal section; large cells in epidermal row belong to annulus; within are the thickening walls (shaded) of a layer of amphithecial cell, to form the peristome, which is anchored by special cells to the rim of the capsule below the annulus; three sporogenous cells (shaded) represent the top of the sporogenous layer, to the left of which is the large air-chamber developed in the amphithecium. — After CHAMBERLAIN.

artificial. The two main divisions are (1) *Cleistocarpae* (or cleistocarps), characterized by the absence of an operculum, and hence with no peristome, the capsule opening by irregular rupture or decay; and

(2) *Stegocarpae* (or stegocarps), characterized by an operculum and generally a peristome. The stegocarps are much the more numerous and representative mosses, comprising two groups: (*a*) *Pleurocarpae*, with the archegonia (and of course the sporophyte) terminal on short lateral branches; and (*b*) *Acrocarpae*, with the archegonia terminal on the main axis. Highest among the stegocarps is the great family Polytrichaceae, of unusual size and complexity in both leafy branch and sporophyte. The leaves have a specially organized chlorophyll tissue; the central region of the stem and seta almost suggest conducting tissue; and there are distinct leaf traces.

Conclusions. — Some of the general conclusions as to bryophytes may be summarized as follows: The gametophyte begins as a simple thallus body and culminates as a filamentous body bearing erect leafy branches. This is the gametophyte at its best, for in the higher groups it is much less highly developed. Such a gametophyte introduces conditions unfavorable for the functioning of sperms.

The sex organs are fairly constant, the archegonia more so than the antheridia. There is a shifting in position from a general distribution over the dorsal surface of the gametophyte to special regions, and finally to the tips of leafy axes, and in this terminal position the archegonia preceded the antheridia. The conspicuous exception in the development of sex organs and their relation to the gametophyte is found in Anthocerotales, in which they are embedded in the tissue of the thallus, the antheridium developing from the inner cell resulting from the periclinal division of the initial, and the archegonium being invested by the growing tissue of the thallus. This relation of the archegonium to the tissue of the thallus is characteristic of pteridophytes.

The sporophyte begins as a simple spore case, being all sporogenous except the single layer of wall cells. But progressive sterilization of potentially sporogenous tissue proceeds through all bryophytes, culminating in the true mosses, in which the sporogenous tissue is much reduced in extent and appears late, and the great bulk of the sporophyte consists of sterile tissue, from which develops a foot, a highly differentiated seta, and a capsule of remarkable complexity.

The sporophyte is dependent upon the gametophyte in all bryophytes, but there is evidently a tendency towards independence, as shown by the development of chlorophyll tissue, which reaches its highest expression in Anthocerotales and in the apophysis of certain mosses.

CHAPTER III — PTERIDOPHYTES

Introductory. — The gap between bryophytes and pteridophytes is perhaps the greatest in the plant kingdom. To pass from the leafless, dependent sporophyte of bryophytes to the leafy, independent, vascular, root-bearing sporophyte of pteridophytes is a very sudden and complete change. One of the great problems in the evolution of plants is to explain how the leafless sporophyte became a leafy one; and a part of the problem is to discover the most primitive sporophyte among pteridophytes, concerning which there is great diversity of opinion. For convenience of presentation, the sequence of groups suggested by BOWER will be used.

(1) LYCOPODIALES

General character. — The club mosses are widely distributed and comprise about one eighth of the living pteridophytes. The group includes four living genera and also numerous extinct forms, among which are some of the oldest known vascular plants. The three genera *Lycopodium*, *Phylloglossum*, and *Selaginella* are evidently closely related, forming a very natural group, while the fourth genus, *Isoetes*, has given rise to much discussion as to its affinities.

Lycopodium

General character. — This genus, comprising about 100 living species, is in all probability one of the oldest living genera of vascular plants, and possibly is represented in the Paleozoic. It deserves a somewhat full description, as it is possibly the best living representative of the earliest forms of vascular plants.

Sporophyte. — The sporophyte in its simplest form is a simple stem covered with very numerous small leaves, and on the upper side of each leaf there is a single large sporangium (fig. 265). Leaves bearing sporangia are called *sporophylls*, and therefore this simplest vascular sporophyte is a simple leafy stem, with every leaf a sporophyll. An assemblage of sporophylls is a *strobilus*, and therefore this primitive sporophyte is a strobilus. The problem, therefore, is how such a leafless sporophyte (sporogonium) as occurs among bryophytes could become a strobilus or rather a strobiloid body.

An explanation of the origin of this body has been suggested by BOWER's theory of the strobilus. The partially independent sporophyte of *Anthoceros* is selected as illustrating a possible ancestral condition of vascular plants at the level of bryophytes, and the possible successive changes are outlined as follows: (1) the sporogenous tissue becomes more and more superficial (a change begun when the sporogenous tissue is transferred from the endothecium to the amphithecium); (2) the continuous sporogenous layer becomes broken into separate masses by intercalated sterile tracts (a condition present among Anthocerotales); (3) the separated sporogenous masses become more superficial, resulting in an alternation of green tissue and sporogenous tissue; (4) the intervening green tissue develops green expansions (small

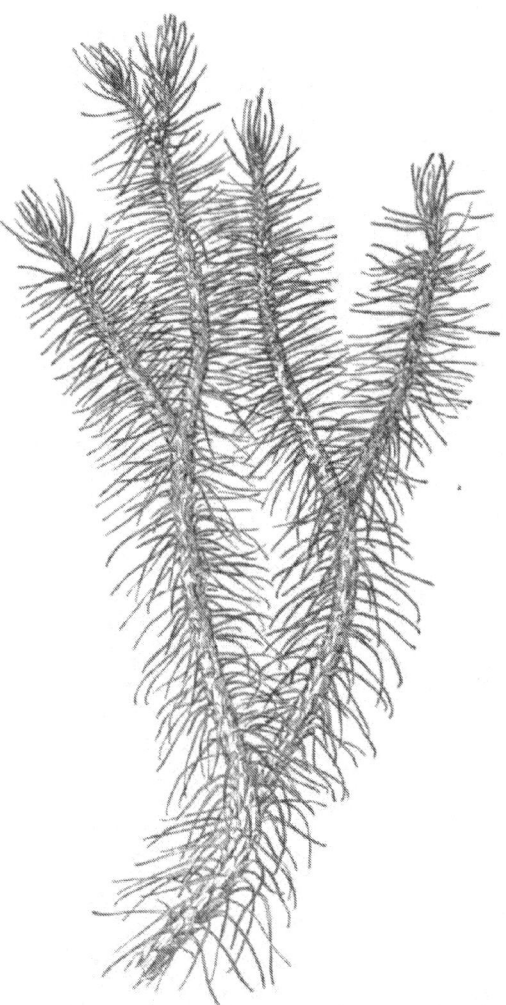

FIG. 265.—*Lycopodium pithyoides:* a sporophyte consisting of a branching stem covered with small leaves, each leaf bearing a sporangium; the simplest type of *Lycopodium* sporophyte, except that it is branching.

leaves), each one having at base a mass of sporogenous tissue (*sporangium*). This final structure is the simple *Lycopodium* body just described. It is the so-called *Selago* type, in which all or nearly all the leaves are sporophylls, and hence practically the whole body is a strobilus. It must be understood that this proposed origin of the *Lycopodium* sporophyte is simply a theory, but it is a very suggestive one.

The more complex sporophytes of *Lycopodium* are branching bodies (fig. 265). There is a gradual sterilization of the lower sporophylls, which thus become simply foliage leaves. Finally the sporophyte becomes differentiated into two distinct regions: that bearing foliage leaves and that bearing sporophylls. The sporophylls finally become quite different in appearance from the foliage leaves and are organized into a compact strobilus, which is sometimes separated from the branching leafy body by a long stalk bearing only rudimentary leaves (fig. 266).

Vascular system. — The anatomy of the stem emphasizes further the primitive character of this sporophyte. A cross section shows two regions: the *cortex*, an outer region of living cells; and the *central cylinder* or *stele*, in which the vascular system (conducting system) is developed. The vascular system has been found to be of great importance in any study of the evolution of vascular plants, and, therefore, the outline of its history must be indicated. In the simpler lycopodiums, or in young stems, the vascular system of the stem forms a solid axial cylinder, in which the *xylem* (the group of water-conducting vessels) is completely surrounded by the *phloem*

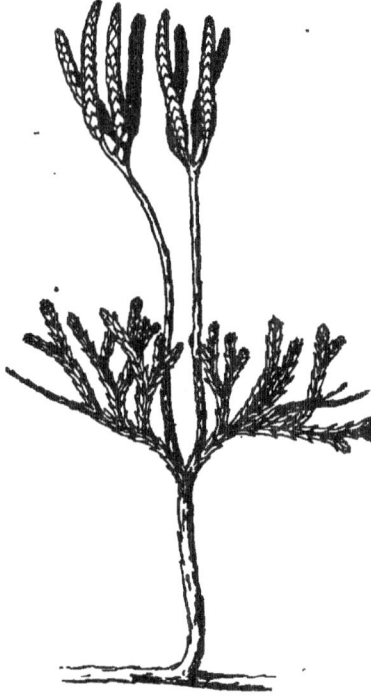

FIG. 266. — *Lycopodium complanatum*: a sporophyte showing distinct differentiation between foliage region and strobilus.

(food-conducting cells), such an arrangement being called the *concentric* arrangement. This most primitive vascular system of the stem, therefore, consists of a single, solid cylinder with concentric xylem and phloem (commonly spoken of as a concentric cylinder), to which type the name *protostele* has been given. In mature stems of *Lycopodium*, the solid xylem strand may divide into branches which run through the stele as several strands separated by pithlike tissue

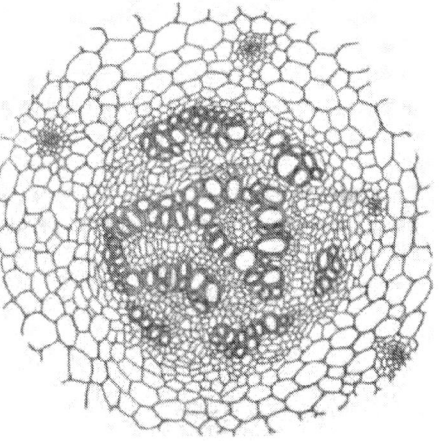

FIG. 267. — Cross section of the central region of an adult stem of *Lycopodium*, showing the inner region of the cortex surrounding the central stele, in which the branches of the xylem mass are irregularly distributed; section of four leaf traces are seen in the cortex, each of them showing the simple concentric arrangement (xylem surrounded by phloem).

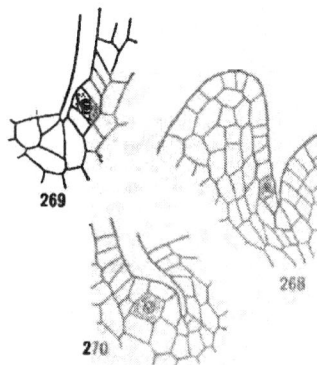

FIGS. 268-270. — Sporangium of *Lycopodium*: 268, section showing a young sporophyll bearing a superficial initial cell (one of a transverse row) on its adaxial face near the base; 269, further development of the initial; 270, division of initial into primary wall cell (outer) and primary sporogenous cell (inner). — After BOWER.

(fig. 267). From the vascular cylinder strands pass out through the cortex, where they are called *leaf traces* (fig. 267), and enter the leaves, where they become continuous with the *veins*.

Sporangium. — The large sporangium is borne upon the upper (*adaxial*) surface of the sporophyll, near the base. The sporangium initial is superficial (fig. 268), and is a transverse row of six to twelve cells; in some cases it consists of two or three such rows. Each of these initial cells divides by a periclinal wall (parallel with the surface), resulting in an outer and an inner transverse row of cells (figs.

270, 271, 272). The outer cells are the *primary wall cells*, which by subsequent divisions give rise to a sporangium wall of at least three layers of cells. The inner cells are the *primary sporogenous cells*, which by subsequent divisions give rise to a considerable mass of sporogenous tissue (fig. 273). This method of sporangium formation, by which the inner cells, following periclinal division of the superficial initials, give rise to the sporogenous tissue, is called the *eusporangiate* method, and plants exhibiting it are often spoken of as *eusporangiates*. All vascular

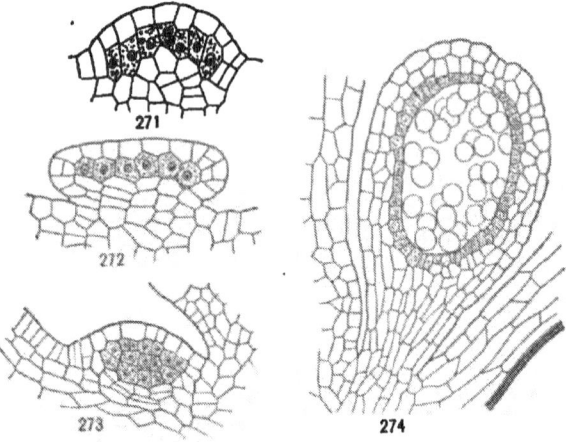

FIGS. 271-274.—Sporangium of *Lycopodium*: 271, 272, view of young sporangium in different planes, showing primary wall layer, primary sporogenous tissue (shaded), and the underlying subarchesporial pad; 273, section showing further development of sporogenous tissue; 274, older sporangium, showing stalklike subarchesporial pad, three wall layers, the innermost of which is the tapetum (shaded), and the rounded off and separated spore mother cells.—After BOWER.

plants are eusporangiates except the modern ferns, whose peculiar method of sporangium formation will be described later.

The sporogenous tissue is invested by a special nutritive layer known as the *tapetum* or *tapetal layer* (fig. 274). In *Lycopodium* the outer portion of the tapetal layer is composed of the innermost wall layer, and the inner portion of the sterile tissue contiguous to the sporogenous tissue. The tapetum, therefore, is simply the layer of sterile cells abutting against the sporogenous tissue, which have been transformed into feeding cells. This function gives to the layer a very characteristic appearance, making it quite distinct from the sterile tissue outside and the sporogenous tissue inside. When the tapetal layer has become a complete investment, the sporogenous cells cease dividing by ordinary division and become *mother cells*, each of which forms a tetrad of spores by two successive divisions, known as the reduction divisions (see p. 61).

Beneath the sporangium, which in section is often somewhat kidney-shaped, there is developed a cushion of sterile cells or even a short stalk, known as the *subarchesporial pad* (figs. 271, 272, 274), in which the vascular elements end. In certain extinct lycopods with very large sporangia, sterile strands or plates radiate from this subarchesporial pad into the large mass of sporogenous tissue, probably being sterilized sporogenous cells. These sterile strands are important to note, as indicating a tendency to divide a large sporangium into chambers.

Gametophyte. — The gametophyte of *Lycopodium* is a very characteristic structure and suggests very little connection with the gametophytes of liverworts. When the spore germinates, there is produced at first a subterranean tuberous body (*primary tubercle*), which later gives rise to an aerial, lobed, green portion bearing the sex organs. The gametophyte is differentiated, therefore, into two distinct regions (fig. 275). The subterranean tuberous part is variable in form and is often highly differentiated into tissue regions (fig. 276); it always contains a characteristic endophytic fungus, which inhabits a definite region of the body. This may be regarded as the primitive kind of gametophyte body in *Lycopodium*, but there are two variations that are important. In certain species the aerial region is lacking, leaving the gametophyte simply a subterranean, tuberous body (fig. 277), which, of course, bears the sex organs. In certain epiphytic species the tuberous region is lacking, the gametophyte being entirely aerial.

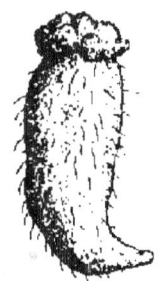

FIG. 275. — Gametophyte of *Lycopodium complanatum*, showing the differentiation into tuberous region and crown. — After BRUCHMANN.

Antheridium. — The antheridium (figs. 278–282) begins as a superficial cell, which enlarges and then divides by a periclinal wall. The outer cell following this division is the *primary wall cell*, which forms an outer wall of one layer of cells; the inner cell is the *primary spermatogenous cell*, which produces a large number of spermatogenous cells, those of the last division being sperm mother cells. This method of antheridium development resembles closely the eusporangiate method of sporangium development, and is always associated with it. It is interesting to note that only the Anthocerotales among bryophytes approach this method of antheridium formation in the fact that the inner cell following the periclinal division gives rise to the spermatogenous tissue. The sperms are remarkable among pteridophytes in being biciliate, a character which belongs to the sperms of bryophytes (fig. 282).

Archegonium.— The archegonium also resembles that of the Anthocerotales in being an embedded structure. The outline of its development is as follows: It begins as a superficial cell, which divides by a transverse wall (fig. 283), the outer cell being the *primary neck cell*, the inner one the *inner cell*. The inner cell divides by a transverse wall, resulting in a row of three cells (fig. 284), a condition of the archegonium very commonly seen. Beginning with the

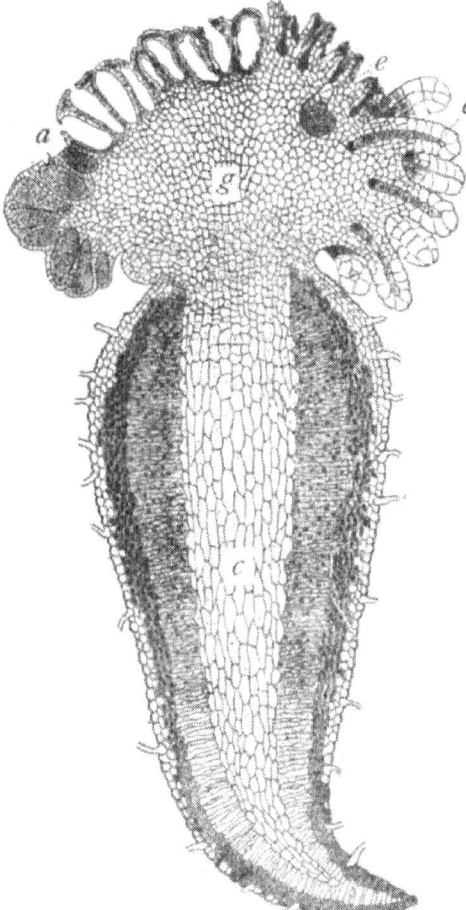

FIG. 276.— Section of gametophyte of *Lycopodium complanatum*, showing crown (*g*) bearing antheridia (*a*) and archegonia (*a'*) (in one, *e*, the embryo sporophyte has developed), and the tuberous region (*c*) with highly differentiated tissues.— After BRUCHMANN.

outermost one of this row of cells, they are called *primary neck cell*, *central cell*, and *basal cell*. The primary neck cell, by successive divisions, develops a neck consisting of several tiers of cells (figs. 284–286), with four cells in each tier. The central cell develops the axial row as follows: the first transverse division results in the *primary neck canal cell* (the outer one) and the *primary ventral cell* (the inner one, fig. 285). By successive transverse divisions, the primary neck canal cell produces a variable

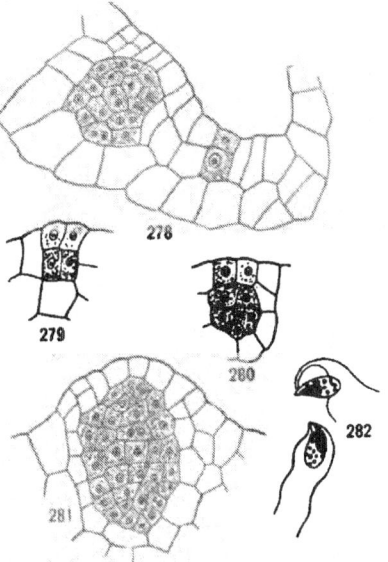

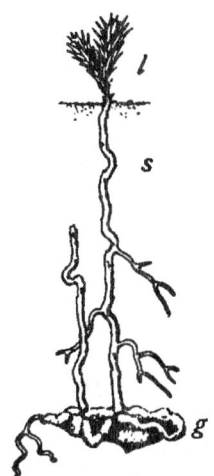

FIG. 277.— Gametophyte (*g*) of *Lycopodium annotinum* (entirely tuberous and subterranean), bearing a young sporophyte (*s, l*); the ground line is shown. — After BRUCHMANN.

FIGS. 278-282.— Antheridium of *Lycopodium clavatum*: 278, to the right a young antheridium after the first division (periclinal) of the superficial initial cell; to the left a much older antheridium; 279, young antheridium after division of primary wall cell and primary spermatogenous cell; 280, further development of spermatogenous tissue; 281, nearly mature antheridium, showing the wall (consisting of one layer of cells) and the mass of spermatogenous cells; 282, two sperms, showing the biciliate character. — After BRUCHMANN.

number of neck canal cells (fig. 286); in some cases four to six, but in other cases as many as thirteen have been observed. This extraordinarily large number of neck canal cells is regarded as a low character, since a steady decrease in the number of neck canal cells is observed throughout the groups having archegonia. The primary ventral cell, just before the maturity of the archegonium, divides into the ventral canal cell and the egg, and finally all the canal cells disorganize (fig. 287).

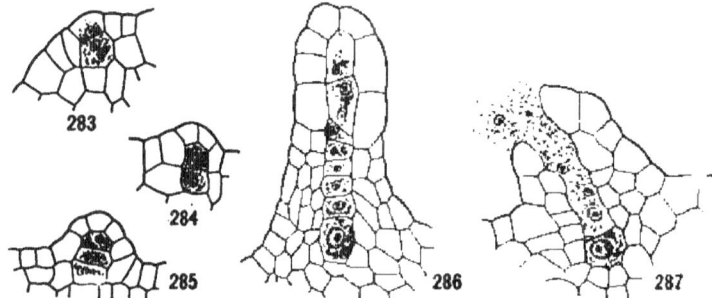

FIGS. 283–287. — Archegonium of *Lycopodium clavatum*: 283, young archegonium after the first division (periclinal) of the superficial initial, resulting in the primary neck cell (outer) and inner cell; 284, division of neck cell and also of inner cell, the latter division resulting in basal cell and central cell (both shaded); 285, division of central cell, giving rise to primary neck canal cell (outermost shaded one) and primary ventral cell (middle shaded one); 286, the completed axial row, consisting of six neck canal cells, the ventral canal cell, and the egg; 287, breaking down of canal cells, leaving a passageway to the egg. — After BRUCHMANN.

Embryo. — The embryo of the *Lycopodium* sporophyte develops in a very characteristic way (figs. 288–293). The fertilized egg divides by a transverse wall, the resulting outer cell being the *suspensor cell*, and the inner one the *embryonal cell* (fig. 288). The suspensor cell may or may not divide, but in any event it usually becomes elongated. The suspensor is an organ of the embryo, but does not enter into its permanent structure, which is developed by the embryonal cell. By successive divisions this cell becomes four cells (figs. 289, 290), which are related to each other as unequal quadrants of a sphere. Two of these quadrant cells develop the *foot*, which is an absorbing organ of the embryo while it is feeding upon the gametophyte. One of the remaining quadrant cells develops the stem, and the other the first leaf. It is to be observed that in this first differentiation of body regions the root is omitted, but it develops later from the tissue produced by the leaf quadrant (fig. 294). The foot is a structure of the sporophyte found among the bryophytes, among which the sporophyte is dependent on the gametophyte through life. The suspensor is a new organ of the

PTERIDOPHYTES

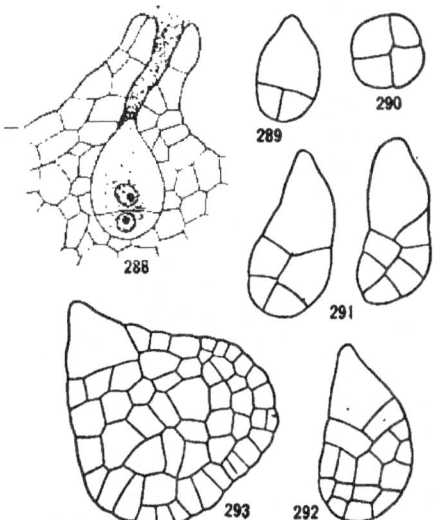

FIGS. 288–293.— Embryo (sporophyte) of *Lycopodium clavatum*: 288, first division of egg into suspensor cell and embryonal cell; 289, 290, division of embryonal cell into four cells (290 being a cross section); 291–293, further stages in the development of the embryo.— After BRUCHMANN.

FIG. 294.— Young sporophyte of *Lycopodium clavatum*, showing foot, primary root, and stem bearing scale leaves.— After BRUCHMANN.

embryo sporophyte, found in certain pteridophytes, as the Lycopodiales, but very characteristic of seed plants

Phylloglossum

This is an Australasian genus of one species, closely allied to *Lycopodium* and thought by some to be the most primitive pteridophyte. The sporophyte body is a tuberous stem bearing a cluster of small leaves. Some of the sporophytes also develop a short, naked stalk bearing a terminal stobilus (fig. 295). Some species of *Lycopodium* begin with this type of body, but the strobilus-bearing stalk becomes branching and leafy, and the tuberous embryonic body disappears. The adult body of *Phylloglossum*, therefore, is like the embryonic body of some species of *Lycopodium*. In other species of *Lycopodium* this kind of embryonic body is absent from the life history. The gametophyte resembles that of *Lycopodium*, in which there is a subterranean tuberous region and an aerial, green, more or less lobed region bearing the sex organs.

Conclusions. — Since *Lycopodium* and its ally represent possibly the most primitive vascular plants, a summary of the important features will be useful. It would follow that the most primitive leafy sporophyte is a strobilus, in the sense that all its leaves are sporophylls. The first foliage leaves are small and scattered, and are sterilized sporophylls. The vascular system consists of a single, solid cylinder, whose xylem and phloem are concentrically arranged. The sporangia are large and solitary on the adaxial face of the sporophyll, and each one is developed from a transverse row of initial cells. The new structures of this sporophyte, as contrasted with that of the bryophytes, are sporophylls, foliage leaves, vascular system, root, and suspensor.

FIG. 295. — *Phylloglossum:* sporophyte bearing a stalked strobilus.

The gametophyte is a subterranean tuberous body with an aerial, green crown bearing the sex organs. The antheridia develop endogenously, and the sperms are bryophytic in type. The archegonia are also embedded, as in Anthocerotales.

Selaginella

General character. — This is the great genus of modern Lycopodiales, comprising nearly 500 species, which belong chiefly to the tropics. It is evidently closely related to *Lycopodium*, and may be regarded as a modern representative of forms that lived during the coal measures, and that had developed *heterospory* (see below).

Sporophyte. — The sporophyte body resembles that of *Lycopodium* in habit (fig. 296), although it is usually much more delicate. It is characterized by two noteworthy features. One is the development of a *ligule*, a flaplike outgrowth from the adaxial surface of the leaf near its base. The ligule is an embryonic organ of the leaf, being very prominent and functional during the growth of the leaf blade. When the blade matures, the ligule becomes merely an inconspicuous and membranous flap. This curious structure is a feature of all the Lycopodiales (including fossil groups) except *Lycopodium* and *Phylloglossum*, and for this reason the former are often called *Ligulatae*, to distinguish them from the latter, which are *Eligulatae*. The other noteworthy feature of the sporophyte body is the occurrence of a single chloroplast in the actively dividing cells (*meristem*). It will be remembered that this same feature appears in the gametophyte body of *Anthoceros* (p. 106).

The vascular cylinder of the stem is generally of the primitive type, being a protostele (p. 125) (fig. 297); but in some cases the cylinder is hollow (a *siphonostele*), containing pith, a type of cylinder derived from the protostele.

Sporangia. — The sporangia, as in all Lycopodiales, are solitary and adaxial with reference to the sporophyll, and derived from a transverse row of initial cells; but in *Selaginella* these initials occur on the stem just above the origin of the sporophyll (figs. 298, 299). This means that sporangia are not always produced by sporophylls, and in such cases the name sporophyll is justified only by its relation to the sporangium. On the basis of their origin, sporangia often are distinguished as *foliar* (on the sporophyll) and *cauline* (on the stem).

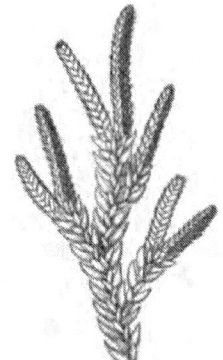

FIG. 296. — *Selaginella*: sporophyte showing strobili and the gradation from foliage leaves to sporophylls.

Heterospory. — The notable feature of *Selaginella*, however, is that all of the sporangia in a strobilus do not mature alike, resulting in heterospory. They all develop alike, and as described under *Lycopodium* (p. 125), as far as the mother cell stage (fig. 300), after which a great difference appears. In some of the sporangia (usually the larger number) all or nearly all of the mother cells function, resulting in the production of numerous spores (fig. 301). In the other sporangia an extensive abortion of mother cells occurs, so

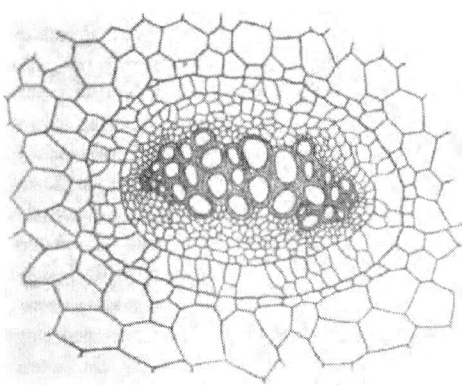

FIG. 297. — Section of stem of *Selaginella*, showing the protostele (a single, solid, concentric vascular cylinder).

extensive that usually only one mother cell functions, all the others contributing to its nutrition (fig. 302). This results in a relatively very

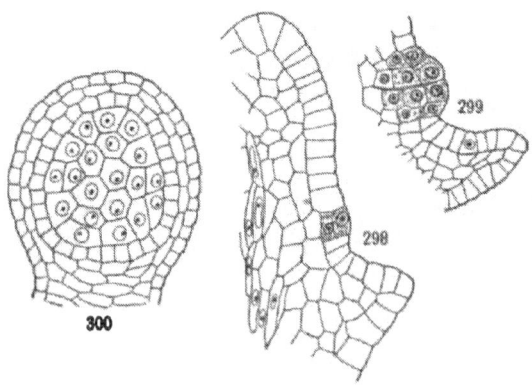

FIGS. 298–300.—Sporangium of *Selaginella*: 298, section through tip of strobilus, showing young sporangium (two shaded cells) on stem, and below it a young sporophyll; 299, further development of sporangium; the superficial cell of the sporophyll containing a nucleus is to give rise to the ligule; 300, sporangium in the mother cell stage.— 298 and 299, after MISS LYON.

large mother cell and a tetrad of four very large spores. In some cases, although a tetrad of spores is started, two or three of them may not develop further, resulting in a sporangium containing only one or two spores. It is this condition of dissimilar spores that is called *heterospory*, in contrast with the condition of similar spores (as in *Lycopodium*), which is called *homospory*. *Selaginella*, therefore, is *heterosporous*, while *Lycopodium* is *homosporous*.

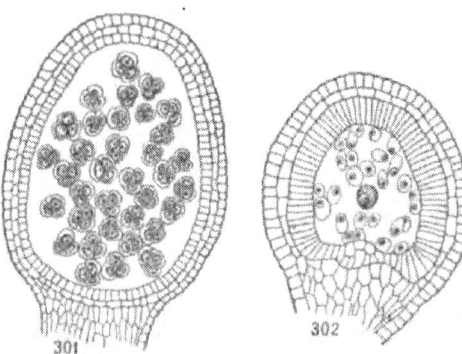

FIGS. 301, 302.—Sporangia of *Selaginella*: 301, microsporangium, showing all the mother cells forming tetrads; 302, megasporangium, showing one functioning mother cell (shaded), the other mother cells acting as nutritive cells.— After MISS LYON.

The terminology applied to the heterosporous condition is simple. The small spores are *microspores*, and the large ones are *megaspores*; the sporangia producing microspores are *microsporangia*, and those producing megaspores are *megasporangia*; the sporophylls related to microsporangia are *microsporophylls*, and those related to megasporangia are *megasporophylls*.

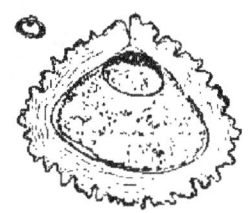

FIG. 303.—Spores of *Selaginella*: mature microspore and megaspore drawn to same scale.

This differentiation of spores in size (fig. 303) is associated with a differentiation in function, for upon germination the microspores produce male gametophytes, while the megaspores produce female gametophytes. The phenomenon of heterospory, therefore, is associated with the sexual differentiation of gametophytes. It is a phenomenon exhibited among pteridophytes only by certain groups, but it is universal among seed plants. In fact, the appearance of heterospory is the necessary antecedent to the formation of a seed. It follows, therefore, that the development of heterospory among pteridophytes made the great group of seed plants possible. In *Selaginella* there is a remarkable approach to the seed condition in the fact that the megaspores are not shed, but are retained within the megasporangium, within which the female gametophyte is developed, the egg fertilized, and the young sporophyte (embryo) formed. Just how far this falls short of being the seed condition will be considered under seed plants.

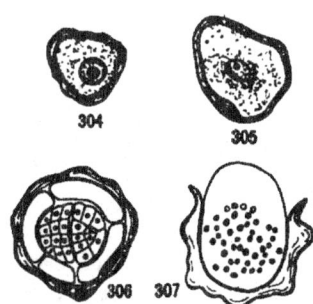

FIGS. 304–307.—Male gametophyte of *Selaginella*: 304, mature microspore; 305, first division, showing antheridium initial (large cell) and vegetative cell (small lenticular cell against the wall); 306, the antheridium (four sterile jacket cells shown surrounding the group of sperm mother cells); the disorganized vegetative cell is also shown (in black); 307, male gametophyte at time of fertilization, the antheridium (jacket cells have broken down) containing free sperms escaping from the microspore wall.—After MISS LYON.

Male gametophyte.—The male gametophyte produced by the microspore is a very simple structure, never outgrowing the spore, and therefore encased by the old spore wall. The two cells formed by the division of the protoplast of the microspore are the antheridium initial and the vegetative cell (fig. 305). This single vegetative cell is the sole representative of the vegetative tissue of more primitive gametophytes. The antheridium initial produces an antheridium with the usual jacket of sterile cells investing sperm mother cells (fig. 306). At maturity the jacket cells break down and the mother cells (with their sperms) are free in the general cavity of the microspore (fig. 307). The male gametophyte, therefore, is reduced to one vegetative cell and one antheridium; and encased by the old microspore wall it is carried to the megasporangium, in which the female gametophytes are developing. There the male gametophyte bursts through the microspore coat (fig. 307). The sperms are very small, with more or less spirally coiled bodies and two terminal cilia. *Selaginella* thus shares with *Lycopodium* and *Phylloglossum* the character of producing biciliate sperms, a type characteristic of bryophytes, and in strong contrast with the sperms produced by other pteridophytes.

Female gametophyte.—The female gametophyte is much more extensive than the male gametophyte, but the greater part of it is invested by the old megaspore wall (fig. 308). The nucleus of the megaspore begins a series of divisions that continue until a large number of free nuclei are produced. This free nuclear division occurs chiefly in the apical (pointed) end of the megaspore, and results in a layer of nuclei, which later become invested by walls. Subsequent divisions result in a cushion of cells at the apex of the megaspore, while the large body of the megaspore is free from cells, acting as a great food reservoir (fig. 308). The wall of the megaspore cracks at the apex and the apical tissue protrudes, developing a more or less expanded mass of tissue in which archegonia develop (figs. 308, 309). Later, the deeper region of the megaspore becomes filled with a tissue of large cells, and continues to act as a food reservoir for the developing embryo. This early differentiation of the female gametophyte into two distinct regions, one that produces archegonia, and the other nutritive, is a marked feature of the female gametophyte in all heterosporous plants.

FIG. 308.—Female gametophyte of *Selaginella*: the apical cushion of cells having broken through the heavy megaspore wall; an archegonium to be observed at the apex.—After MISS LYON.

Fertilization.—The male gametophytes enclosed by the old micro-

PTERIDOPHYTES

spore walls are brought to the megasporangia by the wind or by gravity. The microspores drift among the megaspores with protruding female gametophytes bearing archegonia. Then the sperms are discharged, enter the archegonia, and fertilization occurs (fig. 310). In these female gametophytes, still in the sporangia, the embryo sporophytes develop and then emerge, a strobilus often being beset with young sporelings. Later the strobilus as a whole, with its attached sporelings, drops off.

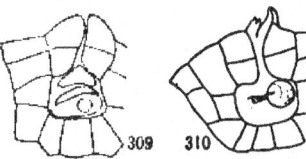

FIGS. 309, 310. — Archegonium of *Selaginella:* 309, the neck and the axial row (neck canal cell, ventral canal cell, and egg); 310, fertilization, the sperm in contact with the egg. — After Miss LYON.

Embryo. — The embryo (sporophyte) is developed much as in *Lycopodium* (figs. 311–314). The suspensor (p. 130) is more extensive than in *Lycopodium*, being of use in relating the embryo to the deep nutritive tissue within the megaspore. The embryonal cell at the end of the suspensor first produces three cells: a terminal cell that develops the stem, flanked by two cells (one on each side) that develop leaves. From one of the leaf segments the foot is developed later (fig. 313); and still later, from the same segment the primary root arises (fig. 314). When fully organized and emerging, the embryo resembles a seedling dicotyledon escaping from its seed. The tuberous foot

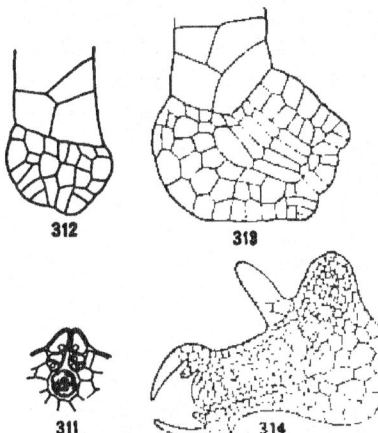

FIGS. 311–314. — Embryo of *Selaginella:* 311, first division of fertilized egg (the outer cell to form the suspensor, the inner cell to form the embryo); 312, early stage of the embryo (attached to suspensor), the apical cell of the stem being evident; 313, later stage of the embryo, showing (to the right) the apical cell of the stem between the apical cells of the first two leaves and (to the left) the developing foot; 314, an older embryo, showing the foot (to the right below), the root (to the right above), the suspensor, the two leaves (to the left) with their ligules, the centrally placed stem tip, and the developing vascular system extending between stem and root tips. — 311, after BRUCHMANN; 312–314, after PFEFFER.

is embedded in the nutritive region of the female gametophyte invested by the megaspore coat, and from it there extends in one direction, outside of the spore coat, an elongating stem bearing at its tip a pair of young leaves, between which is the stem apex; and in the other direction the elongating primary root (fig. 314).

Isoetes

General character. — The genus *Isoetes* (quillworts) comprises about sixty species. It is now usually included among the Lycopodiales, although in certain important features it differs from the other members of the group.

Sporophyte. — In general appearance *Isoetes* suggests a tufted grass, growing on muddy flats or in the water (fig. 315). The stem is very short, unbranched, and covered by overlapping leaf bases. The vascular anatomy of the stem is somewhat confusing, and has been interpreted variously. The stem is so short and the leaves are so numerous that the vascular cylinder is little more than a vascular plate. It seems to be a protostele, however, in which the xylem elements have not completely filled up their region, and there is no recognizable phloem. Such a structure is evidently related to that found among the Lycopodiales, and therefore in vascular anatomy *Isoetes* is to be associated with that group.

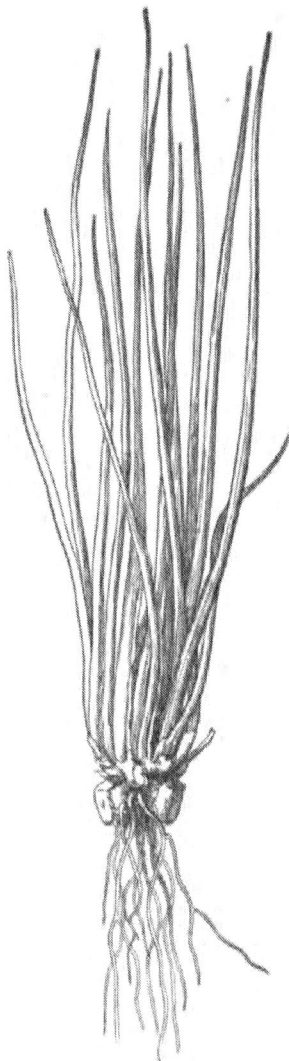

FIG. 315. — *Isoetes*, showing the short unbranched stem bearing dichotomous roots and a tuft of linear leaves.

Leaves. — The leaves are unique in structure, being arranged in a close spiral, and every leaf is a sporophyll, either bearing a sporangium or traces of one. In this sense the whole sporophyte body is a strobilus. Each leaf is distinctly differentiated into sporangium and foliage regions (fig. 317). The foliage portion of the leaf resembles a narrow grass blade, and contains four longitudinal series of air chambers. At the base of this blade, on the adaxial side, the *ligule* appears, socketed in a small pitlike depression. Below the ligule the sporangium region occurs, the sporangium developing in a large deep chamber more or less shut off from the outside by a curtain of tissue (*velum*). This single large sporangium on the adaxial surface of the sporophyll is a very important character relating *Isoetes* to the other Lycopodiales.

Sporangia. — The sporangium resembles also that of the Lycopodiales in arising from a transverse row of initial cells, in this case three or four in number. The method of development is as usual in eusporangiates, beginning with a periclinal division that differentiates the outer wall cells from the inner sporogenous cells. The wall becomes about four-layered, the innermost layer entering into the organization of the tapetal jacket. A large mass of sporogenous tissue is developed, and up to 15,000-25,000 cells all sporangia are alike. At this stage

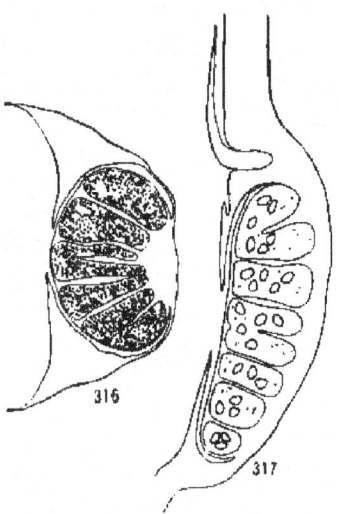

FIGS. 316, 317.—Sporangia of *Isoetes*: 316, cross section of lower region of leaf, showing a microsporangium, with its trabeculae (sterile plates) and numerous microspores; 317, longitudinal section of lower region of leaf, showing a megasporangium, with its trabeculae and relatively few megaspores; also the ligule (above) and the velum extending over the sporangial chamber.

the differences that result in heterospory begin to appear. In those sporangia that are to become microsporangia some of the sporogenous tissue forms plates of sterile cells (*trabeculae*) extending across the sporangium, and all the other cells function in spore formation, producing in a single sporangium 150,000-300,000 microspores (fig. 316). In those sporangia that are to become megasporangia, the trabeculae are more massive, and most of the thousands of sporogenous cells contribute to the nutrition of 40–75 mother cells that function. These mother cells become relatively very large and produce large spores, the total output of megaspores being 150–300 (fig. 317). Both kinds of spores escape by the decay of the sporangium wall.

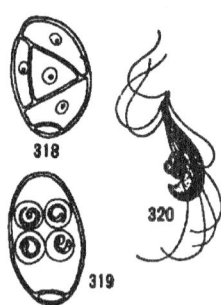

Male gametophyte.—The male gametophyte is still more simple than that of *Selaginella* (figs. 318–320). It consists of a single vegetative cell and a single antheridium, as in *Selaginella;* but the sperm mother cells are only four in number. This is the lowest number reached among pteridophytes, and the nearest approach to seed plants, among which the sperm mother cells are reduced to two. The sperms are large, spirally coiled, and multiciliate (fig. 320), such as characterize all other pteridophytes except Lycopodiales. It is this feature of *Isoetes* that perhaps presents the greatest obstacle to including it among Lycopodiales.

FIGS. 318–320.—Male gametophyte of *Isoetes:* 318, stage showing the vegetative cell (at bottom and without nucleus) and the antheridium (with three wall cells visible and the central primary spermatogenous cell); 319, older stage, in which the wall cells have broken down and the four mother cells (each containing a sperm) are free in the antheridial cavity; 320, sperm.—After BELAJEFF.

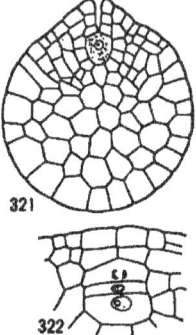

FIGS. 321, 322.—Female gametophyte of *Isoetes:* 321 (after HOFMEISTER), complete gametophyte, bearing an archegonium whose neck is exposed through a crack in the megaspore wall (not shown); 322 (after CAMPBELL), archegonium, showing two tiers of neck cells and an axial row of three cells (neck canal cell, ventral canal cell, and egg).

Female gametophyte.—The female gametophyte develops in the same general way as does that of *Selaginella*, but with some interesting differences. After the free nuclear divisions, followed by the formation of an apical tissue, a layer of cells develops completely about the cavity of the megaspore and then grows centripetally until the megaspore is filled with tissue (fig. 321). The growth of this tissue is precisely like the growth of the endosperm tissue (female gametophyte) in gymnosperms (p. 196). The gametophyte of *Isoetes* does not protrude through the broken megaspore wall and develop tissue outside, as in *Selaginella*, but is exposed only along the triradiate crack through the megaspore wall, along which lines the archegonia appear (fig. 322). The archegonium is notably broad and short, and the primary neck canal cell usually does not divide, resulting in a single uninucleate neck canal cell, which is as far as the reduction of the axial row is carried among pteridophytes (fig. 322).

Embryo. — The embryo sporophyte differs from that of *Selaginella* and *Lycopodium* in several important particulars. In the first place, there is no suspensor, and this feature associates *Isoetes* with the other pteridophytes. The fertilized egg, however, behaves much as does the embryonal cell in *Selaginella* and *Lycopodium*, except that the quadrant cells are assigned differently, two of them forming the foot (as in *Lycopodium*), and the other two forming leaf and root, the stem being the belated member. However, it is characteristic of Lycopodiales to have some member of the body belated in appearance. In *Lycopodium* the belated member is the root, in *Selaginella* the foot and root, in *Isoetes* the stem. The embryo of *Isoetes* has long been recognized to have a remarkable resemblance to the characteristic embryo of monocotyledons among seed plants; and for this reason it was once suggested that perhaps *Isoetes* is a living representative of the ancestors of monocotyledons. In *Isoetes* the axis of the embryo develops the root at one end and a single leaf (*cotyledon*) at the other, the foot arising from the middle region and being embedded in the nutritive tissue within the megaspore. On the free side of the axis a notch appears, from the bottom of which the stem tip arises (fig. 324). The feature of the embryo of monocotyledons is that the single cotyledon is terminal and the stem tip is lateral, and this feature is exactly reproduced in the embryo of *Isoetes*.

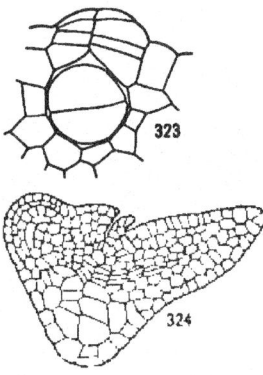

FIGS. 323, 324. — Embryo of *Isoetes*: 323, first division of the fertilized egg, differing from that of *Selaginella* in that the outer (upper) cell does not form a suspensor, but enters into the structure of the embryo; 324, embryo showing foot (below), terminal cotyledon (to the right), root (to the left), ligule (above) from deep notch, and shallow notch (between ligule and root) for stem tip. — After CAMPBELL.

Summary. — A summary of the arguments for and against retaining *Isoetes* among Lycopodiales is as follows: its characters in common

MORPHOLOGY

with Lycopodiales are (1) the vascular anatomy; (2) the solitary sporangium on the adaxial surface of the sporophyll; (3) the development of the sporangium from a transverse row of initial cells; (4) the trabeculae, which also appear in certain fossil Lycopodiales; (5) the ligule, which is present in all Lycopodiales except *Lycopodium* and *Phylloglossum;* and (6) the gametophytes, which resemble closely those of *Selaginella*. The characters not in common with Lycopodiales are (1) the large multiciliate sperms; (2) the absence of a suspensor; (3) the general habit; and (4) the highly specialized leaves.

(2) PSILOTALES

This group of pteridophytes comprises two very small living genera: *Psilotum* (fig. 330), with two species occurring in the tropics of both hemispheres; and *Tmesipteris* (fig. 325), with a single Australasian species (sometimes more species are recognized). These forms are introduced here, not to present their life histories, but to illustrate very briefly certain stages in the evolution of pteridophytes.

Throughout Lycopodiales there appears a tendency to increase the output of spores produced by the sporophyte. The first and simplest method was by branching, thus multiplying strobili. There was also an increase in the size of sporangia; and this led, apparently for nutritive reasons, to the development of sterilized plates through the sporangium, as in certain ancient lycopods; and in *Isoetes* these plates almost divide the sporangium into chambers.

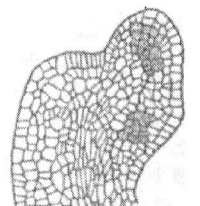

FIGS. 325–328. — *Tmesipteris:* 325, general habit, showing branching leafy stems arising from a tree trunk (epiphytic) and bearing (near tip) the characteristic sporangia; 326–328, various views of the paired sporangia (synangia). — After PRITZEL (ENGLER and PRANTL).

FIG. 329. — *Tmesipteris:* section of sporangia at early stage, showing between the two sporogenous masses a sterile plate of cells which is to form the partition that divides a sporangium (single at the beginning) into two sporangia. — After BOWER.

In *Psilotum* and *Tmesipteris* there are two further stages of development in this direction. In *Tmesipteris* a sterile plate divides the large sporangium into two chambers so distinct that they are called two sporangia (figs. 326–329). That this partition is sterilized sporogenous tissue is proved by its development and by the fact that in exceptional cases it functions as sporogenous tissue. In *Psilotum* the same condition occurs, except that the development of two sterile plates results in three chambers, or a group of three sporangia (figs. 330, 331). The other noteworthy feature of *Psilotum* and *Tmesipteris* is the development of the subarchesporial pad of Lycopodiales into a short stalk, which bears the two or three sporangia and is called the *sporangiophore*.

(3) SPHENOPHYLLALES

This group contains the single large Carboniferous genus *Sphenophyllum*, which illustrates the further development of the sporangiophore. In *Sphenophyllum* there is a distinct strobilus, with whorls of linear sporophylls coalescent at base into spreading funnels. From the adaxial surface of these sporophylls sporangiophores arise, which vary from very short to very long, simple or branching, and bear one to several sporangia. In this genus, therefore, the sporangiophore development is carried much farther than in *Psilotum* and *Tmesipteris*, resulting in a multiplication of sporangia by means of the sporangiophore.

(4) EQUISETALES

This great group is represented in our present flora by the single genus *Equisetum*, comprising about twenty-five species of horsetails or scouring rushes. This is only a remnant of a great group that flourished in the Paleozoic along with the ancient Lycopodiales.

Sporophyte.—The sporophyte body consists of a subterranean, dorsiventral main axis, which gives rise to erect (radial) aerial branches, themselves simple or branched (figs. 332, 333). *Equisetum* is characterized by its remarkably small leaves, which for the most part are insignificant scales that occur in a whorl at each joint and coalesce to form a close sheath. As a conse-

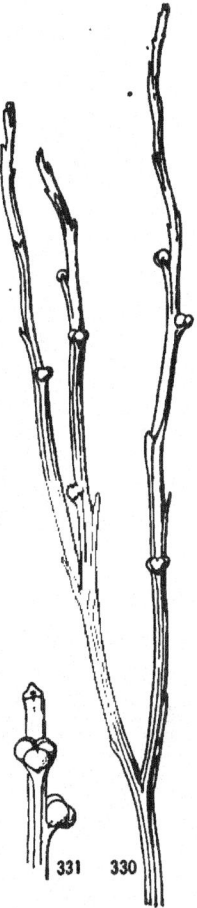

FIGS. 330, 331.—*Psilotum*: 330, general habit, showing the branching body bearing much reduced leaves (scales) and the characteristic three-lobed sporangium (or synangium of three sporangia); 331, the sporangia in greater detail.

144 MORPHOLOGY

quence of this abandonment of leaves as foliage, photosynthesis is entirely a function of the green tissue of the stem. Many of the older forms were leafy, but all Equisetales are characterized by the

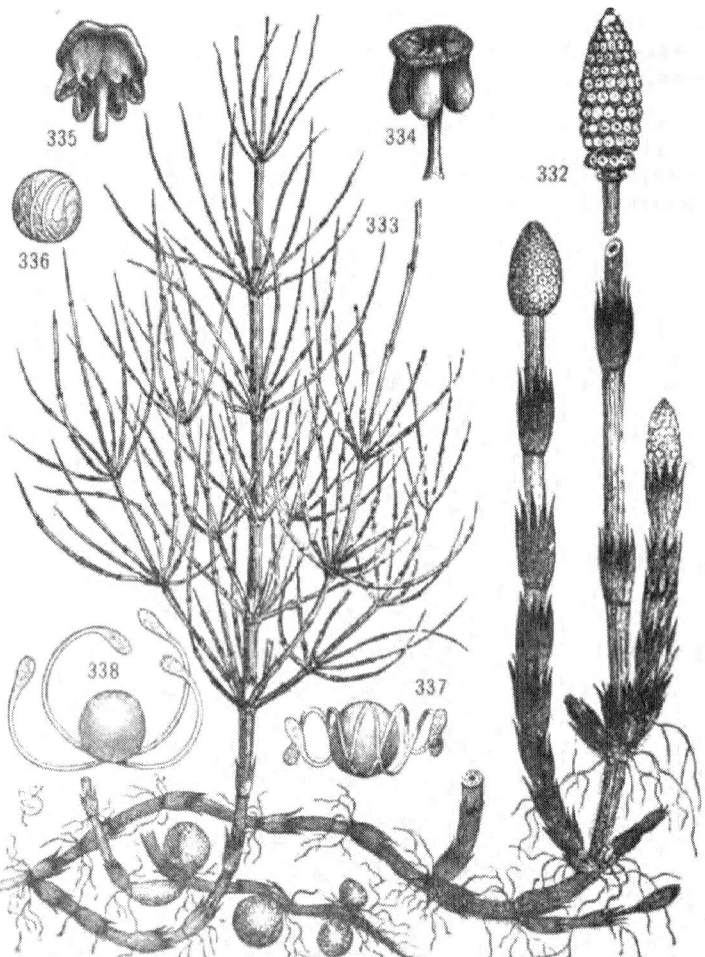

FIGS. 332-338. — *Equisetum arvense:* 332, fertile branches from the dorsiventral stem, each bearing a terminal strobilus, one of them mature; 333, sterile branch; 334, 335, two views of a sporangiophore (so-called "sporophyll"); 336-338, spores, showing the unwinding of the perinium. — After WOSSIDLO.

occurrence of the leaves in cycles (whorls) instead of in the scattered or spiral arrangement observed in the first two groups. In Sphenophyllales the same cyclic arrangement of leaves occurs, and this disposition of the leaves is associated with very distinct differentiation of the stem into *nodes* and *internodes*. Such a differentiation means a localization of the power of producing lateral members, which is not generally distributed, but is restricted to the nodes. It is from the nodes, therefore, that the leaves arise, and from the axils of the leaves that the branches arise. The aerial branches may be all alike, or they may be dimorphic, as in *E. arvense*, in which case special strobilus-bearing branches mature in the spring, and later the green vegetative branches develop (figs. 332, 333).

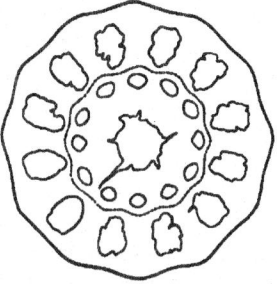

FIG. 339. — Cross section of stem of *Equisetum*: outer zone is cortex containing large air passages (one beneath each furrow); inner region (bounded by dotted line) is the stele, containing a ring (in section) of vascular bundles (one beneath each ridge) enclosing the pith (which is breaking down).

Stem structure. — The structure of the stem is remarkably specialized

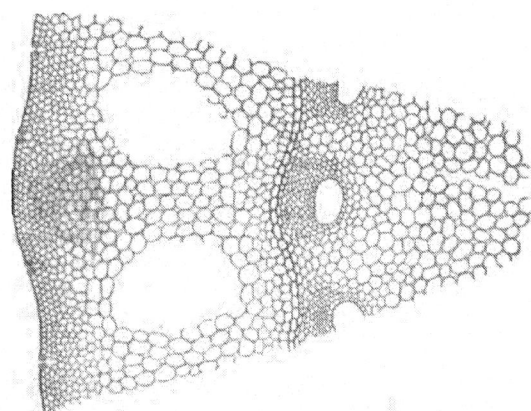

FIG. 340. — Segment of cross section of stem of *Equisetum* in detail, showing epidermis (with stomata), zone of fibrous cells beneath the epidermis, the deeper zone of chlorophyll tissue (penetrating the fibrous zone under the stomata), the large air passages of the cortex, the layer of cortical cells bounding the stele (endodermis), the collateral vascular bundles (each showing phloem, but with xylem replaced by an air passage), and the central pith.

(figs. 339, 340). The outer walls of the epidermal cells are so impregnated by a deposit of silica as to give the characteristic rough feeling to the stem. The stem is fluted, and within the ridges strands of fibrous cells are developed; while in the furrows the chlorophyll tissue reaches the epidermis. It follows that the *stomata* (see p. 250) are in the furrows (usually along the slopes) rather than on the ridges. Deeper within the cortex a zone of large air passages occurs, each one lying beneath a furrow. The central cylinder or stele is remarkably reduced, the vascular bundles being very feebly developed. They are arranged (usually one beneath each ridge) so as to outline a hollow cylinder enclosing a pith, which disappears early; but instead of being concentric bundles, characteristic of most pteridophytes, they are *collateral*; that is, the xylem and phloem strands lie side by side on the same radius, with the xylem towards the center of the stem. In fact, however, in *Equisetum* the xylem is hardly at all developed, its position being occupied by a small air passage (fig. 340).

Sporangium.—The sporangia occur in a very distinct strobilus (fig. 332). The structure usually called a sporophyll has a stalklike base and a peltate top, beneath which five to ten sporangia are borne (figs. 334, 335).

To understand this structure it is necessary to be familiar with certain of the extinct Equisetales. A series can be arranged, beginning with *Sphenophyllum*, passing on to Calamites (an extinct group of Equisetales), and ending with *Equisetum*, which indicates that in the strobilus of *Equisetum* the sporophylls have been suppressed and that the structures bearing sporangia are sporangiophores. In Calamites the strobilus is made up of alternating sets of sporophylls and sporangiophores, and the latter are just such structures as appear in the strobilus of *Equisetum*, without the alternating sets of sporophylls. In *Selaginella* there are sporophylls that do not bear sporangia; and in *Equisetum* there is apparently a strobilus that does not consist of sporophylls.

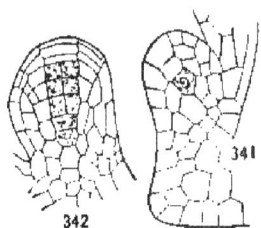

FIGS. 341, 342.—Sporangium of *Equisetum:* 341, early stage, three cells having arisen from the superficial initial, the innermost (shaded) being sporogenous, the two outer being wall cells; 342, further development of wall layers and sporogenous tissue. —After GOEBEL.

The sporangium arises from a single superficial cell, and not from a transverse row as among Lycopodiales. There is the usual periclinal wall, setting apart an outer wall cell from an inner sporogenous cell, as in all eusporangiates (fig. 341).

Several layers of wall cells are formed, and the innermost wall cells by their division add to the sporogenous tissue (fig. 342). The tapetum investing the sporogenous tissue consists of two or three layers of cells. At least one third of the mother cells do not produce spores, contributing to the nutrition of the remaining two thirds.

Spores. — In the development of the spores a remarkable outermost wall layer is formed. In all ordinary spores the wall develops two layers,

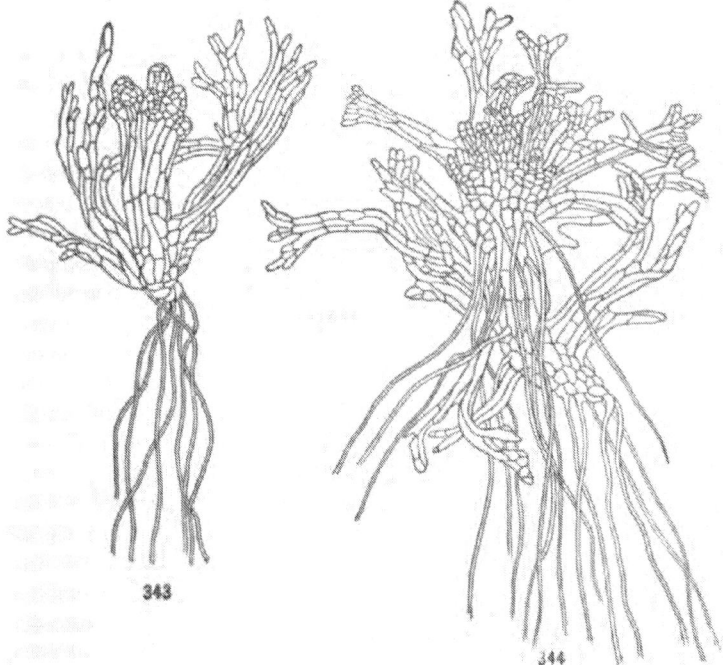

FIGS. 343, 344. — Gametophytes of *Equisetum:* 343, male gametophyte, showing antheridia at some of the branch tips; 344, female gametophyte. — After GOEBEL.

the inner called *intine*, the outer *exine;* but in *Equisetum* another layer is laid down on the exine, called the *perinium*, which cracks into two spirally wound bands that remain connected at one pole of the spore. In shedding, these bands unwind (figs. 336–338), become entangled with the bands of other spores, and thus the spores fall in clumps. This seems to be advantageous since the gametophytes are mostly dioecious;

at least it secures the development of male and female gametophytes in close proximity.

Gametophyte. — The gametophyte is a small, green, branching ribbon, being strictly a thallus, without any of the subterranean development that characterizes *Lycopodium*. Although the gametophytes are usually dioecious, and the female gametophytes are larger and more massive than the male (figs. 343, 344), the spores are all approximately the same size. Certain of the ancient representatives of the Equisetales, however, have been found to be heterosporous.

Antheridium. — The antheridium is interesting in that it shows two kinds of development, dependent upon its position. If it occurs in the axial region of the thallus, it develops as usual among eusporangiates; that is, a superficial initial cell is divided by a periclinal wall, the outer cell producing the wall of the antheridium, the inner cell producing the spermatogenous tissue (figs. 345, 347, 348). If it develops in a terminal position on the thallus, the superficial initial cell forms first a papillate outgrowth, which is cut off by a periclinal wall, and it is this protruding cell that develops the antheridium (fig. 346). In this cell an apical cell with three cutting faces is formed, and then a domelike cap cell is cut off, leaving a central cell, which produces the spermatogenous tissue, invested by four peripheral cells, which develop the wall of the antheridium. This type of antheridium development is characteristic of certain modern ferns. The sperms are very large, spirally coiled, and multiciliate (fig. 349).

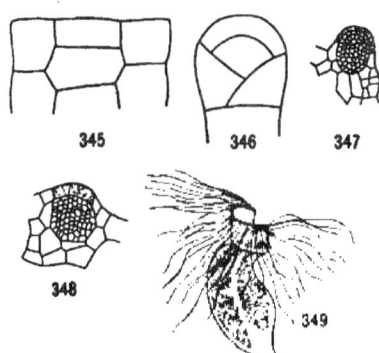

FIGS. 345–349.— Antheridium of *Equisetum*: 345, one type of development, showing the periclinal division, the inner cell being spermatogenous; 346, the other type of development, showing the papillate protruding cell (periclinal wall below), in which are shown two segments (the third behind) cut off by the apical cell, the dome or cap cell, and the enclosed spermatogenous cell; 347, 348, nearly mature antheridia of the first type; 349, a sperm. — 345–348, after GOEBEL; 349, after BELAJEFF.

Archegonium. — The archegonium always develops from the massive axial region and in the axil of a branch. It develops as among other pteridophytes, but is noteworthy in the fact that its neck canal cells are reduced to two in number.

Embryo. — The development of the embryo differs from that of the Lycopodiales in several particulars. There is no suspensor, and the fertilized egg divides into quadrants, among which all the body regions are distributed; foot and root being developed by the inner quadrants, and stem and leaf by the outer ones (figs. 350, 351). A very heavy calyptra is formed, which is broken through by the vigorous young shoot.

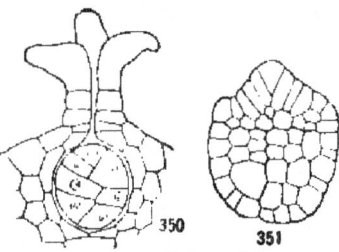

FIGS. 350, 351. — Embryo of *Equisetum:* 350, early stage of embryo, the four body regions having begun to develop; the general structure of the archegonium still evident; 351, more advanced embryo, showing the apical cell that is developing the stem. — After SADEBECK.

Conclusions. — The sporophyte is to be regarded as highly specialized in its leaves, stem anatomy, and strobilus; but its embryogeny appears to be simpler than among Lycopodiales. The gametophyte is entirely aerial; certain antheridia show a specialized form of development; and the archegonia are well advanced, as indicated by the reduction of the neck canal cells.

(5) OPHIOGLOSSALES

General character. — This group of pteridophytes is associated often with Filicales. The three genera usually recognized are *Ophioglossum* (adder's tongue, fig. 352), *Botrychium* (moonwort, fig. 353), and *Helminthostachys* (a New Zealand genus with a single species, fig. 354).[1] The distinguishing character of the group is the so-called fertile spike (a stalk bearing the sporangia), which arises from the adaxial face of the leaf.

Sporophyte. — The sporophyte consists of a subterranean stem covered by the leaf bases, and there are no aerial branches. The leaves are relatively few in number and large, especially in *Botrychium*, and develop very slowly, in some cases becoming aerial only after two or three years of subterranean development. The vascular cylinder is remarkably advanced in structure. It is not only a siphonostele (containing

---

[1] A fourth genus (*Sceptridium*) has been suggested, including some of the species usually referred to *Botrychium*.

pith), but is made up of collateral bundles (p. 146), separated from one another by *pith rays* (radiating plates of tissue extending from pith to cortex). This is the general structure of the vascular cylinder of the majority of seed plants, and this resemblance is further emphasized

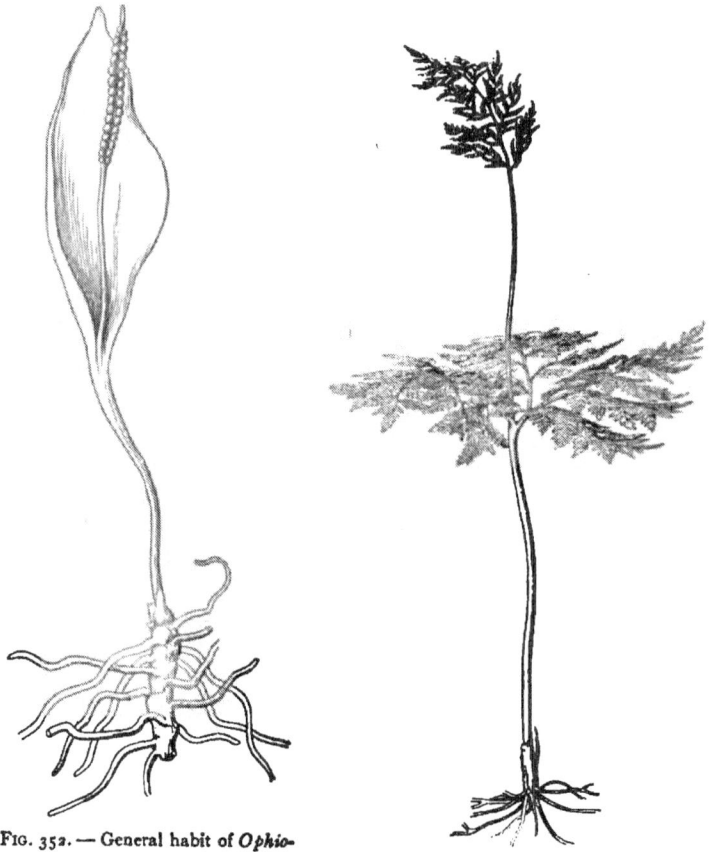

Fig. 352. — General habit of *Ophioglossum*. — After Sachs.

Fig. 353. — General habit of *Botrychium*.

by the presence of a *cambium cylinder* (a meristematic tissue between the xylem and phloem that adds new elements to both). This means increase in diameter by the formation of secondary wood (xylem), and among the elements of this secondary wood there appear *tracheids* with bordered pits, elements characteristic of gymnosperms (fig. 547), but not of pteridophytes.

Fertile spike. — In *Ophioglossum* the fertile spike begins to appear very early in the history of the leaf. As it begins to project from the adaxial face of the young leaf, a superficial band of cells becomes differ-

FIG. 354. — General habit of *Helminthostachys*. — After HOOKER.

entiated on each side, from near the apex downwards. As the spike elongates, these two bands elongate and deepen, eventually giving rise to two continuous bands of sporogenous tissue (figs. 355, 356, 359). Later, sterile plates appear across the band, and the individual sporangia become outlined, the single large sporogenous mass being broken up into a great number of sporangia by sterilization (figs. 357, 358).

The situation has suggested the idea that the fertile spike of Ophioglossales is a sporangiophore extremely developed. If this interpretation is true, sporangiophore development can be traced from the subarchesporial pad of Lycopodiales to the fertile spike of Ophioglossales, whose leaf would thus become a sporophyll. This conception of the simple spike of *Ophioglossum*, with its sessile sporangia, is difficult to apply to *Helminthostachys* with its stalked sporangia, and to *Botrychium* with its more or less branching spike. Recent anatomical studies, however, suggest that this "fertile spike" may have arisen by the fusion of lateral branches

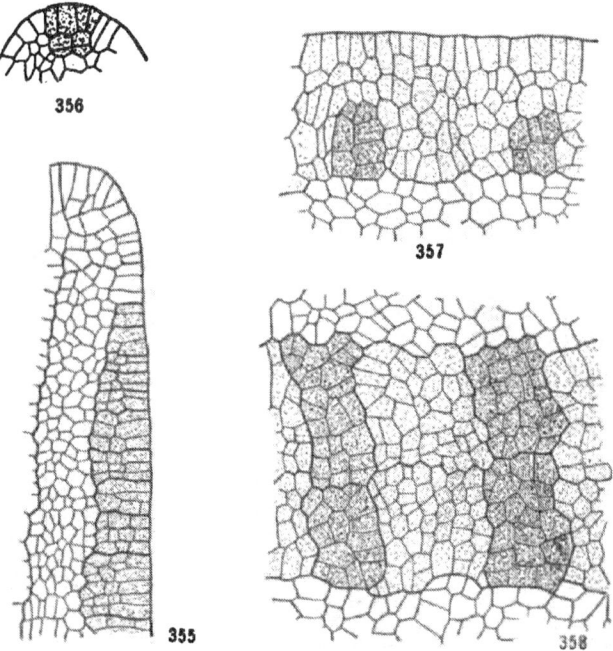

FIGS. 355-358. — Sporangia of *Ophioglossum:* 355, the band of sporogenous tissue developing on one side of the fertile spike; 356, cross section of the sporogenous band; 357, 358, different stages in sterilization, breaking up the band into separate sporogenous masses, each of which develops a sporangium. — After BOWER.

on opposite sides of the main axis. If this is the case, the relationship with the Marattiaceae and other ferns is clear. It is interesting to note that the spike branches as the leaf branches, being simple in the simple-leaved species of *Ophioglossum* and branching in the compound-leaved species of *Botrychium*.

Sporangium. — The development of the individual sporangium is of the usual eusporangiate type, but the remarkable behavior of the tapetum deserves special mention. The walls of the tapetal cells break down, and the protoplasts thus liberated unite to form a nutritive plasmodium that grows among the blocks of sporogenous cells and ramifies into every intercellular space (fig. 360).

Gametophyte. — The gametophyte is of the *Lycopodium* type. In *Ophioglossum*, which is regarded as the most primitive genus, the gametophyte is a tuberous, subterranean body that gives rise to aerial green lobes that bear the sex organs. In *Botrychium* there is no aerial portion, the gametophyte being completely subterranean and tuberous (fig. 361). In *Helminthostachys* the gametophyte is somewhat intermediate in structure, the tuberous body giving rise to a cylindrical aerial process that bears the sex organs. In every case the tuberous body contains an endophytic fungus, as in the gametophyte of *Lycopodium*. It is evident that the gametophyte of the Ophioglossales suggests that of the Lycopodiales; but that the sporophyte is more like that of Filicales.

FIG. 359. — Sporangia of *Ophioglossum*: diagrammatic cross section of fertile spike, showing the two sporogenous bands at different stages. — After BOWER.

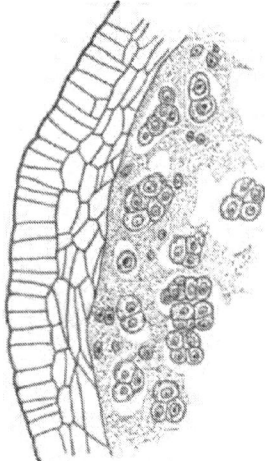

FIG. 360. — Portion of a nearly mature sporangium of *Ophioglossum*, showing the tapetal plasmodium (with nuclei) among the groups of mother cells. — After BOWER.

Sex organs. — The antheridia develop as usual among the eusporangiates, the inner cell, following the periclinal division of the superficial initial, giving rise to the spermatogenous tissue. The sperms are large, coiled, and multiciliate, a type not found among the Lycopodiales, but characteristic of the Filicales.

The archegonium of *Ophioglossum* has a very short neck, the neck canal cells being only two in number, the same reduced number as in *Equisetum*. In *Botrychium* (figs. 362–365) the neck of the archegonium is long, but contains only four neck canal cells.

Embryo. — In general there is no suspensor, but in the recently described genus *Sceptridium* a massive suspensor is reported, at least for one species (formerly *Botrychium obliquum*). There is no differentiation of the great body regions at the quadrant stage, but in *Botrychium*, for example, there is formed first a rather large, undifferentiated mass of tissue (fig. 365) in which at least three growing points (foot, root, and stem) become organized, the leaf appearing later. In this embryogeny of *Botrychium* there is a general resemblance to the Lycopodiales in the belated organization of some body region; and a still further resemblance to those species of *Lycopodium* in which the embryo begins with the development of a protocorm (p. 131). The same belated appearance of one or more body regions has been observed also in species of *Ophioglossum*. In the whole group there seems to be no such early and complete differentiation of the body regions as in Equisetales and Filicales.

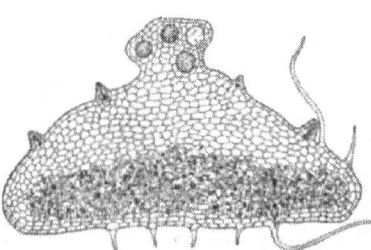

FIG. 361. — Gametophyte of *Botrychium*: antheridia in dorsal ridge; archegonia along the slopes; region of endophytic fungus in ventral region. — After JEFFREY.

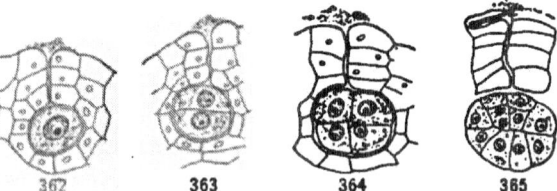

FIGS. 362-365. — Archegonium and embryo of *Botrychium Lunaria*: 362, fertilized egg, in venter of archegonium; 363, first division of egg; 364, quadrant stage; 365, later stage of embryo, the body regions not yet differentiated. — After BRUCHMANN.

Conclusions. — The Ophioglossales have certain features in common with the Lycopodiales, notably the structure of the gametophyte, the adaxial relation of sporangia to sporophylls, and the irregular and somewhat indefinite development of the embryo in its early stages. The "fertile spike," however, may have arisen from lateral branches, which would eliminate this feature of the resemblance to Lycopodiales. The same kind of irregular and indefinite development of the embryo probably also occurs among the Marattiaceae, so that this feature finds its resemblance among both Filicales and Lycopodiales. In the reduced number of foliage leaves and their corresponding increase in size, and in the sperms, the resemblance is decidedly with the Filicales. In vascular structure, the Ophioglossales are more advanced than the majority of pteridophytes. On the whole, the association is evidently with the Filicales of the *Marattia* type.

(6) FILICALES

General character. — The ferns constitute by far the largest group of pteridophytes, including at least 3000 living species, and perhaps many more. The group as a whole is very ancient, but most of the living families are very modern. Two groups of Filicales are recognized: *Filicineae* (true ferns), which are homosporous; and *Hydropteridineae* (water ferns), which are heterosporous.

(a) Filicineae

General character. — Nearly all of the living ferns are true ferns. They are well represented throughout the temperate regions, but are especially abundant in the tropics. The sporophyte displays a great variety of habits — ordinary terrestrial forms, epiphytes (perchers), climbers, aquatics, and trees. Ferns are characterized generally by their comparatively few, large, and usually branched leaves, which bear numerous sporangia, usually upon the *abaxial* surface. The multiplication of sporangia is thus facilitated, not by sporangiophore development, but by distribution over a large leaf surface.

Families. — In so large a group it is necessary to have in mind the principal families. Disregarding the smaller families that have been proposed, the following seven may be considered, conveniently but not completely distinguished from one another by the character of the *annulus*. The annulus is a group or band of thick-walled cells developed in the wall of the sporangium and related to its dehiscence.

1. *Marattiaceae* (ringless ferns). — Annulus wanting. About 25 tropical species in 5 genera.

2. *Osmundaceae* (royal ferns). — Annulus rudimentary (fig. 366). About 15 temperate and tropical species in 3 genera.

3. *Gleicheniaceae.* — Annulus equatorial and indusium (see p. 165) wanting (figs. 367, 368). About 25 tropical species in 2 genera.

4. *Hymenophyllaceae* (filmy ferns). — Annulus equatorial and indusium present (figs. 369, 370, 371). About 155 species, chiefly tropical, in 2 genera.

5. *Schizaeaceae.* — Annulus apical (figs. 372, 373, 374). About 95 species, chiefly tropical, in 4 genera.

6. *Cyatheaceae* (tree ferns). — Annulus vertical and complete (figs. 375, 376). About 280 tropical species in 7 genera.

7. *Polypodiaceae.* — Annulus vertical and incomplete (figs. 384, 385, 390). About 2000 species in 109 genera, including most of the ferns of ordinary observation in temperate regions.

It must not be supposed that the characters given above are the only ones used in separating the families. There are much more funda-

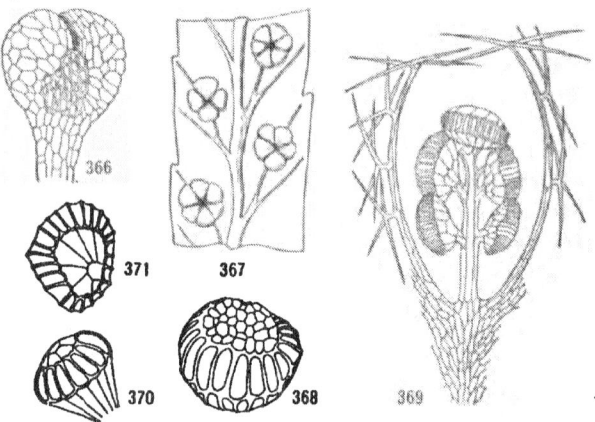

FIGS. 366–371. — Types of annulus: 366, sporangium of *Osmunda*, with a group of thick-walled cells representing the annulus, and a vertical line of dehiscence (after LUERSSEN); 367, sori of *Gleichenia*, showing relation to vein system and absence of indusium (after DIELS); 368, sporangium of *Gleichenia*, with equatorial annulus (after DIELS); 369, marginal sorus of *Hymenophyllum*, showing the stalklike receptacle bearing sporangia with an equatorial annulus, and the investing indusium (after KARSTEN); 370, 371, sporangia of *Trichomanes*, with equatorial annulus (after SADEBECK).

mental ones that will appear as the groups are considered. The sequence of the families as given represents the general relationship, the Marattiaceae being recognized as the most primitive in structure, while the Polypodiaceae are the most specialized and the most recent.

Sporophyte. — The sporophyte is characterized by a subterranean stem, except in the tree ferns, climbers, and epiphytes. In Marattiaceae this stem is short, tuberous, and radial, and covered by the persistent leaf bases (fig. 377). In the other families it is dorsiventral and more or less elongated (fig. 382), a habit apparently acquired by modern ferns, and derived from the older radial type.

PTERIDOPHYTES 157

Vascular system. — At least four kinds of vascular cylinder are represented in the stems of this great group, and there is much discussion as to their historical sequence. They are as follows: (1) the *protostele* (see p. 125), recognized as being the most primitive type (as in *Gleichenia*, fig. 378); (2) the *amphiphloic siphonostele*, in which the phloem occurs on both sides of the xylem in the pith-containing cylinder (as in *Adiantum*, fig. 379); (3) the *polystele*, in which several concentric bundles traverse the stele without organization into a definite cylinder (as in *Pteris*, fig. 380); and (4) the *ectophloic siphonostele*, in which the phloem occurs only on the outer side of the xylem in the pith-containing cylinder (as in *Osmunda*, fig. 381), which is thus composed of collateral bundles (p. 146). This last type of cylinder is regarded as the most advanced, since it is the characteristic cylinder of the majority of seed plants.

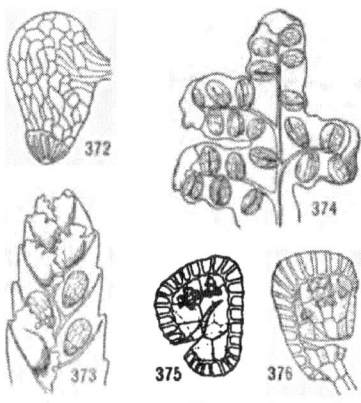

FIGS. 372–376. — Types of annulus: 372, sporangium of *Lygodium* with apical annulus (after PRANTL); 373, sporangia of *Lygodium* in position; some indusia shown (after SADEBECK); 374, sporangia of *Aneimia*, showing apical annulus and the vertical dehiscence (after SADEBECK); 375, 376, two views of sporangium of *Hemitelia*, showing the complete vertical annulus and the transverse dehiscence (after KARSTEN).

An important variation in the character of the xylem must be noted. The first xylem elements to appear are spiral vessels of small caliber. This initial group of vessels is called the *protoxylem*, and its position with reference to the subsequent xylem (*metaxylem*) is important to note. In a stele usually several protoxylem regions appear, and if all the metaxylem develops centripetally (towards the center of the stele), the xylem is *exarch*, which means that the protoxylem regions are external to the metaxylem. Exarch bundles are regarded as the most primitive, and are characteristic of all roots, of the protostele of *Lycopodium*, etc. If the metaxylem develops in all directions from the protoxylem, the xylem is *mesarch* (figs. 380, 381), which means that the protoxylem is surrounded by metaxylem. Mesarch bundles are very characteristic of ferns, and all of the four kinds of bundles described above as occurring among ferns are prevailingly mesarch. If all the metaxylem develops centrifugally (away from the center of the stele), the xylem is *endarch*, which means that the protoxylem is internal with reference to the metaxylem. Endarch bundles are characteristic of seed plants, and are attained by some pteridophytes, as in Equisetales and Ophioglossales. A fern whose vascular cylinder is composed of collateral bundles resembles seed plants in this feature; but in such a case the bundle of

FIG. 377.— *Marattia*: growing on a steep slope, and showing the short tuberous stem covered by an armor of persistent leaf bases.

the fern is mesarch collateral, while that of the seed plant is endarch collateral. It must be remembered that to all such general statements in reference to great groups there are exceptions, and that the statement refers only to the prevailing condition in a group. Metaxylem must not be confused with the *secondary xylem*, which is formed by the cambium.

Another feature of the vascular cylinder of ferns is noteworthy. Where the leaf traces leave the cylinder to pass through the cortex, a gap immediately above the trace is left in the cylinder, which closes again further up. These *leaf gaps* are characteristic of the vascular cylinder of

Filicales and Ophioglossales, and they seem to be associated with the production of large leaves. On the basis of this character, these groups are said to be *phyllosiphonic*, as contrasted with the other groups of pteridophytes, which are *cladosiphonic*, meaning that they have branch

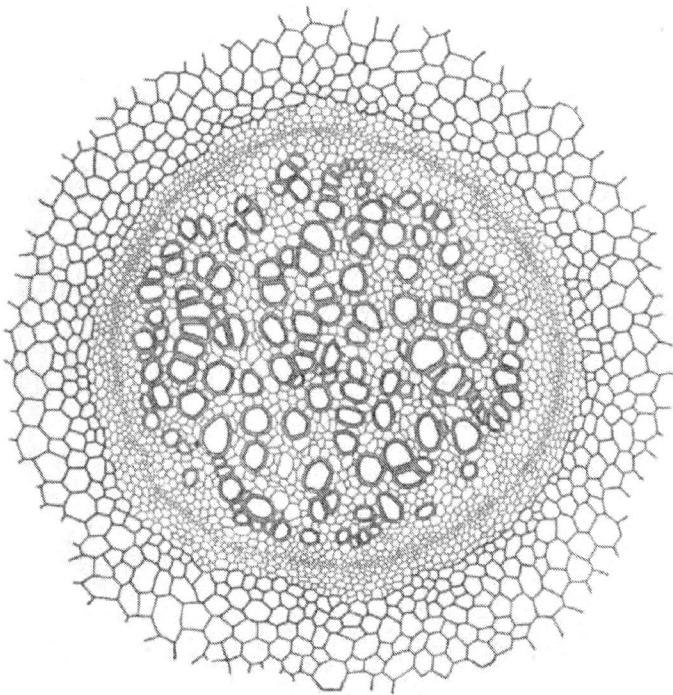

FIG. 378.—The protostele of *Gleichenia*: the xylem vessels, recognized by their large caliber and thick walls, occupy the entire central region of the stele; investing them is a zone of sieve vessels (phloem), which in turn are surrounded by the cortex.

gaps, but no leaf gaps. This distinction has been found to be a very important one in connection with the study of the origin of seed plants.

Leaves.—The leaves of ferns are the only aerial structures in ordinary terrestrial forms. They were formerly called *fronds*, with the idea that they were not ordinary leaves, but a combination of leaf and stem. They are usually branched, either pinnately or palmately, and are characterized by *dichotomous* (forking) venation (figs. 383, 386) and *circinate* vernation (fig. 382), which means that the young leaf is enrolled from the tip downwards, and in expanding unrolls from the base upwards. The internal structure of the leaf is practically the same as that of the leaves of seed plants, with epidermis containing stomata, mesophyll (both palisade and spongy), and abundant veins (see p. 250).

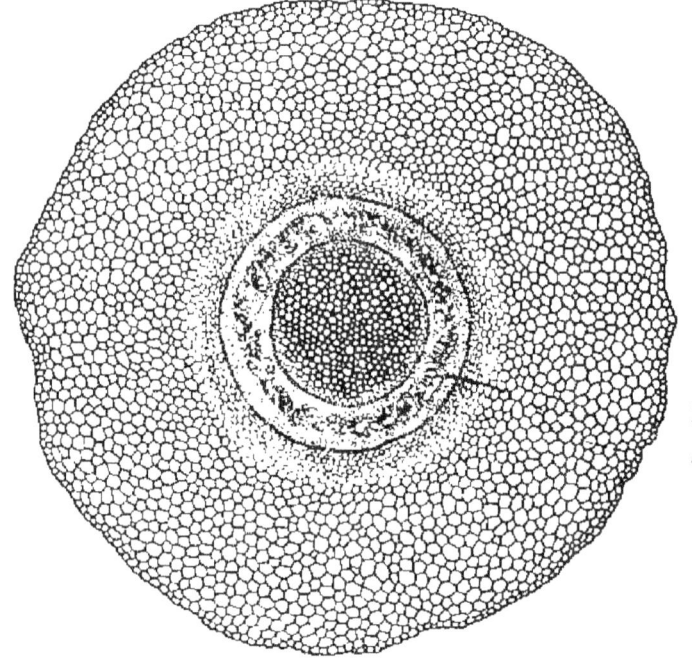

FIG. 379. — The amphiphloic siphonostele of *Adiantum:* beginning at the outside the general regions of the section are epidermis, a thick cortex, endodermis (the epidermis-like innermost layer of the cortex which bounds the stele), the outer phloem, the xylem, the inner phloem, the inner endodermis, and the pith.

Sporangia. — It will be impossible to describe all the methods of sporangium development, but the sporangia of Marattiaceae and Polypodiaceae will be described, with the understanding that the intermediate families show intergrading conditions.

Marattiaceae. — The Marattiaceae are eusporangiate, as are all the pteridophytes previously considered, and also the seed plants. Following the periclinal division of the superficial initial cell, the outer cell develops a wall of several layers of cells, the innermost layer or two functioning as the tapetum; while the inner cell develops a large mass of sporogenous tissue. The number of mother cells in the different genera of Marattiaceae ranges from 128 to 2048, which means a theoretical output of 2048-8192 spores. Most of the Marattiaceae are further distinguished by the fact that the sporangia form what is called a

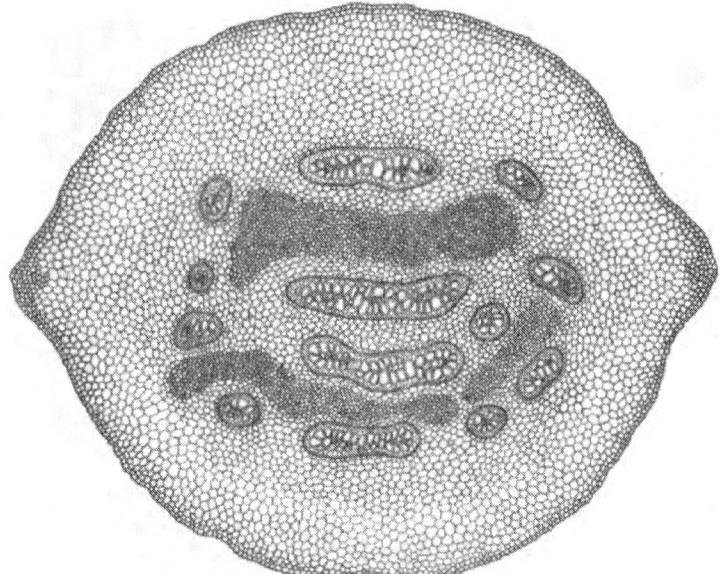

FIG. 380. — The polystele of *Pteris*: in the ill-defined stele there occur several (in this case thirteen) vascular bundles of varying size and form, each one of which is concentric (xylem surrounded by phloem) and invested by a distinct endodermis; in some of them the mesarch character is evident, the group of protoxylem elements (of small caliber) being more or less centrally placed (at least surrounded by metaxylem); the heavy-walled tissue represented by the three irregular masses associated with the vascular bundles is mechanical tissue.

synangium (fig. 386). These synangia appear like small groups of coalescent sporangia distributed over the surface of the leaf, as are the sori (see p. 165) in other ferns. In fact, in some of the Marattiaceae the sporangia are not in synangia, but form sori of distinct sporangia. It is evident that synangia and sori are equivalents; and it is probable that synangia are not coalescent sporangia, but rather sporangia that have not become completely separated from one another.

162   MORPHOLOGY

Polypodiaceae. — The Polypodiaceae are *leptosporangiate*, a peculiar feature belonging to all the Filicales except the Marattiaceae. It means that the sporogenous tissue is developed from the *outer* cell that follows the periclinal division of the superficial initial, instead of from the *inner*

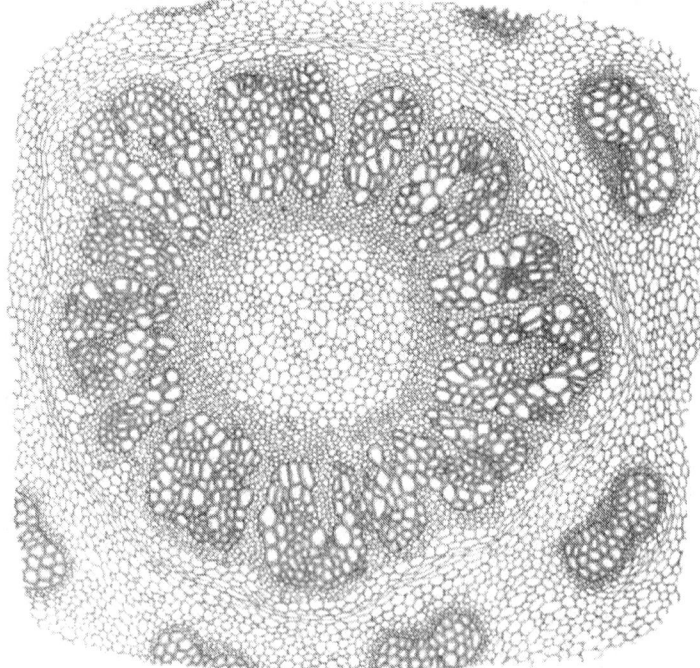

FIG. 381. — The ectophloic siphonostele of *Osmunda*: the central pith is surrounded directly by the xylem (internal phloem having disappeared), which occurs in distinct strands (separated from one another by the pith rays), the mesarch character of which is often very evident; investing the xylem is a thin sheath of phloem; the bundles shown in the cortex are sections of leaf traces.

cell, as in eusporangiates. The outer cell develops as a papillate-projecting cell (fig. 387), in which three oblique walls appear so as to form an apical cell with three cutting faces. This apical cell cuts off segments to form the elongated stalk. When segment formation ceases, a transverse wall through the apical cell cuts off a cap cell, and leaves a four-sided inner cell completely invested by the three uppermost segments and the cap cell. This centrally placed cell is the primary spo-

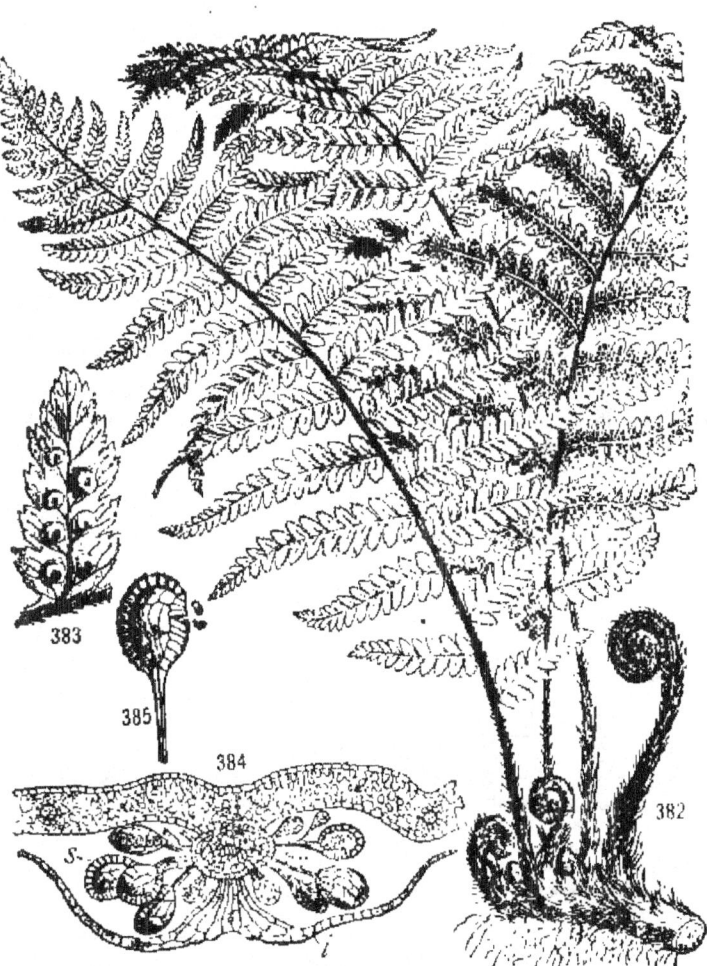

FIGS. 382–385. — *Aspidium:* 382, general habit, showing leaves and circinate vernation, dorsiventral (subterranean) stem, and secondary roots; 383, a single pinnule, showing dichotomous veins and sori with shieldlike indusia; 384, section through a sorus, showing the indusium and long-stalked sporangia; 385, a single sporangium, showing the incomplete vertical annulus and the transverse dehiscence. — After WOSSIDLO.

rogenous cell (fig. 388). The three uppermost segments and the cap develop the wall of the capsule, which is only one layer of cells thick. At the junction of the cap cell with the last segment is developed the *stomium*, which is a group of cells so arranged as to permit a cleavage in the wall of the capsule when it begins to dehisce. The *annulus* is a

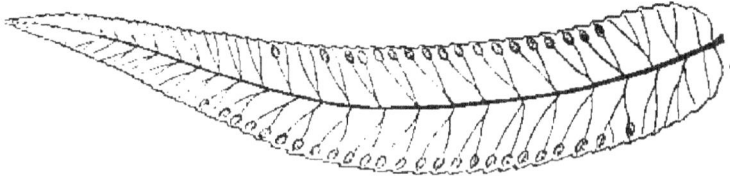

FIG. 386. — Leaflet of *Marattia*, showing dichotomous venation and synangia (instead of sori).

band of thick-walled cells which extends from the stomium over the top of the capsule and down on the other side to the stalk (figs. 385, 390).

The primary sporogenous cell cuts off a sterile cell from each one of the four faces, these four cells developing the tapetum (figs. 388, 389).

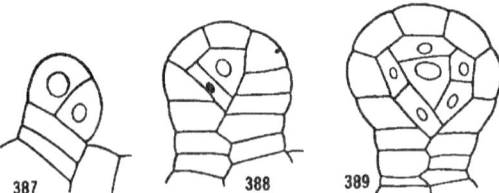

FIGS. 387-389. — Sporangium of one of the *Polypodiaceae*: 387, early stage, in which the outer papillate cell has begun to form the apical cell; 388 later stage, in which the cap cell and upper segments invest a central cell (primary spermatogenous), which has cut off one tapetal cell; 389, later stage, in which all the tapetal cells have been cut off and have begun to divide; the central cell, by a series of divisions, forms 16 mother cells.

The centrally placed sporogenous cell then begins a series of divisions until 16 mother cells are formed, which means a maximum output of 64 spores. Sometimes there are only 8, or 4, or even 2 mother cells. The tapetal cells break down, leaving the mother cells free in the enlarged cavity (fig. 390).

These two kinds of sporangia, one from each extremity of the fern series, indicate not only a passage from the eusporangiate to the leptosporangiate habit, but also a striking reduction in the output of spores per sporangium. In this latter feature there is complete intergrading through the intermediate families.

In passing from Marattiaceae to Polypodiaceae, it is interesting to note the changes in the character of the sporangium stalk. Beginning with sessile sporangia, there is a transition to very short stalks, and finally the very long slender ones that characterize the Polypodiaceae are reached. This change in the character of the stalk accompanies the reduction in the output of spores, so that perhaps among leptosporangiate ferns the development of an elongated sporangium stalk is of more importance than a large output of spores from a single sporangium.

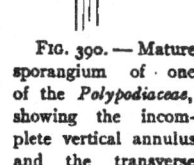

FIG. 390. — Mature sporangium of one of the *Polypodiaceae*, showing the incomplete vertical annulus and the transverse dehiscence.

Sorus. — The *sorus* is a feature of most Filicales, being a definitely limited group of sporangia (figs. 383, 384). Sori vary in form and in arrangement, and are useful as taxonomic characters. Sporangia do not always form sori; in some cases they are scattered over the surface of the leaf, in other cases they form in a continuous band along the margin.

Indusium. — The *indusium* is a flaplike outgrowth from the surface of the leaf which protects the developing sorus (figs. 369, 373, 383). It is exceedingly variable in form; in some cases forming a pouch, in others an overarching shield (fig. 383), in others a cup, etc. It is sometimes lacking entirely, and in certain cases it is replaced by the inrolled leaf margin, which is then spoken of as a "false indusium." These variations in the indusium are so constant for different groups as to be very useful as taxonomic characters.

Gametophyte. — The gametophyte of the Filicineae, better known as the *prothallium*, is a small green thallus, with rhizoids, and resembles the gametophyte of very simple liverworts (fig. 391). The most primitive ferns (Marattiaceae) have the largest and most massive gametophytes. In general, the development of the gametophyte passes through the stages indicated for liverworts (p. 98). In germination there protrudes from the spore a papillate outgrowth which is cut off by a wall as a cell and develops into the filamentous stage, the length of the filament being related to available light. Following this stage is that of the apical cell with two cutting faces, by means of which the gametophyte is broadened. Then follows the group of initials, by means of which the gametophyte is matured, in the course of which the usual apical notch is developed. The axial region of the gametophyte is much thicker than the wings, giving a midrib appearance. In general the gametophytes are monoecious.

Antheridium.—The antheridia appear very early in the history of the gametophyte (fig. 392), being abundant even in the filamentous stage. In the mature gametophyte they occur on the ventral surface in the older part, among the rhizoids (fig. 391). No single type of development can

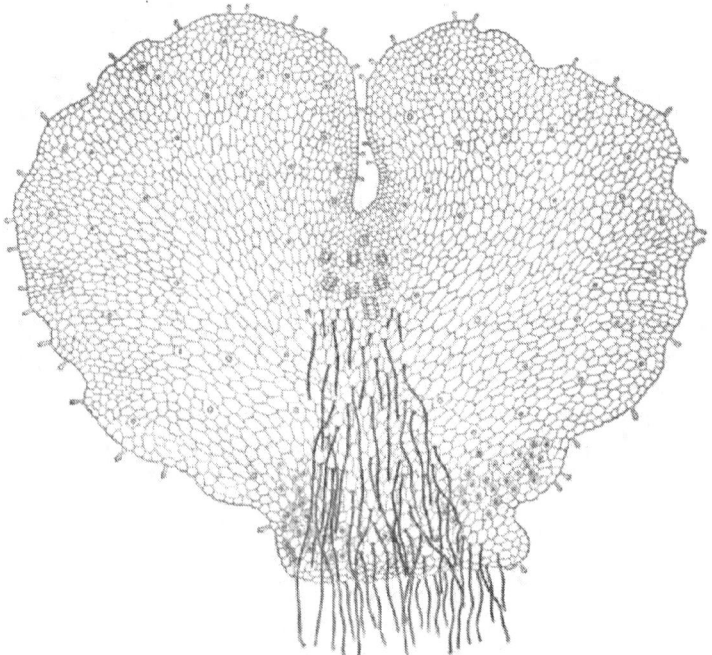

FIG. 391.—Gametophyte of *Aspidium*, looking at the ventral surface, which bears the sex organs and rhizoids; just behind the notch is a group of archegonia, and at the base of the thallus there are numerous antheridia.

be given for all the antheridia of Filicineae, for they are as variable in this regard as are the sporangia. The two extremes (Marattiaceae and Polypodiaceae) will be given, with the understanding that the intermediate families show intergrades.

Marattiaceae.—In the Marattiaceae there is the type of antheridium development usual among eusporangiates. The outer cell following the periclinal division of the superficial initial produces a wall consisting of a single layer of cells; while the inner cell develops 100-200 or more sperm mother cells.

Polypodiaceae. — In the Polypodiaceae the antheridium is derived from the outer cell following the periclinal division, as in the case of the leptosporangiate sporangium. In this cell there appears first the *funnel wall*, which cuts off the *basal ring cell;* then the *dome wall* appears, intersecting the funnel wall and outlining the *central cell;* and finally the *cap* or *cover* cell is cut out of the dome cell, completing the *ring cell* (fig. 392). These divisions result in three peripheral cells investing a central one, the former producing the wall of the antheridium, the latter the sperm mother cells, usually thirty-two in number (sometimes sixty-four). There is thus a decrease in the output of sperms in passing from Marattiaceae to Polypodiaceae, just as in the case of the spores, but it is much less extensive. The sperm is large and spirally coiled, consisting of a large body (chiefly nucleus) and a conspicuous cytoplasmic beak, from which forty to fifty long retrorse cilia arise.

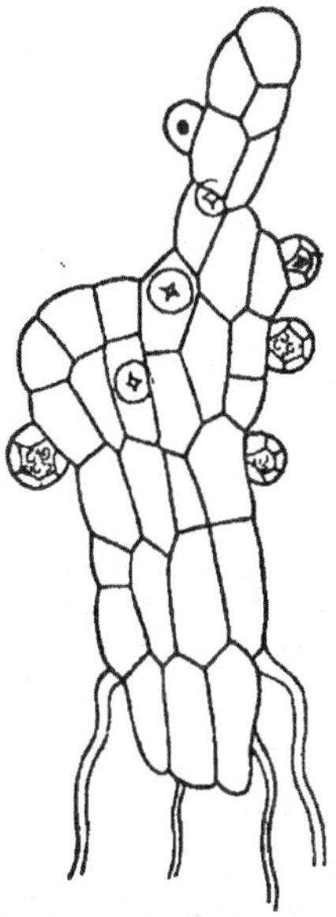

Archegonium. — The archegonia appear late in the history of the gametophyte, being developed on the ventral side in the region of the apical notch (fig. 391). Their development is very uniform, and follows the usual course among pteridophytes. By a periclinal wall the superficial initial is divided into the primary neck cell and the inner cell; and by another transverse division the latter becomes the central cell and the basal cell (fig. 393, *a*). This row of three cells — primary neck cell, central cell, and basal cell — is perhaps the most commonly observed stage in the development. The primary neck cell produces a neck of three or four tiers (fig. 393, *b–d*), with four cells in each tier. The central cell produces the axial row, the first division resulting in the primary neck canal cell and the primary ventral cell. Among the Marattiaceae the primary neck canal cell produces two neck canal cells;

FIG. 392.—Young gametophyte of fern bearing antheridia; in the uppermost antheridium on the right side the funnel and dome walls have appeared; in the three other complete antheridia the cover cell has appeared, completing the three peripheral cells; the central cell has developed sperm mother cells.

but among the Polypodiaceae usually only the nucleus divides, resulting in a single binucleate neck canal cell. The primary ventral cell divides, as usual, into the ventral canal cell and the egg (fig. 393, c). In passing from Marattiaceae to Polypodiaceae, one passes from broad canal cells to small ones, and from two distinct neck canal cells to the elimination of the wall (binucleate condition). There is thus a gradual disappearance

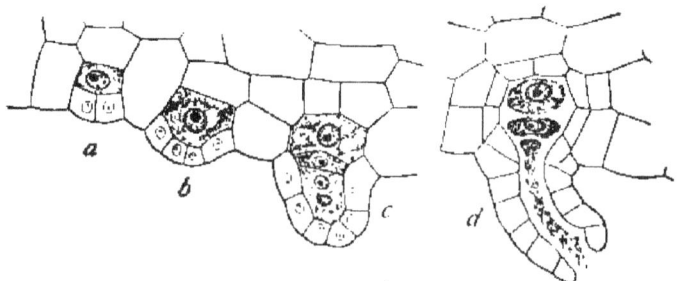

FIG. 393.—Archegonium of a fern: a, young stage, showing two neck cells, central cell (shaded), and basal cell, all from single initial; b, older stage, showing further development of neck and enlargement of central cell preparatory to forming the axial row; c, neck further developed and axial row complete (binucleate neck canal cell, ventral canal cell, and egg); d, mature archegonium, with neck complete, neck canal cell disorganized, ventral canal cell breaking down, and egg rounded off.

of the neck canal cells, a process which is completed when seed plants are reached.

Fertilization. — In fertilization the sperm enters the neck of the archegonium, ciliated end first; and then the ciliated beak ceases to function. As the sperm enters the cytoplasm of the egg, the cytoplasmic sheath of the sperm, including the beak, is often left behind, and the male nucleus moves alone through the egg cytoplasm to the female nucleus; but in some cases the whole sperm has been observed within the egg nucleus.

Embryo. — In the development of the embryo, the four great body regions are said to be differentiated at the quadrant stage; but in passing from Marattiaceae to Polypodiaceae the quadrants are directed differently. Among Marattiaceae the first division of the egg is transverse to the long axis of the archegonium (fig. 394), by far the most common plane. The current account is that this first division differentiates the shoot (stem and leaf) from the foot and root, the former being represented by the inner cell, the latter by the outer; and that at the quadrant stage the two outer (ventrally directed) quadrants develop the foot and root, while the two inner (dorsally directed) quadrants develop the stem and leaf, which pierce through the tissue of the overlying thallus (fig. 394). Recent investigations, however, indicate that both the outer (ventral) quadrants may develop the foot, the two inner (dorsal) quadrants forming a tissue that gives rise to leaf, stem, and root. This method of development suggests that of the embryo of Ophioglossales, with which group the Marattiaceae seem to be closely allied.

Among Polypodiaceae the first division of the egg is parallel with the long axis of the archegonium (fig. 395), the shoot cell being directed towards the apex (notch) of the prothallium. At the quadrant stage (fig. 395) the two apically directed quadrants give rise to stem and leaf (the latter being ventral); while the two basally directed quadrants give rise to foot and root (the latter being ventral). The stem and leaf, directed towards the notch, grow under the prothallium and the leaf turns up through the notch. In such a case, the foot is the most temporary organ, functioning only so long as the gametophyte endures, while the primary root does not exist for a long time. The relatively permanent structures of the sporophyte are the stem, giving rise to secondary roots, and the leaves.

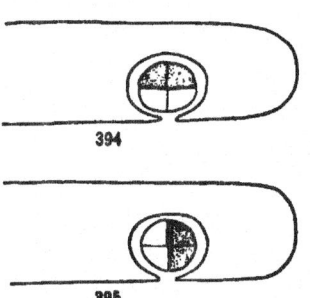

FIGS. 394, 395.—Diagram of quadrant stage of embryo: 394, *Marattia*, in which the first wall is transverse to the long axis of the archegonium, the shaded quadrants giving rise to stem and leaf; 395, a polypod, in which the first wall is parallel with the long axis of the archegonium, the shaded quadrants (directed towards the notch) giving rise to stem (upper quadrant) and leaf (lower quadrant); in both cases the notch is to the right.

Apogamy and apospory.—The phenomenon of *apogamy* is so prevalent among Filicineae that it deserves special mention. Apogamy is the production of a sporophyte by a gametophyte without the act of fertilization. Such a sporophyte may arise either from the unfertilized egg, in which case the apogamy is called *parthenogenesis;* or it may arise from the vegetative tissue of the prothallium, in which case it is called *vegetative apogamy.* It is found to be very common among ferns, and can be induced with little difficulty.

The companion phenomenon is *apospory*, in which a gametophyte is produced by a sporophyte without the formation of a spore. These aposporous gametophytes in ferns arise usually from checked sporangia, but sometimes directly from the leaf margin (usually a tooth), and occasionally from other regions of the leaf.

An interesting question connected with apogamy and apospory is the effect on the number of chromosomes. A sporophyte has the double (diploid) number ($2x$) of chromosomes because it has come from a fertilized egg. Therefore, does an apogamous sporophyte have the reduced (haploid) number (x)? A gametophyte has the reduced number (x) because it has come from a spore produced by the reduction divisions. Therefore, does an aposporous gametophyte have the double number ($2x$)? Recent investigations, both among ferns and seed plants, indicate that both of these questions may be answered in the affirmative.

Conclusions. — The important features of this great group may be summarized as follows: There are represented all the pteridophyte types of vascular cylinder, from the most primitive to the most advanced; but the cylinders are peculiar among pteridophytes (Ophioglossales excepted) in being phyllosiphonic. The leaves are the most highly developed among pteridophytes (Ophioglossales excepted), being reduced in number and increased in size. The sporangia are multiplied on the lower surface of the leaves; there is very little differentiation of foliage leaves and sporophylls; and there is no organization of strobili. The conspicuous features are the development of the leptosporangiate habit, found in no other group of vascular plants (water ferns excepted); and along with this the appearance of a special kind of antheridium development. There is a gradual diminution of spore output per sporangium, and a corresponding diminution of sperm output; also a persistent retention of homospory. The gametophyte is a thallose, aerial structure. The line as a whole appears to be highly specialized, the only group containing the possibilities of the higher plants being the Marattiaceae, probably the oldest family.

(b) Hydropteridineae

General character. — The water ferns are probably an aquatic branch from the true ferns that has developed heterospory. They are leptosporangiates, and hence are doubtless derived from the only other known group of leptosporangiates. They comprise two distinct families that seem to be of separate origin. It is evident, therefore, that heterospory has arisen independently in almost every group of pteridophytes.

Salviniaceae

These are the floating ferns, comprising two genera, *Salvinia* and *Azolla*, with few species, but some of them are widely distributed.

Sporophyte. — The sporophyte body is a floating, dorsiventral stem, that develops by an apical cell with two cutting faces, instead of the apical cell with three cutting faces usual among ferns. The segments are cut off right and left, and subsequent divisions result in eight rows of cells, four ventral and four dorsal. In *Salvinia* (fig. 396) the dorsal rows of cells give rise to four rows of broad, flat, overlapping, aerial leaves; while the two central ventral rows give rise to submerged and much dissected leaves that bear the sporangia. The two lateral ventral rows give rise to the branches, and roots are entirely lacking. In *Azolla* the two central dorsal rows of cells do not give rise to lateral members, but the two lateral dorsal rows produce leaves which are dorsiventrally lobed

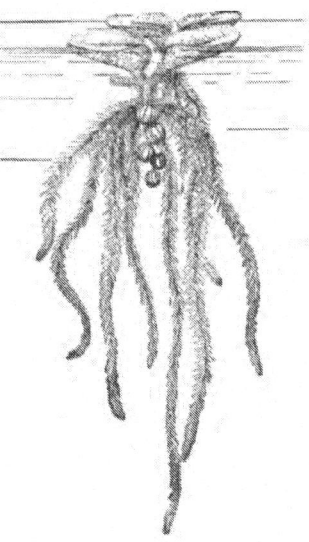

FIG. 396. — *Salvinia*, showing the broad floating leaves, and the dissected submerged leaves bearing sporocarps.

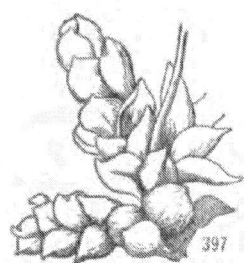

FIGS. 397, 398. — *Azolla*: 397, ventral surface of branch, showing leaves and sporocarps; 398, megasporocarp and microsporocarp. — After CAMPBELL.

(fig. 397). The submerged ventral lobes bear the sporangia, and a chamber in the aerial dorsal lobe is inhabited by an endophytic alga (*Anabaena*). The two central ventral rows produce roots, and the two lateral ventral rows produce branches.

Sporocarp. — The sporangia are submerged, as described, and each sorus is completely invested by the indusium,

172   MORPHOLOGY

which becomes hard at maturity, forming a small nutlike body called the *sporocarp* (fig. 396). In Salviniaceae, therefore, the sporocarp is a sorus invested by an indusium. Microsporangia and megasporangia

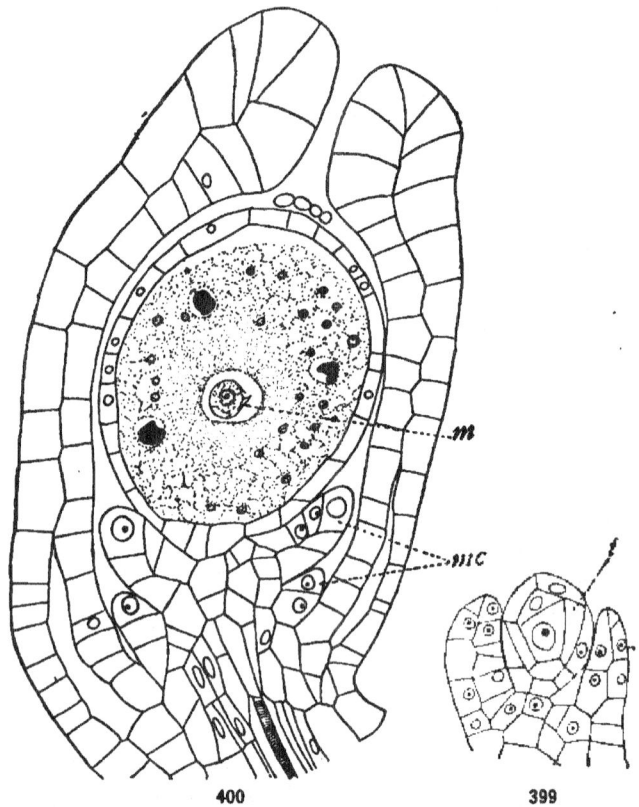

FIGS. 399, 400. — *Asolla*: 399, young sporocarp, showing a young megasporangium and the developing indusium; the megasporangium has advanced to the cutting off of tapetal cells (*t*); 400, megasporocarp, showing the terminal megasporangium with one megaspore (*m*) surviving the degeneration of he others, and the microsporangia (*mc*) checked. — After MISS PFEIFFER.

begin to develop in each sorus, but only one kind matures, so that at maturity there are two kinds of sporocarps (*megasporocarps* and *microsporocarps*, fig. 398), both kinds occurring on the same plant and even on the same leaf segment. All the sporangia have long

PTERIDOPHYTES

slender stalks, and are distinctly leptosporangiate of the more advanced type.

In both kinds of sporangia sixteen mother cells are developed (eight in the megasporangium of *Azolla*), as among the most advanced of the true ferns. In the microsporangium sixty-four spores are formed; but in the megasporangium only one megaspore matures, a single mother cell functioning and three spores of the tetrad not maturing. Each sorus begins by developing a terminal megasporangium (fig. 399), and beneath this microsporangia begin to appear. The megasporangium of *Azolla* develops mother cells and forms eight tetrads (32 spores). If thirty-one of these megaspores degenerate and one persists, the microsporangia develop no further, and the structure becomes a megasporocarp containing one megaspore (fig. 400). If all thirty-two megaspores degenerate, the microsporangia continue to develop (fig. 401), and the structure becomes a microsporocarp (fig. 402).

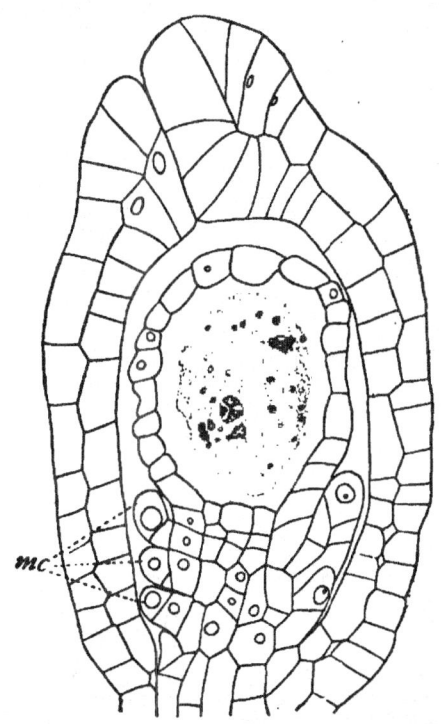

FIG. 401. — *Azolla*: young microsporocarp, in which all the megaspores have degenerated in the single megasporangium and the microsporangia (*mc*) are appearing in abundance. — After MISS PFEIFFER.

The tapetal cells break down and discharge their cytoplasm into the sporangial cavity, forming a remarkable matrix about the spores. In *Salvinia* the microspores lie firmly embedded in hardened cytoplasm; while in *Azolla* the cytoplasm organizes into two to eight masses (*massulae*), embedding the microspores. These massulae are invested by a membrane, from the surface of which there arise remarkable appendages (*glochidia*) that resemble hairs with sagittate tips (fig. 403). About the single megaspore the matrix forms a heavy and often elaborate *perinium* (p. 147) or *epispore* (fig. 406).

Male gametophyte. — The microspore germinates within the sporangium of *Salvinia*, and within the discharged massulae of *Azolla*, in both cases sending out a tube to the surface, the external part of which is cut off by a wall (fig. 404). This external, water-exposed cell is the anthe-

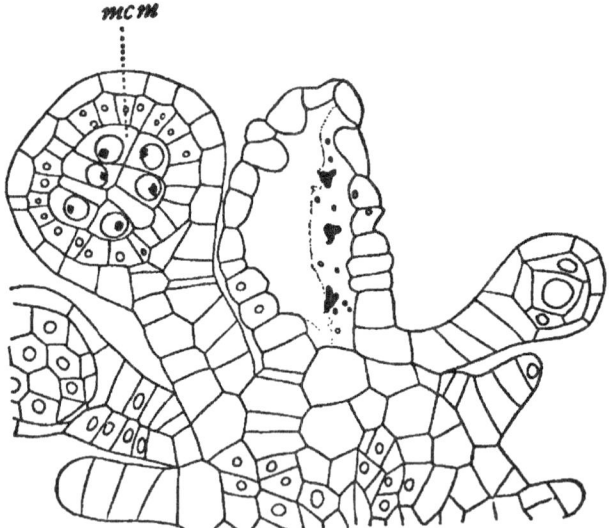

FIG. 402. — *Azolla*: older microsporocarp, in which the microsporangia have developed to the mother cell stage (*mcm*) and the terminal megasporangium has collapsed. — After MISS PFEIFFER.

ridium initial; and therefore the male gametophyte, as in *Selaginella* and *Isoetes*, is reduced to one vegetative cell (within the microspore) and one antheridium. The antheridium initial begins a series of two or three transverse divisions, after which a central cell is cut off by periclinal walls and produces eight sperm mother cells (fig. 405).

Female gametophyte. — The development of the female gametophyte differs in several important particulars from that of *Selaginella* and *Isoetes*. The nucleus of the megaspore divides near its apex and a relatively small apical cell is cut off. The wall thus formed separates the nutritive region from the reproductive region. The small apical cell protrudes through the megaspore wall and develops an exposed tissue containing archegonia (fig. 406). The nucleus of the large nutritive cell (almost the entire body of the megaspore) remains undivided in *Salvinia*, but in *Azolla* it initiates a series of free nuclear divisions, no cell walls

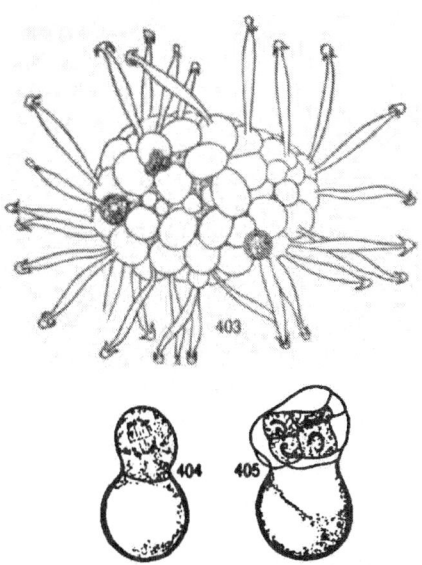

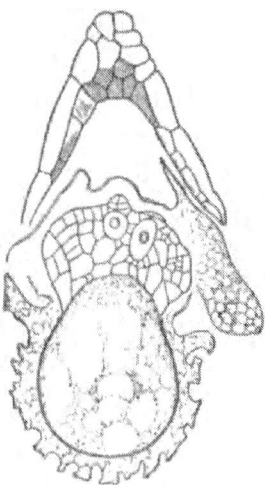

FIGS. 403-405.—*Azolla*: 403, massula, with inclosed microspores (shaded) and glochidia; 404, development of male gametophyte, the extruded cell (antheridium initial) beginning to divide; 405, male gametophyte with antheridium complete (wall cells enclosing spermatogenous cells).—After CAMPBELL.

FIG. 406.—*Azolla*: female gametophyte, showing the extruded, archegonium-producing tissue and the large nutritive cell (invested by the megaspore wall); around the gametophyte are remains of the perinium, and above a part of the indusium is represented.—After CAMPBELL.

being formed. The two chief points of contrast in this developmental history, as compared with *Selaginella* and *Isoetes*, are (1) the development of a wall across the spore in connection with the first nuclear division, forming a *diaphragm* between the nutritive and reproductive regions; and (2) the failure to develop a nutritive tissue.

Embryo.—The development of the embryo differs in no way from that of true ferns, except that the first division of the egg is transverse to the long axis of the archegonium, a feature characterizing the primitive Marattiaceae, but not the modern leptosporangiates.

FIG. 407.—*Marsilea:* showing dorsiventral stem giving rise to roots below and leaves above, circinate vernation of developing leaves, and adaxially borne sporocarps.

Marsileaceae

This family comprises the genera *Marsilea* and *Pilularia*, whose species root in the mud, under water or in muddy flats.

Sporophyte.—The stem is dorsiventral, as in the Salviniaceae, but it develops from an apical cell with three cutting faces, thus forming three longitudinal rows of segments. The leaves alternate from the dorsal segments, and the roots are produced by the ventral segments. The leaf of *Marsilea* has a long petiole and four leaflets peltately arranged (fig. 407); the first leaves, however, produce no blades, only the petiole developing, and this is the permanent condition in *Pilularia*.

Sporocarp.—The so-called sporocarp is borne on a stalk that arises adaxially from the leaf (petiole), the whole structure apparently being a spore-bearing branch of the leaf (fig. 407). This adaxial structure may have arisen as did that of the Ophioglossales;

that is, by the fusion of lateral branches (p. 152). The sporocarp seems to be a modified leaf blade or blades enclosing a group of sori (fig. 408). In *Marsilea* the sporocarp is somewhat bean-shaped, each sorus being in a cavity that extends from the ventral side towards the dorsal (fig. 409). Lining each cavity is a delicate indusium completely investing the sorus, which contains both microsporangia and megasporangia (fig. 410). In the microsporangia all the mother cells function in producing microspores; while in each megasporangium only one megaspore matures, as in the Salviniaceae. The sori are attached to a tissue which swells remarkably upon exposure to water, dragging

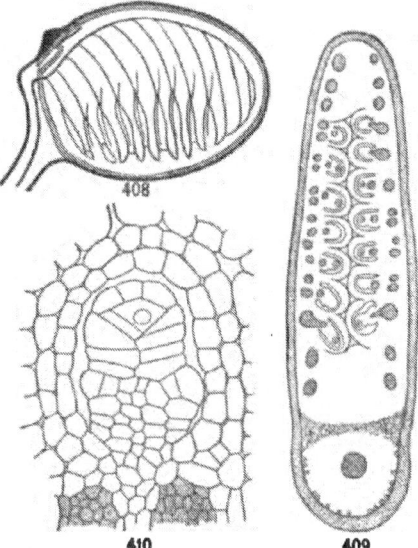

FIGS. 408-410.—*Marsilea:* 408, inside of one of the "valves" of the sporocarp, showing the system of veins, the short branches supplying the sori; 409, section through a sporocarp, showing the two rows of sori beginning to develop (terminal cell in each is a young megasporangium); 410, section through a young sorus, showing a developing megasporangium (cutting off tapetal cells) above, and a microsporangium initial appearing on each side below; the investing indusium is evident. — After JOHNSON.

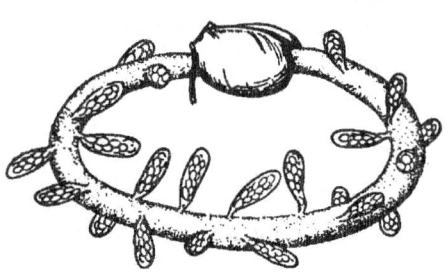

FIG. 411.—*Marsilea:* the swelling mucilaginous ring dragging out sori (indusia enveloping sporangia) from the sporocarp.

the sori out, from the ventral side of the sporocarp, attached to a mucilaginous ring formed of the swollen tissue (fig. 411). In *Pilularia* the sporocarp is globular, four soral cavities extending from the base towards the apex, the microsporangia being above and the megasporangia below. There is also a swelling tissue which in this case bursts out at the top of the sporocarp. The remarkable longevity and resisting power of the sporocarps of *Marsilea* deserve mention. Sporocarps preserved on herbarium sheets for fifty years and others kept in 95 per cent alcohol have resumed activity when placed in water.

In contrasting the structures called sporocarps in Salviniaceae and Marsileaceae, it is evident that they are very different. In Salviniaceae

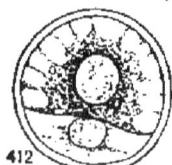  

FIGS. 412-414. — Male gametophyte of *Marsilea*: 412, first division of the microspore into vegetative cell (the smaller) and antheridium initial; 413, first division of antheridium initial; 414, antheridium with wall of sterile cells investing spermatogenous cells (shaded). — After CAMPBELL.

the sporocarp is an indusium investing a sorus, while in Marsileaceae it is a leaf blade inclosing a group of sori with their indusia.

Gametophytes. — The male gametophyte does not emerge from the microspore, as it does in Salviniaceae, remaining entirely within the spore coat, as in *Selaginella* and *Isoetes*. As in all the previously mentioned

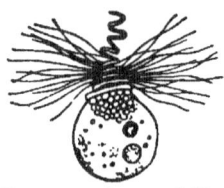

FIG. 415. — Sperm of *Marsilea*. — After CAMPBELL.

cases of heterospory, a single vegetative cell and a single antheridium make up the male gametophyte (figs. 412-414); but in Marsileaceae the output of sperms is 32, much larger than in Salviniaceae (8) and in *Isoetes* (4). The sperms of *Marsilea* are remarkable for the great number of coils in the beak, reaching 13 or 14, the upper 12 or 13 having no cilia (fig. 415). The female gametophyte closely resembles that of the Salviniaceae, and the nucleus of the great nutritive cell remains undivided, as in *Salvinia* (figs. 416, 417).

Embryo. — The embryo develops as in all the leptosporangiate ferns, the first wall of the egg being vertical (parallel with the long axis of the archegonium), and the four body regions being differentiated at the quadrant stage. It is noteworthy that the Marsileaceae have retained the primary vertical wall of the egg, characteristic of the leptosporangiate ferns, and that Salviniaceae have the transverse wall of the older eusporangiate Marattiaceae.

Conclusions. — It is evident that the water ferns are a very specialized aquatic group, probably derived from the leptosporangiate ferns. Moreover, the features of the sporangium, in development and output, indicate an origin from one of the higher leptosporangiate families. The

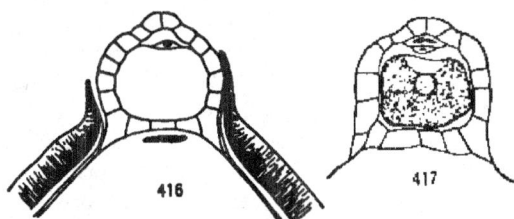

FIGS. 416, 417. — Female gametophyte of *Marsilea*: 416, the tissue protruding from the heavy megaspore wall developing a single large archegonium; the top of the large nutritive cell with its single nucleus seen; 417, the mature archegonium. — After CAMPBELL.

annulus characters, which might have determined the point, are lacking. It is interesting if heterospory has developed in these aquatic conditions; and it is noteworthy that the development of the female gametophyte is very different from that of *Selaginella* and *Isoetes*, which resemble gymnosperms in this regard. The fern connections of Marsileaceae are clearer than those of Salviniaceae, which in habit are further removed from the terrestrial leptosporangiates.

CHAPTER IV — SPERMATOPHYTES

Introductory. — The Spermatophytes (seed plants) include the most highly organized plants, and are distinguished from the lower groups by the production of seeds. Once they were called *Phanerogams*, a name contrasted with *Cryptogams*, which included all the lower groups. *Phanerogam* means "sexual reproduction evident," and *cryptogam* means "sexual reproduction concealed." This distinction was based upon the belief that stamens and pistils are sexual organs, and that no such organs are evident in the lower groups. In fact, the sexual organs are very evident in the groups included under cryptogams; while they are very obscure in the so-called phanerogams.

The seed plants were also generally called *flowering plants*, but the flower is not a structure that defines the group. There are two possible definitions of a flower. A very common one is that it is essentially a group of sporophylls (stamens and carpels); but this definition includes the strobilus, a structure well represented among pteridophytes. Another definition of a flower is that it is a structure in which a perianth (sepals and petals) is associated with the group of sporophylls; but this definition excludes many seed plants, and especially all the gymnosperms. The limit of the flower, therefore, is either more extensive than seed plants or less extensive; and since the structure does not fit the group, the name flowering plants has been abandoned. The seed is a structure that seems to agree exactly with the boundary of the group, and therefore the name seed plants (spermatophytes) seems to be the most appropriate.

The two groups of spermatophytes are *Gymnosperms* and *Angiosperms*, the names expressing the conspicuous difference; for in gymnosperms the seeds are exposed, and in angiosperms they are enclosed in a case. This difference is very far from expressing the full contrast between these two groups, but the characters will be developed as the groups are described. It is sufficient to state here that the gymnosperms are very ancient and form a comparatively small part of the present seed plant vegetation; while the angiosperms are comparatively modern and include the great bulk of the present seed plant vegetation.

A. GYMNOSPERMS

This group includes the primitive seed plants, and to understand their relation to pteridophytes it will be necessary to consider them in their historical sequence. Seven great groups are recognized: (1) *Cycadofilicales*, (2) *Bennettitales*, (3) *Cycadales*, (4) *Cordaitales*, (5) *Ginkgoales*, (6) *Coniferales*, and (7) *Gnetales*. The first, second, and fourth of these groups are extinct.

(1) CYCADOFILICALES

Discovery. — The discovery of the existence of this most primitive group of seed plants, known only in the Paleozoic and chiefly in the Carboniferous, is so recent that a brief outline will be of interest. The Coal-measure deposits are notable for the remains of fernlike plants, and such plants constitute about one half of the known vegetation of the time. Until recently all of these plants were thought to be ferns, the evidence from their leaf forms and venation appearing to be conclusive. Most of them show no sporangia, and such sporangia as do appear are mostly of the *Marattia* type. The first expressed doubt (1883) that these fernlike plants were all ferns arose from the persistent absence of sporangia. Later the anatomy of the stems of several forms was discovered to show characters combining those of ferns and of cycads, and for such forms the group name *Cycadofilices* was proposed (1896). In 1903 seeds were found on the leaves of certain of these Cycadofilices, and the group name *Pteridosperms* was proposed to include the Cycadofilices that bear seeds. Finally, in 1905 the microsporangia were discovered; and curiously enough some of these microsporangia were the sporangia of so-called ferns. Therefore, a knowledge of the existence of ferns during the Carboniferous came to depend more upon inference than upon any sure recognition of their remains. In any event, it seems certain that almost all of the so-called fern vegetation of the Carboniferous belongs to these primitive seed plants. The oldest name for the group is here adopted, its termination being adapted to that of the other groups with which it is coordinate.

Sporophyte. — The habit of the sporophyte body is conspicuously fernlike, including not merely the usual fern habit, but also climbers and trees. The vascular anatomy, which first separated the group from ferns, deserves brief mention. Three of the four conspicuous types of vascular cylinder found among ferns (see p. 156) are found in the stems of Cycadofilicales, the three representative genera illustrating them being *Heterangium* (protostele), *Lyginodendron* (ectophloic siphonostele), and *Medullosa* (polystele). Among the Cycadofilicales, however, there is a development of secondary wood in varying amount, but always distinct (fig. 418). This character distinguishes Cycadofilicales from ferns, but it would not serve to separate them from pteridophytes, for secondary wood was formed by many of the older pteridophytes (as the extinct Lycopodiales and Equisetales).

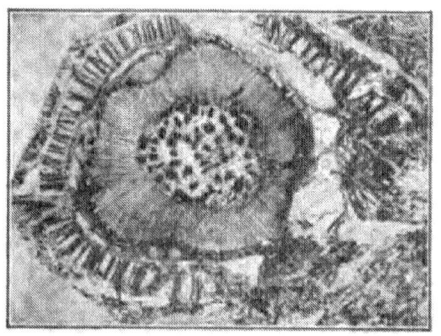

FIG. 418. — Photograph of cross section of vascular cylinder (ectophloic siphonostele) of *Lyginodendron*, showing the secondary wood characteristic of Cycadofilicales. — Photograph by BOODLE.

Seeds. — The seeds of Cycadofilicales have now been found in connection with all the great frond genera of the Carboniferous. The leaves or the pinnae which bear seeds usually differ in form from the sterile

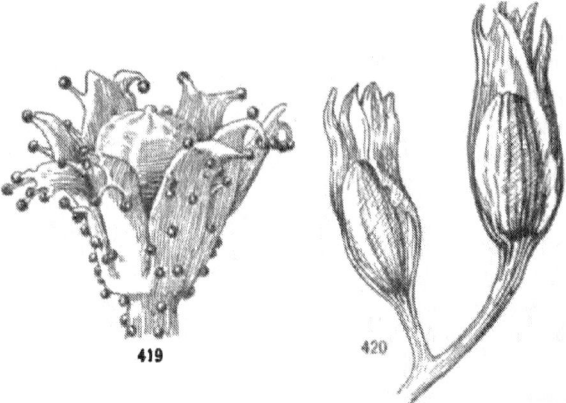

FIGS. 419, 420. — Seeds of Cycadofilicales: 419, seed of *Lagenostoma Lomaxi* (restored by OLIVER), showing the investing glandular cupule; 420, two seeds of *L. Sinclairi* terminating naked branches. — After ARBER.

leaves or pinnae, the seeds terminating naked branches and often being invested by husklike cupules (figs. 419, 420, 421), as if the lamina had disappeared and only the prominent ribs persisted. In some cases, however, the seeds replace sori on ordinary fernlike leaves (fig. 422). There are very many detached paleozoic seeds which have never been connected with the plants that produced them; but doubtless many of them belonged to the Cycadofilicales. So far as these attached and detached seeds have been sectioned, they show certain features in common which are regarded as primitive. In seed plants the megasporangium has long been called an *ovule*. In general structure it consists of a central region (the real sporangium) called the *nucellus*, which is invested by one or two coats called *integuments*. A passageway (*micropyle*) is left through the integument at the tip of the nucellus. When the changes occur that transform the ovule into the seed, the integument develops in various ways to form the seed coat or *testa*. In fossil seeds it is evident that the structure of the ovule must be inferred from the structure of the seed.

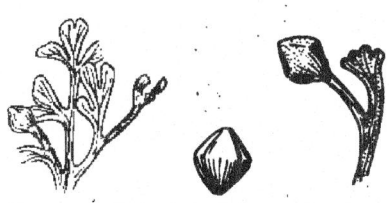

FIG. 421. — Seeds of *Aneimites* (an American form). — After WHITE.

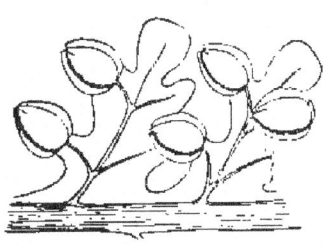

FIG. 422. — Seeds of *Pecopteris* on ordinary fernlike leaves. — After GRAND' EURY.

In the seeds of Cycadofilicales there is a three-layered testa, which is often peculiarly free from the nucellus. The vascular strand that enters the seed divides into two sets of branches, one set traversing the testa, and the other traversing the outer region of the nucellus, in case the testa and nucellus are free. The nucellus is beaked, and contains a deep chamber (*pollen chamber*), which serves as a gathering place for microspores, and which in living gymnosperms is associated with swimming sperms. A remarkable feature of the seed, and of all paleozoic seeds that have been sectioned, is that there is no trace of an embryo. Since the embryo is present in mesozoic seeds, its absence from paleozoic seeds must be due to other causes than failure to be preserved.

Stamens. — The microsporangiate structures (stamens), first recognized in 1905, have been found to be of at least three types. They are leaves or pinnae more or less modified, and may be said to take the following forms: (1) epaulet type (*Crossotheca*), in which the microspo-

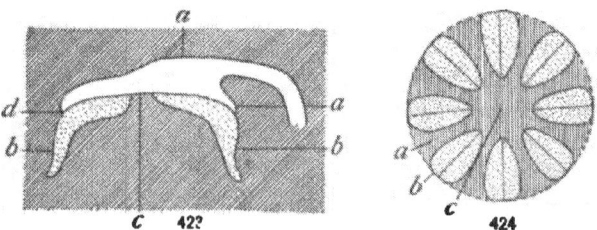

FIGS. 423, 424. — Microsporangia of Cycadofilicales, epaulet (*Crossotheca*) type: 423, diagram of cross section, showing the limb (*a*), the sporangia (*b*) showing their attachment (*d*), and the "central boss" (*c*); 424, diagram of horizontal section, showing the two-chambered sporangia; letters as before. — After KIDSTON.

rangia are pendulous from a more or less peltate and stalked lamina (figs. 423, 424); (2) cupule type (*Calymmatotheca*), in which the microsporangia occur in cupule-like structures terminating naked branches (fig. 425); and (3) synangium type, in which the microsporangia occur as synangia upon the abaxial face of fernlike leaves.

Female gametophyte. — The female gametophyte is hardly at all preserved, so far as found, and sections of the seed give no evidence as to its structure.

Conclusions. — The chief features of this most interesting group may be summarized as follows: It is evidently very closely related to the ferns, the resemblance in external appearance being remarkably close. The vascular anatomy is distinctly of the fern type, but with the additional feature of secondary wood, which is a gymnosperm feature. The microsporangia are hardly changed from fern sporangia; but the megasporangia are enormously changed, a well-developed ovule replacing a sorus or a synangium. It seems clear that this, the most ancient group of seed plants, was derived from still more ancient ferns.

FIG. 425. — Microsporangia of Cycadofilicales, cupule (*Calymmatotheca*) type: *Codonotheca*; sporangia on the inner surface of the cupule valves. — After SELLARDS.

(2) BENNETTITALES

General character. — The members of this extinct group were very conspicuous during the Mesozoic, and they have been called fossil cycads. In fact, the Mesozoic has been called the age of cycads, so far as plants are concerned. Recent investigations have shown, however, that the Bennettitales are very distinct from the living cycads. They were extraordinarily abundant during the Jurassic, numerous remains having been found in North America, Europe, and Asia, and extending into the arctic regions. The richest display of forms occurs in the United States (Maryland, South Dakota, and Wyoming), the conspicuous American genera being *Cycadeoidea* and *Cycadella*, and in Mexico.

Sporophyte. — The sporophyte body is generally tuberous in form, sometimes very large, but short columnar trunks (three to four meters high) also occur. This stem is covered by a heavy armor of leaf bases, among which there are wedged numerous short axillary branches, each bearing a terminal strobilus (fig. 426). The occurrence of numerous strobili on lateral branches is in striking contrast with the usually solitary terminal strobilus of the cycads. A second striking external feature is the occurrence of an abundance of membranous scales (*ramentum*), which are packed among the leaf bases and sometimes sheath the whole body with a feltlike mass. This ramentum is characteristic of ferns, and is often conspicuous upon the trunks of tree ferns.

FIG. 426. — Photograph of fossil trunk of *Cycadeoidea*, showing the tuberous body and the armor of leaf bases, wedged among which may be seen numerous strobili. — After WIELAND.

The anatomy of the stem is exactly like that of the cycads; with a very thick cortex, a comparatively thin vascular cylinder, and a large pith. The vascular bundles composing the cylinder are collateral, with the protoxylem in contact with the pith (endarch). In the leaves, however, the protoxylem occurs in the midst of the xylem (mesarch), a feature characteristic of ferns. The wood of the stem, therefore, has advanced to the endarch condition, while in the leaves the old mesarch character of the ferns remains. The leaf trace is a single and direct vascular strand, in striking contrast with the leaf traces of cycads. The tuberous or columnar body bears a crown of huge cycad-like (fernlike) leaves.

Strobilus. — The strobili of certain European forms have been known for a long time, but their real structure was not known until the recent study of the American forms. It seems clear now that probably the strobili of the whole group were bisporangiate, a most remarkable condition among gymnosperms, for in all the other groups the strobili are either staminate or ovulate, except in cases that are regarded as abnormal. The structure of a representative strobilus may be described as an illustration of the general condition (figs. 427, 428). The strobilus is sheathed by a series of sterile, overlapping bracts. Within (and above) these there arise ten to twenty microsporophylls (stamens); and within the stamens, covering the rest of the axis of the

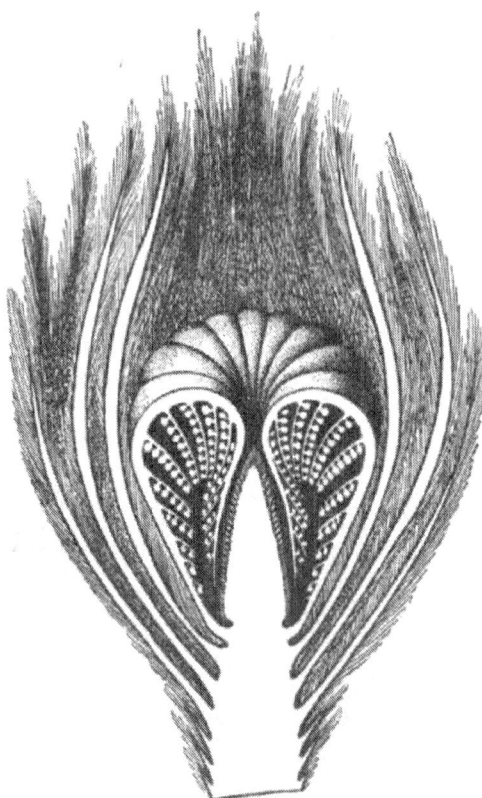

FIG. 427. — Diagram of strobilus of *Cycadeoidea*, showing the hairy sheathing bracts, the set of branched stamens (bent inward so that the backs are towards the ovules), and the tip of the axis covered by ovules. — After WIELAND.

SPERMATOPHYTES 187

strobilus, are the megasporophylls (carpels). The whole structure is like that of a huge flower (like a *Magnolia*), with perianth, stamens, and conical mass of carpels. When the stamens are present, the ovules are immature; when the seeds are mature, the stamens have disappeared, but their place of insertion is evident in the form of a shoulder between the seeds and the enveloping bracts (fig. 429).

FIG. 428. — Diagram of strobilus of *Cycadeoidea*, showing the relation of parts and a stamen unfolded. — After WIELAND.

Stamens. — The stamens are like fern leaves that are twice pinnate (fig. 428), and underneath the pinnules (sometimes twenty in number) there are two lateral rows of synangia (fig. 430), which are sori of the *Marattia* type. The stamens are united below into a broad disk, becoming free and pinnate above the ovule-bearing apex of the axis. The synangia are almost identical in structure with those of *Marattia*, so that the microsporangia have advanced very little beyond the fern level.

Ovulate structures. — The megasporangiate structures, however, have advanced very far beyond the fern level, and are very peculiar (fig. 431). The seeds terminate long and slender stalks, which are packed among *interseminal scales* that are also stalked structures. The stalked seeds and interseminal scales are arranged so as to form an ovoid, fruitlike body, with a mosaic surface composed of the flaring tops of the interseminal scales, wedged between which the micropylar tubes of the seeds protrude. If this structure be compared with the seed-bearing structures of the Cycadofilicales, especially those in which the seeds terminate the naked branches of a pinna, it will be observed that if these branches be reduced to a single axis, the condition in Bennettitales is obtained. The interseminal scales are probably sterile megasporophylls; and all the megasporophylls, leaflike and spreading in Cycadofilicales, are compacted into a strobilus in Bennettitales.

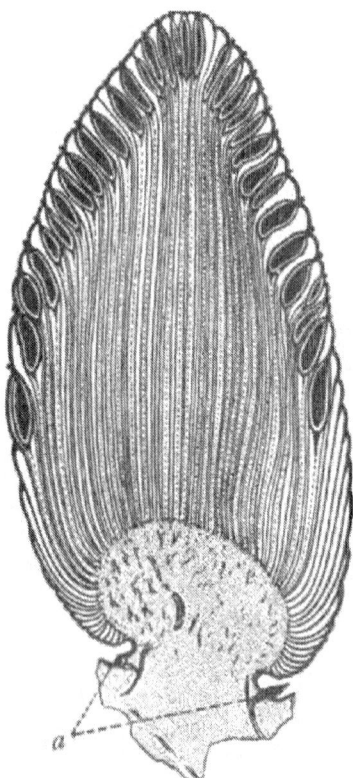

FIG. 429. — Strobilus of a species of *Cycadeoidea*, in which the seeds are mature, and showing the shoulder (*a*) which bore the stamens. — After WIELAND.

Seeds. — The structure of the seeds has been obtained from sections, which show a basal cupule, suggesting a rudiment of the investing and husklike cupule of some of the Cycadofilicales; a two or three layered testa; and a large dicotyledonous embryo completely filling the seed (fig. 432). This embryo is unlike that of any living gymnosperm, in that in developing it destroys all of the endosperm (see p. 202).

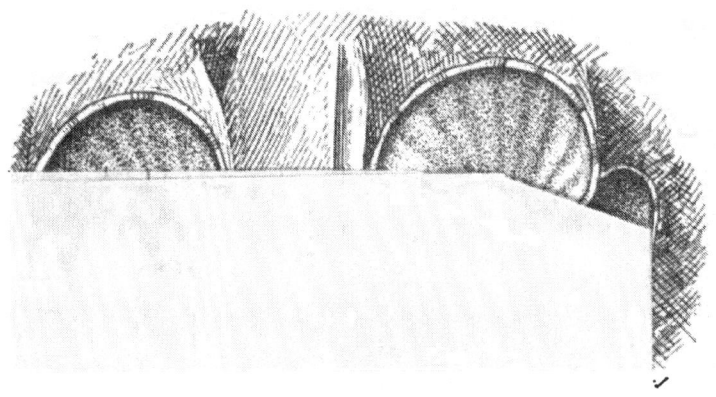

tion of
ietties,
dicoty-
—After

Conclusions. — The characters presented by this group are a combination of the characters of Cycadofilicales, of Cycadales, and of characters peculiar to itself. In lateral branches, ramentum, direct leaf traces, and synangia, it resembles Cycadofilicales and Filicales. In general habit and anatomy it resembles Cycadales. In its bisporangiate strobilus, its united and pinnate and synangium-bearing stamens, its mixture of sterile and fertile megasporophylls bearing terminal ovules, and its peculiar embryo, it is unlike any other gymnosperm group.

(3) CYCADALES

General character. — The cycads are tropical plants, including almost one hundred species, constituting nine genera. They are distributed almost equally between the oriental and occidental tropics, *Cycas* being the conspicuous oriental genus, and *Zamia* the conspicuous occidental one. The cycads are the modern living representatives of the line that began with the Cycadofilicales of the Paleozoic, and was continued by the Bennettitales of the Mesozoic.

FIG. 433. — *Cycas media* (middle and right) and *C. Normanbyana* (left), from oriental tropics. — After F. VON MÜLLER.

SPERMATOPHYTES

Sporophyte. — The sporophyte body consists of a tuberous or columnar stem, covered by an armor of leaf bases, and bearing a crown of large branched leaves and an apparently terminal strobilus (figs. 433–437). All the stems are tuberous when young, but in some species the tuberous body passes into the columnar, which in certain species of *Cycas* reaches

FIG. 434. — *Dioon edule* (Mexican). — After CHAMBERLAIN.

a height of 10 or even 20 m. (fig. 433). In those forms with the persistently tuberous habit, the stem is sometimes subterranean and very small (fig. 437). While the stem usually appears to terminate in a single strobilus, the strobili are in fact lateral, although close to the apex, and a succession of them may appear near the stem tip. In fact, in an African form strobili have been observed arising in a cycle about the vegetative point. It will be remembered that the strobili of Bennettitales are lateral, but distributed along the stem; while in Cycadales they are lateral, but restricted to the tip of the stem.

Vascular anatomy. — The anatomy of the stem resembles that of the Bennettitales, with a thick cortex, a thin vascular cylinder, and a large pith (fig. 438). The vascular bundles of the stem are collateral and endarch, as usual among gymnosperms; but in leaf traces, or leaf veins, or axes of strobili, the old fern connection is indicated by mesarch bundles and sometimes even by concentric bundles. It is in these so-called peripheral regions of the body that the older features of the vascular structure persist the longest. The primary cambium of the stem may persist (as in *Zamia*), although the amount of secondary wood it forms is always small; or it may be of short duration (as in *Cycas*), in which case a series of successive cambium cylinders is formed in the cortex, resulting in a concentric series of vascular cylinders. The leaf traces differ very much from those of the Bennettitales. Instead of being direct, as in the latter group, some of them (usually two) pass around the stem through the cortex, and often enter a leaf on the opposite side of

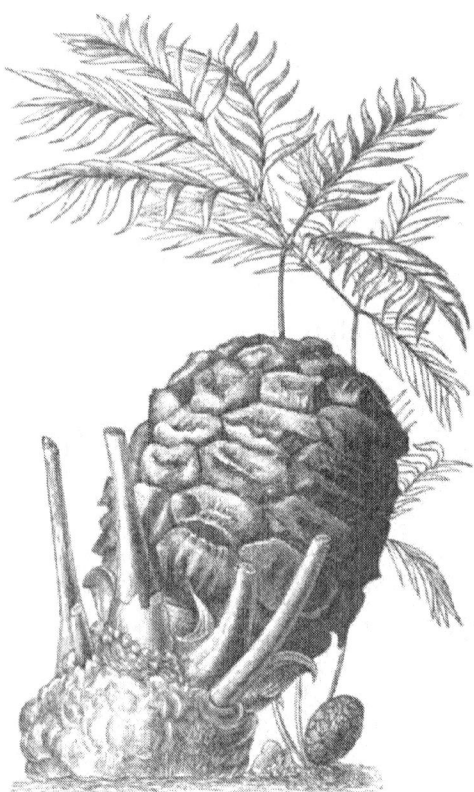

FIG. 435. — *Bowenia* (oriental), showing tuberous stem with heavy armor of leaf bases. — After EICHLER (ENGLER and PRANTL).

the stem from their emergence from the cylinder. These leaf traces curving about through the cortex are called *girdles*, and are conspicuous objects in any cross section of the stem (fig. 438).

Leaves.—The leaves are very large, pinnate, and generally leathery. The mesophyll is peculiar in containing cells elongated parallel with the leaf surface, and so loosely arranged as to appear like bridles of tissue traversing a large cavity.

Strobilus.—The strobili are dioecious, in striking contrast with those of Bennettitales, in which the staminate and ovulate structures are not only on the same plant, but also in the same strobilus.

FIG. 436.—*Zamia* (from Florida), showing small, tuberous, mostly subterranean stems, one bearing a staminate strobilus.

FIG. 437.—*Zamia*, bearing an ovulate strobilus.

Staminate.—In the staminate strobili the sporophylls are closely imbricate (figs. 436, 439), narrowed below, and broadened above into a more or less expanded terminal sterile portion (figs. 440, 441). The sporangia are borne on the abaxial surface of the sporophyll, varying in number from 1000 or more in *Cycas* (fig. 440) to very few in *Zamia* (fig. 441). They may cover the whole face of the sporophyll, or may occur only on the two flanks. Usually they are in definite sori of two to six sporangia, and often they are more or less united at base.

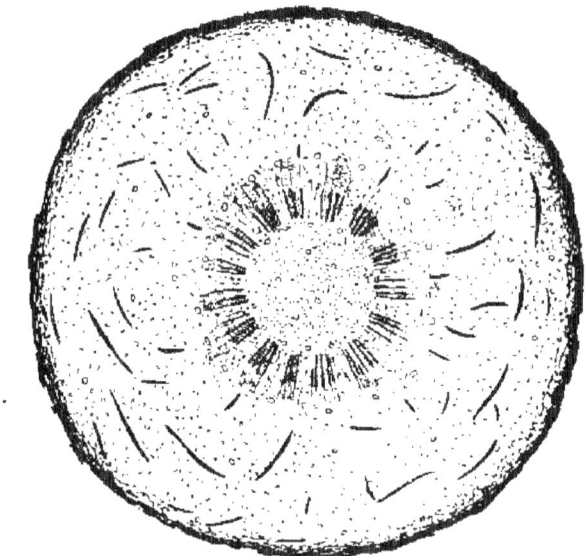

FIG. 438. — Cross section of a stem of *Zamia*, showing the thick cortex, thin vascular cylinder, large pith, and curving leaf traces (girdles); the vascular cylinder is seen to consist of vascular bundles (xylem next the pith, phloem next the cortex) separated by pith rays; partly diagrammatic.

The sporangia are eusporangiate in development, but the initial cell or cells are *hypodermal* (under the epidermis), and not superficial as among the pteridophytes. The initials usually form a hypodermal plate of four cells which divide periclinally into two plates, the outer giving rise to the four to seven wall layers (overlaid by the epidermis), the inner giving rise to the mass of sporogenous tissue. The tapetum is organized from the peripheral layer of sporogenous cells. The output of spores per sporangium varies from 500 in *Zamia* to 26,000 in *Encephalartos*.

The abaxial distribution of sporangia, the sori, the large output, the dehiscence, all resemble ferns of the *Marattia* type.

Ovulate. — The ovulate strobili (fig. 442) are sometimes very large. The genus *Cycas* is peculiar in its ovulate strobilus, in that it is not a compact strobilus, but a rosette of sporophylls resembling reduced foliage leaves, in which ovules replace the lower pinnae or teeth (figs. 443, 444). In general, the sporophylls vary from the leaflike (pinnate) forms of *Cycas* to peltate forms (as in *Zamia*, fig. 441, and *Ceratozamia*, fig. 445). Between these extreme forms there is a complete series of transitions, but there is always a terminal sterile region of varying form. The ovules vary in number from five or six to two.

FIG. 439. — Staminate strobili of *Dioon*. — After CHAMBERLAIN.

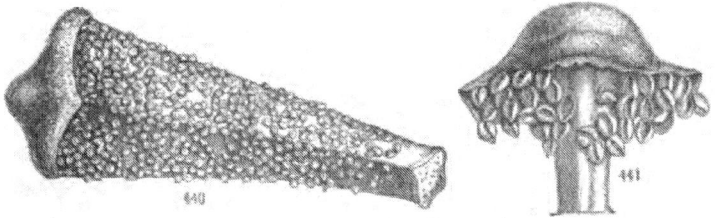

FIGS. 440, 441. — Stamens (microsporophylls) of *Cycas circinalis* (440) and *Zamia integrifolia* (441). — After RICHARD.

Ovules. — The structure of the ovule (fig. 446) is of the same general type as those of Cycadofilicales and Bennettitales. The thick integument is free from the nucellus in the region of the nucellar beak, and develops a testa of three layers: a stony layer between an outer and an inner fleshy layer. Among the Cycadofilicales, it will be remembered, the vascular supply to the ovule is divided into two sets of vascular strands, the outer set traversing the integument, the inner set the peripheral region of the nucellus; but in that case the integument and nucellus are almost completely free. Among the Cycadales, where the integument and nucellus are free only above, the outer set of vascular strands traverses the outer fleshy layer of the testa and the inner set traverses the inner fleshy layer (fig. 446). The nucellus develops a sharp beak, within which a conspicuous pollen chamber is formed. The first evidence of sporogenous tissue is the appearance of a spore mother cell deep within the nucellus, which soon differs conspicuously from the neighboring cells in size and contents. This mother cell, by the reduction divisions, forms a linear tetrad, the innermost megaspore functioning, and in its growth encroaching upon the other megaspores and the neighboring cells.

FIG. 442. — Ovulate strobilus of *Zamia*.

Female gametophyte. — The female gametophyte develops in a general way as in *Selaginella* and *Isoetes*, and as in nearly all gymnosperms. At least five stages in the development should be borne in mind : (1) free nuclear division, by which a varying number of free nuclei are distributed through the cytoplasm of the megaspore; (2) parietal placing of these nuclei by the development of a central vacuole; (3) continued free nuclear division; (4) formation of parietal tissue by

SPERMATOPHYTES 197

the development of cell walls separating the free nuclei; (5) centripetal growth of this tissue until it fills the cavity of the enlarging megaspore (which is now known as the *embryo sac*, fig. 446). At least two regions

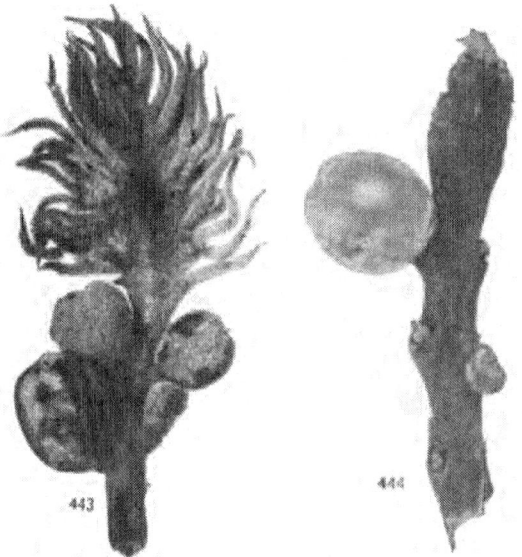

FIGS. 443, 444.—Megasporophylls of *Cycas*: 443, *C. revoluta*; 444, *C. circinalis*.

may be distinguished in the completed gametophyte; a region of smaller cells at the micropylar end of the embryo sac, in which archegonia are developed; and a deeper region of larger cells, which are nutritive in function (compare *Selaginella*, p. 136).

Archegonia.—The archegonia vary widely in number, but three to five are most common. The archegonium initial is a superficial cell, which divides periclinally into a primary neck cell (the outer one) and a central cell (the inner one).

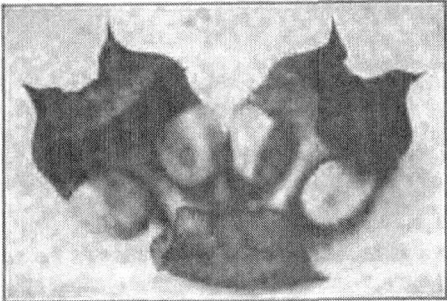

FIG. 445.—Megasporophylls of *Ceratozamia*.

The primary neck cell divides vertically, and these two neck cells, lying side by side, are constant among the Cycadales. The central cell then begins a remarkable enlargement, and becomes invested by a special jacket of cells, known as the *archegonial jacket*, which functions as a nutritive layer. Finally the nucleus of the central cell divides into the ventral nucleus, which soon disorganizes, and the egg nucleus, about which the cyto-

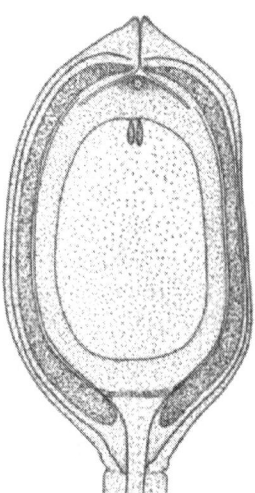
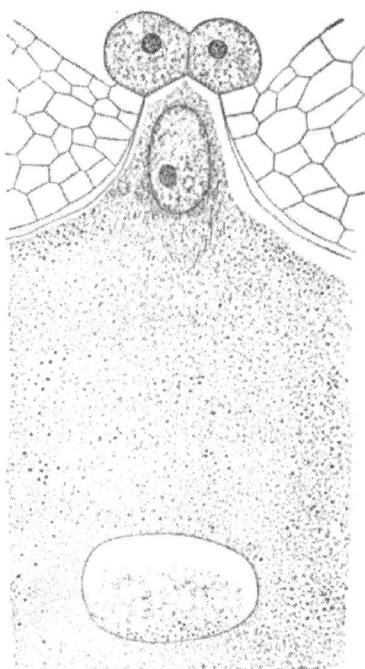

Fig. 446. — Diagrammatic section of ovule of *Dioon*, showing the thick integument free from nucellus at beak (in which the pollen chamber is evident, but not open); the three layers of the testa, outer fleshy (traversed by vascular strands), stony (thick and shaded), and inner fleshy (distinct in region of beak, but merged with nucellus below, and traversed by vascular strands); the embryo sac containing the female gametophyte (endosperm), in which two archegonia are present. — After CHAMBERLAIN.

Fig. 447. — Micropylar end of a mature archegonium of *Dioon*, showing the two neck cells, the ventral nucleus (in the apex), and the egg nucleus (below). — After CHAMBERLAIN.

plasm is organized to form the egg (fig. 447). The notable feature of this archegonium, in contrast with the archegonia of bryophytes and pteridophytes, is the complete elimination of neck canal cells. The cycad egg and its nucleus are the largest known among plants. As the archegonium develops at the micropylar surface of the gametophyte, the neighboring cells continue growth, and the archegonium is left in a depression known as the *archegonial chamber* (fig. 448).

Male gametophyte. — The male gametophytes differ from those of *Selaginella* and *Isoetes* in certain important particulars. The first division within the microspore (pollen grain) cuts off a persistent vegetative cell. The next division gives rise to the *generative cell* (primary spermatogenous cell) and the *tube cell*. This is the usual condition of the gametophyte at the shedding of the pollen grain, which is therefore seen to contain three nuclei: those of the persistent vegetative cell, of the generative cell, and of the tube cell (fig. 449).

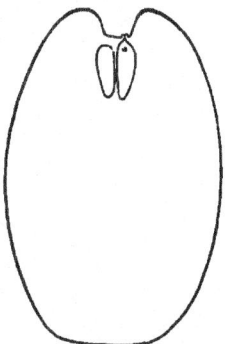

FIG. 448. — Diagram of embryo sac (containing female gametophyte) of *Dioon*, showing two archegonia and the archegonial chamber. — After CHAMBERLAIN.

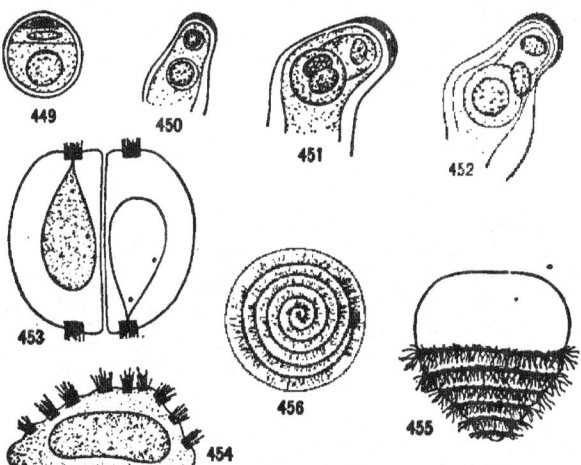

FIGS. 449-456. — Male gametophyte of *Cycas revoluta*: 449, shedding stage of microspore (pollen grain), showing persistent vegetative cell, generative cell, and tube cell; 450, later stage (after shedding), showing rounded-off vegetative and generative cells (tube nucleus has passed into the pollen tube); 451, division of nucleus of generative cell into nuclei of stalk and body cells; 452, enlargement of nucleus of body cell, and thrusting out of the stalk nucleus; 453, division of body cell to form the two sperm mother cells, in each of which a ciliated sperm is beginning to form; 454, section of a developing sperm; 455, 456, two views of a mature sperm. — 449-454, after IKENO; 455, 456, after COULTER.

200 MORPHOLOGY

The subsequent development of the gametophyte occurs after the pollen grain has reached the pollen chamber. In this position the tube begins to develop and to penetrate the tissue of the nucellus, the tube nucleus passing into it. Then the generative cell, remaining within the

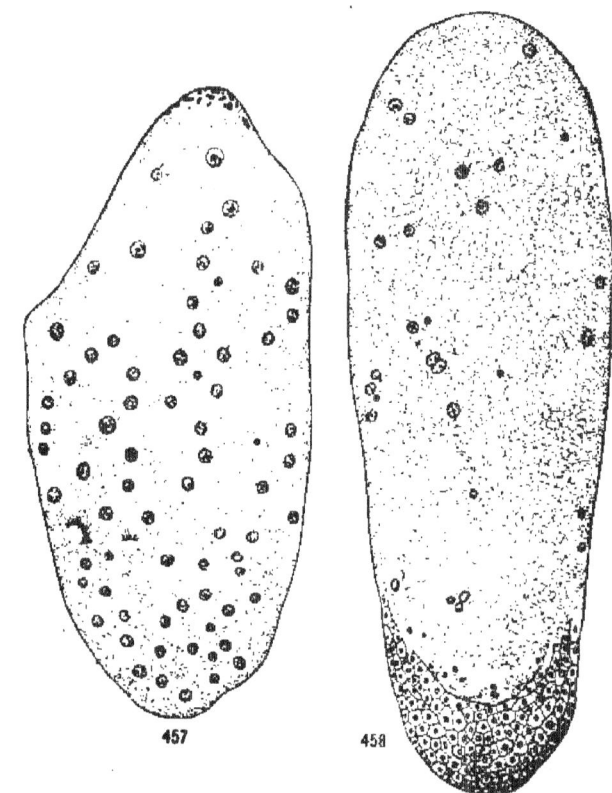

FIGS. 457, 458. — Development of the embryo of *Zamia:* 457, the stage of free nuclear division; 458, tissue-formation at base of egg, with numerous free nuclei remaining in the general cytoplasm. — After COULTER and CHAMBERLAIN.

grain, divides into the *stalk cell* and the *body cell* (fig. 451). The stalk cell is sterile and produces nothing; but the body cell enlarges (fig. 452), and there appear within it, near the nucleus, two remarkable bodies, the *blepharoplasts*. The body cell then divides to form the two *sperm mother* cells (fig. 453), in each of which is one of the blepharoplasts. In

SPERMATOPHYTES

a Cuban cycad (*Microcycas*) recently studied, as many as sixteen mother cells and sperms have been found in a single pollen tube. Within each mother cell a large, spirally grooved, multiciliate sperm is formed (figs. 453, 454), which is discharged and swims freely (figs. 455, 456). The blepharoplast has received its name from the fact that it develops the cilia. The discovery of these swimming sperms of Cycadales was quite unexpected, since it had been supposed that all seed plants had abandoned swimming sperms; but the discovery served to emphasize the fern connections of the cycads.

Fertilization. — The pollen tube penetrates the tissue of the nucellus in various directions, often branching, and always functioning as an absorptive structure (*haustorium*). Finally it collapses, and the tube nucleus may return to the grain end of the tube. In the meantime the tissue of the nucellus lying between the pollen chamber and the archegonial chamber has broken down, and the two chambers become continuous. Then the sperms are discharged into the archegonial chamber, and finding their way into the archegonium fertilize the egg. It is evident that the pollen tube in these primitive seed plants is not a means of

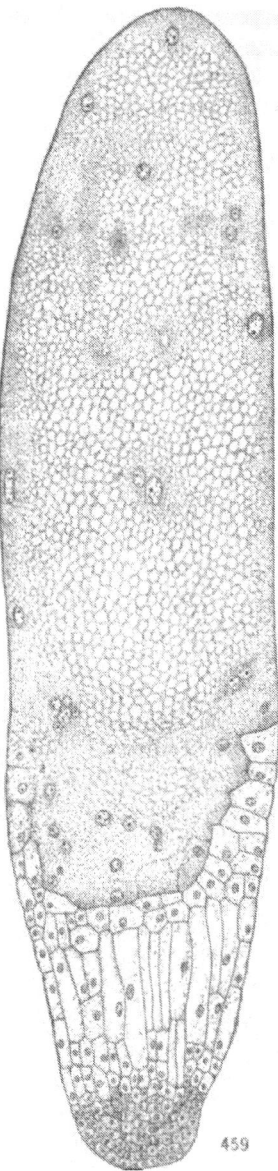

FIG. 459. — Differentiation of proembryo of *Zamia* by elongation of cells of suspensor region; unelongated cells above suspensor forming the "rosette"; apical group of small meristematic cells (note spindles) to form the embryo. — After COULTER and CHAMBERLAIN.

carrying the sperms to the archegonia, but is simply an absorptive organ.

Embryo. — The development of the embryo differs in detail among the cycads, but the general features are fairly constant (figs. 457, 458). The first stage is that of free nuclear division, resulting in a distribution of nuclei through the cytoplasm of the huge egg (fig. 457). For example, in *Zamia* there are eight successive divisions, resulting in 256 free nuclei. The next stage is that of wall formation, which varies in extent, sometimes resulting in a tissue which nearly fills the egg, but sometimes (as in *Zamia*) being restricted to the lower region of the egg (fig. 458). This tissue, which in *Zamia* occupies the lower end of the egg, is the *proembryo*. The cells behind the tip cells of the proembryo begin to elongate remarkably (fig. 459), forcing the tip cells out of the archegonium into the nutritive tissue of the gametophyte (*endosperm*), and continue to elongate until they form an exceedingly long, tortuous, and often spirally coiled massive filament (*suspensor*), sometimes 5 cm. or more long (fig. 460). The tip cells at the end of this long suspensor form the embryo, which develops two cotyledons, a constant feature of cycads. In the germination of the seed these cotyledons remain within the testa.

FIG. 460. — Embryo of *Cycas circinalis*, showing (above) the remains of proembryonic tissue, the long and coiled suspensor, and the terminal embryo. — After TREUB.

Changes in terminology. — In passing from pteridophytes to spermatophytes, it is sometimes confusing to the beginner to fit the older terminology of the seed plants to the more recent terminology of the lower groups. It is important that this change in terms should not give rise to the idea that there is any change in the character of the structures. The following list should prevent any possibility of confusion in this transition from one set of terms to another. The real name of the structure, as used in the lower groups, is followed in each case by the older name applied in seed plants before any such relationship was known : microsporophyll (stamen), megasporophyll (carpel), microsporangium (pollen sac), megasporangium (ovule), microspore (pollen grain), megaspore (embryo sac), female gametophyte (endosperm).

Conclusions. — The fernlike characters of the cycads appear in the vascular anatomy, mesarch and even concentric bundles still being present; in the form and general character of the leaves; in the microsporophylls with their abaxial sporangia in sori; and in the swimming sperms. These characters are shared with Cycadofilicales and Bennettitales, the ovules of which groups those of cycads further resemble in the three-layered testa (the outer and inner layers fleshy and the middle one stony), the two sets of vascular strands, and the nucellar beak with its pollen chamber. The general habit of the sporophyte body further resembles that of the Bennettitales; but the relatively terminal and monosporangiate strobili are peculiar to cycads.

The cycads evidently represent the modern end of one seed plant line, which has come from the fernlike Cycadofilicales of the Paleozoic, and which gave rise to the Bennettitales during the Mesozoic.

(4) Cordaitales

General character. — This is an extinct paleozoic group of gymnosperms that was contemporary with the Cycadofilicales, and these two groups made up most of the seed plant vegetation of the Paleozoic, the Cordaitales being the dominant gymnosperm forest type. The two groups appear side by side as far back as the records go, but intergrading forms indicate that the Cordaitales probably arose from the Cycadofilicales at a very early period.

Sporophyte. — The Cordaitales were tall and slender trees, often 10 to 30 m. high before branching, with a dense crown of branches, and a great abundance of simple and large leaves (fig. 461). The general appearance of these trees differs from that of any living gymnosperm.

Vascular anatomy. — The structure of the stem combines the characters of other groups and suggests its relationships. The siphonostele composed of collateral endarch vascular bundles is common to all gymnosperms; the mesarch bundles of the leaves, a character shared with the gymnosperm line beginning with Cycadofilicales and ending with Cycadales, testifies to the connection with ferns; the large pith is shared with the same gymnosperm line; the double leaf trace is also a feature of the Cycadofilicales; but the branching habit, the simple leaves, and especially the thick cylinder of secondary wood are characters of the Coniferales. These characters indicate a connection with the Cycadofilicales, and a development towards the Coniferales instead of towards the Cycadales.

Leaves. — The leaves are simple, elongated (fig. 461), with parallel veins that branch dichotomously, except in certain forms with very narrow leaves. In some forms the leaves are short and obovate, suggesting those of Ginkgoales. The structure of the leaves is like those of the cycads, with the very characteristic mesophyll (see p. 193). In form, therefore, the leaves in general resemble those of the conifers; but in structure they resemble those of the cycad line.

Strobili. — The strobili are small and monosporangiate, both kinds of strobili usually occurring on the same plant (monoecious), characters which belong to the conifers. They occur in clusters on lateral branches (fig. 461), and both kinds are sheathed by bracts.

Staminate. — The staminate strobilus is made up of spirally arranged sterile bracts, among which the stamens occur, either solitary or grouped near the apex (fig. 462). Each stamen is a slender stalk bearing a terminal cluster of three to six erect sporangia with longitudinal dehiscence. It is only among the Cycadofilicales that such terminal and erect microsporangia are found (cupule type, see p. 184).

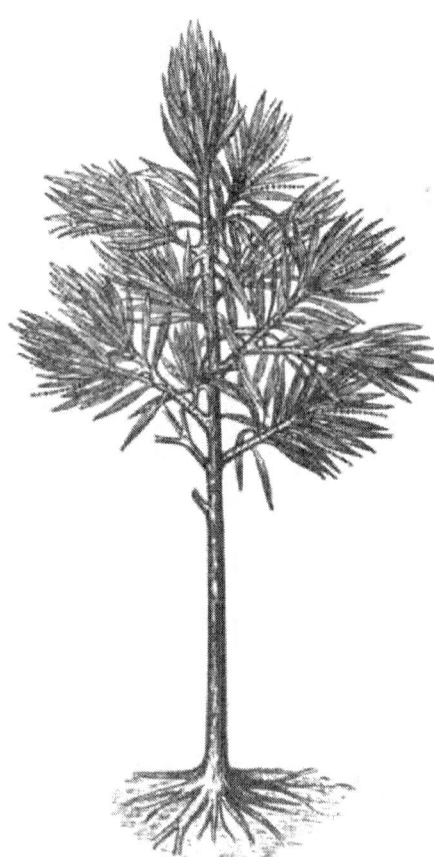

FIG. 461. — Restoration of *Dorycordaites*, one of the Cordaitales, showing the branching habit, the simple, elongated, parallel-veined leaves, and the clusters of strobili borne on lateral branches. — After GRAND'EURY.

Ovulate. — The ovulate strobilus is made up of conspicuous overlapping bracts, in whose axils short branches appear, each of which bears one or two bractlets and a terminal ovule (fig. 463). The bearing of ovules on secondary axes of the strobilus results in what is called a *compound strobilus*, a type of strobilus characteristic of certain conifers.

Ovules. — Although the structure of the testa is not clear in the sections that have been made (fig. 463), two layers are evident (the outer fleshy and the stony), and it is probable that an inner fleshy layer was also present. This type of testa is characteristic of the whole cycad line of gymnosperms. Another primitive feature of the ovule is that the nucellus is quite free from the integument, and that one of the sets of vascular strands traverses the outer fleshy layer, and the other set traverses the peripheral region of the nucellus. This structure is duplicated only among the Cycadofilicales. There is also a prominent nucellar beak and a large pollen chamber, a structure which indicates the existence of swimming sperms.

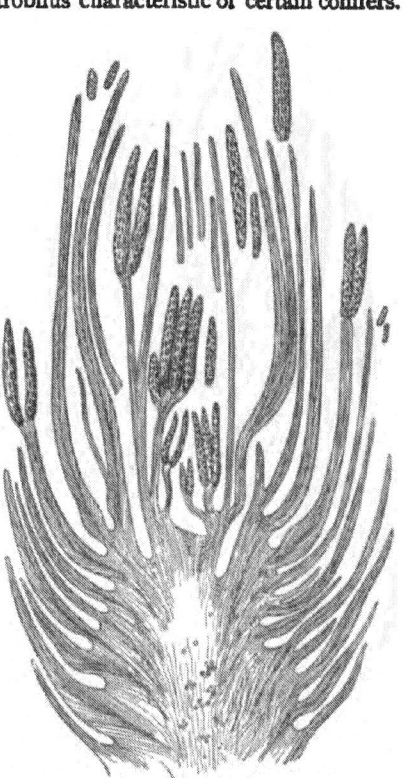

FIG. 462. — Section of staminate strobilus of one of the Cordaitales, showing the spirally arranged sterile bracts, and the stalked stamens bearing terminal sporangia (the longitudinal dehiscence of the sporangia not shown). — After RENAULT.

Male gametophyte. — The pollen grains are preserved in abundance, and in favorable specimens a group of internal cells is evident (fig. 464), which must represent a male gametophyte; but whether these cells are vegetative or spermatogenous or both cannot be determined. In either case, the number of cells indicates a very primitive condition.

Female gametophyte. — The female gametophytes resemble those of modern gymnosperms. Two archegonia have been seen, and between them a beaklike projection of the endosperm, a structure that characterizes *Ginkgo*. No seeds have been found containing embryos; and

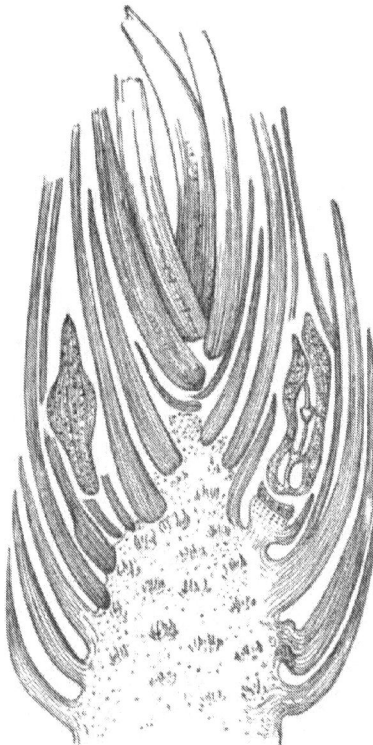

since the same fact is true of the Cycadofilicales, it is evident that all the seed plants of the Paleozoic shared this peculiarity.

Conclusions. — A summary of the characters of Cordaitales shows an interesting combination. There are primitive characters which indicate connection with the Cycadofilicales and the cycad line, such as the large pith, the structure and mesarch bundles of the leaf, the structure of the ovule, and the swimming sperms. The advanced characters are the lofty and branching habit, the thick cylinder of secondary wood, the form of the leaves, and the compound ovulate strobilus, all of which are characters of the Coniferales. It

FIG. 463. — Section of ovulate strobilus of one of the Cordaitales, showing the large overlapping bracts, in the axils of two of which there appear short branches bearing terminal ovules; that to right also shows a bractlet. — After RENAULT.

FIG. 464. — Pollen grains of one of the Cordaitales, showing the group of internal cells that probably belong to the male gametophyte. — After RENAULT.

seems evident, therefore, that the Cordaitales represent a second great branch from the Cycadofilicales stock, a branch which leads towards the Coniferales. This branch seems to have separated from the Cycadofilicales long before the other branch which ends in the modern Cycadales.

SPERMATOPHYTES

(5) GINKGOALES

General character. — *Ginkgo biloba*, the maidenhair tree, is the only living representative of a gymnosperm line that reaches back to the paleozoic Cordaitales, and was most extensively displayed during the Mesozoic. Its extensive cultivation by the Chinese and the Japanese, especially in temple grounds, first brought it into notice, and for a long time it was supposed that it did not exist in the wild state. In recent years, however, it has been found growing wild in the mountains of western China.

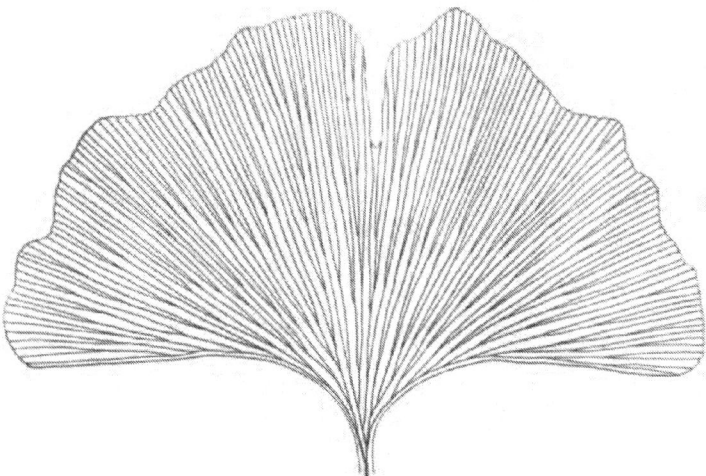

FIG. 465. — The leaf of *Ginkgo*.

Sporophyte. — *Ginkgo* is a tree with the general habit of a conifer, and therefore very unlike a cycad. As in both Cordaitales and Coniferales, it develops two kinds of branches: long shoots bearing scattered foliage leaves, and dwarf shoots bearing a few crowded leaves.

Vascular anatomy. — The anatomy of the stem closely resembles that of the Coniferales, with its thick cylinder of secondary wood and its relatively small pith, the latter character contrasting with the large pith of Cordaitales. All traces of mesarch bundles have disappeared from the stem, and also from the leaves, but they occur in the cotyledons. It is evident that in vascular anatomy *Ginkgo* has departed farther from the ferns than have the Cordaitales or the cycad line.

Leaves. — The leaf is very characteristic in form and venation (fig. 465), the broadly wedge-shaped outline, often more or less lobed, and the forked veins resembling somewhat the leaves of maidenhair fern and suggesting the common name. The mesophyll has the peculiar character (transversely elongated and very loosely arranged cells) described under Cordaitales and Cycadales (p. 193).

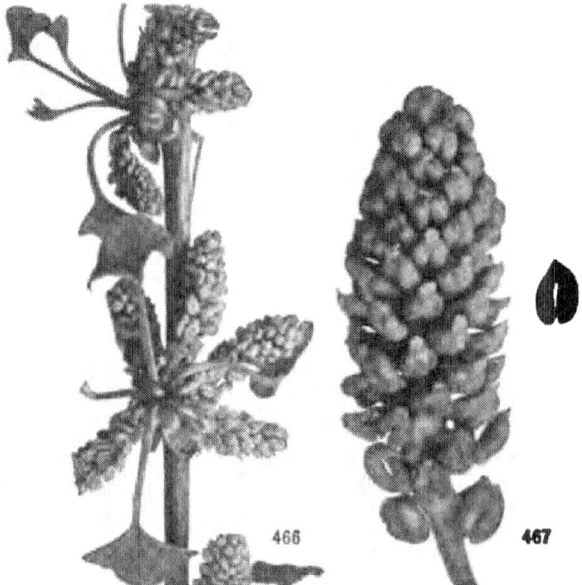

FIGS. 466, 467. — Staminate strobilus of *Ginkgo*: 466, the clusters of strobili borne on dwarf branches; 467, a single strobilus, showing the character of the individual stamens (a stalk ending in a knob and bearing two pendent sporangia).

Strobili. — The strobili are monosporangiate, and the two kinds of strobili occur on different trees (dioecious).

Staminate. — The staminate strobili occur in loose catkin-like clusters borne on the dwarf branches (fig. 466). The sporophyll (stamen) consists of a stalk ending in a knob, from beneath one side of which two (sometimes three to seven) pendent sporangia are borne (fig. 467). This type of stamen suggests the epaulet type found among Cycadofilicales (see p. 184). The development of the sporangium is regularly eusporangiate, as described under Cycadales (p. 194).

SPERMATOPHYTES

Ovulate. — The ovulate strobili are also borne on the dwarf branches and are very much reduced (fig. 468). A strobilus consists of a long stalk, near the tip of which usually two ovules are borne, only one of which usually matures a seed (fig. 469). At the base of each ovule there is a little cupule or *collar*, which is the rudiment of the sporophyll (fig. 470). Sometimes there are three or four ovules on a strobilus, and sometimes the collar becomes leaflike; so it is evident that the strobilus is remarkably reduced, usually producing only two ovules upon very rudimentary sporophylls.

FIG. 468. — Ovulate strobili of *Ginkgo*, borne in clusters on dwarf branches, and each bearing two ovules.

Ovules. — The ovules resemble in general structure those of Cordaitales and the cycad line already described (fig. 470), with the three-layered integument (outer fleshy, stony, and inner fleshy layers), the nucellar beak, and the pollen chamber; but the set of vascular strands, which in the groups referred to traverse the outer fleshy layer, are not present in *Ginkgo*, only the inner set appearing in the inner fleshy layer.

The megaspore mother cell is first observed deep within the nucellus, and it becomes invested by a distinct zone of glandular tissue. This glandular zone is digestive in function, invading and destroying the surrounding tissue of the nucellus. Surround-

FIG. 469. — Ovulate strobili of *Ginkgo* bearing developing seeds; the strobili to the right have developed single seeds; those to the left have developed both seeds.

ing the mother cell, therefore, there are three distinct concentric zones of tissue: (1) the invading digestive zone; (2) the invaded and disorganizing zone; and (3) the storage zone, outside of the disorganizing zone, and containing food surplus in the form of starch. After the female gametophyte (endosperm) is organized, it in turn invades and destroys the digestive zone and all the surrounding tissues of the nucellus. The mother cell forms the usual linear tetrad of megaspores, only the innermost one enlarging and functioning.

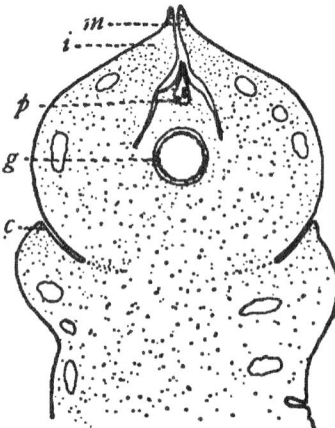

FIG. 470. — Section of ovule of *Ginkgo*, showing thick integument (*i*), micropyle (*m*), nucellar beak with pollen chamber (*p*), collar (*c*), and young female gametophyte (*g*). — After COULTER and CHAMBERLAIN.

Female gametophyte. — The female gametophyte develops as described for Cycadales (see p. 196), with free nuclear division (up to 256 free nuclei), parietal tissue (fig. 470, *g*), and centripetal growth. It is a remarkable fact that this female gametophyte becomes green, although enclosed within a three-layered testa, one layer being thick and fleshy and another compact and stony. The gametophyte continues its growth until it destroys all the nucellar tissues and reaches the testa.

Archegonia. — The archegonia are usually two in number (sometimes three), and develop as described for the cycads, including the organization of the archegonial jacket (see p. 197). In cycads a ventral nucleus is formed and speedily disorganizes, but in *Ginkgo* a cell wall is developed separating the ventral nucleus from the egg, so that there is a ventral canal cell, a feature which persists in some of the conifers. In *Ginkgo* the archegonial chamber is formed as usual, but between the two archegonia the endosperm grows into a conspicuous central beak, which reduces the archegonial chamber to a circular crevice (fig. 471). This peculiar feature appears also in the Cordaitales, but is not known in any other group of gymnosperms.

Male gametophyte. — The male gametophyte develops two vegetative cells (the first one lasting only until shedding, the second one persisting), a generative cell, and a tube nucleus. This is the shedding stage, and the subsequent development occurs in the pollen chamber, after the pollen tube has begun to develop. In that position the nucleus of the generative cell divides, but no wall is formed, the stalk nucleus being thrust out to one side of the general cytoplasm, which organizes the body cell in connection with the other nucleus. The events that follow are exactly as in the cycads: two blepharoplasts appearing in the body cell; the body cell dividing into two sperm mother cells, each

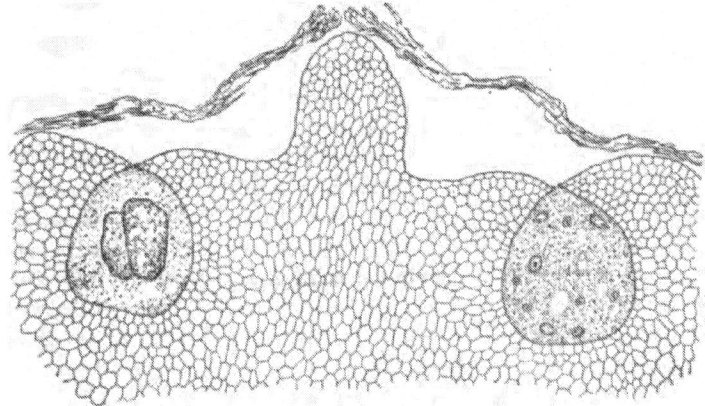

FIG. 471. — Micropylar end of female gametophyte of *Ginkgo*, showing the endosperm beak developed in the archegonial chamber, and the two archegonia; in the left archegonium the sperm and egg nuclei are fusing; in the right archegonium the early free nuclear division of the embryo is occurring.

with one blepharoplast; and each mother cell developing a spirally grooved, multiciliate sperm, which later is discharged.

Fertilization. — The details of fertilization also resemble those in the cycads. The pollen tube is a branching and absorptive (haustorial) organ; the pollen chamber and archegonial chamber become continuous by the breaking down of the small amount of intervening tissue; the grain end of the tube is thus brought into position favorable for the discharge of sperms into the archegonial chamber; and fertilization is accomplished (fig. 471).

Embryo. — The embryo is peculiar among gymnosperms in the absence of a slender, elongated, and tortuous suspensor, but a real suspensor is present. Free nuclear division (fig. 471) results in the distribution of 256 nuclei through the cytoplasm of the egg, and then walls form, filling the egg with tissue (proembryo) more completely and permanently than in any other known gymnosperm (fig. 472). The cells of the upper two thirds of this proembryo remain inactive; while the cells of the lower third (which are much smaller) grow actively, forming a broad cylinder that invades the endosperm. This cylinder is really a massive suspensor, and at its tip the embryo is formed. This embryo, as in cycads, has two cotyledons, but sometimes three have been observed, and they also remain in the seed during germination.

FIG. 472. — Proembryo of *Ginkgo*, filling the egg with tissue. — After STRASBURGER.

Conclusions. — *Ginkgo* resembles the Cordaitales and the cycad line in the structure of its ovules, and in its swimming sperms; but it is like the conifers in the habit of its sporophyte body and in its stem structure. Its origin from the Cordaitales seems clear, but the primitive reproductive characters which persist also distinguish it from Coniferales as a separate line.

(6) CONIFERALES

General character. — This is the large group of living gymnosperms, comprising approximately 350 recognized species, included in forty genera. In contrast with the tropical distribution of the cycads, the conifers are characteristic of the north and south temperate zones. Two families are recognized: *Taxaceae*, in general with fleshy seeds and freely exposed ovules; and *Pinaceae*, in general with dry seeds and ovules covered by scales. The Taxaceae comprise about eleven genera and 100 species; while the Pinaceae comprise about twenty-nine genera and 250 species. The two families differ so much that they must be treated separately.

(a) Taxaceae

General character. — The Taxaceae comprise two well-marked tribes or subfamilies: *Podocarpineae* (the podocarps) and *Taxineae* (the taxads). The podocarps in general are south temperate, *Podocarpus* being the largest genus (about sixty-five species), and as characteristic

SPERMATOPHYTES

of the southern hemisphere as are the pines of the northern hemisphere. The taxads in general are north temperate, *Taxus* (yew) being the most widely distributed genus.

Sporophyte. — The habit of the sporophyte body is familiar, in general being the branching habit established in *Ginkgo* and common to all conifers. In size the body ranges from large trees to straggling bushes. The mesarch type of bundle, characteristic of ferns, occurs in the stem of at least one species (a *Cephalotaxus*), but in most of them it is found only in the cotyledons, as in *Ginkgo*. The leaves are entire, as in all conifers, and range in breadth from the needles of *Taxus* to the broad blades of certain species of *Podocarpus*.

Staminate strobilus. — The staminate strobilus is always a distinct strobilus, enveloped by sterile bracts (as among Cordaitales, fig. 473). The sporophylls differ in form in the two tribes. Among the podocarps the sporophyll is bract-like, with two abaxial sporangia and a sterile tip (fig. 474); while among the taxads the sporophyll is peltate (epaulet type), as in *Ginkgo*, and bears a variable number of pendent sporangia (figs. 475, 476). The development of the microsporangium is as usual among eusporangiates. The microspores (pollen grains) of the podocarps are peculiar in being winged, each pollen grain developing two winglike extensions from the exine, as among the pines.

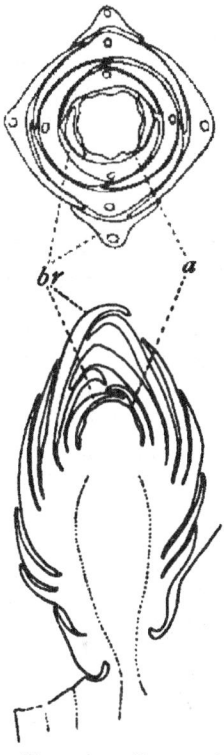

FIG. 473. — Cross and longitudinal sections of young staminate strobilus of *Torreya*, showing the overlapping bracts (*br*) and the position of the developing stamens (*a*). — After COULTER and LAND.

Ovulate strobilus. — The ovulate strobilus is much reduced, usually containing a single terminal ovule. For example, in *Torreya* (nearly related to *Taxus*) the ovulate strobilus resembles a simple ovulate flower, with four bracts (two decussate pairs) investing a terminal ovule (fig. 477).

Ovule. — The integument of the ovule is of the ancient type, developing three distinct layers (outer fleshy, stony, and inner fleshy); and a set of vascular strands traverses the outer fleshy layer, the inner set

214   MORPHOLOGY

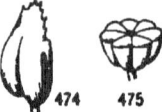 

FIGS. 474-476. — Microsporophylls (stamens) of Taxaceae: 474, *Podocarpus* (after HOOKER); 475, *Taxus* (after RICHARD); 476, *Torreya* (after HOOKER). — From ENGLER and PRANTL.

(belonging to the inner fleshy layer) being suppressed. This is just the reverse of the vascular condition in *Ginkgo*, in which the set of vascular strands belonging to the outer fleshy layer is suppressed, and the set belonging to the inner fleshy layer is developed. In early stages of the ovule the nucleus is entirely free from the integument, but as the ovule develops largely from beneath, the region in which the nucellus and integument are free from one another is carried to the tip of the ovule. A notable change in the ovule, as contrasted with the preceding groups of gymnosperms, is that there is no nucellar beak or pollen chamber (fig. 477); nor is there developed about the megaspore mother cell any special digestive (glandular) zone of cells, as in *Ginkgo*. The development of the linear tetrad and the selection of the innermost megaspore for functioning are as usual.

Female gametophyte. — The female gametophyte develops by the usual stages: free nuclear division (up to 256 nuclei), parietal wall formation, and centripetal growth. It is important to note the variation in the appearance of the archegonial initials. In some cases they are not differentiated until the gametophyte has become quite extensive; that is, they appear comparatively late in its history. In other cases, however, notably in *Torreya*, the archegonium initials appear as soon as wall formation has filled the embryo sac with tissue (figs. 478, 479).

Archegonia. — The archegonia range in number from one to eleven, the neck

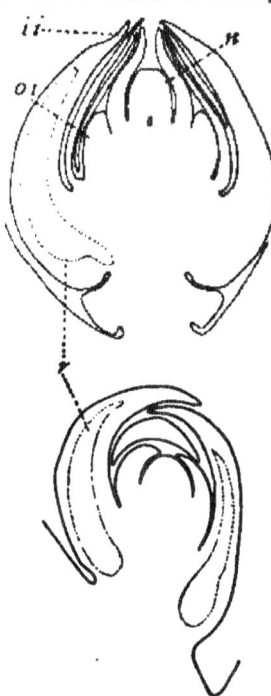

FIG. 477. — Longitudinal sections of ovulate strobilus of *Torreya* at different ages, showing the enveloping bracts and the solitary terminal ovule; upper section (the older) shows the two integuments (*ii, oi*), nucellus (*n*), and deep-placed mother cell. — After COULTER and LAND.

consisting usually of two (fig. 478) or three cells, but in *Podocarpus* it sometimes becomes a massive structure of about twenty-five cells. There is no well-defined archegonial jacket, and when it is remembered that there is no special digestive zone about the mother cell, it is evident that the nutritive mechanism is not differentiated in this group as it is in *Ginkgo*, or even in the cycads. In the division of the nucleus of the ventral cell, which precedes the formation of the egg, there is no separating wall formed, and hence no ventral canal cell. The ventral nucleus is its only representative, and in *Torreya* it is doubtful whether even this appears. The disappearance of the ventral canal cell and its nucleus is the last stage in the reduction of the axial row, which thereafter is represented only by the egg.

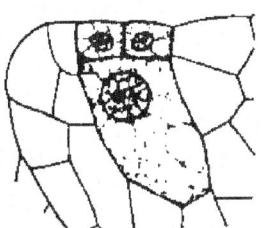

FIG. 478. — Young archegonium of *Torreya*, showing the two neck cells and the central cell. — After COULTER and LAND.

Male gametophyte. — In the development of the male gametophyte, the podocarps and taxads show a striking contrast. In the podocarps two to six vegetative (prothallial) cells appear (fig. 480); while in the taxads no vegetative cells have been discovered. The division of the generative (primary spermatogenous) cell into the sterile stalk cell and the body cell is as described for the preceding groups (fig. 480); but a striking change appears in the fact that there are no blepharoplasts in the mother cell, which means that ciliated (hence swimming) sperms are not formed. The nucleus of the body cell divides, and this division may be accompanied by a separating wall, so that two sperm mother cells are formed (taxads); or the nuclear division may not be accompanied by wall formation, so that there are only two mother cell nuclei in the general cytoplasm of the body cell (podocarps). In either case the division is unequal, so that only one cell or one nucleus functions (fig. 479). No sperms are formed, but the mother cell functions directly as a sperm, its nucleus being the structure essential in fertilization. It has become the habit to call these mother cells that do not form sperms internally and discharge them, but function themselves as sperms, simply *male cells*.

Fertilization. — In pollination (by the wind) the pollen grains come to rest on the tip of the nucellus, and in the absence of a pollen chamber

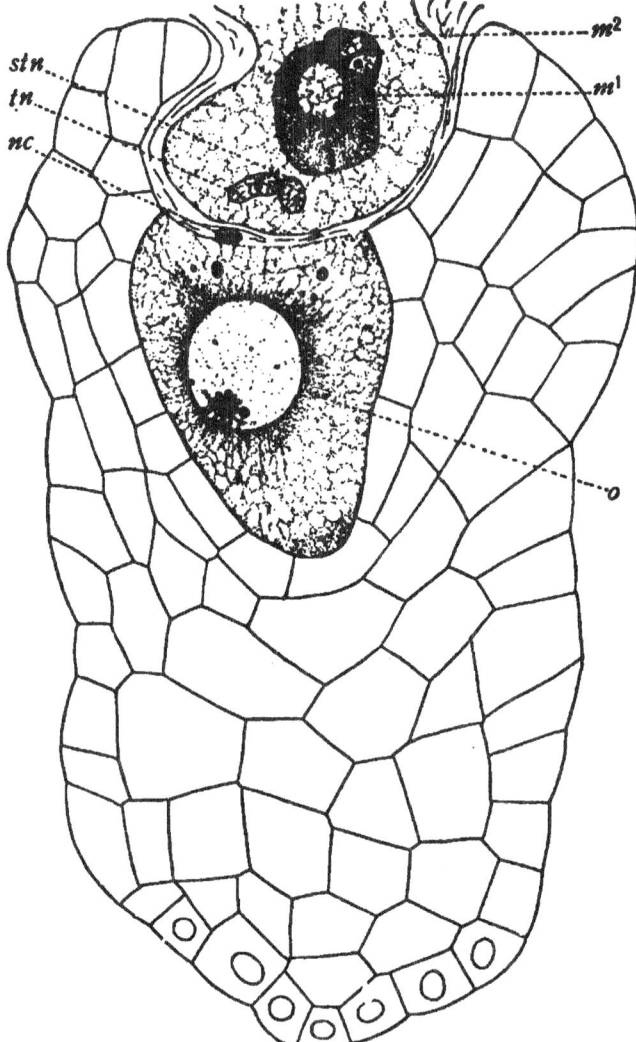

FIG. 479.—Mature female gametophyte of *Torreya*, showing the single archegonium containing a large egg nucleus (*o*), remnants of the neck canal cell nucleus (*nc*), and the tip of the pollen tube containing tube nucleus (*tn*), stalk cell nucleus (*stn*), and the two unequal male cells (m^1, m^2).—After COULTER and LAND.

there is much nucellar tissue to be traversed before the female gametophyte with its archegonia is reached. For the first time, the pollen tube acts as a carrier of the male cells, the body cell, which is to divide, entering the tube and remaining near its tip as it advances through the tip of the nucellus (fig. 479). The tube may advance directly towards the archegonia or it may pursue a devious route, in some cases not reaching the archegonia until during the second season. When an archegonium is reached, its neck is broken through and the contents of the tip of the pollen tube are discharged into the egg (fig. 481).

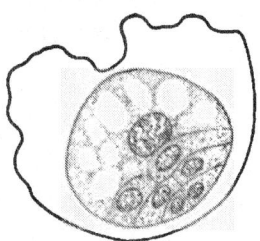

FIG. 480. — Male gametophyte of *Dacrydium* (one of the podocarps) at shedding stage of pollen, showing four vegetative cells, stalk and body cells (formed by the generative cell), and the tube nucleus. — After MISS YOUNG.

Embryo. — In the development of the embryo from the fertilized egg, there is a variable amount of free nuclear division, from four free nuclei (*Torreya*, fig. 482) up to thirty-two, in strong contrast with the very numerous free nuclei appearing in the embryogeny of cycads and of *Ginkgo*. After the free nuclei are formed, walls appear, and the resulting tissue (proembryo) fills the egg. In general, there are about three tiers of cells in the proembryo, the lowest (innermost) one usually consisting of a single cell, so that the proembryo has a general conical outline (fig. 483). An elongation of cells begins in the upper (outermost) tier (fig. 484), and this is continued by the middle tier, so that the terminal cell, which is to form the embryo, is thrust out of the archegonium and

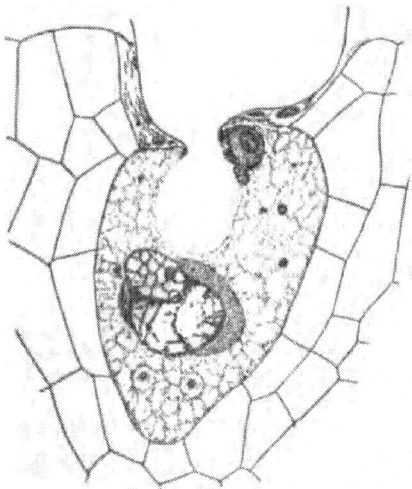

FIG. 481. — Fertilization of *Torreya*: the pollen tube has discharged its contents into the egg, and the male and female nuclei are fusing. — After COULTER and LAND.

218   MORPHOLOGY

deep into the endosperm by the rapidly and extensively elongating suspensor. In the organization of the embryo two cotyledons appear, as in all the preceding groups of gymnosperms. *Torreya* is peculiar in the irregular growth of its endosperm (female gametophyte), which

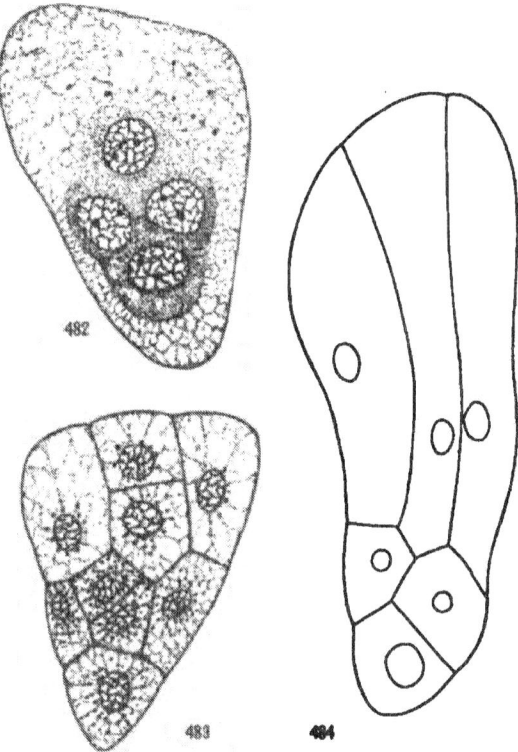

FIGS. 482–484. — Embryo of *Torreya*: 482, the stage of four free nuclei; 483, the completed proembryo (filling the egg), the cells approximately in three tiers; 484, uppermost tier of proembryo elongating to form suspensor. — After COULTER and LAND.

encroaches upon the surrounding nucellar tissue in such a jagged way as to give the appearance in the seed called *rumination*, which may be seen also in sections of nutmegs.

Conclusions. — The Taxaceae have not been traced with certainty below the middle of the Mesozoic, so that it seems to be a comparatively modern group among gymnosperms. It has made a decided advance beyond the groups previously considered in the loss of swimming sperms and the related structures of the ovules, and also in other features; nevertheless, it has also retained certain primitive features, as, for example, the presence of mesarch bundles in the cotyledons and even in the stem. The general relationships of the family will be considered in connection with the Pinaceae.

(b) Pinaceae

General character. — This family, characterized in general by its conelike ovulate strobili and dry seeds, includes the conspicuous

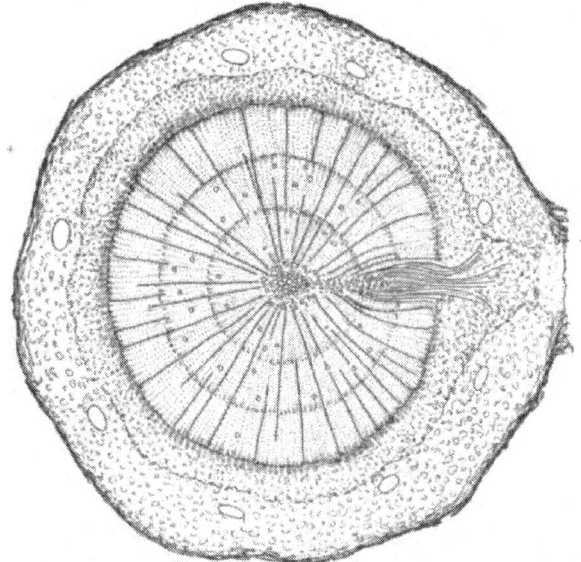

FIG. 485. — Transverse section of a three-year-old twig of *Pinus sylvestris*, showing the small pith, the thick and compact vascular cylinder of secondary wood, and the cortex; radiating lines through the wood represent the narrow pith rays; resin ducts in both wood (small) and cortex (large); to the right is a branch gap in the cylinder.

gymnosperm vegetation of north temperate regions. Four tribes are recognized, as follows:

Abietineae (9 genera and about 140 species), including pines, spruces, firs, hemlocks, larches, and cedars, the large genus being *Pinus*, with about 80 species.

220   MORPHOLOGY

Taxodineae (8 genera and about 15 species), including the characteristic American genera *Sequoia* (redwood) and *Taxodium* (bald cypress).

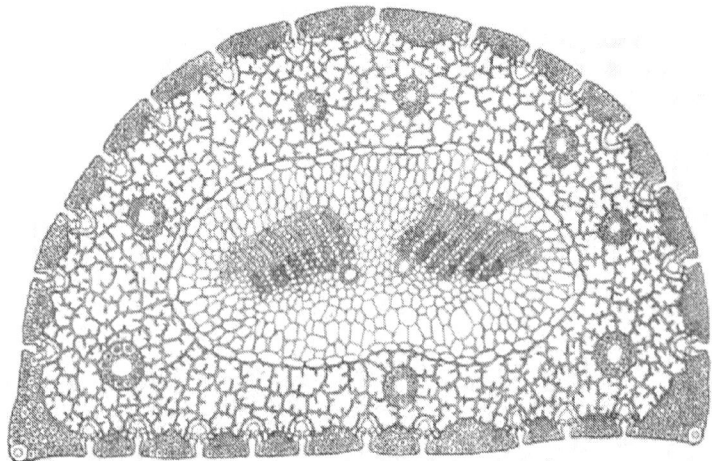

FIG. 486. — Transverse section of a pine needle, showing the epidermis (in which are deeply sunken stomata) underlaid by several layers of heavy-walled cells (sclerenchyma), the mesophyll with characteristic infolded walls and containing resin ducts, the distinct bundle sheath (endodermis) surrounding the vascular region (stele), and the two parallel vascular bundles (xylem directed towards the flat face of the leaf).

Cupressineae (9 genera and about 80 species), including the cypress, arbor vitae (false cedar), and junipers, the large genus being *Juniperus*, with about 30 species. This tribe is peculiar among Coniferales in its opposite (cyclic) leaves.

Araucarineae (2 genera and about 20 species), known as araucarians or araucarian pines, and characteristic of the southern hemisphere.

Sporophyte. — The general habit of the sporophyte body is sufficiently indicated by the familiar forms mentioned above (also see fig. 955). The vascular cylinder, with its endarch bundles, its thick cylinder of secondary wood composed of radially arranged tracheids with bordered pits, is well known (fig. 485). So far as known,

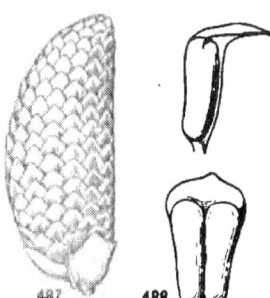

FIGS. 487, 488. — Staminate cone (487) and microsporophylls (488) of pine (the latter in two views), showing the two abaxial sporangia and the sterile tip.

all traces of the mesarch structure have disappeared, even from the cotyledons. The leaves vary from narrow needles (fig. 486) to broad blades and concrescent disks. When the blades are broad, transversely elongated mesophyll cells appear.

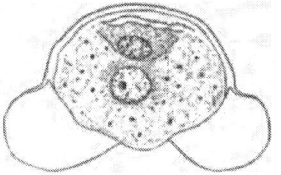

FIG. 489. — The winged and shedding pollen grain of pine, containing an early stage of the male gametophyte. — After COULTER and CHAMBERLAIN.

Staminate strobilus. — The staminate strobilus (fig. 487) is made up of sporophylls (stamens) which are exceedingly variable in form. In general, the stamen is bractlike, with sterile tip and abaxial sporangia (as in cycads and podocarps), the sporangia most frequently two in number (fig. 488), though sometimes more numerous; but in the araucarians

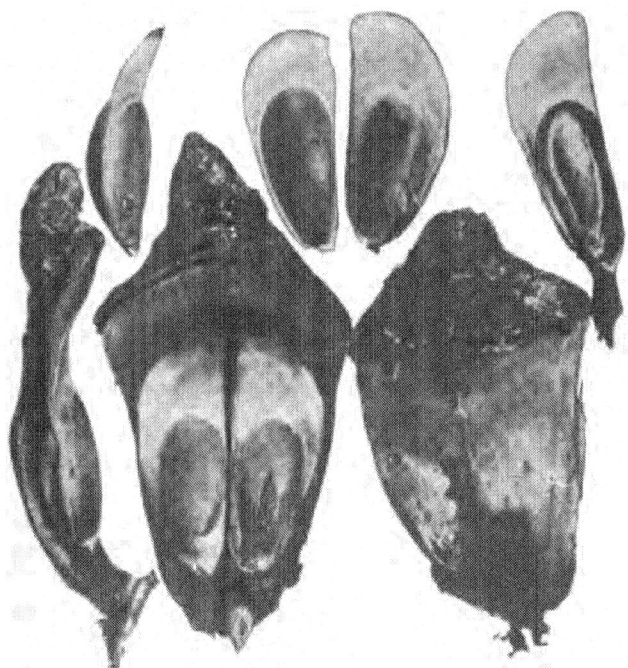

FIG. 490. — Various views of the ovuliferous scales and ovules of pine: on upper surface are borne two ovules (megasporangia) with micropyles directed towards the base of the scale; the seeds become winged by tissue developed from the scale.

the stamen is peltate (as in taxads), and one-sided peltate (as in *Torreya*). The sporangia are developed as usual, and in the Abietineae the pollen grains (microspores) are winged (as in podocarps, fig. 489).

Ovulate strobilus. — The ovulate strobilus of Pinaceae has been the subject of much discussion. In the Abietineae the strobilus is made up of a series of bracts, in the axil of each of which a so-called *ovuliferous scale* appears, which usually bears two ovules whose micropyles are directed towards the base of the scale (fig. 490). In the other tribes the bract and ovuliferous scale are more or less united. The discussion

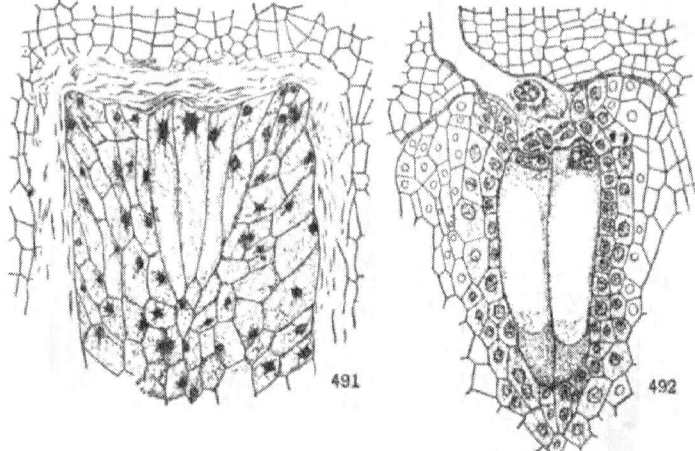

FIGS. 491, 492. — Archegonium complex of *Thuja*: 491, group of archegonium initials; 492, two mature archegonia (reached by a pollen tube, in which the body cell has not yet divided) with a common archegonial chamber and a common archegonial (nutritive) jacket. — After LAND.

referred to has to do with the nature of the ovuliferous scale, and many facts indicate that it represents a fused pair of leaves of a dwarf axillary branch. This means that the ovules are borne in the strobilus on axes of the second order, as in Cordaitales, and that the ovulate strobilus of Pinaceae is a compound strobilus.

Ovule. — The structure of the ovule is as described for Taxaceae, except that the outer fleshy layer does not develop, and the seed is dry; that both sets of vascular strands have been eliminated; and also that there is the same elaborate nutritive mechanism that was described for *Ginkgo*. The development of the ovule and the seed is usually a very prolonged process. Probably in no case is the period between first appearance of the ovule and the shedding of the seed less than two growing seasons; and in some cases the seed is not shed until the third season after the ovule appears, pollination taking place during the second season.

Female gametophyte. — The development of the female gametophyte proceeds as in the previous groups, until an extensive endosperm is formed. At least two distinct regions of the endosperm are always evident; namely, a region of smaller cells towards the micropyle, in which the archegonia develop, and a deeper region of larger cells, which functions as a nutritive region.

Archegonia. — The archegonia range in number from one to sixty, the usual numbers among the Abietineae being three to five. In the Taxodineae and Cupressineae an *archegonium complex* is organized; that is, a group of archegonia is invested by a common archegonial jacket and has a common archegonial chamber (figs. 491, 492). The necks of the archegonia are remarkably variable in the number of cells, ranging from the ordinary two-celled neck to that in *Pinus*, which consists usually

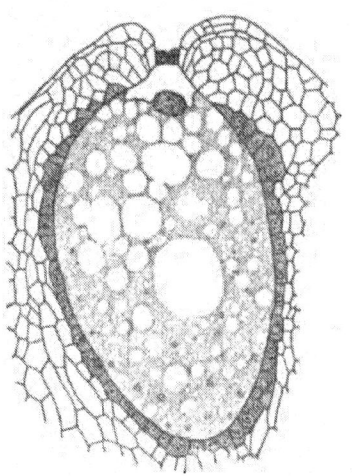

FIG. 493. — Archegonium of *Pinus*, showing two neck cells, the central cell (whose nucleus is just about to divide to form ventral canal and egg nuclei), and the archegonial jacket. — After COULTER and CHAMBERLAIN.

of two tiers with four cells in each tier, but may reach four tiers with as many as sixteen cells in each tier. In the Abietineae a definite ventral canal cell is formed (fig. 493), but in Taxodineae and Cupressineae only a ventral nucleus appears (as in Taxaceae); while in Araucarineae the situation is unknown.

Male gametophyte. — The male gametophyte is quite variable as to the number of vegetative (prothallial) cells, but the condition is usually constant in each tribe. In Abietineae there are two vegetative cells, both of which are ephemeral (figs. 494-500); in Taxodineae and Cupressineae there are no vegetative cells (as in taxads); while in Arau-

224   MORPHOLOGY

...ineae the vegetative cells are numerous (as in podocarps). As in Taxaceae, the generative cell divides into stalk and body cells, and the body cell passes into the pollen tube, where either it divides into two

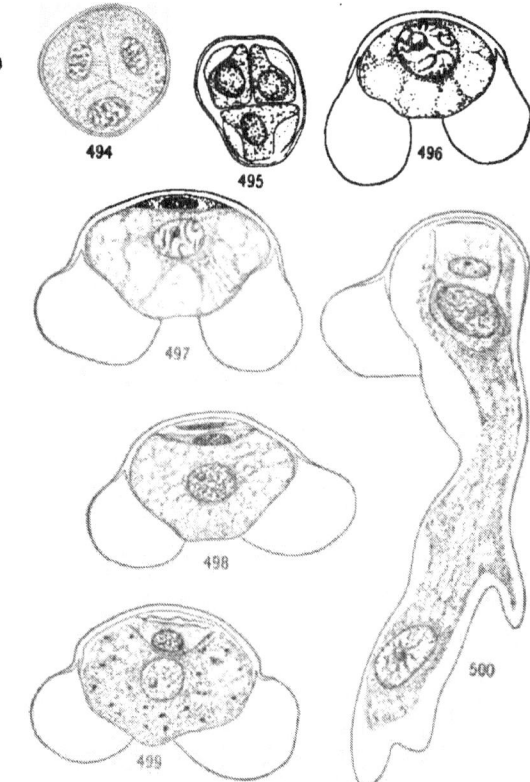

Figs. 494–500. — Male gametophyte of *Pinus:* 494, the forming tetrad of spores (pollen grains) within the mother cell; 495, young pollen grains forming wings; 496, a single mature pollen grain; 497, first vegetative cell cut off; 498, second vegetative cell cut off (first one disorganizing); 499, division to generative cell and tube nucleus (both vegetative cells disorganized) (shedding stage); 500, growth of the pollen tube, into which the tube nucleus has descended; division of generative cell into stalk (upper) and body cells. — After COULTER and CHAMBERLAIN.

cells (male cells), or its nucleus divides into two nuclei (male nuclei). The male cells in Abietineae are generally unequal, a condition apparently connected with the fact that only one functions; but in Taxodineae and Cupressineae the male cells are equal, since both may function by the tube entering the chamber of an archegonium complex. The tip of the pollen tube, just before fertilization, contains the two male cells and also (usually in advance of them) the stalk and tube nuclei (fig. 501).

Fertilization. — The general features of fertilization are as described for the Taxaceae, the pollen tube acting as a carrier of the male cells to the archegonia, in addition to its old function as an haustorium.

Embryo. — In the development of the embryo (figs. 502–509), free nuclear division occurs until four to sixteen nuclei are formed, and sooner or later become placed at the bottom of the egg. With the next nuclear division walls appear, and division of cells continues until three or four tiers of cells are formed, the tiers containing approximately the same number of cells. This proembryo, therefore, by no means fills the cavity of the egg, as in the preceding groups of gymnosperms, the greater bulk of the egg being a large reservoir of surplus food material.

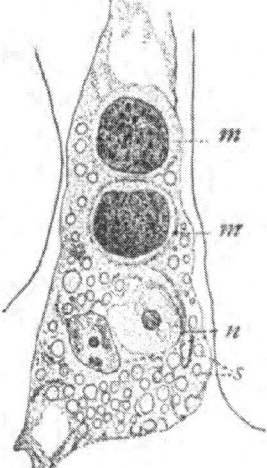

FIG. 501. — Tip of pollen tube of *Pinus*, just before fertilization, containing the two male cells (*m*), stalk and tube nuclei (*n*), and abundant starch grains (*s*). — After COULTER.

The proembryo of *Pinus* may be used to illustrate the general structure of the proembryo and the functions of its different regions (figs. 502–509). This proembryo is made up of four tiers of cells, with four cells in each tier. The uppermost tier consists of four cells, open (without walls) towards the food reservoir of the egg. The next tier, which is the part of the proembryo that remains within the egg, constitutes the so-called *rosette*. The third tier of four cells forms the suspensor, each cell elongating enormously, so that the four-celled suspensor becomes a long and tortuous filament. At the tip of the suspensor, thrust by its elongation deep into the endosperm, is the lowest tier of four cells, which forms the embryo (figs. 509, 510). All four of these cells may form one embryo, or each of the four cells may form a separate embryo. In any event, although several eggs may begin to form embryos, one embryo soon dominates and the others disappear.

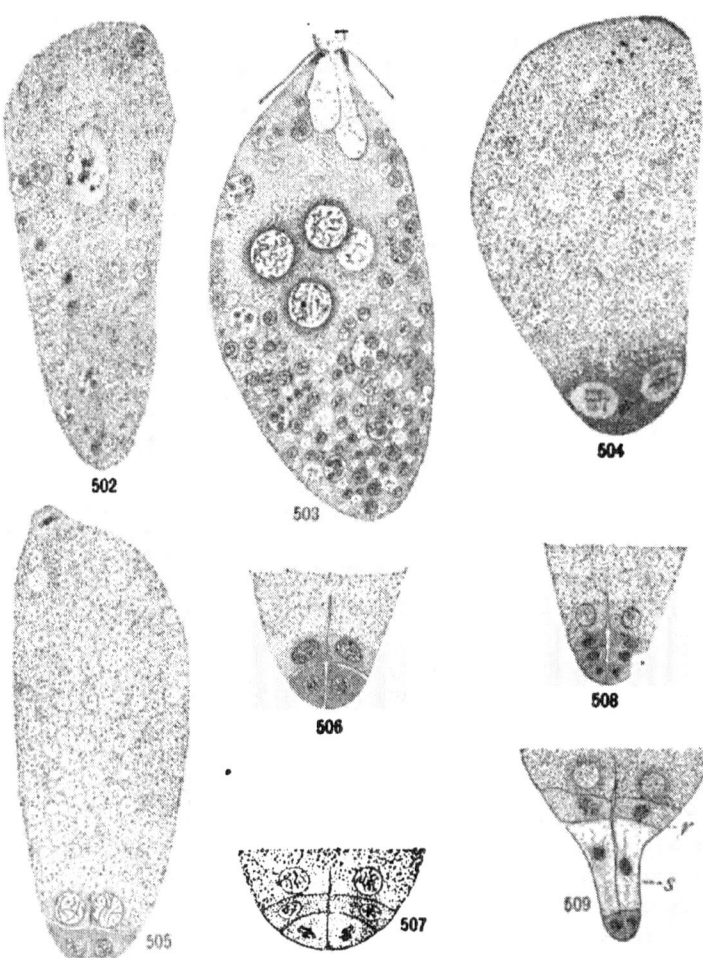

FIGS. 502-509. — Development of embryo of *Pinus*: 502, fusion of male and female nuclei in the large egg; 503, four free nuclei (one in background) derived from fusion nucleus; 504, the four nuclei (two visible) at base of egg and dividing; 505, eight-nucleate stage (four nuclei visible); 506, the same a little further advanced; 507, next division, resulting in twelve cells in three tiers; 508, completed proembryo (four tiers of cells, uppermost open towards the general cytoplasm of the egg); 509, beginning of suspensor-formation (s), leaving within the egg the rosette cells (r), and thrusting out of it the four tip cells, which will form the embryo. — After COULTER and CHAMBERLAIN.

The cotyledons are not steadily two in number, as in the preceding groups of gymnosperms, but vary from two (mostly so in Cupressineae and Araucarineae) to as many as fifteen (in the Abietineae). It is because the pines and their allies are the most familiar gymnosperms that gymnosperms are commonly described as *polycotyledonous;* but it should be remembered that the occurrence of more than two cotyledons is a feature of only two tribes of Coniferales (Abietineae and Taxodineae), and that two cotyledons occur in some of the members even of these tribes.

Conclusions. — It seems most reasonable to conclude that the Coniferales have been derived from the paleozoic Cordaitales, which also gave rise to the Ginkgoales. The Coniferales, however, have retained fewer primitive characters than the Ginkgoales, and are especially noteworthy in having lost the swimming sperms.

In comparing the six tribes of Coniferales, the testimony as to their relationships is very confusing. The testimony obtained from the geological record is necessarily incomplete, but so far as it is available the relative ages of the tribes are as follows: The Abietineae have been traced to the Paleozoic, and in all probability are the oldest of the Coniferales. The Araucarineae have been traced through the Mesozoic, in which period they were very abundant; and in all probability they are but little younger than the Abietineae. The Taxodineae and Cupressineae are recognizable in the Lower Mesozoic; while the Taxaceae (Podocarpineae and Taxineae) are not known below the middle Mesozoic. It may be that this sequence indicates the actual sequence of the tribes, but it is

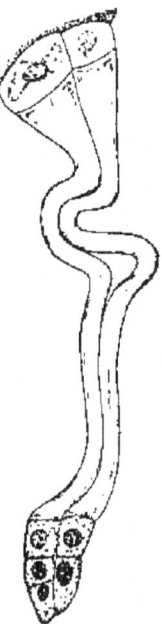

FIG. 510. — Embryo of *Pinus*, showing (above) two cells of the rosette, two cells of the suspensor, and an early stage of the terminal embryo. — After COULTER and CHAMBERLAIN.

hard to reconcile it with the morphological characters detailed above. In any event, the fact that Coniferales as a whole have developed from the Cordaitales seems to be sufficiently clear, and is all that need concern the elementary student of the group. It should be remembered that origin from Cordaitales means also a connection through them with the ferns, and therefore that all gymnosperms have descended from ferns.

MORPHOLOGY

(7) GNETALES.

General character. — This group comprises three very distinct genera: *Ephedra*, with about fifty species distributed throughout the arid regions of the Mediterranean basin and adjacent Asia, and also in the arid regions

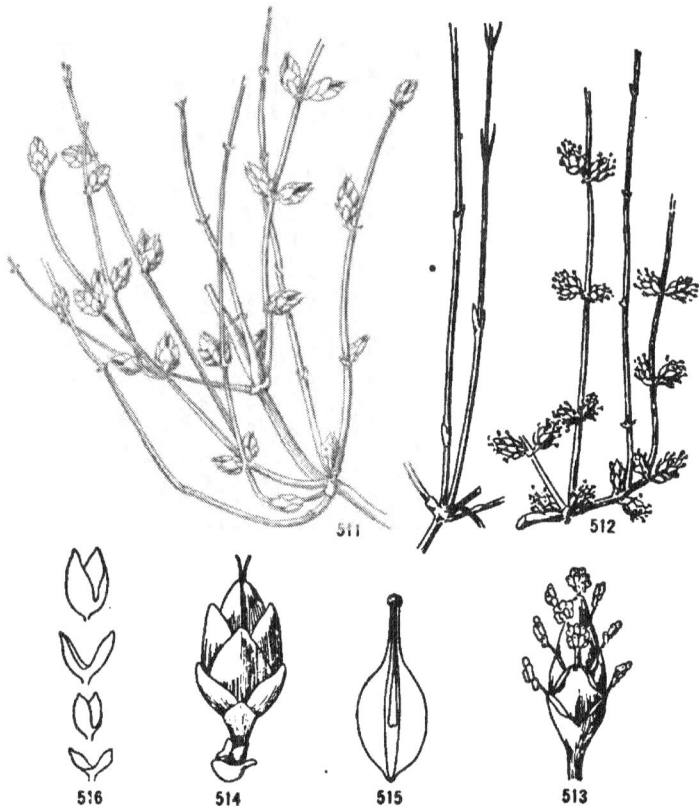

FIGS. 511-516. — *Ephedra:* 511, branches bearing ovulate strobili; 512, branches bearing staminate strobili; 513, staminate strobilus, showing staminate "flowers" in axils of bracts; 514, ovulate strobilus; 515, an ovulate "flower"; 516, decussating bracts of the ovulate strobilus. — After WATSON.

of western North America and South America; *Tumboa* (often called *Welwitschia*), represented by a single species in the arid districts of western South Africa; and *Gnetum*, with about fifteen species distributed throughout the tropics of both hemispheres. Gnetales have always attracted attention from the fact that in certain characters they resemble angiosperms more nearly than do the other gymnosperms.

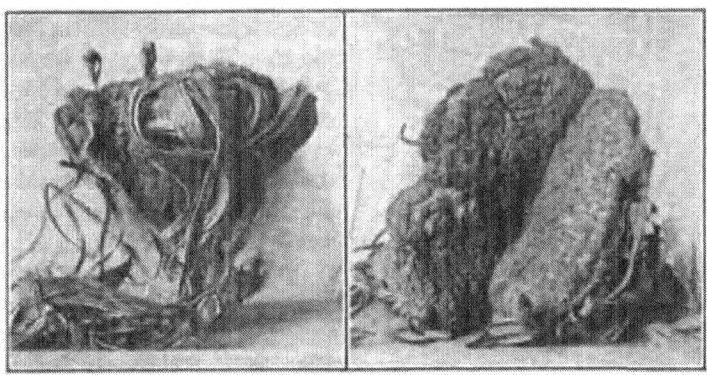

FIG. 517. — *Tumboa*, showing the heavy conical body and the two-lobed crown bearing two broad parallel-veined leaves (in the photograph split into shreds) and strobilus-bearing branches.

Sporophyte. — The species of *Ephedra* are straggling shrubs, with long-jointed and fluted green stems, and scalelike opposite leaves forming at each joint a two-toothed sheath (figs. 511, 512, 975). *Tumboa* has a huge, woody, turnip-shaped body, whose crown bears a single pair of elongated, strap-shaped, parallel-veined, and persistent leaves (fig. 517). The species of *Gnetum* are small trees or woody twiners with leathery, net-veined, opposite leaves, resembling those of dicotyledons (fig. 522). It will be observed that a constant character of the group is the cyclic (opposite) leaves, a feature found among Coniferales only in the Cupressineae.

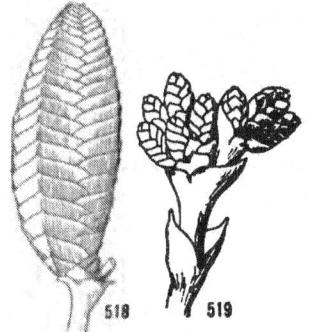

FIGS. 518, 519. — Ovulate (518) and staminate (519) strobili of *Tumboa*. — 518, after LE MAIOUT and DECAISNE; 519, after HOOKER.

Vascular anatomy. — It is in their vascular anatomy that the Gnetales show a striking angiosperm character. The secondary wood does not consist exclusively of tracheids with bordered pits, as in the other gymnosperm groups, but in addition to these gymnosperm tracheids there are also true vessels of the angiosperm type.

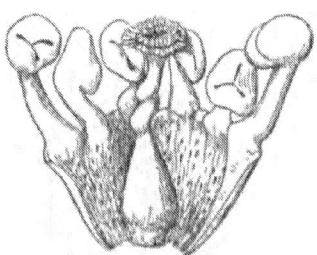

Fig. 520.—*Tumboa*: staminate "flower" (with bracts removed), showing the six trisporangiate stamens united below, and the sterile ovule with long and twisted micropylar tube.— Adapted from HOOKER.

Staminate strobili.— The staminate strobili are made up of pairs of decussate bracts, which are imbricate in *Ephedra* (fig. 513) and *Tumboa* (fig. 519), and connate in *Gnetum* (fig. 523). In the axils of these bracts are the so-called staminate flowers. In *Ephedra* and *Gnetum* a staminate flower consists of an axis bearing at its tip two or more sporangia (figs. 513, 524), and invested below by two or four bracts, which are free or coalescent in a tube. In *Tumboa* the structure is very different and quite remarkable. Within the investing bracts there is a whorl of six united (*monadelphous*) stamens, each of whose free tips bears three sporangia; and within the cycle of stamens there is a central (terminal) sterile ovule, whose remarkably long micropylar tube is spirally coiled and broadly flaring at the tip (fig. 520). This remarkable structure indicates that the ancestors of *Tumboa* had flowers that contained functioning stamens and ovules, and that in the case of *Tumboa* staminate and ovulate flowers arose by the disappearance of ovules in certain flowers, and of stamens in others. No such close association of stamens and ovules is known among gymnosperms, except in Bennettitales, where they occur in the same strobilus.

In attempting to interpret the staminate strobilus of the Gnetales, it is evident that the microsporangia are borne upon secondary axes (which are the so-called flowers), and therefore the strobilus is compound. In Cordaitales and in certain of the Coniferales there are compound ovulate strobili, but only in Gnetales do com-

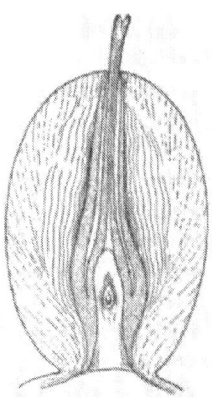

Fig. 521.—*Tumboa*: ovulate "flower," showing the enveloping and winged bracts, the two integuments (the inner forming the long micropylar tube), and the nucellus containing the embryo sac.— Adapted from STRASBURGER.

pound staminate strobili occur. The bractlets of this secondary axis, which invest the stamens, were interpreted as representing the *perianth* of a flower, and the presence of a perianth was regarded as another striking angiosperm character of Gnetales; but if these bracts represent a perianth, those in the compound ovulate strobilus of Cordaitales also represent a perianth, as well as all bractlets on secondary axes of strobili. To extend the term *perianth* to include these vague conditions

FIGS. 522-524. — *Gnetum latifolium:* 522, branch bearing staminate strobili and the characteristic leaves; 523, part of staminate strobilus, showing the "connate" bracts, and in their axils numerous staminate "flowers"; 524, a single staminate "flower." — After BLUME.

is to make it difficult to define, and perhaps is to mislead as to the origin of the perianth of angiosperms.

Ovulate strobilus. — The ovulate strobili have the same general structure as the staminate, the so-called ovulate flowers arising in the axils of the bracts (figs. 514, 518, 526, 527). There is the same perianth structure observed in the staminate flowers, and in *Tumboa* there is said to appear outside of the ovule the rudiments of a stamen set.

232	MORPHOLOGY

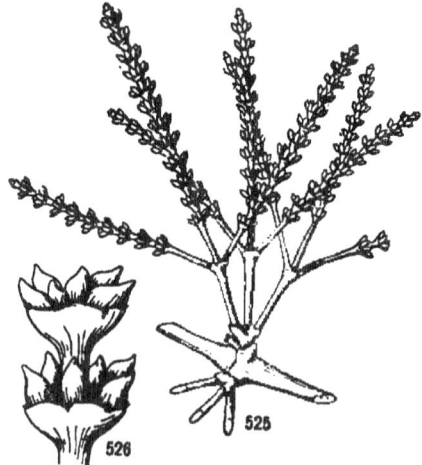

FIGS. 525, 526.—*Gnetum latifolium*: 525, branches bearing ovulate strobili; 526, part of ovulate strobilus.—After BLUME.

Ovule.—The ovule has two integuments, the inner one forming a long tubular micropyle, which is a marked feature of the group (figs. 521, 528, 530). The nucellus has the usual gymnosperm feature of a heavy mass of sterile tissue overlying the megaspore mother cell (and later the embryo sac). In all the preceding groups of gymnosperms, except Coniferales, this overlying tissue is beaked and contains a pollen chamber, a structure associated with the presence of swimming sperms. In *Ephedra* a remarkable funnel-shaped pollen chamber is developed by the breaking down of the nucellar tissue (fig. 528), which extends to the embryo sac and exposes the necks of the archegonia; hence in pollination the pollen grains may come to rest in contact with the archegonium necks. In *Gnetum* the tip of the nucellus is more or less disorganized, and this is the only trace of a pollen chamber (fig. 530); while in *Tumboa* there is not even a trace.

Female gametophyte.—The structure of the female gametophyte in Gnetales is of great interest, for there is an evident approach towards the angiosperm condition.

FIG. 527.—Ovulate strobili of *Gnetum*, with fleshy seeds maturing.

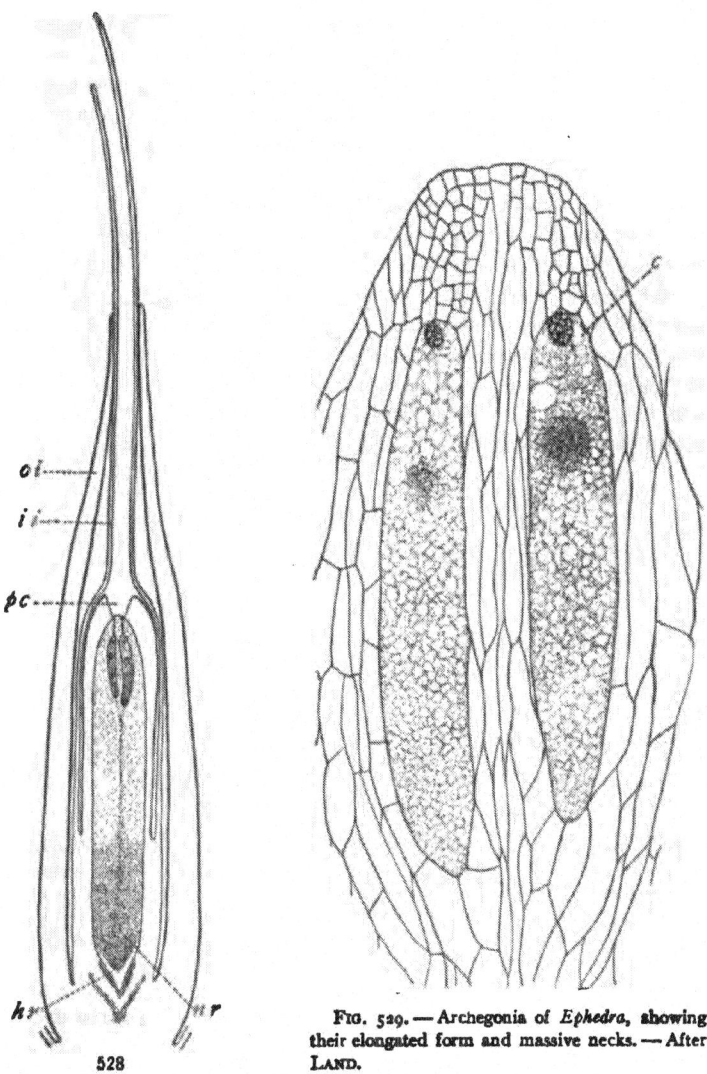

Fig. 529.—Archegonia of *Ephedra*, showing their elongated form and massive necks. — After LAND.

Fig. 528.—Diagrammatic section of ovule of *Ephedra*, showing outer integument (*oi*), inner integument (*ii*) forming the long micropylar tube, the remarkable pollen-chamber (*pc*), and the elongated female gametophyte (within the embryo sac) with two long-necked archegonia. — After LAND.

The three genera differ widely in this regard, and therefore must be considered separately.

Ephedra. — The female gametophyte is developed as in other gymnosperms, with free nuclear division (up to 256 nuclei), parietal wall formation, centripetal growth, and differentiation of the endosperm into distinct micropylar and antipodal regions. In this case, however, the antipodal tissue (nutritive) is relatively small-celled and compact, and the micropylar tissue is more loosely organized and has thinner walls. In this loose micropylar tissue usually two archegonia are formed, their very long, many-tiered necks extending to the pollen chamber described

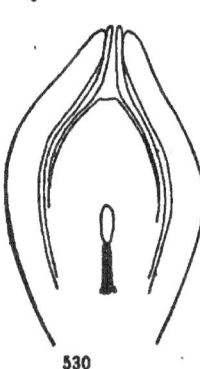
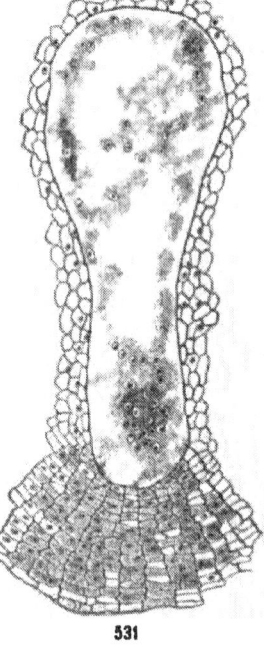

FIGS. 530, 531. — *Gnetum Gnemon:* 530, diagrammatic section of ovule, showing the two integuments (inner one forming the micropylar tube), nucellus with disorganized tip, and deep-placed embryo sac, beneath which is a mass of feeding (glandular) tissue; 531, enlarged view of same embryo sac (ready for fertilization), in which the female gametophyte consists of free nuclei (each a potential egg), and below which is the mass of feeding tissue. — After COULTER.

above (figs. 528, 529). In the organization of the egg, a ventral nucleus is cut off, and not a ventral cell.

Tumboa. — The female gametophyte is developed as in *Ephedra* as far as wall formation; but in the differentiation of the endosperm into two regions (one fourth micropylar and three fourths antipodal) there is very incomplete wall formation. As a consequence, the cells of the antipodal region are multinucleate, and those of the micropylar region become so (two to five-nucleate). Since there is no uninucleate cell in the micropylar tissue, there is no archegonium initial, and hence no archegonium. Instead, several of the multinucleate cells develop what have been called *prothallial tubes*, which penetrate the overlying nucellar tissue, and into them the nuclei pass, each nucleus being a potential egg nucleus. It is at this point that the archegonium disappears; which seems to be associated with the fact that the egg nuclei are differentiated before wall formation in the endosperm has been completed.

Gnetum. — In this genus there is free nuclear division as before, but wall formation does not occur, so that the embryo sac at the time of fertilization contains only free nuclei (fig. 531), and each one of these free nuclei is a potential egg nucleus. This

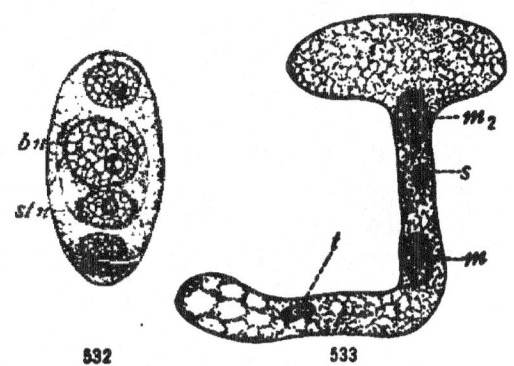

FIGS. 532, 533. — Male gametophyte of *Ephedra*: 532, pollen grain in shedding stage, containing two vegetative nuclei (below), stalk (*stn*) and body (*bn*) nuclei, and tube nucleus (above); 533, completed male gametophyte (after beginning of pollen tube), showing in the tube the male cells (*m*), stalk nucleus (*s*), and tube nucleus (*t*). — After LAND.

is the general angiosperm condition. Below the antipodal end of the sac a remarkable nutritive (glandular) tissue is developed.

Male gametophyte. — The male gametophyte of Gnetales is known only in *Ephedra*. In its shedding condition the pollen grain of *Ephedra* contains two persistent vegetative cells, and conspicuous stalk, body, and tube nuclei (fig. 532). In this condition the pollen grain rests on the exposed archegonium necks, and before the pollen tube is formed the body nucleus divides into two equal male nuclei (fig. 533).

Fertilization. — The phenomena of fertilization vary with the structure of the female gametophyte. In *Ephedra* the pollen tube breaks through the long and massive neck of the archegonium (fig. 529); in *Tumboa* it comes into contact with the prothallial tubes that are penetrating the overlying nucellar tissue; while in *Gnetum* it enters the embryo sac and encounters the free egg nuclei (fig. 531).

Embryo. — The development of the embryo of Gnetales shows a remarkable modification of the usual gymnosperm method, and varies in accordance with the structure of the gametophyte in each genus. In all cases the embryo has two cotyledons.

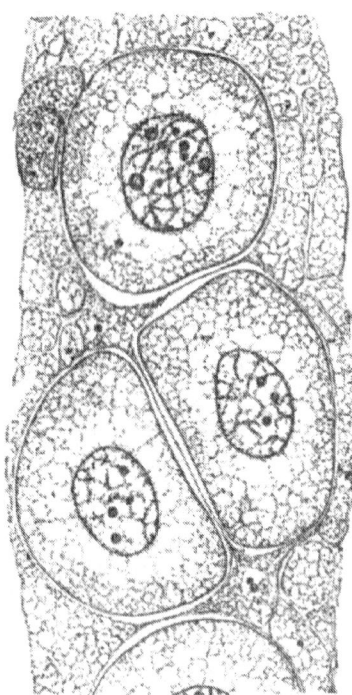

FIG. 534. — Embryo of *Ephedra*: three of the eight free proembryonal cells. — After LAND.

Ephedra. — In *Ephedra* there is free nuclear division within the egg until eight free nuclei appear, and then these nuclei enter into the organization of eight free cells (the proembryonal cells, fig. 534). Two or more of these independent proembryonal cells may function as follows: the nucleus divides; the cell develops a prolongation like a pollen tube (fig. 535), which penetrates the surrounding endosperm, and into its tip one of the nuclei passes. Later the tip of this tube, containing the nucleus, is cut off by a wall (fig. 536), and from this cell the embryo is developed (fig. 537).

Tumboa. — In *Tumboa* the fusion nucleus (within the prothallial tube) is used in the formation of a free and independent cell, which then behaves as do the independent proembryonal cells of *Ephedra*. It should be noted that in this case the stage of free nuclear division in embryo formation has disappeared, and the first division of the fertilized egg is accompanied by wall formation, which is an angiosperm condition.

Gnetum. — In *Gnetum* the fertilized eggs in the micropylar chamber of the embryo sac behave as in the case of *Tumboa*, and as do the proembryonal cells of *Ephedra*, the tubular prolongation penetrating the endosperm tissue, which finally replaces the nucellar tissue. In both *Tumboa* and *Gnetum*, therefore, the general behavior of the angiosperm egg has been reached.

Conclusions. — It is evident that Gnetales show remarkable angiosperm tendencies, which may be summed up as follows : true vessels in

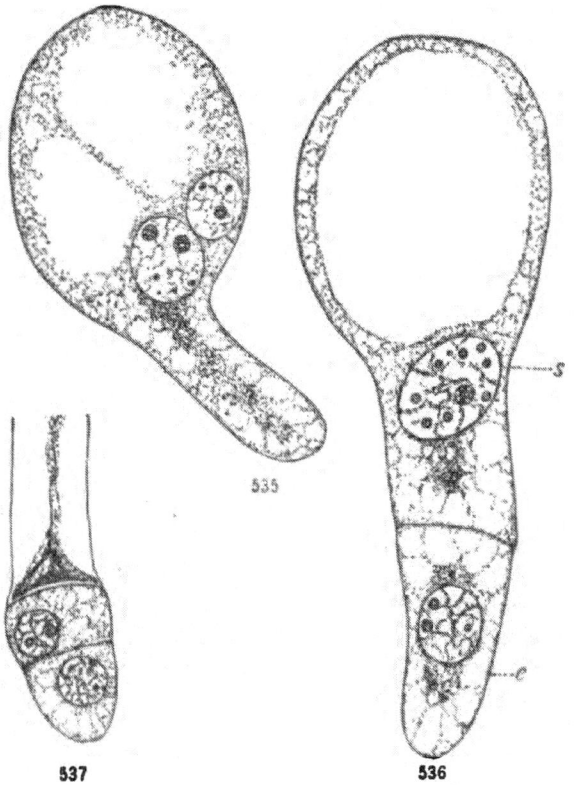

FIGS. 535–537. — Embryo of *Ephedra:* 535, one of the proembryonal cells whose nucleus has divided and which has begun to form a tubular elongation; 536, both nuclei in the tubular elongation and a wall formed between them, one cell (*s*) elongating to form the suspensor, the other (*e*) to form the embryo; 537, embryo beginning to form at the end of the suspensor. — After LAND.

the secondary wood; the final elimination of archegonia and the organization of independent eggs; and an embryogeny in which free nuclear division in the fertilized egg has disappeared. The elimination of archegonia seems to be associated with the tendency to differentiate the egg nucleus earlier and earlier in the history of the gametophyte, and when this differentiation occurs before wall formation, archegonia are no longer possible. The compound strobili of Gnetales also, both staminate and ovulate, with their more or less differentiated bractlets investing the stamens and ovules, suggest the inflorescence of certain angiosperms.

There is no sure record of Gnetales as fossils, and therefore all the evidence available indicates that they are relatively modern among gymnosperms. *Ephedra* is evidently related to the Coniferales; and *Tumboa* and *Gnetum* are just as evidently related to *Ephedra;* so that it is altogether probable that the Gnetales represent a somewhat modern offshoot from the Coniferales.

B. ANGIOSPERMS

General character. — The angiosperms represent the culmination of the plant kingdom, and are plants not only of the highest rank, but also of the greatest importance to man. Probably they constitute also the greatest group of plants in the number of species, which is approximately 125,000. When this vast assemblage of species is contrasted with the 450 living gymnosperms and the 4000 living pteridophytes, it is evident that the angiosperms form by far the largest part of our vascular vegetation. It is also the most modern vascular group, being absolutely unknown in the Paleozoic, and not very abundant until late in the Mesozoic. The conspicuous superficial character of the group, as contrasted with gymnosperms, is implied in the name, the ovule being enclosed by the *carpel* (megasporophyll), so that the pollen grain does not reach the ovule, but rests on the surface of the carpel.

The great groups. — The two primary divisions of angiosperms are the *Dicotyledons* and the *Monocotyledons*, and the four prominent characters used in distinguishing them are as follows: (1) the embryo of a monocotyledon has a single terminal cotyledon and a laterally developed stem tip; while the embryo of a dicotyledon has a terminal stem tip and laterally developed cotyledons (usually two); (2) in the stem of a monocotyledon the vascular bundles are scattered; while in a dicotyledon they are arranged so as to form a vascular cylinder enclosing a pith; (3) the leaves of monocotyledons have a closed venation, that is, veinlets do not end freely in the margin, which is therefore entire; while the leaves of dicotyledons have an open venation, veinlets ending freely in the margin, which is often variously toothed or lobed; (4) the flowers of monocotyledons have their members in sets of three; while the flowers of dicotyledons have their members in sets of five or four.

These characters are by no means of equal value, the character of the embryo being the only one without serious exception. There are monocotyledons with vascular cylinders, with open venation, and with flowers not in threes; and there are dicotyledons with scattered vascular bundles, with closed venation, and with flowers in threes. It is not so much a single character, therefore, that distinguishes a monocotyledon from a dicotyledon, as a combination of characters.

There are recognized also two great divisions of dicotyledons, the *Archichlamydeae* and the *Sympetalae*, and the conspicuous character which distinguishes them is implied in their names. The Archichlamydeae have either no petals or petals entirely separate from one another (free), and this is recognized as the primitive condition of the perianth (*chlamys*); while in the Sympetalae the petals develop so as to form tubes of various kinds. This distinction is superficial and breaks down in certain cases, but it holds generally and is convenient.

These three great groups of angiosperms are related to one another as follows: the Archichlamydeae are recognized as including the most primitive angiosperms; from the more primitive Archichlamydeae the monocotyledons probably have arisen as a special branch; while from the more advanced Archichlamydeae the Sympetalae have arisen and are clearly the highest group of angiosperms. It will be necessary to keep in mind these three groups and their relationships in order to understand the following discussion.

STEM

A description of the general structure of a vascular stem has been deferred to angiosperms, whose stem may be taken as an illustration of the general features of all vascular stems.

Elongation. — The tip of the stem is the *growing point*, consisting of a group of very actively dividing (*meristematic*) cells. Among pteridophytes this group of meristematic cells is usually represented by a single apical cell. All the tissues of the stem are derived from the cells of the growing point, whose activity very soon results in the appearance of three more or less distinct generative regions: (1) *dermatogen*, which later forms the *epidermis;* (2) *periblem*, which later forms the *cortex;* and (3) *plerome*, a central cylinder which forms the *stele*, in which the vascular elements appear (fig. 538).

Epidermis. — The dermatogen passes into the epidermis, which is usually a single layer of protective cells closely interlocked and with relatively impervious walls, but pierced by stomata. In case the stem increases in diameter, as in dicotyledonous trees, the epidermis is usually ruptured and destroyed, and another protective layer is developed by the cortex, as described below.

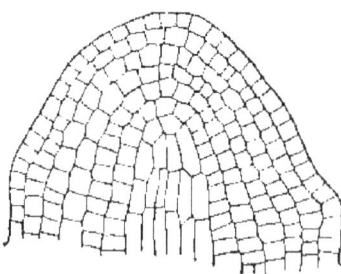

FIG. 538. — Stem tip of *Hippuris* (a dicotyledon), showing dermatogen (outermost layer), periblem (the five layers beneath the dermatogen), and the plerome (central region of more elongated cells). — After DEBARY.

Cortex. — The periblem produces the cortex (figs. 539, 541), which is a hollow cylinder of living cells. It is exceedingly variable in structure, but is characterized by containing chlorophyll tissue abutting against the epidermis; and if it is thick enough, there is also a deeper region of the cortex free from chlorophyll. The layer of cortical cells abutting against the stele often forms a very distinct bounding layer, like an inner epidermis, and is called the *endodermis* (fig. 379). In the cortex, strands of fibrous cells may be developed, and cavities or canals of various kinds may occur.

In case the stem increases in diameter, the cortex develops a meristematic layer known as the *phellogen* or *cork cambium* (fig. 539), which forms *cork cells*, a very impervious kind of cell (see p. 318). Continuous activity of the phellogen within results in an increasing thickness of the sheet of cork cells without, and such sheets form a most efficient protection. The chlorophyll tissue beneath the cork cells maintains connection with the air for a time through special structures, called *lenticels* (fig. 540), interrupting

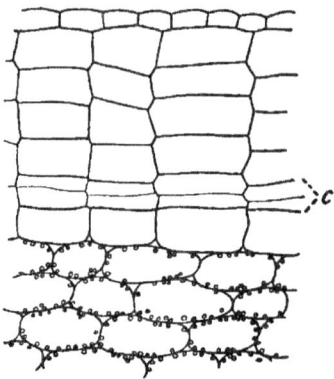

FIG. 539. — Transverse section of outer portion of cortex of a geranium, showing the cork cambium or phellogen (*c*) cutting off layers of cork cells (four such layers beneath epidermis); below are chlorophyll-containing cells of the cortex.

SPERMATOPHYTES

the cork. The phellogen layer may be developed at various depths in the cortex, and all the cortical cells outside the cork die, being cut off from the supplies within.

Stele. — The plerome cylinder behind the growing point passes below into the stele containing the vascular elements. The outermost layer of stelar cells, abutting against the endodermis, is called the *pericycle*. The first xylem elements to appear are small in caliber, and of the *spiral* kind (fig. 542), a kind especially adapted to a region of rapid elongation. These groups of spiral vessels are called the *protoxylem* (fig. 541), and the later vascular elements form the *metaxylem* (fig. 541). In case there is a cambium, a *secondary xylem* is

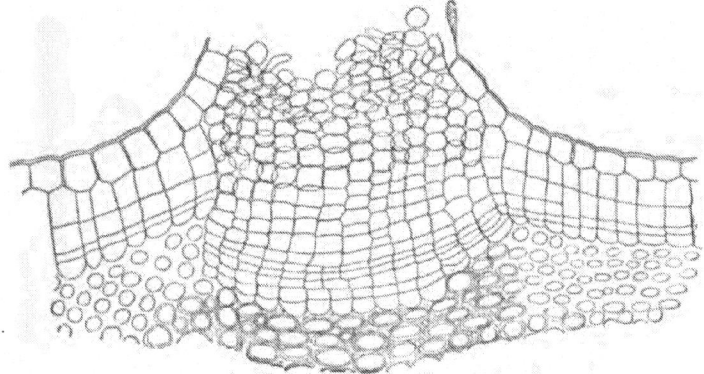

FIG. 540. — Section of the lenticel of elder. — After STRASBURGER.

formed. In neither metaxylem nor secondary xylem do vessels of the spiral kind usually occur, but vessels of larger caliber (fig. 541), notably the *pitted vessels* or *dotted ducts* so called on account of the thin spots left in a generally thickened wall (fig. 544). In gymnosperms (except Gnetales) there are no true vessels (*tracheae*), but *tracheids* (single cells tapering at each end) with thin spots in the wall, so characteristic in appearance as to be called bordered pits (fig. 547). In pteridophytes, this same kind of xylem element is represented by tracheids with transversely elongated pits, known as *scalariform* (ladder-like) vessels (fig. 548).

In forming tracheids or tracheae, the protoplasts of the living cells gradually disappear as the characteristic thickening of the wall is formed, so that the completed vessels are dead cells. Tracheids are single cells thus formed; while tracheae (true vessels) are developed by a fusion of cells end to end, so that a continuous tube of considerable length may be formed. A system of tracheae always ends in tracheids, which are therefore at least the end cells of any vascular system.

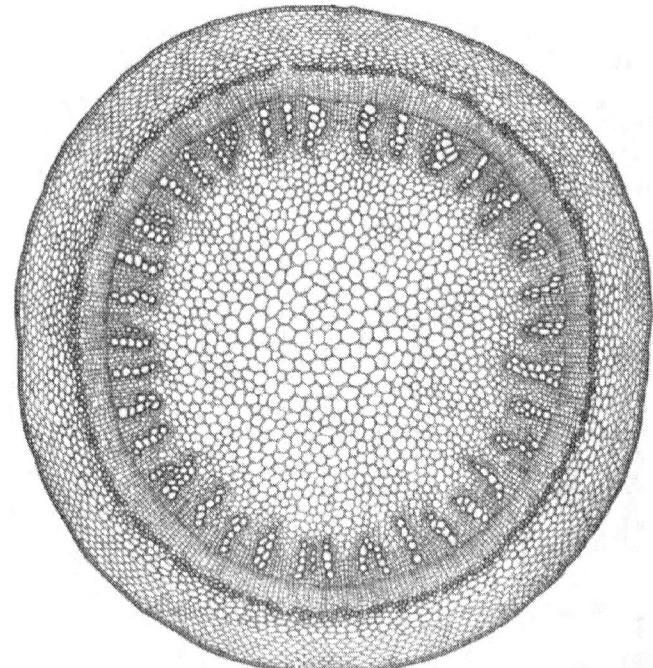

FIG. 541. — Transverse section of vascular cylinder of a young dicotyledon (*Ricinus*): the regions, beginning outside, are epidermis (single layer of cells); cortex (a zone of several layers), including an almost continuous band of fibrous cells (heavy walls); a zone of several layers (the outer ones being phloem, the inner cambium); the zone of xylem strands (separated by pith rays, the innermost vessels in each strand being protoxylem, the outer and larger ones metaxylem); and the pith.

The characteristic element of the phloem is the *sieve vessel* (fig. 545), so named because in the wall there occur definite areas full of perforations known as *sieve plates* (fig. 546). These vessels also arise by cell fusion, as do the tracheae.

The vascular system. — The vascular system of dicotyledons and of monocotyledons is so different that the two groups must be considered separately.

SPERMATOPHYTES

Dicotyledons. — The vascular system of dicotyledons is by no means uniform, nor should it be expected in so large a group, but its general features can be indicated.

In the mature stem the vascular system consists of a hollow cylinder composed of vascular bundles and inclosing the pith (a siphonostele) (figs. 541, 549). Traversing the vascular cylinder from the pith to the cortex, and hence separating the bundles, are the pith rays. The bundles are collateral endarch, and also *open;* that is, there is a *cambium* between the xylem and phloem strands which forms secondary xylem

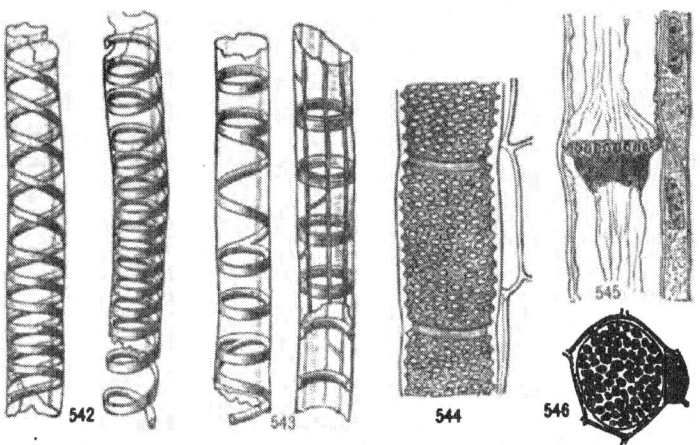

FIGS. 542–546. — Vascular elements of an angiosperm: 542, spiral vessels (of protoxylem); 543, spiral and annular vessels; 544, dotted duct (characteristic of metaxylem and secondary xylem); 545, sieve vessel (of phloem) with companion cell; 546, sieve plate, with section of companion cell. — 542, 543, after BONNIER and SABLON; 544, after DEBARY; 545, 546, after STRASBURGER.

and phloem. The secondary wood (xylem) differs from that of the gymnosperms in containing true vessels (*tracheae*) instead of tracheids, and most characteristic among these vessels are the dotted ducts (fig. 544). The phloem also differs from that of the gymnosperms in that the sieve vessels have *companion cells* (figs. 545, 546). No trace of mesarch structure is seen, even in the cotyledons, which seems to indicate that the angiosperms are further removed from the ferns than are the gymnosperms.

The only primitive suggestion that remains in the vascular system of the stem is the presence of leaf gaps in the vascular cylinder, connected with the insertion of the leaf traces. It will be remembered that the presence of leaf gaps is a feature of the ferns, in contrast with the other groups of pteridophytes; and their appearance in the dicotyledons is taken to be one indication that this group is connected with ferns, either through gymnosperms or directly. In tracing the development of the vascular system in a seedling dicotyledon, it is interesting to note that the stem cylinder often begins as a protostele, and more or less rapidly becomes a siphonostele.

Monocotyledons. — The monocotyledons were once thought to be the primitive angiosperms, but the study of their vascular anatomy has been chiefly instrumental in suggesting the probability that they are derived from dicotyledons. The evidence is obtained from a study of the development of the vascular system from the earliest stages of the seedling to the adult stem. A transverse section of an adult stem usually shows " scattered " vascular bundles (fig. 550), quite unlike the arrangement into a hollow vascular cylinder characteristic of the dicotyledons. In studying the development of this stem, however, four stages are often recognized. In the earliest stage the cylinder may be a protostele; and this passes more or less quickly into the second ·stage, that of the siphonostele, in which the cylinder is just that of a dicotyledon, with its collateral bundles. This means that an embryonic stage of a monocotyledon is the permanent, adult condition of a dicoty-

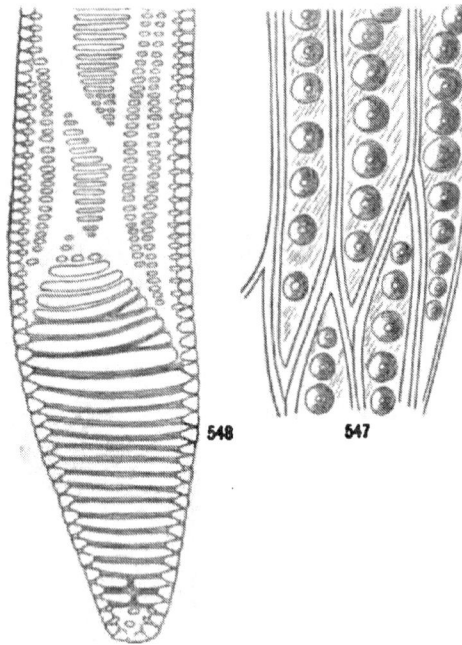

FIGS. 547, 548. — Tracheids: 547, those of gymnosperms, with bordered pits (after CHAMBERLAIN); 548, the scalariform tracheids of ferns (after DEBARY).

ledon. In some monocotyledons this stage persists, and in these cases the adult stems resemble those of dicotyledons.

In the third stage of development the collateral bundles gradually become transformed into *amphivasal* bundles; that is, bundles in which the xylem surrounds the phloem (fig. 551). This transformation is very evident, the xylem of the collateral bundle gradually extending about the phloem until finally it surrounds it completely. All the intermediate stages in this extension of the xylem about the phloem may be found. The amphivasal bundle is characteristic of the mature stems of monocotyledons. In the seedlings, the leaves, and floral axes, the bundles are collateral (the dicotyledon type);

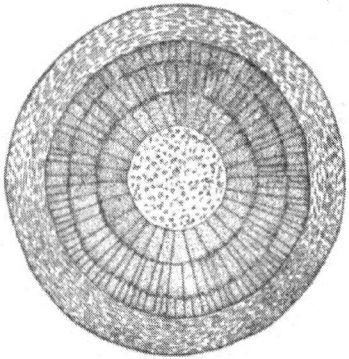

FIG. 549. — Transverse section of stem of dicotyledon (box elder), showing vascular cylinder composed of three growth (annual) rings of xylem formed by the cambium.

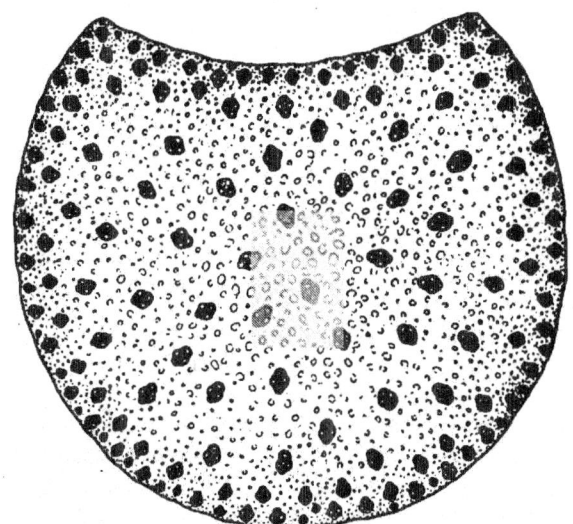

FIG. 550. — Transverse section of stem of monocotyledon (corn), showing the "scattered" vascular bundles.

so that it seems evident that the amphivasal (monocotyledon) type of bundle is more recent than the collateral (dicotyledon) type.

While the transformation of collateral to amphivasal bundles is progressing, the bundles of the cylinder become more and more dissociated; some bundles enter the pith region, the definite outline of a hollow cylinder is broken up, and a transverse section of the stem shows

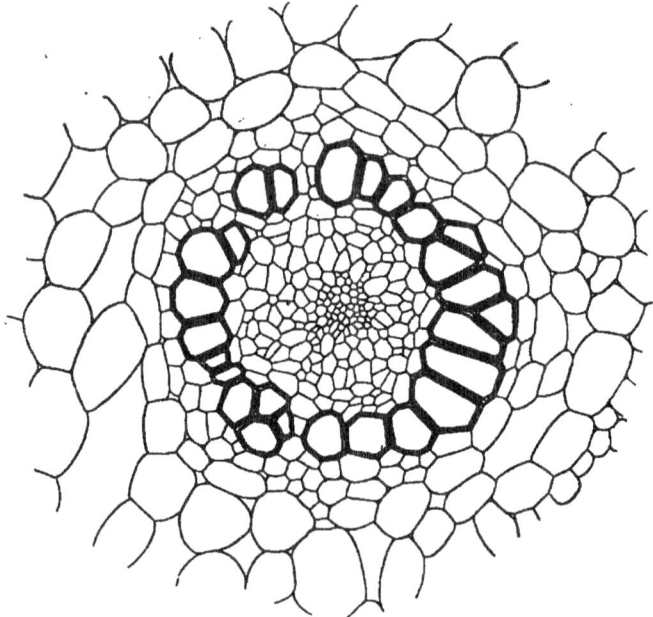

FIG. 551. — Transverse section of amphivasal bundle of *Acorus* (a monocotyledon), showing the xylem completely surrounding the phloem.

vascular bundles scattered through the stele (fig. 550). This development of pith (medullary) bundles and the disorganization of the cylinder is the fourth stage.

Of course there are monocotyledons which do not pass through all these stages, stopping at the second (when they are like dicotyledons), or at the third (when the cylinder is retained but the bundles are amphivasal). There are also dicotyledons in which medullary bundles develop and the cylinder is broken up (as in *Castalia, Podophyllum*, certain species of *Ranunculus*, etc.), and even some in which amphivasal

SPERMATOPHYTES

bundles are formed (as in *Rheum*). It is interesting to note that these dicotyledons with broken-up cylinders belong in the region of the Archichlamydeae from which the monocotyledons are believed to have arisen.

Root

The structure of roots is relatively uniform throughout vascular plants, so that a general description may apply to all groups.

Elongation. — The growing point of the root is not at the surface of its tip, but just beneath, being covered by a tissue of protective cells called the *root cap* (fig. 552). As a consequence, the group of meristematic cells within the root tip forms four generative regions: (1) dermatogen, (2) periblem, and (3) plerome, as in the stem; to these is added (4) *alyptrogen* which forms the root cap, the latter renewed from beneath as it wears off outside (fig. 552).

Root hairs. — Behind the root cap the *root hairs* appear, which are produced by the epidermal cells, and are really enormous extensions of the surface of epidermal cells (figs. 553, 554). Root hairs are relatively short lived, but new ones are formed constantly as the root elongates.

The vascular system. — The vascular anatomy of the root is of the same general type throughout vascular plants. The vascular cylinder

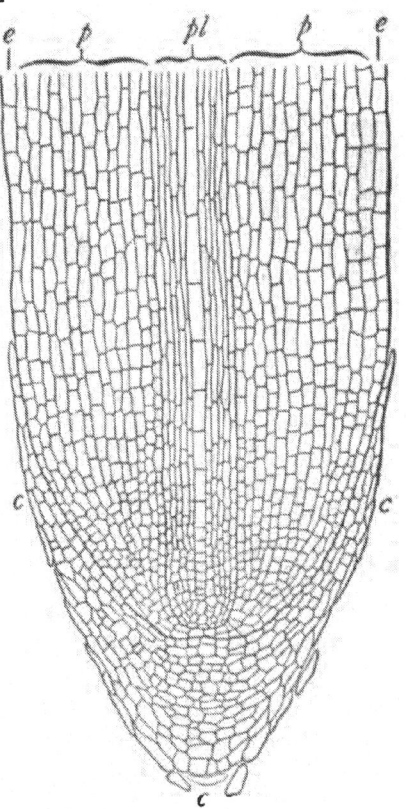

FIG. 552. — Longitudinal section of root tip of spiderwort (*Tradescantia*), showing root cap (*c*), dermatogen (*e*), periblem (*p*), and plerome (*pl*). — After COULTER.

is of the most primitive type, being solid (with xylem at the center) and exarch. However, it is not concentric, the xylem developing towards the center from two or more protoxylem points near the periphery of the stele, and between these radiating strands of xylem separate phloem strands occur (fig. 555). This arrangement of phloem and xylem, in which they occur on alternating radii, is called the *radial* arrangement.

In the secondary thickening of roots (figs. 556, 557), a cambium is developed, which forms secondary xylem inside the phloem; the two,

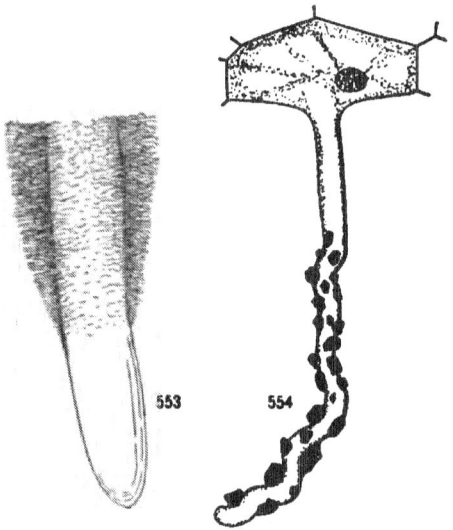
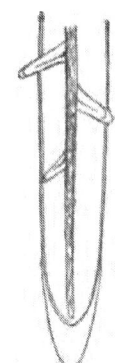

FIGS. 553, 554.— Root hairs: 553, of corn, showing relation to root tip; 554, of wheat, showing relation to an epidermal cell and the close contact with soil particles.

FIG. 558.— Endogenous origin of root branches: longitudinal section of root of arrow leaf, showing the branches starting from the vascular cylinder and penetrating the cortex.— After COULTER.

therefore, hold the same relation to one another as do the xylem and phloem of a collateral bundle. Continued activity of this cambium results in a cylinder of collateral bundles, made up of phloem and secondary xylem; and the radiating arms of the primary xylem are at the bottom of the primary pith rays. Of course, the cambium also forms secondary phloem within the older phloem. By this secondary growth the vascular cylinder of a root may soon lose any appearance of its primitive radiate structure, and assume the appearance of a dicotyledonous stem, with collateral bundles.

SPERMATOPHYTES

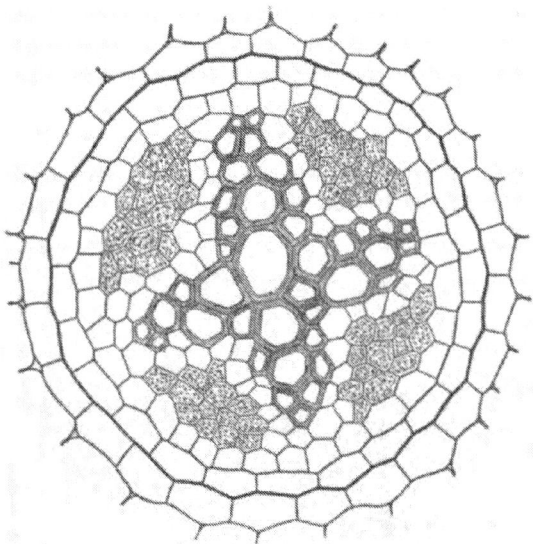

Fig. 555. — Partly diagrammatic transverse section of vascular cylinder of root of *Ranunculus*: the two outermost layers belong to the cortex, the inner one being the endodermis; the next layer (outermost one of the stele) is the pericycle; in the center is the group of xylem vessels, extending in four rays to the pericycle; the outermost xylem vessels of each ray are protoxylem, the metaxylem having developed towards the center in four converging lines; between the xylem rays are the four groups of phloem (shaded).

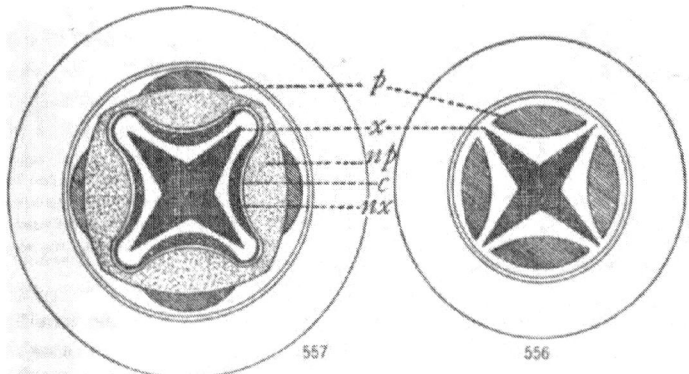

Figs. 556, 557. — Diagrams to show secondary thickening in root, 556 being the primary condition, 557 the secondary; x, primary xylem; p, primary phloem; c, cambium; nx, secondary xylem; np, secondary phloem. — After COULTER.

250   MORPHOLOGY

The branches of a root are formed at the periphery of the vascular cylinder and push through the cortex, this *endogenous* origin being in sharp contrast with the method of origin of stem branches (fig. 558).

LEAF

The structure of an angiosperm leaf is in every essential the same as that of a pteridophyte leaf, and should be clear at this point. For those

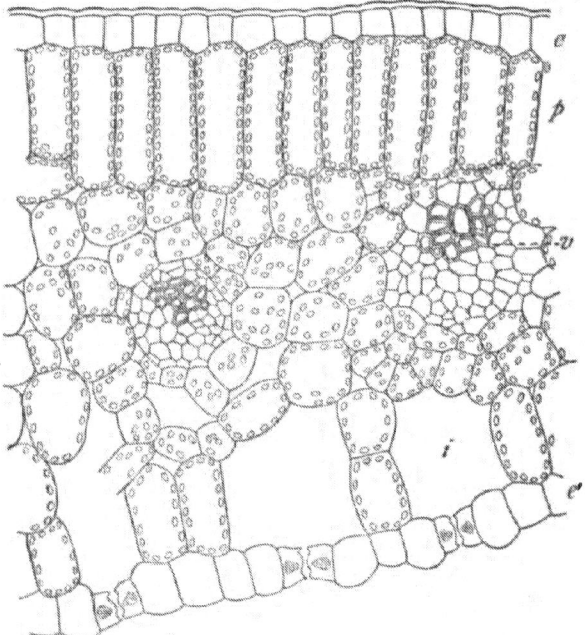

FIG. 559. — Transverse section of lily leaf: beginning above, the regions are the upper epidermis (*e*); the palisade layer (*p*); the region of spongy tissue (extending to the lower epidermis), with intercellular spaces and vascular strands (*v*), the cells containing chlorophyll; and the lower epidermis (*e'*), in which sections of three stomata are seen, each opening into a large intercellular chamber (*i*). — After COULTER.

unfamiliar with this structure, it may be pointed out that the essential features of an ordinary dorsiventral leaf are as follows: a layer of close-fitting or even interlocked epidermal cells above and below, in which stomata are developed (figs. 559-561); between the epidermal layers the *mesophyll* region, whose cells contain chloroplasts (fig. 559);

often two regions of mesophyll (the *palisade region* of vertically elongated and close-lying cells, and the *spongy region* of rounded and loosely packed cells, leaving a labyrinth of intercellular spaces); and the *veins*, of varying order (fig. 559, *v*), which traverse the mesophyll and contain the vascular strands (conducting system) connecting with

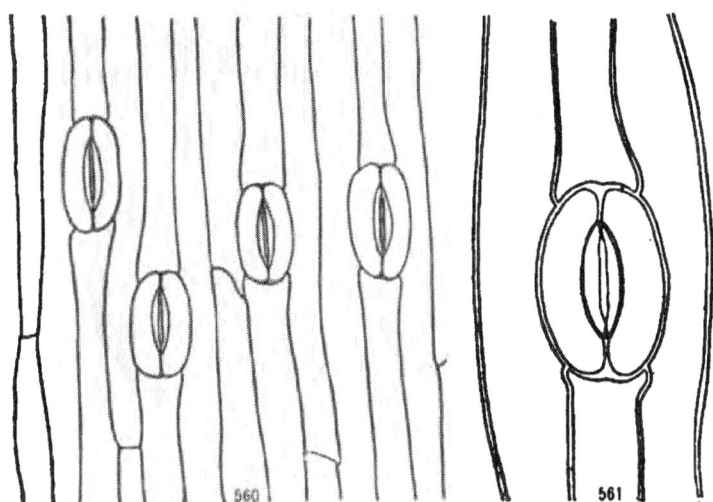

FIGS. 560, 561. — 560, surface view of epidermis of leaf of lily, showing epidermal cells and stomata; 561, a single stoma more highly magnified. — After COULTER.

those of the stem and root, and also strands of mechanical or supporting tissue. Such a structure provides protection (epidermal layers) for the mesophyll cells, an internal atmosphere bathing the mesophyll cells and communicating with the external atmosphere through the stomata, a conducting system, and a mechanical framework.

FLOWER

General character. — The flower is a very characteristic structure of angiosperms, but it is impossible to define it with exactness, so as to apply to all angiosperms and to no other group. In passing from gymnosperms to angiosperms there is a gradual transition from the structure called a strobilus to that called a flower or an inflorescence. The most characteristic feature of the flower of angiosperms is the presence of a perianth associated with the sporophylls. In its full expression, the perianth consists of two sets of members, *sepals* and *petals*, which in general are foliar in nature, but differ more or less distinctly from the ordinary bracts or leaves of the plant (fig. 562). They seem to have been derived, historically, from adjacent sporophylls and adjacent bracts or foliage leaves; in any event, they are intercalated as distinct members between the bracts or foliage leaves on the one side, and the sporophylls on the other. It is not clear what was the most primitive condition of the flower among angiosperms; whether it began with

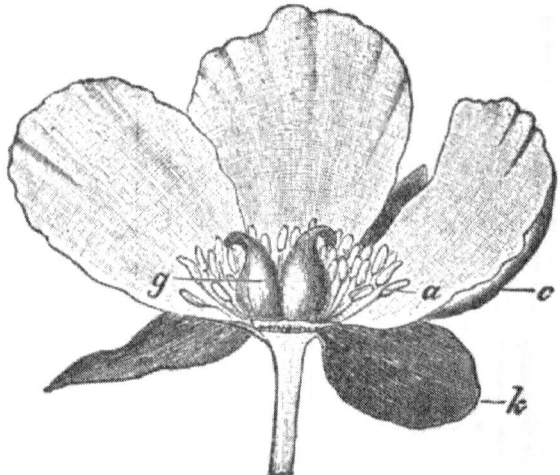

FIG. 562. — Section of flower of peony, showing sepals (*k*), petals (*c*), numerous stamens (*a*), and apocarpous carpels (*g*). — After STRASBURGER.

a fully developed perianth, which in certain groups became reduced or even suppressed; or whether it began with no perianth, which first appeared in very simple form and gradually became more highly developed and complex. Both views have support. In any event, there are certain general facts and tendencies of the flower which are evident.

Differentiation of perianth. — A series of flowers can be arranged with those having no perianth (*naked*) at one end, and those with a sharply differentiated *calyx* (sepals) and *corolla* (petals) at the other. Between these two extremes there will be found flowers with inconspicuous bracts, those with bracts more distinctly perianth-like in arrangement, those with a perianth differing in texture from bracts but not differentiated into two sets. It is evident that this series may have developed in either direction; that is, either by the gradual reduction and final elimination of the perianth (a reduction series), or by the gradual appearance and differentiation of the perianth (an ascending series). In the one case the naked flowers, for example, would be reduced flowers; in the other case they would be primitive flowers. There is every reason to believe that evolution has taken place in both these directions, and

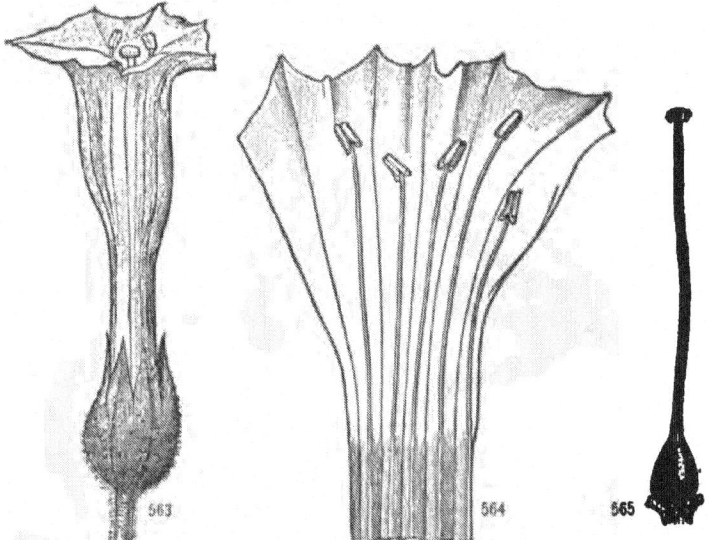

FIGS. 563–565. — 563, sympetalous flower of tobacco (*Nicotiana*); 564, an opened corolla tube, showing the stamens apparently attached to it; 565, the syncarpous pistil. — After STRASBURGER.

that what are known as simple flowers are sometimes primitive and sometimes reduced.

Spiral to cyclic. — A very evident tendency in the evolution of the angiosperm flower is to pass from what is called the spiral condition to the cyclic condition. In a strobilus the bracts and sporophylls are spirally arranged upon a more or less elongated axis, and are indefinite in number; and this same condition occurs in the flowers of certain angiosperms. Beginning with this strobilus-like flower there is a tendency to shorten the floral axis (*receptacle*), which results in a closer spiral of flower parts, and finally reaches the cyclic stage, in which there is a cycle for each kind of organ. At the same time, the receptacle broadens, so that the final stage is one in which the succession of cycles seems to be centripetal rather than acropetal.

Associated with the appearance of the cyclic stage is the establishment of a definite number of organs for each cycle. For example, the definite floral number for cyclic monocotyledons is three, but there are many spiral monocotyledons with no definite number; the definite floral number for cyclic dicotyledons is usually five or four, but there is a host of spiral dicotyledons in which the numbers are indefinite. The cyclic condition is not necessarily attained simultaneously by all the regions of

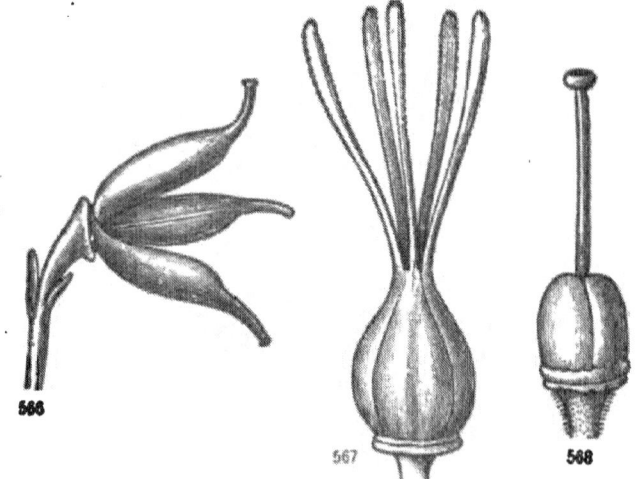

FIGS. 566–568. — Pistils: 566, apocarpous; 567, syncarpous with free styles; 568, completely syncarpous. — After BERG and SCHMIDT.

the flower. For example, in the buttercup the sepals and petals usually show the definite cyclic number five, but the stamens and carpels are still in the spiral condition of indefinite numbers (fig. 562).

Zonal development. — Another evident tendency among the flowers of angiosperms is the so-called coalescence of members of the same set. For example, the zone of tissue upon a receptacle which is giving rise at several points to a cycle of separate petals, sooner or later begins to develop uniformly, resulting in a corolla tube instead of several petals (fig. 563). This is called *zonal development*, and the sooner it begins the more completely tubular does the corolla become. This tendency to zonal development is observed in all the floral cycles, and this condition is poorly expressed in the terms *synsepalous, sympetalous, monadelphous,* and *syncarpous.* The syncarpous condition (*syncarpy*) is extremely common (fig. 568); but the sympetalous condition (*sympetaly*) is noteworthy as giving name to one of the three divisions of angiosperms.

All such terms as "united," "fused," "coalescent," and their technical equivalents suggest a very wrong impression as to the origin of the structure concerned. The separate parts implied in the words "united," etc., never had a separate existence. For example, in many cases separate petals occur; and where there is zonal development they are not separate, but this does not mean that they have "united" or "coalesced."

Hypogyny to epigyny. — Zonal development often involves more than a single set. In sympetaly the stamen zone is also usually involved, so

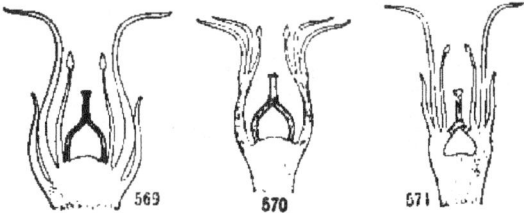

FIGS. 569–571. — Diagrams to show structure of hypogynous (569), perigynous (570), and epigynous (571) flowers. — After GANONG.

that the stamens seem to arise from the tube of the corolla (fig. 564). There are three conditions in reference to zonal development that includes more than one set which are important to note, for they have to do with a disinct evolutionary tendency of the flowers. The most primitive condition is one in which the sets are entirely free from one another (unless it be the corolla and stamens), in which case the flower is *hypogynous*, meaning that the three outer sets arise from beneath the carpel set (fig. 569). In another condition, zonal development involves the three outer sets, resulting in an urnlike structure surrounding the carpels, from the rim of which the distinct sepals, petals, and stamens arise. In this case the flower is *perigynous*, meaning that the three outer sets seem to arise around the carpel set (fig. 570). In the last condition the zonal development involves all of the sets, leaving a cavity in the center, so that all of the sets seem to arise from the top of the ovary. In this case the flower is *epigynous*, meaning that the floral members seem to stand upon the ovary (fig. 571). Epigyny is regarded as an advanced character, and is one of the prominent features of the families considered as highest.

Irregularity. — There is also often a tendency for one or more of the sets to become *irregular* (zygomorphic), a tendency noteworthy chiefly among petals. This means that the corolla is not composed of similar petals, as is true of *regular* (actinomorphic) flowers, but that the petals differ decidedly in form, as, for example, in a sweet pea. This tendency to irregularity is not a general one, but is characteristic of certain groups.

These various tendencies are found in the different groups in all stages of development, so that the relative rank of a group is determined by the combination of its stages. For example, a naked, spiral, hypogynous flower, in which there is no zonal development, would have the most primitive combination; while a cyclic, sympetalous, syncarpous, and epigynous flower would have the most advanced combination.

Organogeny. — The *organogeny* of a flower has to do with the development of the floral members, the most noteworthy fact being the order of succession of the different sets. In a spiral flower the order of succession is necessarily *acropetal;* that is, the sets arise successively towards the apex of the receptacle. This succession, therefore, is sepals, petals, stamens, carpels. If this succession is maintained in a cyclic flower, the acropetal succession, of course, appears centripetal. But with the shortening and broadening of the floral axis (receptacle), the primitive succession is often broken up. For example, in Compositae (the highest family) the succession is petals, stamens, carpels, sepals, which is a striking shift in the position of the sepals; while in *Capsella* (shepherd's purse) the succession is sepals, stamens, carpels, petals.

Relation of sporangia. — The flowers of angiosperms are prevailingly bisporangiate; that is, stamens and carpels occur in the same flower (fig. 562). In the case of monosporangiate flowers two conditions are possible: the staminate and carpellate flowers may occur upon the same plant (*monoecious*) or upon different plants (*dioecious*).

STAMEN

General character. — The stamen is the organ bearing microsporangia, and therefore is the equivalent of the microsporophyll of gymnosperms. The sporangia are usually four in number, but they vary from one to many. Usually the stamen is differentiated into two distinct regions: the *anther*, which is the region bearing the sporangia; and the *filament*,

SPERMATOPHYTES

which is the more or less elongated, stalklike region (figs. 572–574). It should be noted that such a term as anther is one of convenience rather than of morphological exactness, for it is made up of a complex of sporangia and sporophyll.

Microsporangia. — The sporangia develop as in gymnosperms, being of the eusporangiate type. A transverse section of a very young anther shows a mass of homogeneous tissue invested by the epidermis. The layer just beneath the epidermis (hypodermal layer) is potentially sporogenous; but usually it becomes actually sporogenous in four regions, which in transverse section show a variable number of cells (one to several). Of course these regions of initial cells are really four longitudinal, hypodermal bands of varying width. Each one of these bands of initials divides periclinally, forming two layers of cells (fig. 575). The outer layer (just beneath the epidermis) is the primary wall layer; the inner one is the primary sporogenous layer. The primary wall layer divides further, forming several (usually three to five) wall layers (fig. 576). The outermost wall layer is usually

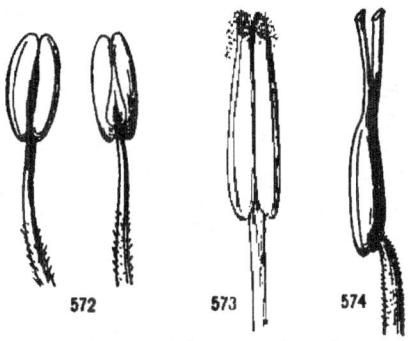

FIGS. 572–574. — Stamens of angiosperms, showing anther and filament: 572, ordinary type, with longitudinal dehiscence; 573, *Solanum*, with dehiscence by terminal slit or pore; 574, *Vaccinium*, with tubular prolongations of pollen sacs for dehiscence. — After KERNER.

much modified, the cells becoming large and conspicuously banded, forming the so-called *endothecium* (fig. 580), a layer that assists in the dehiscence of the sporangium. The innermost wall layer usually becomes transformed into a portion of the *tapetum*, the nutritive layer of the sporogenous tissue (figs. 576, 577). The intermediate layers are the *middle layers*, and usually become more or less flattened and disorganized through the activity of the tapetum. A section through a completed sporangium wall, therefore, reveals the epidermis, the endothecium, one or more middle layers, and the tapetum (fig. 577).

The cells of the primary sporogenous layer usually divide two or three times (sometimes oftener, and sometimes not at all), forming the spore mother cells (fig. 577). In the two successive divisions of the mother

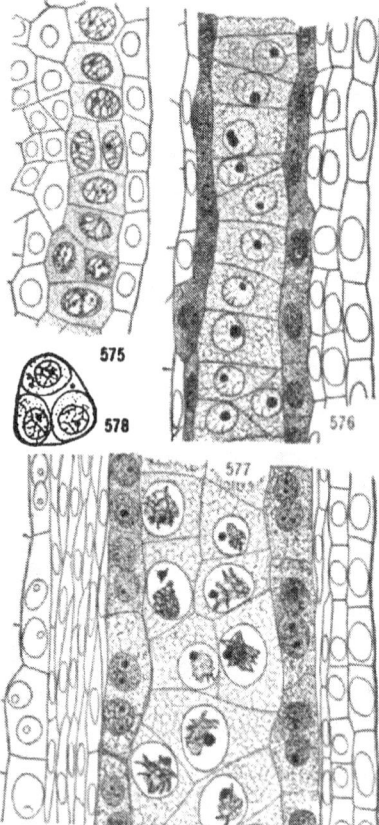

FIGS. 575-578. — Development of the microsporangium of *Silphium*: 575, transverse section of a small portion of a very young anther, showing the hypodermal initial cells (shaded and with large nuclei), which are beginning the periclinal division into primary wall cells (outer) and primary sporogenous cells; 576, later stage, the primary wall cells having formed three layers, the innermost (shaded) being the tapetum (nutritive layer), which is continuous about the sporogenous cells; 577, later stage, showing endothecium (layer beneath epidermis) forming, middle layer of flattened cells, tapetum conspicuous and its cells binucleate, and sporogenous tissue (after one division of primary sporogenous cells) in the mother cell stage; 578, a mother cell containing a tetrad. — After MERRELL.

cells to form the tetrads of spores (fig. 578), the reduction of chromosomes occurs. Usually the tetrads within the mother cells are of the tetrahedral type, but in some cases the arrangement is different, the four spores being in a linear series. The mature microspores (pollen grains) usually round off and separate, forming a powdery mass (fig. 580). The spore walls are two-layered, the outer layer (*exine*) being thicker and more brittle and often variously sculptured, the inner layer (*intine*) being delicate and very elastic. In the exine there are always one or more thin spots where the pollen tubes emerge, most monocotyledons having one such spot, and dicotyledons having two to many. In the pollen grains of *Ranunculus* (buttercup), for example, fifteen to thirty thin spots may be observed.

In some groups of angiosperms the spores of a tetrad do not separate, a condition once described as a compound grain. In certain cases still larger groups of spores cling together, and this tendency reaches its extreme expression in such plants as orchids and milkweeds, where all the

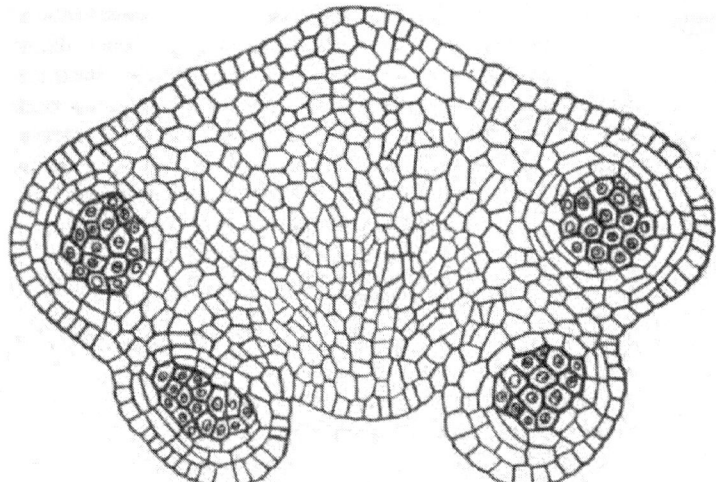

FIG. 579.—Transverse section of a young anther of lily, showing the four sporangia well advanced. — After COULTER.

spores of a sporangium cling together in one mass, called the *pollinium*.

As the four sporangia of an anther increase in size (fig. 579), the sterile tissue separating the two sporangia on each side of the anther breaks

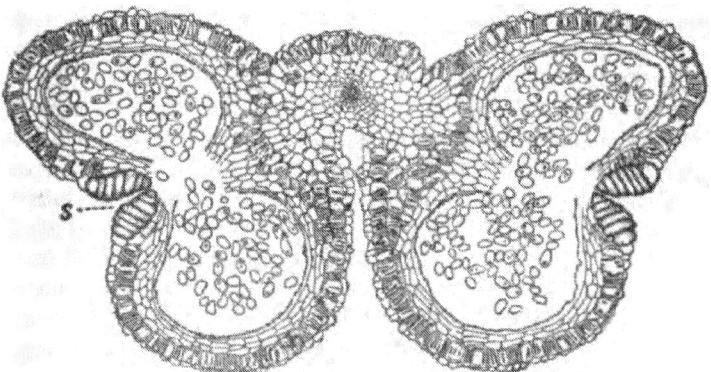

FIG. 580. — Transverse section of a mature anther of lily, showing the sporangial cavities fused to form two pollen sacs (which are full of pollen grains); the endothecium conspicuous (just beneath a more or less fragmentary epidermis), and also the remarkable cells formed by the epidermis at the line of dehiscence (*s*); the tapetum has broken down (dotted line), and several middle layers are evident. — After COULTER.

down, and each pair becomes one continuous spore chamber or sac, called the *pollen sac* (fig. 580). The pollen sac of angiosperms, therefore, is usually composed of two coalesced sporangia. The dehiscence of the pollen sacs, in the discharge of the spores (pollen grains), is most commonly by a longitudinal slit, developed where the two coalesced sporangia join (figs. 572, 580); but sometimes they open by terminal slits or pores (fig. 573), or by openings in tubular prolongations of the pollen sacs (fig. 574), or sometimes by hinged valves.

CARPEL

General character. — The carpel is a megasporophyll, and though often it does not produce the megasporangium (ovule), it always incloses it. Ovules, on account of their relation to its tip, frequently arise from the axis; so that ovules among angiosperms are both cauline and foliar in origin. The carpel is usually organized into two distinct regions: the *ovary*, in which the ovules occur; and the *style*, usually a more or less elongated and stalklike region arising from the top of the ovary (figs. 566–568). Upon the style, usually at its tip, sometimes along one side, there is exposed a special tissue that receives the pollen, known as the *stigma*. This stigma is the exposed part of a tissue which extends through the style (sometimes lining a stylar canal) and along the wall of the ovarian cavity, and forms the nutritive path of the pollen tubes on their way from the stigma to the ovules. This tissue in the style has been called *conducting tissue*, and in the ovarian cavity the *placenta*.

In cases of syncarpy, two or more carpels are organized together, forming a single ovary (fig. 567), and often a single style (fig. 568). In such cases the ovary may contain as many chambers as there are carpels, or there may be only one chamber. Since carpels may be organized singly or collectively, it is convenient to have a general term that can be applied to either kind of carpel organization, and that term is *pistil*. A *simple* pistil is one composed of a single carpel (fig. 566); while a *compound* pistil is composed of more than one carpel (fig. 567), and may contain as many chambers as there are carpels in the organization, or it may contain a single chamber.

Ovule. — The ovule may arise from any free surface within the cavity of the ovary; and since this free surface involves both the carpels and the tip of the axis (sometimes prolonged into the cavity of the ovary), the ovules may be foliar or cauline. In the different groups of angiosperms, however, the ovules are borne in very definite ways.

General structure. — In the development of the ovule, the nucellus first appears as a protrusion from the surface which bears it; later a ring arises around its base, which develops into an integument; and still

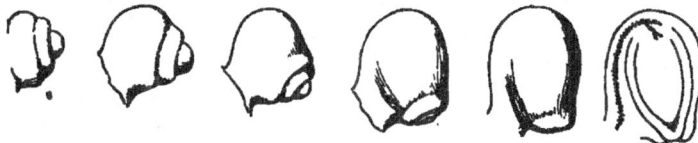

FIG. 581. — Development of an anatropous ovule, the series beginning at the left; the two integuments appear successively and gradually overtop the nucellus as the ovule becomes curved; last figure a section showing relation of the two integuments and the nucellus at maturity of ovule. — After GRAY.

later a second ring may arise outside of the first, which develops into a second integument (fig. 581). Soon the integument (or integuments) overtops the nucellus, and where it closes in over the nucellus there is left a narrow, more or less elongated passageway, the *micropyle* (fig. 582). Among the Archichlamydeae and monocotyledons there are

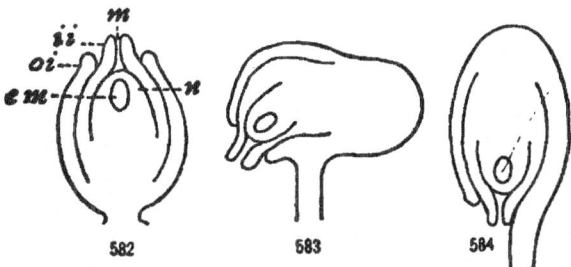

FIGS. 582–584. — Directions of ovules; 582, orthotropous; 583, campylotropous; 584, anatropous; also showing outer (oi) and inner (ii) integuments, micropyle (m), nucellus (n), and embryo sac (em). — After COULTER.

usually two integuments; while among the Sympetalae there is almost invariably a single massive integument.

Direction. — Important differences are shown in the directions assumed by mature ovules. Some grow straight outward from their place of origin, the axis being straight and the micropyle directed away from the point of origin; such ovules are called *orthotropous* (fig. 582), and this condition is regarded as the most primitive. In other ovules the axis becomes curved, the micropyle being directed thus towards the surface of origin; such ovules are called *campylotropous* (fig. 583), and they are much less common than the other kinds. Far the most common kind of ovule among angiosperms is one which develops a stalk (*funiculus*) that becomes curved at the apex, so that the body of the ovule lies against it, and although the axis of the body is straight, the micropyle is directed towards the surface of origin; such ovules are called *anatropous* (inverted), the funiculus appearing as a ridge along one side of the body of the ovule (figs. 581, 584). The advantage of the anatropous ovule may be recognized when it is remembered that the pollen tube is advancing along the wall of the ovary, and the micropyles are thus brought near the wall.

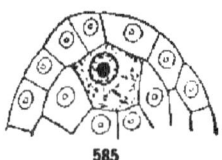
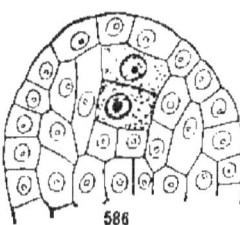

FIGS. 585, 586.—Development of megasporangium of *Salix:* 585, single hypodermal initial; 586, division of initial into primary wall cell (outer shaded one) and primary sporogenous cell.—After CHAMBERLAIN.

Development.—The megasporangium (really the nucellus) is eusporangiate in its development, resembling the microsporangium at every stage. There is usually a single hypodermal initial cell, which is soon recognized among the other hypodermal cells by its larger size and the different appearance of its contents (fig. 585). Sometimes there are two or more of these initial cells, as is the usual case in microsporangia. The large hypodermal initial divides by a periclinal wall into two cells, the outer cell being the primary wall cell, the inner one being the primary sporogenous cell (fig. 586). The wall cell may not divide (fig. 587), or there may be one or more divisions (fig. 588), or in some cases there may be several wall layers developed, as in microsporangia. The primary sporogenous cell does not divide and form more sporogenous cells, and therefore it is the megaspore mother cell. This means that when it divides, a tetrad is formed by two successive divisions, which are the reduction divisions. The tetrad of megaspores is almost always a linear row (fig. 587), which is an exceptional arrangement among microspores. It is very seldom that more than one of the megaspores matures, and that one is almost invariably the innermost one of the row, that is, the one farthest from the micropyle. In its growth the developing megaspore encroaches upon and destroys the other megaspores and more or less adjacent tissue of the nucellus, becoming a very large cell (fig. 587), which is later the embryo sac.

This account of the development of the megasporangium includes all the events that ever occur, but in certain groups of angiosperms one or more of these events are omitted. Among the Sympetalae, for example, the hypodermal initial cell never divides into a primary wall cell and a primary sporogenous cell, but is itself the primary sporogenous cell or mother cell. This means that in this great group the wall tissue of the megasporangium has been eliminated. The same condition is found here and there in the other groups.

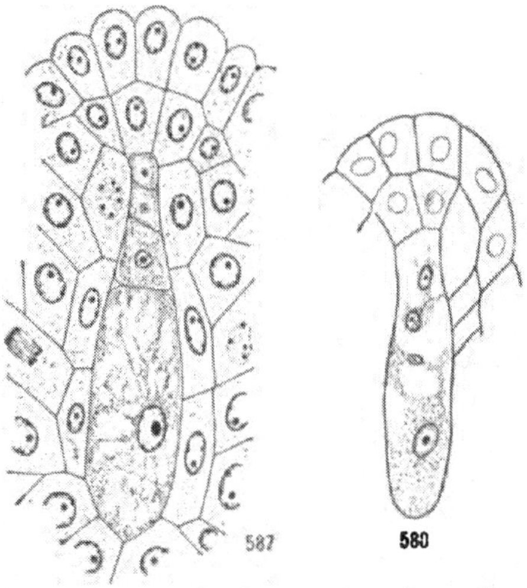

In some cases the nucleus of the mother cell divides, forming four nuclei, but walls do not separate them. Sometimes when this happens (as in *Eichhornia*) three of the nuclei degenerate and the fourth one functions (fig. 588).

In other cases the mother cell divides only

FIGS. 587, 588. — Development of megasporangium: 587, tetrad of *Canna* (after WIEGAND), in which the innermost megaspore has very much enlarged; single undivided wall cell; 588, tetrad of *Eichhornia* (after WILSON SMITH), in which no walls have appeared, but three of the megaspore nuclei are degenerating; primary parietal cell divided once.

once, and one of the daughter cells functions as an ordinary megaspore in producing a female gametophyte (as in *Cypripedium*). The cell thus functioning is not really a megaspore, but two megaspores, which together form the gametophyte.

In *Lilium* and certain other forms a remarkable shortening of the history occurs. The hypodermal initial cell does not produce a wall cell, and therefore is the primary sporogenous cell or mother cell. This mother cell does not divide and form a tetrad of megaspores of the usual kind, but the megaspores are represented by four nuclei. The mother cell, therefore, seems to behave like a megaspore in producing the female gametophyte, and the hypodermal initial thus directly produces the female gametophyte. Of course this really means that four megaspores enter into the formation of the gametophyte, and the two successive reduction divisions are the first two divisions in the formation of the gametophyte.

FEMALE GAMETOPHYTE

Development. — The development of the female gametophyte of angiosperms begins with free nuclear division, as in gymnosperms, but the nuclei thus produced are definitely eight in number, following three successive divisions from the nucleus of the megaspore. It is in this free nuclear stage that the egg is differentiated, which is the condition of *Gnetum*, except that here the nuclei are much fewer in number. In

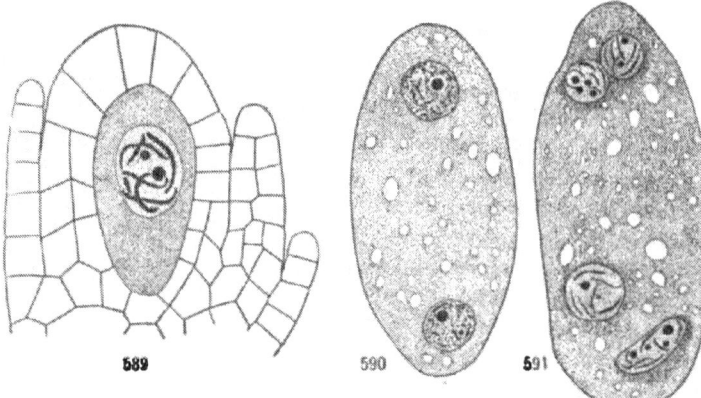

FIGS. 589–591. — Development of female gametophyte of angiosperms, as shown by a lily: 589, megaspore (in the ovule); 590, first division; 591, second division.

connection with these free nuclear divisions two remarkable features appear. One is the polarity exhibited by the nuclei. After the first division the two nuclei separate and pass to the poles of the embryo sac, one to the micropylar end, and the other to the antipodal end (fig. 590). There follow two successive divisions, so that first two (fig. 591) and then four (fig. 592) nuclei are produced at each pole of the sac. The other feature referred to is the *polar fusion*, which means that a nucleus from each end passes toward the center of the sac, where the two come into contact and fuse (figs. 593, 594), forming the *fusion nucleus* (primary endosperm nucleus).

Egg apparatus and antipodals.—The three nuclei in the micropylar end of the sac are organized into a group of three naked cells called the *egg apparatus* (figs. 593, 594). The cells are all potential eggs, but only one of them (the central one) matures as a functional egg. The other two are called *synergids* (helpers), because they are apparently of some service in connection with fertilization. Often the synergids become beaked, the beaks sometimes even extending into the micropyle. The three nuclei at the antipodal end of the sac form a group of three naked cells or walled cells, called *antipodal cells* (figs. 593, 594), or merely *antipodals*, and their history is exceedingly variable. Usually they are ephemeral; sometimes they are quite persistent; and in some cases they form a very active tissue. In the last case, the activity is shown either by the great enlargement of the three cells, or by their division to form a variable amount of tissue. In any case, when the antipodals are active, they serve as nutritive cells, and in general they serve this purpose until the endosperm is formed.

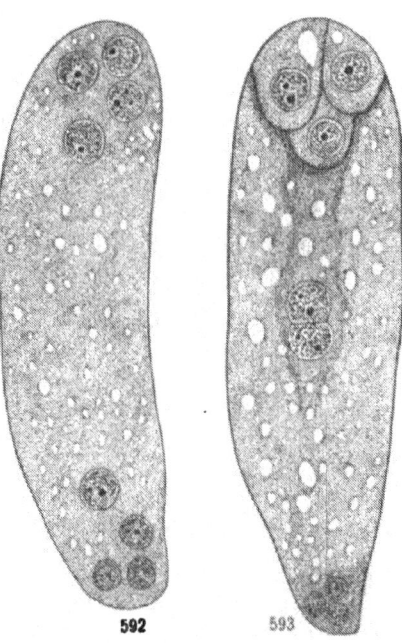

FIGS. 592, 593.—Development of female gametophyte of angiosperms, continued from fig. 591: 592, third division, resulting in four nuclei in each end of the sac; 593, organization of egg apparatus (upper end of sac), fusion of polar nuclei (center of sac), and antipodal nuclei (base of sac).

Exceptions.—The sequence of events described above is remarkably uniform for so great a group as the angiosperms; but there are certain interesting exceptions. For example, in a member of the pepper family

(*Peperomia*) there are sixteen free nuclei in the embryo sac. These nuclei show no polarity, and a large number of the nuclei enter into the formation of the large fusion nucleus, which in this case is the result of multiple fusion. This same general condition has been found also in *Juglans* (walnuts), *Ulmus* (elms), the aroids, etc.; but probably in all these cases two or four megaspore nuclei are involved.

Nutritive mechanism. — The nutritive mechanism of the embryo sac is varied and sometimes complex. In all cases there is an enlargement of the sac, which encroaches in every direction upon the adjacent tissue of the nucellus, which is thus used as a nutritive tissue. In some cases, notably among the Sympetalae, there is organized about the sac a definite nutritive jacket, which obtains food from the surrounding tissue and from which it enters the embryo sac. In other cases the antipodal end of the sac extends into the tissue beneath (*chalaza*), sometimes becoming conspicuously tubular and prolonged. In still other cases tubular extensions of the sac are put out in other directions, especially into the heavy integument from the micropylar end. Occasionally all of these methods of nutrition are combined, resulting in a complicated and very efficient nutritive mechanism.

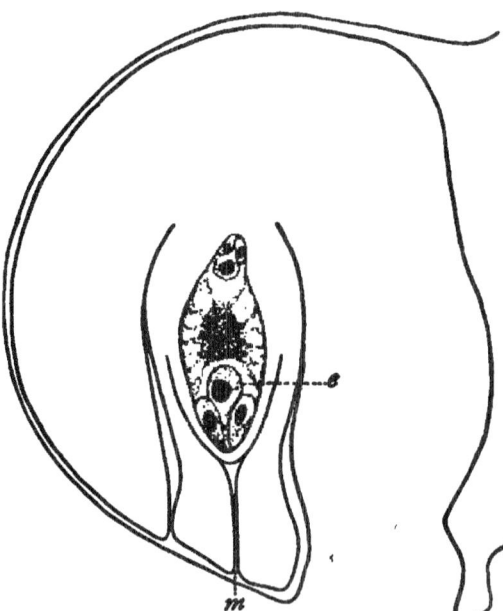

FIG. 594. — Mature female gametophyte of lily within the anatropous ovule, showing the egg apparatus (*e*, the egg; the two other cells the synergids) directed towards the micropyle (*m*), the three antipodals at the other end of the sac, and the two polar nuclei in contact in the center. — After COULTER.

MALE GAMETOPHYTE

Development. — In the development of the male gametophyte of angiosperms no vegetative cell appears (except in very rare cases), so that the gametophyte is reduced to an antheridium, and the pollen grain is an antheridium initial (fig. 595). The first division of the nucleus of the microspore produces the generative and tube nuclei, and this is the usual condition of the pollen grain at shedding (fig. 596). The generative cell is usually organized as a naked cell, which assumes various forms, generally from spherical to lens-shaped. This cell may divide before the shedding of the pollen grain, in which case three nuclei are observed within the mature grains (fig. 597); or it divides after passing into the pollen tube. The generative cell is the primary spermatogenous cell, and there is only one division, resulting in two equal male cells.

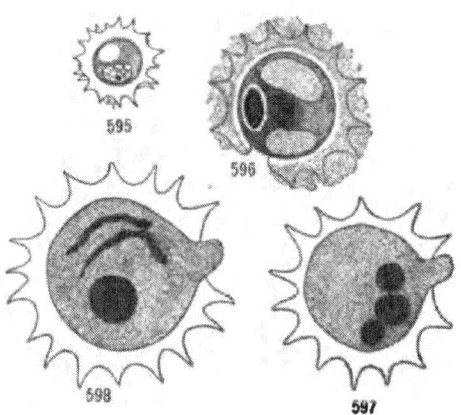

FIGS. 595–598. — Male gametophyte of angiosperms, as shown by *Silphium*: 595, pollen grain, with its single nucleus and spiny outer coat; 596, first division, forming generative and tube nuclei (shedding condition in many cases); 597, second (and last) division, resulting in the two male cells from the generative cell (shedding condition in some cases), a division which often occurs in the pollen tube; 598, the two male cells having elongated. — After MERRELL.

The gradual reduction in the number of spermatogenous cells produced by the antheridium of a heterosporous plant has reached its extreme expression among angiosperms. In *Selaginella* the generative (primary spermatogenous) cell produces a large number of mother cells, each of which produces a sperm. In *Isoetes* the generative cell produces four mother cells, each of which develops a sperm. In cycads and *Ginkgo* the generative cell produces three cells (by two successive divisions), two of which are mother cells developing sperms. In conifers the generative cells produce the same number and character of cells as in cycads, but the two mother cells do not develop sperms, functioning themselves as male cells.. In angiosperms there is only one division, the generative cell producing two male cells. These male cells are variable in form, being spherical, lens-shaped (very common), spindle-form, curved, or even spirally twisted.

FERTILIZATION

Pollination. — Pollination is the transfer of pollen from stamen to stigma, and is a necessary antecedent to fertilization. The term *fertilization* is often used when pollination is meant, but no student of morphology should confuse the two. In angiosperms pollination is a very extensive subject, for insects as well as wind are agents of transfer; in other words, they are insect-pollinated as well as wind-pollinated. This use of insects, which has developed among the higher angiosperms, has involved a variety of mechanism and of habit that is fairly bewildering; but the whole subject lies within the domain of ecology (see Part III). It is sufficient to note that in some cases the pollen is transferred to the stigma of its own flower (*close pollination*), and in other cases to the stigma of another flower (*cross pollination*). Dioecious plants are necessarily cross pollinated. Hybrids may be produced by cross pollinating (or *crossing*) individuals belonging to different species or varieties.

Pollen tube. — After the pollen grain lodges on the stigma, the pollen tube is developed and penetrates from the stigma to the embryo sac. This involves penetration of the style, entrance into the ovarian cavity, passage along the wall of the ovarian cavity to the insertion of the ovule, passage along the ovule to the micropyle, passage through the micropyle to the tip of the nucellus, penetration of the tissue of the nucellus overlying the embryo sac, and finally penetration of the sac wall (fig. 599). The time involved in this journey holds no relation to the distance traversed. For example, in *Crocus*, with a style 6 to 10 cm. long, the time is one to three days; while in *Arum*, with a style only 2 to 3 mm. long, the time is five days. The range of time, so far as known, is from a few hours to thirteen months (in certain oaks). These long periods are found among angiosperms which are regarded as primitive (the so-called *Amentiferae*), and suggest the similar condition among gymnosperms. Among these same primitive angiosperms, also, there are found branching pollen tubes, suggestive of the old haustorial habit of the tube.

Chalazogamy. — Among the Amentiferae there also occurs the phenomenon of *chalazogamy*, which means that the pollen tube does not enter the embryo sac by way of the micropyle, but pierces directly through the region of the ovule beneath the embryo sac (*chalaza*) and enters the embryo sac from below. Among the more familiar plants in which chalazogamy has been found are the walnuts and elms. Entrance by the micropyle is called *porogamy;* and there are other routes used by the pollen tubes of certain plants, intermediate between true chalazogamy and porogamy.

Fertilization. — After the tip of the pollen tube has entered the sac, it enlarges very much, usually destroys one of the synergids, and finally discharges the two male cells or nuclei (fig. 599). One of the male cells passes to the egg and fertilization is accomplished. The other male cell passes deeper into the sac, comes into contact with the fusion nucleus, and fuses with it. Into the structure of the primary endosperm cell (or nucleus), therefore, three nuclei have entered: an antipodal polar, a micropylar polar, and a male nucleus. This participation of both male cells in nuclear fusions in the same embryo sac has been called *double fertilization*, and it is perhaps the greatest puzzle connected with the embryo sac of angiosperms.

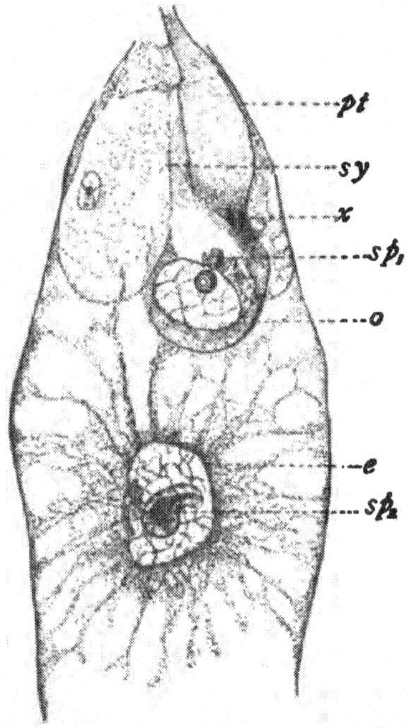

FIG. 599. — Fertilization in *Silphium:* sy, undestroyed synergid; pt, swollen tip of pollen tube, still with some contents (x); sp_1, coiled male cell in contact with egg nucleus (o); sp_2, curved male cell in contact with fusion nucleus (e). — After LAND.

Double fertilization. — This phenomenon was first described in 1898, but subsequent investigation has indicated that it is probably of universal occurrence among angiosperms. It means that one male cell enters into the formation of the embryo, and the other into the formation of the endosperm. This raises a question as to the nature of the endosperm of angiosperms. The old view was that it is belated tissue of the female gametophyte, which in some way is stimulated to develop by the polar fusion. But when the part played by the male cell was discovered, it was suggested that this *triple fusion* is a real fertilization, which would mean that the so-called endosperm is a sporophyte, the twin of the embryo. If this is true, the endosperm of gymnosperms is not the same as that of angiosperms. If the test of the number of chromosomes be applied, to decide whether the endosperm is gametophytic (x) tissue or sporophytic ($2x$) tissue, it is found that it is at least $3x$ tissue. To call $3x$ tissue gametophytic seems to make the test of little value. If the triple fusion be analyzed, it will be noticed that one cell is the micropylar polar, which is sister to the egg, and another is a male cell. If only these two cells fused, it could hardly fail to be regarded as fertilization; but the third cell that enters into the fusion is a vegetative cell (or nucleus) from the antipodal end of the sac, so that the real nature of the fusion is confused. Perhaps it would be better to speak of the endosperm of gymnosperms as *female gametophyte*, and to reserve the name *endosperm* for this problematical tissue in the embryo sac of angiosperms.

ENDOSPERM

Development. — As described above, the endosperm of angiosperms is produced by the triple fusion nucleus. It usually begins with free nuclear division, but sometimes it begins with wall formation that chambers the sac. In its completest development it forms a tissue that fills the embryo sac and is packed about the embryo. In some groups the endosperm may develop only as a few free nuclei, so that it may be regarded as suppressed, as in Helobiales and orchids (groups belonging to monocotyledons). There is also great variation in the permanency of endosperm which has been fully developed. It may be used up by the embryo during the ripening of the seed, as in peas and beans (Leguminosae); or it may persist in the mature seed, being used up by the embryo during germination, as in the cereals. In structure, permanent endosperm tissue has no intercellular spaces, and the cell wall may be thin or thick, an excessive thickening occurring in bony seeds, notably in the date and in the so-called vegetable ivory, both from the seeds of palms. Sometimes by its continued growth the endosperm has been observed to burst the seed coats, turn green, and form intercellular spaces.

Perisperm. — The storage region of some seeds is not the endosperm but the *perisperm*, which is the nucellar tissue surrounding the embryo

SPERMATOPHYTES

sac. In this case the endosperm functions as an intermediary between the perisperm and the embryo, obtaining the food stored in the former and passing it on to the latter.

Xenia.—The phenomenon known as *xenia* is the appearance in the seed of characters belonging to the pollen parent, when the pollen is foreign (belonging to another race). For example, when a race of white or yellow corn is crossed with pollen from a race of red corn, many of the resulting kernels are red or mottled. It is found that this color belongs to the endosperm, and that it is introduced by the male cell that enters into the triple fusion. This means that in this case the endosperm is a hybrid as well as the embryo.

EMBRYO

The embryo of angiosperms does not begin with free nuclear division, as in gymnosperms (*Tumboa* and *Gnetum* excepted), but the first division is accompanied by a wall. As the most fundamental difference between dicotyledons and monocotyledons is found in the embryo, the two groups must be considered separately.

Dicotyledons.—The embryo of *Capsella* (shepherd's purse) is most commonly used as a representative of the dicotyledonous embryo. The egg divides transversely and subsequent tranverse divisions result in a filament of varying length (fig. 600). This filament is the *proembryo*, which later becomes differentiated into suspensor and embryo. The terminal cell of the proembryo divides into octants (fig. 601), the four terminal octants forming the stem and cotyledons, the four basal octants forming the hypocotyl except its tip. In the octant stage the dermatogen (the layer that produces the epidermis) is cut off by periclinal walls (fig. 602). In the interior the two other body regions are soon outlined, the periblem (producing the cortex) and the plerome (producing the stele) (fig. 603).

At the tip of the hypocotyl the plerome is complete, but the periblem and dermatogen are incomplete (fig. 603). This gap in the tip of the hypocotyl is filled by the adjacent (second) cell of the proembryo as follows: This cell divides transversely, and the daughter cell next to the embryo is the *hypophysis*, which fills out the hypocotyl. The hypophysis divides transversely, the inner cells completing the periblem, and the outer cells completing the dermatogen (figs. 603–608). The second cell of the proembryo, therefore, contributes both to the embryo and to the suspensor, and the boundary between these two regions is

272   MORPHOLOGY

established when that cell divides and forms the hypophysis. While this method of embryo formation may be regarded as characteristic of dicotyledons, there are numerous variations, conspicuous among which are the following:

Variations. — The proembryo may be a spherical mass of cells (as in the water lilies), in which the growing points are organized, but with little or no differentiation of a suspensor.

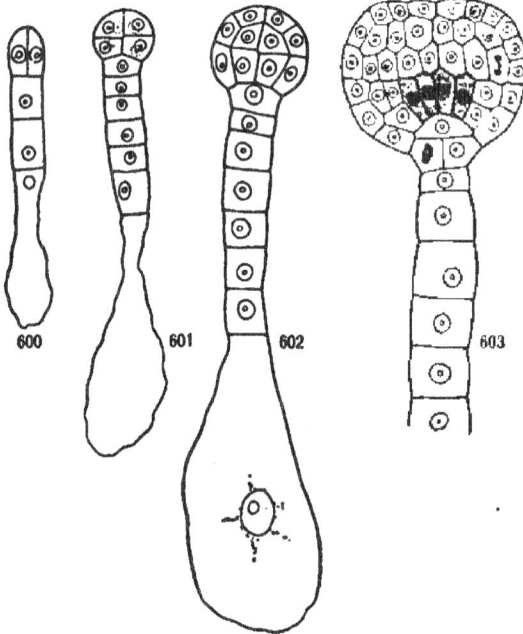

Figs. 600–603. — Development of embryo of *Capsella* (a dicotyledon): 600, the filamentous proembryo, in which the terminal cell has divided and the basal cell has become large; 601, later stage, in which the terminal cell has divided to octants; 602, later stage, in which the dermatogen has been cut off; 603, later stage, in which plerome (shaded) and periblem (between plerome and dermatogen) are distinguishable in the hypocotyl region; hypophysis (divided to three cells in the figure) completing periblem (by inner cell) and dermatogen (by two outer cells). — After Coulter and Chamberlain.

In other cases the proembryo is massive, but of no definite form, filling the micropylar end of the embryo sac.

SPERMATOPHYTES

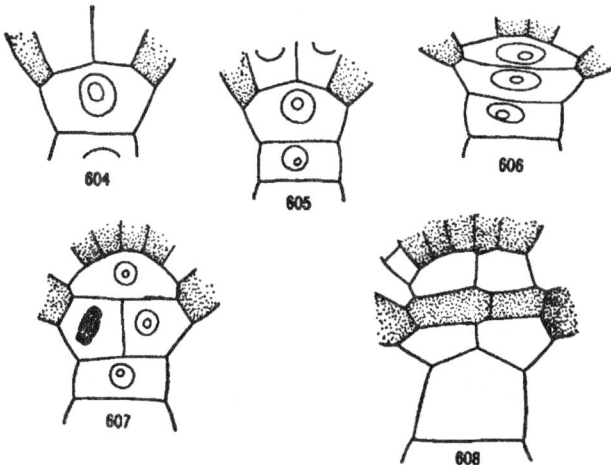

FIGS. 604–608. — The hypophysis in *Capsella*: 604, cell with nucleus is the cell of the filamentous proembryo next to the terminal one (which has formed most of the embryo); 605, division of this cell into hypophysis (cell next to the embryo) and end cell of suspensor (it is this division that finally differentiates embryo and suspensor); 606, division of hypophysis into two cells; 607, division of the outer daughter cell of the hypophysis; 608, final product of the hypophysis (six cells visible, in three tiers), innermost tier completing the periblem (plerome shaded), middle tier (shaded) completing the dermatogen (shaded), and outermost tier starting the root cap. — After COULTER and CHAMBERLAIN.

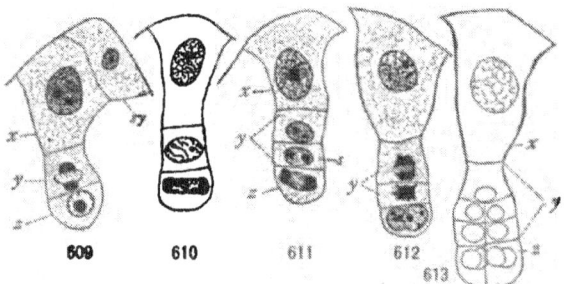

FIGS. 609–613. — Development of embryo of *Sagittaria* (a monocotyledon): 609, the three-celled filamentous proembryo, the terminal one (*z*) forming the cotyledon (*sy*, the undestroyed synergid); 610, the same; 611, division of middle cell; 612, 613, later stages; *x*, enlarged basal suspensor cell; *y*, middle cell; *z*, terminal cell. — After SCHAFFNER.

Among the Leguminosae there is often developed a conspicuous and very active suspensor, which may almost girdle the sac with its turgid cells.

274 MORPHOLOGY

Among certain plants without chlorophyll (*Monotropa*, etc.) the embryo is very simply organized, consisting of a few cells, the differentiation into body regions proceeding during germination.

Monocotyledons. — The embryo of *Alisma* or of *Sagittaria* is most commonly used to represent the monocotyledonous embryo. The proembryo is usually a filament of three cells (figs. 609, 610), the terminal cell forming the cotyledon. The middle cell begins a series of divisions, some of the resulting cells forming the stem tip, hypocotyl, and root tip, and the others belonging to the suspensor (figs. 611–617). In

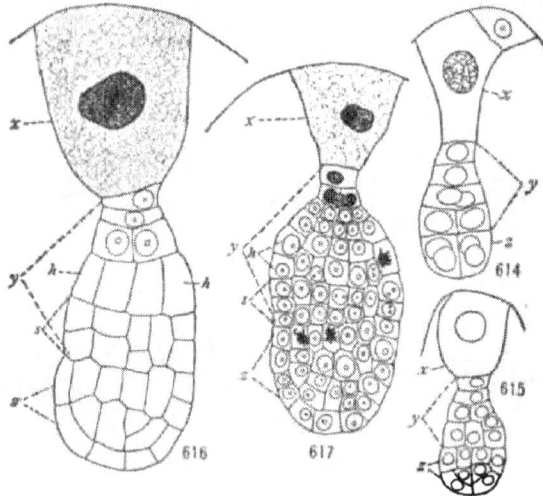

FIGS. 614–617. — Further development of embryo of *Sagittaria*: stages later than the series shown in figs. 609–613; *x*, enlarged basal cell; *y*, middle cell, giving rise to stem-tip (*s*), hypocotyl (*h*), and some suspensor cells; *z*, the terminal cotyledon. — After SCHAFFNER.

this case, also, the boundary between embryo and suspensor is established by a division of the second cell of the proembryo, which contributes both to the embryo and to the suspensor (fig. 617); but in this monocotyledon type the whole of the embryo except the terminal cotyledon is derived from the second cell. The basal cell of the proembryo usually becomes very much enlarged, forming the conspicuous part of the suspensor (figs. 616, 617). The notable monocotyledonous feature is the terminal cotyledon and the laterally developed stem tip, which appears in a notch developed in the side of the axis of the embryo (fig.

SPERMATOPHYTES

618). Notable variations in this method of embryo formation are as follows:

Variations. — Among the aroids the proembryo is usually a spherical mass of cells.

In *Lilium* and its allies the suspensor becomes massive, sometimes filling the micropylar end of the sac, and occasionally giving rise to extra embryos.

In orchids the embryo is very simply organized at the maturity of the seed, consisting of only a few cells, with no differentiation into body regions.

PARTHENOGENESIS

Parthenogenesis is the development of an embryo from an unfertilized egg, and it seems to be a rare phenomenon among angiosperms,

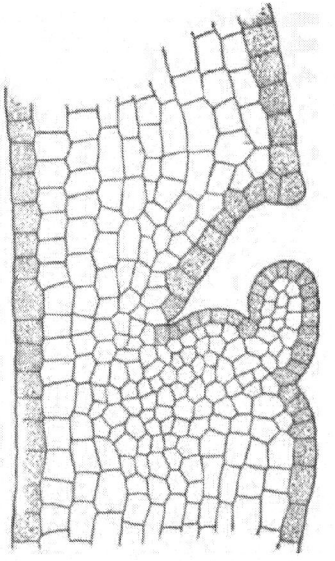

FIG. 618. — Stem tip of *Sagittaria* developing in notch on side of embryo. — After SCHAFFNER.

having been recorded thus far in only six or eight scattered genera, conspicuous among which are species of *Thalictrum, Alchemilla, Antennaria,* and *Taraxacum.* In these cases, since there is no fusion of nuclei in the act of fertilization, there is no doubling of the chromosomes; but it has also been found that in them there is no reduction division in the formation of the megaspores, so that the egg already has the $2x$ number, which is transmitted to the young sporophyte (embryo).

POLYEMBRYONY

The occurrence of more than one embryo in a seed is not so common among angiosperms as among gymnosperms, but the cases are numerous. The synergids and the antipodals have been observed to produce embryos, and since these cells are gametophytic, these embryos arise by vegetative apogamy (see p. 169). Very commonly also the cells of the nucellus adjacent to the embryo sac or even those of the integument may form embryos that push into the sac. Since the nucellus and integument belong to the sporophyte, these embryos arise by sporophyte budding. A remarkable case is that of an *Allium* (onion) with five embryos in the sac : one from the fertilized egg, one from a synergid, two from the antipodals, and one from the integument. There are thus four possible ways by which embryos may appear in an embryo sac: (1) from a fertilized egg, (2) by parthenogenesis, (3) by vegetative apogamy, and (4) by sporophyte budding.

CLASSIFICATION OF ANGIOSPERMS

In so vast a group as angiosperms, it is impossible to present so complete a classification as was given for the gymnosperms or even for the pteridophytes. However, it seems necessary to indicate the larger groupings. The scheme presented is known as that of ENGLER, and although it will doubtless be very much modified, it will serve to introduce the great groups.

MONOCOTYLEDONS

Among Monocotyledons about 25,000 species are recognized, which are distributed among 42 families; and these families are grouped into ten great alliances. These alliances may be considered under two categories, six of them having spiral flowers (with indefinite numbers), and four of them having cyclic flowers (with definite numbers). The spiral alliances are regarded as the more primitive, and the cyclic alliances represent the more advanced monocotyledons. The six spiral alliances are as follows:

1. *Pandanales* (3 families, 100 species). — The screw pine is the representative form, but the cat-tail flag (*Typha*) is a representative in our flora. The group is regarded as low in rank, which means either that it is primitive or reduced, because it has naked flowers with indefinite numbers, and is wind-pollinated. It is also an aquatic group, and the flower cluster is protected by the sheathlike base of the leaf.

2. *Helobiales* (7 families, 235 species). — This is also an aquatic and wind-pollinated group, whose lowest members have naked flowers, as the pondweed (*Potamogeton*), but whose higher members have a calyx and corolla, as the water plantain (*Alisma*). In this group, also, the sheathing base of the leaf encloses the young flower cluster.

3. *Glumales* (2 families, 7000 species). — These are the grasses and sedges, which form one of the greatest of angiosperm alliances. While there are aquatic members, it is chiefly a terrestrial group, covering the

earth's surface more completely than any other. The flowers are naked and wind-pollinated, and the floral numbers fluctuate widely. The peculiarity of the group, which has suggested the name, is that the individual flowers are protected by bracts (*glumes*), the flower clusters being composed of these overlapping bracts. This method of protection is in strong contrast with that of the preceding groups.

The three preceding alliances are those which contain naked flowers, and if this is a primitive character, these are the most primitive alliances of the monocotyledons. It must be remembered, however, that this condition may have arisen through reduction.

4. *Palmales* (1 family, 1100 species). — These are the palms, the one group including trees among the monocotyledons. The flowers have a perianth, but it is not differentiated into calyx and corolla. In general the floral numbers are indefinite, but there is occasional evidence of a settling to three, especially in the carpels, which are not only usually three in number, but also syncarpous. With the appearance of a perianth, there is also the appearance of insect pollination, so that the group as a whole is both wind-pollinated and insect-pollinated. It is also characterized by the large sheathing bases of the leaves, which invest the young flower clusters, a feature in common with the first two groups.

5. *Synanthales* (1 family, 45 species). — This is a small and peculiar South American alliance, which needs no description in this connection.

6. *Arales* (2 families, 1025 species). — These are the aroids, a very distinct group of monocotyledons. The best known representatives are probably Jack-in-the-pulpit (*Arisaema*) and calla lily, but numerous tropical forms are in common cultivation in greenhouses. The flowers are clustered on a fleshy axis (*spadix*), enveloping and often overarching which is a great bract (*spathe*). The spathe is as variable in form and variegated in color as are ordinary flowers, and associated with it there is a development of insect pollination. In fact, the brightly colored spathe seems to play the same part in aroids as does the corolla in the higher groups. The flowers clustered on the spadix are exceedingly variable as to the perianth; and although the stamens and carpels are indefinite in number, the number is small (1-4). A very distinct feature of aroids among monocotyledons is the production of broad, net-veined, and frequently lobed leaves, which resemble those of dicotyledons. One of the families is made up of the duckweeds (*Lemna*), which are very much reduced aquatic forms.

The preceding alliances are the so-called spiral alliances, in which the floral members are not definitely and constantly of the same number. While the floral number three is a feature of monocotyledons, it is evident that it does not apply to the spiral alliances in the same sense that it does to the cyclic alliances.

In the following cyclic alliances the almost constant floral formula is: perianth 3 + 3, stamens 3 + 3, carpels 3 (and syncarpous). Furthermore, the perianth is the conspicuous floral feature rather than bracts, and insect pollination is well established. In other words, the real flowers of monocotyledons, as ordinarily recognized, belong to the cyclic alliances.

7. *Farinales* (11 families, 2000 species). — This alliance is in a certain sense a transition group between the spiral and cyclic alliances; for although the cyclic number is established, many of the forms are grasslike herbs with bractlike perianth, as in the rushes (Juncaceae); but there are also forms with showy corolla, as the spiderwort (*Tradescantia*).

8. *Liliales* (9 families, 5000 species). — These may be regarded as the representative monocotyledons, with conspicuous and usually regular perianth, and well-established insect pollination. Most of the monocotyledonous flowers of ordinary experience belong here. The group shows a distinct development from hypogyny, as in the amaryllises (Amaryllidaceae), to epigyny, as in the flags (Iridaceae).

The two remaining cyclic alliances are characterized not only by epigyny, but also by the extreme irregularity of the flowers.

9. *Scitaminales* (4 families, 800 species). — These are the cannas, bananas, and gingers of the tropics. One peculiar feature of the group is the so-called false stem, which may be seen in the banana. The stemlike structure, which often rises to a considerable height, is built up of the heavy and overlapping bases of the leaves.

10. *Orchidales* (2 families, 7000 species). — The orchids are notable for the great irregularity and showiness of their flowers, and for their extreme specialization in insect pollination. The number of species runs very high, but orchids cannot be regarded as abundant. By contrasting the 7000 species of grasses and sedges with the 7000 species of orchids, it becomes evident that although the species of two groups may number the same, the number of individuals may be very different. The orchids may be regarded as the culmination of monocotyledons in floral structure, and that culmination is expressed by epigyny and extreme irregularity.

SPERMATOPHYTES

ARCHICHLAMYDEAE

This vast group contains a maze of forms whose relationships are very confusing. Over 61,000 species and 180 families are recognized, which are grouped into 26 great alliances. Archichlamydeae include primitive angiosperms, and although they are prevailingly spiral, the cyclic condition, with a definite number in all of the floral members, is established in several of the higher alliances. It would be unprofitable to name all of the alliances, for many of them would suggest nothing to the elementary student. Some of the more significant will be selected for brief description, and the others grouped.

1-12. (26 families, 5900 species.) — This group of alliances is especially puzzling as to relationships. They are regarded as relatively primitive forms, and include many of the most common trees, as willows, walnuts, beeches, oaks, etc. Many of them were formerly grouped as Amentiferae, a name referring to the characteristic flower cluster called *ament* or *catkin*, a cluster perhaps most familiar in the willows and alders. The flowers are naked or have a bractlike perianth, the floral numbers are generally indefinite, and wind pollination prevails. This assemblage does not seem to be related to any of the higher alliances.

13, 14. (11 families, 4070 species.) — This is another apparently isolated group, including such plants as smartweed (*Polygonum*), pigweed (*Amaranthus* and *Chenopodium*), pinks (Caryophyllaceae), etc. In structure the flowers range from a bractlike perianth to distinct sepals and petals, and are mostly cyclic, three, four, and five being the prevailing floral numbers. Insect pollination is established only among the pinks.

15. *Ranales* (16 families, 4050 species). — This is recognized as the great genetic alliance, which means that the higher alliances are thought to have been derived from it. Familiar families are the crowfoots or buttercups (Ranunculaceae), the water lilies (Nymphaeaceae), and the magnolias (Magnoliaceae). There is a distinct calyx and corolla; the flowers are hypogynous; and the numerous carpels form separate pistils (*apocarpous*). Although the cyclic number is often evident in the calyx and corolla, the stamens and carpels at least usually retain the spiral condition and are indefinitely numerous. By some it is thought that the Ranales are the most primitive Archichlamydeae, not only giving rise to the other dicotyledons, but also to the monocotyledons.

16, 17. (9 families, 2760 species.) — These families are clearly special branches from Ranales, the most specialized one probably being the mustards (Cruciferae).

18. *Rosales* (16 families, 14,270 species). — This is the greatest alliance among the Archichlamydeae, including far the largest family — the Leguminosae, with over 11,000 species. Another prominent family is the Rosaceae, which gives name to the alliance. These two families are plainly branches from the Ranales; and among the Leguminosae the flowers become conspicuously irregular. The irregularity is of a special type, illustrated by the sweet pea, so that a large part of the family is easily recognized. In the development of irregularity in connection with insect pollination, the Leguminosae hold the same position among Archichlamydeae that the orchids (Orchidaceae) hold among monocotyledons.

19–25. (99 families, 27,358 species.) — This is a tangle of seven alliances leading off in every direction from the preceding ones, each alliance characterized by some special feature. Each one, however, gradually becomes more definitely cyclic and approaches the epigynous condition.

26. *Umbellales* (3 families, 2660 species). — This is easily the highest of the alliances of Archichlamydeae and it is kept from being included among the higher Sympetalae only because it is polypetalous. The dominant family is the parsley family (Umbelliferae), and associated with it are the dogwoods (Cornaceae). The floral formula is definitely as follows: sepals 5, petals 5, stamens 5, carpels 2, and this is also the most advanced floral formula found among Sympetalae. Associated with this high formula is epigyny. Another high character is that the flowers are small and massed, the cluster being more or less invested by a rosette of bracts (*involucre*). Apparently as a result of the massing of the flowers, the sepals are much reduced, and the whole cluster shows more or less division of labor, some flowers (the peripheral ones) often being more showy, and the others more fertile.

SYMPETALAE

This is a much better defined group than the Archichlamydeae, from which they are certainly derived. The combination of characters is as follows: completely cyclic flower, sympetalous corolla, ovule with a single massive integument, and complete absence of wall tissue in the ovule (see p. 263). About 42,000 species and 51 families are recognized, which are grouped into eight alliances, whose characters and sequence are quite evident.

The first three alliances are called the *pentacyclic* and *isocarpic* alliances. The former term means that there are five cycles of floral members, the stamens being in two cycles; the latter term means that the number of carpels is the same as that of other cycles. The floral formula which expressses both of these facts is as follows: sepals 5, petals 5, stamens 5 + 5, carpels 5 (syncarpous). These pentacyclic Sympetalae are most nearly related to the Archichlamydeae, and in fact contain some polypetalous forms. They are not very numerous, including only about 3500 species.

1. *Ericales* (6 families, 1700 species). — The heaths constitute the dominant family (Ericaceae), very characteristic of northern latitudes. Some of the forms are polypetalous, but they are so related to sympetalous forms that they cannot be separated from them; and in some of the sympetalous forms the stamens are free from the corolla. One of the features of the alliance is the characteristic dehiscence of the anthers, which is by means of terminal openings in the tubular prolongations of the pollen sacs.

2. *Primulales* (3 families, 850 species). — Two features of this alliance, of which the primroses (Primulaceae) are representatives, are the opposite stamens and free central placenta. The five stamens are opposite the five petals, instead of alternate with them, as is usual; but this is explained when it is discovered that the outer cycle of stamens is abortive, being represented by rudiments called *staminodia*. The axis of the flower extends into the ovary cavity like a central column, and upon it the cauline ovules are developed, a condition which was formerly called free central placentation.

3. *Ebenales* (4 families, 900 spec es). — These are mostly tropical shrubs and trees, represented in our flora by the persimmon (*Diospyros*). As the name suggests, the characteristic family is the ebony family (Ebenaceae). It is a curious mixture of primitive and advanced characters, with frequent lapses into indefinite numbers, especially of stamens.

The remaining alliances are *tetracyclic* and *anisocarpic*. This means that there are usually only four floral cycles, and that the number of carpels is not equal to that of the other cycles. The general floral formula is as follows: sepals 5, petals 5, stamens 5, carpels 2 (syncarpous). In the more primitive alliances the carpels fluctuate between five and two, often being four or three. The five tetracyclic alliances fall naturally into two groups, the first three having hypogynous flowers, and the other two having epigynous flowers. The hypogynous alliances are as follows:

4. *Gentianales* (6 families, 4200 species). —The combination of characters that distinguishes this alliance from the next is the uniformly opposite leaves and twisted *aestivation* (petals in the bud appearing as if twisted around each other). As the name suggests, the gentian family (Gentianaceae) is the characteristic representative of the alliance. The curious and highly specialized milkweeds (Asclepiadaceae) are also included here, characterized not only by their milky juice, but chiefly by their elaborately insect-pollinated flowers and pollinia (see p. 258).

5. *Tubiflorales* (20 families, 14,600 species). —This great alliance represents the culmination of the hypogynous Sympetalae, with conspicuous tubular corollas. The flowers range from regularity, as in the morning glories (*Ipomoea*) and polemoniums (Polemoniaceae), to irregularity, as in the mints (Labiatae) and figworts (Scrophulariaceae). The type of irregularity in this case is called *bilabiate*, which means that the corolla develops a two-lipped mouth. These Tubiflorales with irregular flowers hold the same position in reference to insect pollination among Sympetalae that the Leguminosae do among Archichlamydeae, and the Orchidaceae among monocotyledons.

6. *Plantaginales* (1 family, 200 species). —This small alliance, comprising the single family of plantains (Plantaginaceae), is characterized by flowers with a membranous corolla and the cyclic number four. Its relationships are obscure, but it is probably a reduction group.

The two following epigynous alliances represent the culmination of Sympetalae, and therefore of angiosperms.

7. *Rubiales* (5 families, 4800 species). —The madders constitute the characteristic family (Rubiaceae), and associated with it are the honeysuckles (Caprifoliaceae). The cyclic number is prevailingly four, and there is a strong tendency to aggregate the flowers in close clusters.

8. *Campanales* (6 families, 14,500 species). —This highest alliance is dominated by the great family Compositae (sunflowers, asters, goldenrods, dandelions, etc.), which is not only the highest, but the greatest of angiosperm families, including at least 12,500 species. It adds to its sympetaly epigny, a seedlike fruit (*achene*), a special development of its sepals as *pappus*, a complex organization of flowers into a head so compact as to simulate a single flower, and usually a differentiation of the flowers of a head into those that are showy (the peripheral *ray flowers*) and those that are fertile (*disk flowers*).

CHAPTER V — ORGANIC EVOLUTION

THE morphology of plants, as presented in the preceding chapters, is in reality a somewhat detailed illustration of the evolution of the plant kingdom. The theory of descent is the working theory of modern biology, and no student of morphology should omit some consideration of it. The subject has developed so extensively that it can be presented here only in very brief outline, an outline that may serve as an extended definition, and also as an introduction to a real study of organic evolution. Many names connected with the doctrine of evolution and many important views in reference to it must be passed over, and only the most conspicuous features presented.

Definition. — The doctrine of organic evolution claims that the existing plants and animals are the modified descendants of earlier forms; that in some way new forms have arisen from the old ones, and have given rise in turn to still other forms. According to this view, the whole plant kingdom, for example, may be likened to a profusely branching tree, the tips of whose myriad branchlets represent our present flora. The morphologist attempts to trace these branchlets from their tips, which he sees, to their connections, which he can only infer. His proofs are obtained from the structure and development and behavior of living plants, and also from the form and structure of ancient plants, so far as they are available in suitable fossil form. His conclusions, it must be remembered, are reasonable inferences, and cannot be based upon actual demonstrations. It is evident that opinions may differ widely as to the actual historical connections of plant groups; but it is practically unanimous that there are such connections.

The idea of organic evolution is not modern, being in the thought of man as far back as records of thought have been found; but it is only in modern times that it has been based upon direct observation of the facts, that is, has become scientific. It is not necessary to recite the facts that underlie the widespread belief in organic evolution, for many of these facts, so far as they concern plants, have been given in the preceding chapters. To believe in organic evolution, however, is one thing, and to explain it is a very different thing. The well-known names associated with the doctrine of evolution often are thought of as the names of men who may be called authors of the theory of evolution; but they are really men who have proposed explanations of evolution. For example, Darwin, perhaps more than any other evolutionist, is spoken of as the author of the doctrine of organic evolution; but if his explanation and every other explanation should be disproved, the fact of evolution would still remain to be explained. No proposed explanation of evolution is entirely satisfactory, but biologists are daily becoming more convinced of the truth of evolution.

With this distinction between the fact of evolution and its explanation made clear, it will be possible to outline briefly the conspicuous explanations that have been offered. The problem to be solved is how new forms may arise from old ones, which is the problem of the origin of species.

Environment. — Perhaps the oldest explanation of organic evolution, based upon observation, is that plants and animals may be changed by their environment. Such facts as the seasonal changes in the plumage of birds and in the covering of mammals, and also the changes in plants in relation to their environment, suggested that plants and animals are plastic and can be molded by a changing environment. This explanation was offered, during the last decade of the eighteenth century, by Erasmus Darwin of England, St. Hilaire of France, and Goethe of Germany. It was assumed that any change induced by environment would be transmitted to the offspring, to be retained so long as the environment remained constant.

It is evident that organisms respond more or less in certain ways to decided changes in the environment, but such direct responses are regarded generally as too superficial and fluctuating to account for the production of new forms. The influence of environment, however, while insufficient to explain organic evolution, is still recognized as an important factor of the problem, whose value may vary widely. If there are such things as "ecological species," their origin is due by definition to environment.

Use and disuse. — In the early part of the nineteenth century, Lamarck offered an explanation of evolution, which he called "appetency," meaning the effect of desire. The theory is better known as Lamarckism, and it has strong defenders, in modified form, to the present day. It is really the effect of use and disuse. It is well known that persistent use develops such an organ as a muscle, and that persistent disuse causes it to dwindle and to lose its power of functioning, leading eventually perhaps to abortion or even to suppression. If this law is conceived of as applying to every organ of a plant or an animal, the results might be as deep-seated and general as could be demanded by the origin of new forms.

According to this theory, the use or disuse of an organ is determined by the environment. A change in the environment might shift the demands upon the different organs, and so build up or modify some and allow others to degenerate, resulting in a different kind of plant or animal. This process is sometimes called " adaptation," the idea being that plants and animals can " adapt " themselves to fit their environment. Lamarck used the neck of the giraffe as one of the striking illustrations of his theory. He imagined that a grazing animal, thrust into an environment where feeding upon the foliage of trees became more or less necessary, would call upon its neck in such a way that it would become somewhat elongated; and that the gain in length secured by any individual would be transmitted to its offspring, so that generations of such animals would gradually build up the enormously elongated neck of the modern giraffe. Such a result would mean the transmission of small changes acquired during the lifetime of an individual, and the possibility of such transmission is now generally disbelieved.

The three factors recognized by this theory are (1) a changing environment, (2) the effect of use and disuse, and (3) the inheritance of acquired characters. The first two factors are evidently important, but they are of no avail in producing new forms, according to Lamarck, unless the third factor operates.

Natural selection. — The explanation of organic evolution by means of natural selection is more widely known than any other evolutionary theory. Its announcement in 1858 by Charles Darwin and the appearance in 1859 of his book entitled *Origin of species by means of natural selection* introduced a new epoch in scientific thought and method. Modern biology, in a very real sense, may be said to date from this book, and what is called Darwinism has dominated it for nearly fifty years. The enormous mass of facts, obtained from world-wide observations and prolonged experiments, was organized in such a convincing way to support the theory that only wider observation and more careful experiment could make it appear unsatisfactory. In fact, the theory of natural selection as presented by Darwin led to a wide acceptance of the doctrine of evolution. Whether the theory stands or falls as an explanation of the origin of species, its supreme importance in the history of biology demands that it be understood by all students of plants and animals. The bare outline of the theory is as follows:

The theoretical "ratio of increase" of plants and animals is far beyond their actual increase. If an annual plant should produce two seeds, and each seed should "fulfill its mission," there would be two plants in the second season, four in the third, eight in the fourth, and so on in geometrical ratio, until in comparatively few years there would be many millions of descendants from a single individual, enough to populate the whole earth. If this ratio of increase be applied to the myriads of plants and animals of many kinds, the result would be a tremendous competition for space and food, a competition which has been called "the struggle for existence." Since in general the number of adult plants and animals is no greater in one season than in the preceding, it is evident that the "struggle" results in a tremendous destruction of individuals. This leads to the striking conclusion that "death is the rule, and life the exception."

In considering this enormous waste of living forms, Darwin concluded that the survivors of the "struggle" must be better situated or equipped than their less fortunate fellows, and that the competition resulted in what Spencer afterwards called "the survival of the fittest," which is another way of saying "the destruction of the unfit."

The idea that two plants from the same parent might be differently equipped, led to the observation of the facts of variation. No two individuals of the same species, even from the same parent, are alike in every detail; and the variations range from very minute ones to very large and striking ones. It was concluded that there must be a selection from among these variants of those best suited to the conditions of living. There was no attempt at this time to search for the cause of variation; it was simply accepted as a fact which makes evolution possible.

The actual demonstration of the use that can be made of variations was obtained by Darwin from the operations of plant and animal breeders, who had long changed plants and animals under domestication. Some of these changes had been so extensive that it was difficult to believe that the wild form and the highly cultivated form were the same species. In fact, had they both been found growing wild they would probably have been described as two species. The process of the breeders was to select from the variants those which best suited their purpose, and to continue this selection generation after generation. It was found that this continuous selection gradually built up the selected characters, until the desired result was obtained. This could well be called the origin of new forms by artificial selection; that is, selection directed by man.

Darwin concluded that there is a process similar to this going on in nature. Innumerable variants are constantly appearing, in numbers beyond any possibility of their continuance. The more suitable ones are selected by nature for survival, the means of selection being "the struggle for existence." This selection continuing from generation to generation, the favorable variations would be perpetuated and increased, and eventually the variation might become so great that it could be regarded as standing for a new species. The very appropriate name given to this process is natural selection, and its method consists in the slow building up of small variations, in a given direction determined by the environment, to one great enough to cross the boundary of the parent species.

Although natural selection is certainly operative in the destruction of certain forms and the preservation of others, it is thought by many to be doubtful whether this process can result in the production of new species. Some of the reasons for this doubt that have been urged are as follows:

(1) It is generally believed that acquired characters are not inherited; and if so, it is thought that the small variations exhibited by individuals would not be passed on to their progeny with any certainty. An acquired character is one that is "taken on" by the individual during its lifetime, and is no part of its parental inheritance. The variations claimed to be used by natural selection, however, are probably inherited for the most part, and can hardly be included among acquired characters; so that this objection is not a serious one.

(2) It is claimed that the slight variations used by the theory of natural selection cannot be extended by continuous selection beyond the boundary of the species; in other words, that there is a limit of variation for each species, which cannot be passed by variations of this type. Such variations are commonly spoken of as fluctuating variations, and the amount of fluctuation varies in different species. It is claimed that with all the centuries of artificial selection by plant and animal breeders, the species boundary has never been crossed by this process.

(3) It is recognized that the forms improved by artificial selection

are inconstant. If a plant which has been built up in certain characters by culture be left to nature, it reverts or "runs back," and its descendants soon lose the characters of cultivation and resume those of the ancestral stock. It is evident that the establishment of a new species demands constancy in the built-up characters. The only answer to this objection is that the characters for which man selects are not those for which nature selects; and therefore the inconstancy in nature of a plant built up by culture is no proof that a plant built up by natural selection would be inconstant in nature.

(4) It is also urged that many forms and organs continue to exist which are in no sense " adapted." If nature is selecting suitable individuals and organs, that is, those " adapted " to their environment, and is destroying those that are not, why do so many of the latter survive? There are so many cases of this kind, that the selection by nature does not seem to be based upon the suitability of an individual or an organ.

(5) Perhaps the most serious objection to the theory is that it demands a selection among such slight variations that one can hardly be conceived of as having any decided advantage over another, really a " life and death advantage." If broad leaves are of advantage to a certain species growing under certain conditions, selection among individuals with broad and narrow leaves would seem to be easy; but the theory demands that the selection be made before the broad leaves are built up, and continue during the slow process of building. In other words, the advantage given by a completed structure is not evident during the process of building up; but natural selection is supposed to be directing this building up on the basis of a distinct advantage from generation to generation. To select among completely equipped individuals is one thing; but to select so that individuals may become equipped is a very different thing.

Mutation. — In 1901 Hugo DeVries offered an explanation of the origin of species, which he called mutation. He had observed in one of the few vacant fields in Holland an evening primrose (*Oenothera Lamarckiana*), which had been introduced from the United States. Among the numerous individuals he found some so unlike the ordinary form that he was compelled to regard them as distinct species, and inquiry showed that they had never been described. Plants of *O. Lamarckiana* and of the new species were removed to the garden at Amsterdam and studied through many generations.

It was found that when thousands of seeds of *O. Lamarckiana* were germinated, there would appear among the seedlings a few that were very different from the others. These few being brought under cultivation developed into individuals with all the marks of species distinct from the parent. Moreover, they "came true," generation after generation, which is regarded as the final test of a species. In this way *O. Lamarckiana* was observed to give rise to several new species, in some cases the same species appearing repeatedly. Not all of these suddenly produced species would have survived in nature, but some of them had already stood this test in the vacant field. This immediate appearance of a fully equipped new species, without any intermediate stages or any building up by selection, DeVries called *mutation*, the forms thus produced being *mutants*. The rôle of natural selection in this case is not to produce species, but to select among those already produced. It is evident that a mutant is simply a large variation, such as are called "sports."

DeVries investigated the results of plant breeders, as Darwin had done, and distinguished between improved forms and really new forms. The former evidently arose from the continuous selection of small variations, and were always inconstant. The very few new forms produced were constant, and, so far as records of their pedigree were available, were found to have arisen in each case from some individual that had suddenly appeared among the cultures. In other words, new forms were found, not produced; and when found, they remained constant. Naturally DeVries concluded that all the new and permanent forms that have appeared in connection with plant breeding have been mutants, and have not been built up by continuous selection.

It is entirely unknown whether this mutating condition is of general occurrence. Cultures of plants and animals are being carried on by numerous investigators, and the results may indicate presently whether mutation is to be regarded as a general method in the origin of species or as only an occasional one. It is becoming more and more evident that new species may have arisen in several ways, perhaps including all the methods heretofore suggested, and certainly including some that remain to be discovered. Whether mutation stands or falls as an explanation of evolution, the most important contribution of DeVries to evolutionary science is its transfer from the field of observation and comparison to the field of experimental work.

Orthogenesis. — Natural selection utilizes small variations in building up new species, and mutation calls large variations species. In both cases the parent organism is supposed to give rise to progeny that vary in every direction, the successful direction to be determined by natural selection. This has been called indeterminate variation. In tracing the evolution of great groups, however, it becomes clear that the important variations occur in certain definite directions, which have been maintained persistently throughout all possible changes of condition. For example, the history of such a group as gymnosperms shows a tendency to vary in certain definite directions that has persisted from the early Paleozoic to the present time. What is true of the tendencies that result in great groups, has also been found to be true in many cases of related species. In other words, there is much to indicate that while variation may be indeterminate, there are also certain definite and predetermined lines that persist. This origin of new forms (whether by natural selection or mutation or neither), as the result of a persistent determinate variation, is called *orthogenesis*. It certainly removes one of the greatest difficulties in the way of natural selection, and that is the beginning and development of a structure that can be of advantage only when completed. It satisfies also the many known cases of excessive development in certain directions, a development that may be not only disadvantageous, but even destructive.

Even if determinate variation is accepted as a fact, however, what determines the persistent variation? The answer to this question has resulted in many variations of the theory of orthogenesis. In the earlier development of the theory, it was perhaps natural to explain it by means of a mysterious principle inherent in organic life, "an inner directive force" that persistently makes for progress. Of course such an "explanation" could not satisfy modern biologists, who prefer to believe that determinate variation is occasioned by external factors; but it is still very uncertain how these external factors operate, and even what they are.

It should be noted that natural selection, mutation, and orthogenesis are not mutually destructive. They all deal with variations, and may all be operative in producing new forms. Natural selection deals with fluctuating variations, which are small and in every direction; mutation with large variations, which are large and in every direction; and orthogenesis with those small or large and relatively few variations which for some reason persist and increase from generation to generation and carry forward the group as a whole.

Weismannism. — The theories of Weismann have strongly favored Darwin's theory of natural selection by supporting it at its weakest points.

The theory of *panmixia* attempts to explain how organs degenerate, which natural selection cannot explain unless the abandoned organs are injurious. Natural selection is assumed to select favorable structures and make them still more favorable, but not to eliminate structures that have simply become useless. According to Weismann, when selection ceases to operate upon a certain organ because it has become useless under new conditions, individuals with this organ poorly developed will no longer be at a disadvantage and therefore will survive. The crossing of individuals with this organ in all stages of effectiveness will result in the next generation in lowering the general level of efficiency, and the organ as a whole will appear degenerate. This general mixing, which lowers the average of efficiency, is called *panmixia*. It is impossible to explain, however, how panmixia could lead to a continuous degeneration of the organ involved.

Weismann's theory of *germinal selection* (1895) is one of the most ingenious speculative explanations of the beginnings of variation and of determinate variation (orthogenesis) that has been proposed, neither of which natural selection seemed able to explain, for it can operate only upon variations that have been carried forward to the point of distinct advantage, and it cannot carry forward a variation in spite of changing conditions. Weismann differentiated between *somatic* protoplasts, which give rise only to the vegetative cells of the plant or animal body, and *germ* protoplasts (" germ-plasm "), which give rise to the reproductive cells. The nuclei of the protoplasts contain large numbers of imaginary living units (*biophores*), and these units are organized into groups (*determinants*) which determine the character of the cell. Each kind of somatic cell is supposed to be produced by a certain kind of determinant; but a germ cell contains all the determinants that belong to all the cells of the body. The structure of the offspring depends upon the determinants that are favored in development, and this at first seems to be a matter of chance in food supply. There results a "struggle" among determinants, and a "germinal selection." The stronger determinants that become established in the germ-plasm, however, are handed down generation after generation, and therefore a variation once begun may continue until it can be laid hold of by natural selection, or may even continue as the persistent determinate variation recognized by orthogenesis.

Ingenious as this explanation is, it must be stated that it rests upon no demonstration, and that there are serious objections to it.

Isolation. — The importance of isolation in the formation of species is variously estimated, but that it is at least of great assistance seems evident to those best acquainted with species in nature. If a group of individuals possessing a certain variation were associated with a larger number of closely related individuals not possessing it, the intercrossing of the two groups might obliterate the distinction. On the other hand, if the varying group were isolated from all of its near relatives, so that there could be no intercrossing, the variation would be far more likely to persist and increase. In other words, a variation that otherwise might disappear may be established by isolation.

The term *isolation* usually suggests geographical or topographical isolation, which is perhaps the most effective kind. Migration distributes individuals widely, and the various barriers that segregate them into distinct groups are well known and need not be enumerated. The general tendency to dispersal inevitably leads to more or less isolation, and it seems probable to many that most species have been finally established in this way. In any event, it is evident to those familiar with the geographic or topographic position of species in reference to one another that this kind of isolation is a factor of very great importance in their determination. It does not produce them, but it gives them an opportunity.

There is also recognized what is called biologic isolation, which means that such variations may occur among closely related individuals that, although they may be associated in one habitat, they become incapable of crossing. This may result from a difference in the season for fertilization, in some structure that prevents crossing, or in various other ways. At present, this kind of isolation does not stand out as a factor in the determination of species so distinct and effective as does geographic isolation.

Mendel's law. — It is evident that whether new species arise by the cumulative results of natural selection acting upon small variations, or by the occasional sudden appearance of wide variations, a still more fundamental problem is to explain variation, which is one of the features of heredity. The study of heredity, therefore, which is fundamental to all evolutionary doctrine, is being prosecuted to-day with remarkable vigor. Conspicuous among the recently developed doctrines of heredity is Mendel's law, so called because it was first announced by Gregor Mendel, an Austrian monk. Mendel's publication of fifty years ago fell on sterile ground and passed into oblivion, until it was brought to light in recent years by scientific plant breeders, DeVries among others. It is impossible to give an adequate account of Mendelism in this connection, for it has become so extensively developed that only the special investigator can follow its ramifications. Some conception of it may be obtained, however, from the simplest possible illustration.

In the study of heredity the use of hybrids enables the investigator to observe more distinctly the characters of each parent as they appear in the progeny. Using a very simple hybrid, Mendel's law may be illustrated as follows, with the help of the accompanying diagram.

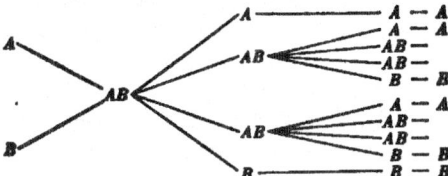

Let A and B represent two species of plants that are crossed; then one of the hybrid plants that result may be represented by AB, which indicates a mixture of the characters of the two parents. When AB produces progeny, the hybrid will "split" in the following ratio: one fourth pure A, one fourth pure B, and one half the mixture AB. In the next generation the A and B plants will produce only A and B plants, and so on through successive generations; but the AB plants (hybrids) will produce offspring that split the characters in the same ratio as before, and so on. It is evident that this provides incidentally a test for hybrids, and that in the case of a hybrid there is a splitting and the separation of a certain proportion of the parent plants. It was this test that DeVries applied to his evening primrose, and as it did not "split" in many generations, he was convinced that he was dealing with a pure species.

It can be understood that such simple hybrids as the one used in the illustration do not represent the general situation in nature or under culture; but they serve to illustrate the fundamental feature of Mendel's law, which is that a hybrid in the second generation splits up in some definite ratio. It is not clear that all hybrids behave in this way; that is, some of them may not be Mendelian hybrids; but the law is prevalent enough to be used as the basis of very much scientific plant breeding and of experimental work related to evolution.

Heredity. — A phase of heredity has been presented under Mendel's law, but the general subject should be considered briefly. Heredity is the most difficult and perhaps the most important problem in biology. It means the transmission from parent to offspring of a similar structure, a transmission that involves fundamental resemblances with differences in detail. The possible machinery of heredity has been observed, but the factors controlling and determining the product are elusive as yet. Little more can be done than to state the problem.

In the simplest plants and animals every cell has the power of reproducing the whole organism. In the more complex plants and animals this power is restricted, being retained only by the reproductive cells. It is evident, therefore, that the reproductive cells possess a very primitive power, a power that the other cells have lost. Reproductive cells are to be thought of not as cells that have acquired some special power, but as cells that have retained a primitive power that once belonged to all cells. All other kinds of cells may reproduce their own kind, but a reproductive cell can reproduce the whole organism.

Reproduction is not simply cell multiplication, but also cell differentiation, and the organization of differentiated cells into organs, and of organs into the complete organism. Reproductive cells have been made to multiply cells under artificial stimulus; but it is this far-reaching directive power that has baffled investigation.

Any theory of heredity must explain not only likeness to the parent, but also variation from the parent and from every other individual, which is individuality. It must explain ancestral likeness, which is often called "atavism"; and also the sudden appearance of new characters, which after all may be very old ones. In short, the mass of observations awaiting explanation by some law of heredity is enormous.

The student of plant morphology is familiar with the general organization of a living cell. He has learned to recognize in the nucleus the probable machinery of heredity; and in the chromosomes the particular nuclear structure whose behavior suggests a definite relation to heredity. The mingling of paternal and maternal chromosomes in the fertilized egg is the beginning of a series of changes that must be followed eventually; but as yet the particular chromosomes are lost to sight, and their fate is followed only by inference or imagination. Later, male and female chromosomes are recognized again, but only to function in reproduction, and their varying influence in determining the structure of the individual remains unknown.

INDEX

[Figures in italics indicate pages upon which illustrations occur.]

Abies, resin gland, *340*.
Abietineae, 219.
Absorption bands, *369*; spectrum, 368, *369*.
Abstriction, of spores, 65.
Acetic fermentation, 411.
Achene, 282.
Acids, organic, 414.
Acorus, vascular bundle, *246*.
Acrocarpae, 121.
Acrogynae, 103.
Acropetal succession, in flowers, 256.
Actinomorphic flowers, 256.
Adder's tongue, 149.
Adhesion, 324.
Adiantum, stem section, *160*.
Aecidiospores, 83.
Aecidium, 83, *84*.
Aerating system, 318.
Aerotaxy, 449.
Aerotropism, 474.
Aestivation, 282.
Aethalium, 3.
Agaricaceae, 88.
Agaricales, 87.
Agaricus, 89.
Albizzia, leaf movements, *456*.
Albugo, *65*, *66*.
Alcoholic fermentation, 409.
Aleurone grains, *392*.
Algae, 14.
Alkaloids, 392, 415.
Allium, absorption spectra, *369*.
Alternation of generations, Coleochaete, 31; Polysiphonia, 60; rusts, 84; higher plants, 92.
Ament, 279.
Amides, 360, 392.
Amphigastria, 104.
Amphithecium, 95, *97*, 99, 108, *113*, 115, *118*, *119*.
Amphivasal bundles, 245, *246*.
Amylase, 400.
Anabaena, 9.
Anabolism, 402.
Anacrogynae, 101; conclusions, 103.
Anaptychia, *80*.
Anatropous ovules, *261*.

Andreaeales, 114.
Androspores, 30.
Aneimia, sporangium, *157*.
Aneimites, *183*.
Aneura, 101.
Angiosperms, 180, 238; classification, 276.
Anisocarpic flowers, 281.
Annual thickening, 346.
Annular vessels, *243*.
Annulus, mushrooms, 89; ferns, 155, *156*, *157*, *163*, 164, *165*, 352.
Anther, 256.
Antheridium, green algae, 27, *30*, *31*, *32*, *36*, *42*, *43*; Fucus, *50*; Nemalion, *56*; Polysiphonia, *59*; fungi, *64*, *66*, 73, 75, *78*; liverworts, 92, *94*, *95*, 99, 102, *104*, *105*, *106*, 107; mosses, *112*, *115*, *117*; lycopods, 127, *129*, *135*, *140*; equisetums, *148*; ophioglossums, *154*; ferns, 166, *167*; water ferns, 174, *175*, *178*.
Antherozoid, 17, 56.
Anthoceros, *106*, *107*, *108*, *109*.
Anthocerotales, 106; conclusions, 109.
Antipodal cells, 265.
Apical cell, *42*, 46, 98.
Aplanospores, *34*.
Aplastic products, 412.
Apocarpous flowers, 279.
Apogamy, ferns, 169; angiosperms, 275.
Apogeotropism, 460.
Apophysis, 119, *120*.
Apospory, ferns, 169.
Apostrophe, *450*.
Apothecium, 71, *72*, *78*, *79*, *80*.
Arales, 277.
Araucarineae, 220.
Archegonium, 92; liverworts, *94*, *96*, 99, 103, 104, *107*; mosses, *112*, *113*, *115*, *117*, *118*; lycopods, 128, *130*, 136, *137*, *140*; equisetums, 148; ophioglossums, 153, *154*; ferns, 167, *168*; water ferns, *175*, 179; gymnosperms, 197, *198*, *199*, 205, 210, *211*, 214, *215*, *216*, *223*, *233*; complex, *223*; jacket, 198.
Archicarp, 79.
Archichlamydeae, 239; classification, 278.
Arthrospores, 9.

A

INDEX

Ascobolus, 73.
Ascocarp, 70, 71, 72, 73, 75, 76.
Ascogenous hyphae, 72, 73.
Ascogonium, 73.
Ascomycetes, 70.
Ascospores, 70, 72, 73, 76, 77.
Ascus, 70, 72, 73, 76, 77, 78, 80.
Ash, 412, 415.
Aspergillus, 74.
Aspidium, habit and sporangia, 163; gametophyte, 166.
Assimilation, 364, 401.
Atrichum, leaf cells, 450.
Atropin, 415.
Auriculariales, 86.
Autobasidiomycetes, 86.
Autonomic movements, 453.
Autotrophic plants, 362, 380.
Auxiliary cells, Polysiphonia, 59, 60.
Auxospores, 53.
Azolla, 171, 172, 173, 174, 175.

Bacillus, 11.
Bacteria, 10, 11; aerobic, 13; anaerobic, 13; iron, 14; nitrifying, 13; nitrogen, 13; pathogenic, 13; saprophytic, 13; sulphur, 14.
Bark, loss of, 355.
Basidiomycetes, 80.
Basidiospore, 80, 83, 89.
Basidium, 80, 82, 83, 89.
Batrachospermum, 57.
Bennettitales, 185.
Bennettites, strobilus and seed, 189.
Bilabiate flowers, 282.
Biophores, 291.
Biophytum, records of responses, 429.
Black fungi, 76.
Black knot, 76.
Black mold, 67.
Bleeding, 332, 334.
Blepharoplast, 200, 211.
Blue-green algae, 4.
Blue mold, 74.
Body cell, 199, 200, 211, 215, 217, 224, 235.
Bog mosses, 110.
Boletus, 88.
Botrychium, 149; habit, 150; gametophyte and archegonium, 154.
Botrydium, 33, 34.
Bowenia, 192.
Box elder, section of stem, 245.
Branches, fall of, 355; origin of, 419.
Brown algae, 44.
Brucin, 415.
Bryales, 115.
Bryophytes, 92.

Bulbochaete, 30, 31.
Butyric fermentation, 411.

Caffein, 415.
Callus, 419.
Calymmatotheca, 184.
Calyptra, 95, 97, 100, 113, 118.
Calyptrogen, 247.
Calyx, 252.
Cambium, 150, 192, 243, 249.
Campanales, 282.
Campylotropous ovule, 261, 262.
Canna, megasporangium, 263.
Capillarity, and ascent of water, 349.
Capillitium, puffballs, 90; slime molds, 3.
Capsella, embryo, 272, 273.
Capsule, liverworts, 100, 103, 105, 108, 109; mosses, 113, 114, 115, 118, 119, 120; ferns, 164.
Carbohydrates, 358, 374.
Carbon assimilation, 363.
Carbon dioxid, admission of, 365; as raw material, 364.
Carnivorous plants, 386.
Carotin, 367, 368.
Carpel, 260.
Carpogonium, 56, 57, 59, 60.
Carpospore, 56, 57, 59, 60.
Catabolism, 402.
Catalysis, 399.
Catalyst, 399.
Catkin, 279.
Cell, organs, 297; rôle of living, 351; wall, 297, 298, 306.
Cellulose, 299, 359; "reserve," 390.
Central body, blue-green algae, 5.
Central cylinder, 124.
Centripetal succession, flowers, 256.
Ceratozamia, megasporophyll, 197.
Chaetophora, 26.
Chalaza, 266, 269.
Chalazogamy, 268.
Chantransia, 58.
Chara, apical cell, 42; habit, 41; sex organs, 43.
Charales, 41.
Chemical stimuli, 438.
Chemotaxy, 447.
Chemotropism, 473; fungi, 473; pollen tubes, 474.
Chlamydomonas, 15.
Chlamydospore, 81.
Chlorenchyma, 366.
Chlorophyceae, 15.
Chlorophyll, 2, 367.
Chlorophyllin, 367.
Chloroplast, 207, 366, 376, 450.
Chlorovaporization, 330.

INDEX

Chromosomes, 32, 51, 60, 92, 170, 275.
Chytridiales, 63.
Chytridium, 63.
Cilia, 445; in action, 446.
Cinchonin, 415.
Circinate vernation, 159, 163, 176.
Citric acid, 414.
Citrus, oil receptacle, 340.
Cladophora, 26, 27; walls, 308.
Cladosiphonic, 159.
Clavariales, 87.
Cleistocarpae, 120.
Cleistothecium, 74, 75.
Clinostat, 462.
Closterium, 37, 38.
Club mosses, 122.
Clustercup, 83, 84.
Cocain, 415.
Coccus, 11.
Codein, 415.
Codonotheca, 184.
Coenocytes, 26, 27, 33, 34, 35, 36, 62.
Cohesion theory, 351.
Cold, cause of death, 483.
Coleochaete, 31, 32.
Coleoptile, and starch grains, 465.
Colony, blue-green algae, 6; green algae, 17, 21.
Columella, Anthoceros, 108, 109; black mold, 67, 68; mosses, 113, 118, 119, 120.
Companion cells, 243; rôle, 394.
Compass plants, 478.
Concentration, 304.
Concentric bundles, 125, 161.
Conceptacle, 50.
Conducting system, 393; origin, 341.
Conducting tissue, in style, 260.
Confervales, 24; conclusions, 33.
Conidia, 65, 74, 75.
Coniferales, 212.
Conjugales, 37; conclusions, 40.
Conjugation, 16, 38, 39, 40.
Contact movements, 454.
Coprinus, 88, 89.
Coral fungi, 87.
Corallina, 55.
Cordaitales, 203, 204, 205, 206.
Cork, cambium, 240; cells, 240; rôle, 318.
Corn, section of stem, 245.
Cornaceae, 280.
Corn smut, 81.
Corolla, 252, 253.
Correlations, 441.
Cortex, angiosperms, 239, 240, 242; gymnosperms, 192, 193, 219; kelps, 48; pteridophytes, 124, 125, 145, 159, 160, 161, 162.
Crossing of pollen, 268.
Crossotheca, 184.

Cryptogams, 180.
Cup fungi, 71.
Cupressineae, 220.
Cupules, 98, 99.
Curvatures, growth, 458; nastic, 442.
Cuscuta, haustorium, 382.
Cutin, 299.
Cutleriaceae, 49.
Cyanophyceae, 4.
Cyatheaceae, 156.
Cycadales, 190.
Cycadella, 185.
Cycadeoidea, habit, 185; strobilus, 186, 187, 188; synangia, 189.
Cycadofilicales, 181.
Cycadofilices, 181.
Cycas, habit, 190; microsporophyll, 195; megasporophyll, 197; male gametophyte, 199; embryo, 202.
Cystocarp, 56, 57, 59.
Cytase, 400.
Cytoplasm, 2, 297.

Dacromycetales, 86.
Dacrydium, male gametophyte, 217.
Daily period, 436.
Death, 480.
Decay, 385.
Deformities, 440.
Dendroceros, 106.
Dermatogen, 239, 240, 247, 465.
Desmidiaceae, 37.
Desmids, 37.
Desmodium, leaflets, 453.
Determinants, 291.
Development, 417.
Dextrinase, 400.
Diageotropism, 467.
Diaphragm, water ferns, 175.
Diastase, 399.
Diatomin, 53.
Diatoms, 52, 54.
Dichotomous, branching, 49; venation, 159, 163, 164.
Dicotyledons, 238; classification, 279; embryo, 271; vascular system, 243.
Dictyotales, 55.
Diffusion, 302, 304, 393; rate, 304.
Digestion, 397; extra-cellular, 398.
Dioecious, 30, 105.
Dioecism, 30.
Dionaea, 386, 387.
Dioon, embryo sac, 199; habit, 191; ovule, 198; staminate strobilus, 195.
Dioscorea, ocella, 479.
Discomycetes, 72.
Disease, 482.
Disk flowers, 282.

C

INDEX

Dodders, 472.
Dorsiventrality, 437.
Dorycordaites, 204.
Dotted ducts, 241, 243.
Double fertilization, 269.
Downy mildews, 65.
Drosera, 387, 454.

Ear fungi, 86.
Earth star, 90.
Ebenales, 281.
Ecology, 295.
Ectocarpus, 45.
Ectoplast, 306.
Efficiency, 371.
Egg, thallophytes, 17, 18, 19, 28, 30, 32, 36, 51, 64; bryophytes, 96, 107, 118; pteridophytes, 130, 137, 140, 154, 168, 179; spermatophytes, 198, 216, 217, 226, 265, 266, 269.
Egg apparatus, 265.
Eichhornia, megaspore tetrad, 263.
Elaterophore, 103.
Elaters, 100.
Electric waves, 438.
Electrotropism, 479.
Eligulatae, 132.
Embryo, angiosperms, 271, 272, 273, 274, 275; Botrychium, 153, 154; Equisetum, 149; ferns, 168, 169; gymnosperms, 189, 200, 201, 202, 211, 212, 218, 225, 226, 227, 236, 237; Isoetes, 141; Lycopodium, 130, 131; Selaginella, 137.
Embryo sac, 197, 198, 199, 234, 261, 264, 265, 266.
Endarch, 157.
Endodermis, 240.
Endogenous, 250; root branches, 248.
Endosperm, 202, 211, 223, 270.
Endothecium, anthers, 257, 258, 259; bryophytes, 95, 97, 99, 108, 113, 115, 118, 119.
Energy, 368; absorbed, 370.
Entomophthorales, 68.
Environment, 284.
Enzymes, 39; carbohydrate, 399; fat, 400; glucoside, 400; protein, 401.
Ephedra, archegonia, 233; embryo, 236, 237; habit, 228; male gametophyte, 235.
Epidermis, angiosperms, 239, 240, 242, 248, 250, 251, 319; bryophytes, 94, 98, 109, 118, 120; pteridophytes, 145, 160, 161.
Epigyny, 255.
Epinasty, 442.
Epistrophe, 450.
Epithem, 332.
Equilibrium, position of, 463.
Equisetales, 143; conclusions, 149.
Equisetum, 143; antheridium, 148; embryo, 149; gametophyte, 147; habit, 144; sporangium, 146; stem section, 145.
Ergot fungus, 77.
Ericales, 281.
Erysiphaceae, 75.
Erysiphe, haustorium, 381.
Etiolin, 367.
Eudorina, 17, 18.
Euglena, 20.
Eumycetes, 62.
Eurotium, 74.
Eusporangiates, 126.
Evaporation, 323.
Evolution, 283.
Exarch, 157.
Excitability, 434.
Exine, 147, 258.
Exoascus, 71.
Exobasidiales, 86.
Exogenous, origin of branches, 419.
Exudation, 332, 333; cause, 335.

Fagus, mycorhiza, 382.
Farinales, 278.
Fat enzymes, 400.
Fatigue, 432.
Fats, 360, 391.
Fermentation, 385, 409; acetic, 411; alcoholic, 409; butyric, 411; lactic, 410.
Ferns, 155.
Fertilization, gymnosperms, 201, 211, 215, 217, 225, 226, 235, 268, 269; mosses, 116; pteridophytes, 136, 168; thallophytes, 18, 28, 66.
Ficus, leaf skeleton, 343.
Filament, of anther, 256, 257.
Filicales, 155.
Filicineae, 155; conclusions, 170.
Filmy ferns, 155.
Flagella, 445.
Flagellates, 20.
Florideae, 55.
Flower, 180, 251.
Flowering plants, 180.
Fluorescence, 370.
Flytrap, 386, 387.
Food, 356; and growth, 363; source of energy, 363; storage, 388; translocation, 388.
Foot, bryophytes, 100, 103, 108, 109, 113, 114; pteridophytes, 130, 131, 137, 141, 149, 154, 168.
Formaldehyde, 360.
Form and light, 437.
Formative stimuli, 435.
Fragmentation, blue-green algae, 7.
Friction, as stimulus, 470.
Fronds, 159.

D

INDEX

Fructose, 359.
Fruits, loss of, 355.
Fucales, 49.
Fucus, fertilization and embryo, *52*; habit, *49*; sex organs, *50*, *51*.
Fuligo, aethalium, *3*; plasmodium, *2*.
Function, 297; unit of, 298.
Fungi, 61; chemotropism of, 473.

Galls, *304*, 440.
Gametangium, 45, 46.
Gamete, 16, *17*, *22*, *23*, *25*, 46, 49.
Gametophyte, 32; thallophytes, 52, 60, 85; liverworts, 92, *93*, 97, 101, 103, 106; mosses, 111, 115; pteridophytes, *127*, *128*, 131, *147*, 148, 153, 165, 166, *167*; female, *136*, *140*, *174*, *175*, *178*, *179*, 196, *199*, 205, 210, 211, 214, *216*, 223, 232, *234*, *264*, *265*, *266*; male, *135*, *140*, *174*, *175*, *178*, .*199*, 205, *206*, 210, 215, *217*, 223, *224*, *235*, *267*.
Gases, diffusion, 302; entry and exit, 322; exclusion, 318; from shoot, 352.
Gasteromycetes, 89.
Geaster, 90.
Gemmae, 98, 104, 117.
Generative cell, *199*, *224*, *267*.
Gentianales, 282.
Geotaxy, 450.
Geotropism, 459; lateral, 467.
Geranium, section of cortex, *240*.
Germinal selection, 291.
Gill, of mushrooms, 88, *89*.
Gill fungi, 88.
Ginkgo, leaf, *207*; female gametophyte, *211*; ovule, *210*; proembryo, *212*; strobili, *208*, *209*.
Ginkgoales, 207.
Girdles, leaf trace, 193, *194*.
Girdling, 347.
Glands, geranium, *337*; form, 338; Syringa, *338*; nectar, *339*; resin, *340*.
Gleba, Gasteromycetes, 90.
Gleichenia, sori, *156*; stele, *159*.
Gleicheniaceae, 155.
Glochidia, 174, *175*.
Gloeocapsa, *5*.
Gloeothece, *5*.
Glucose, 359, 375.
Glucoside enzymes, 400.
Glumales, 276.
Glumes, 277.
Gnetales, 228.
Gnetum, embryo, 236; female gametophyte, *234*; ovule, *234*; strobili, *231*, *232*.
Gonidia, 19.
Gradient, 304.
Grand period, 421, *422*.
Grape mildew, 66.

Gravity, movements, 455; nastic curvatures, 443.
Green algae, 15.
Growing point, angiosperms, 239, *240*, *247*.
Growing regions, 422.
Growth, 417; curvatures, 458; and food, 363; and light, *435*; movements, 457; rapidity, 424; and transpiration, 326; and turgor, 310.
Guard cells, *251*, *320*.
Gulfweed, 52, *53*.
Gums, 413.
Guttation, 332; artificial, 333; in fungi, 333; nightly, 333.
Gymnosperms, 180, 181.

Haustorium, fungi, 61, *381*, 398; pollen tube, 201.
Heat, cause of death, 483; from respiration, 407.
Helminthostachys, 149; habit, *151*.
Helobiales, 276.
Helotism, 382.
Helvellales, 71.
Hemerocallis, nectar gland, *339*.
Hemitelia, sporangium, *57*.
Hepaticae, 93.
Herbarium mold, 74.
Heredity, 293.
Heterangium, 182.
Heterocysts, 7, *8*, *9*.
Heterogamy, 17.
Heterospory, 132, 133, 134.
Heterotrophic plants, 362, 380.
Hippuris, stem tip, *240*, *418*.
Homospory, 134.
Hormogonia, *8*.
Horsetails, 143.
Host, 61, 381.
Humidity, and transpiration, 329.
Hybrids, 268, 293.
Hydnaceae, 88.
Hydnum, 88.
Hydrodictyon, 21, *22*, *23*, 445.
Hydropteridineae, 170; conclusions, 179.
Hydrotropism, 475.
Hymenium, 71.
Hymenogastrales, 90.
Hymenomycetes, 86.
Hymenophyllaceae, 155.
Hymenophyllum, sorus, *156*.
Hyphae, 61.
Hypogyny, 255.
Hyponasty, 442.
Hypophysis, 271, *273*.

Imbibition, 300.
Impatiens, geotropic curvature, *461*.

E

INDEX

Income, material, 297.
Indusium, *156, 157, 163,* 165, *172, 175, 177*.
Injury, 440; mechanical, 482.
Insectivorous plants, 386.
Integument, 183, 196, 205, 209, 210, 213, 214, *230*, 232, *233*, *261*, 280.
Internodes, 41, 145.
Intine, 147, 258.
Inulase, 400.
Inulin, 391.
Invertase, 400.
Involucre, 280.
Irregularity, flowers, 256, 278, 280, 282.
Irritability, 426; loss of, 434.
Isocarpic flowers, 281.
Isoetes, embryo, *141;* gametophytes, *140;* habit, *138;* sporangia, *139.*
Isogamy, 16.
Isolation, 292.

Jungermanniales, 101; contrast with Marchantiales, 105.

Laboulbeniales, 77.
Lactic fermentation, 410.
Lactuca, root hairs, *312.*
Lagenostoma, *182.*
Laminariaceae, 47.
Laminaria, *46*.
Latex system, 396.
Leaf, angiosperms, *250, 251;* fall of, 354; gaps, 159; gymnosperms, *190, 191, 192, 193,* 203, *204, 207, 208,* 220, 229; liverworts, 101, *104;* mosses, *111, 112, 116;* pteridophytes, 122, *133, 138,* 150, 151, *158, 163, 164, 171, 176;* traces, 125, 192, *194*.
Leafy liverworts, 101.
Lecithins, 360.
Leguminosae, 280; relation to nitrogen, 379.
Lenticel, 240, *241*.
Leptosporangiates, 162.
Lessonia, 48.
Leucoplast, *389*.
Lichens, 78, 91.
Life, 408.
Light, exposure to, 370; and form, *437;* and growth, *435;* and nastic curvatures, 443; photosynthesis, 368; position, 478; source of, 372.
Ligulatae, 132.
Ligule, Lycopodiales, 132, *134, 137, 139, 141.*
Liliales, 278.
Lily, anther section, *259;* leaf epidermis, *251;* leaf section, 250, *319*.
Liquids, 302.
Liverworts, 93.
Locomotion, 444.

Lycoperdales, 90.
Lycoperdon, 90.
Lycopodiaceae, conclusions, 132.
Lycopodiales, 122.
Lycopodium, 122; antheridium, *129;* archegonium, *130;* embryo, *131;* gametophyte, *127, 128, 129;* habit, *123, 134;* sporangium, *125, 126;* stele, *125.*
Lyginodendron, stem section, *182.*
Lygodium, sporangium, *157.*
Lyngbya, 6.

Macrocystis, habit, *47.*
Malic acid, 414.
Maltase, 400.
Manubrium, *43.*
Maple sap, 334.
Marattia, embryo, *169;* habit, *158;* leaflet, *164.*
Marattiaceae, 155; antheridium, 166; sporangia, 160.
Marchantia, *98, 99, 100,* 435.
Marchantiaceae, 97.
Marchantiales, 93; contrast with Jungermanniales, 105.
Marsilea, female gametophyte, *179;* habit, *176;* male gametophyte, *178;* sporocarp, *177.*
Marsileaceae, 176.
Massulae, water ferns, 173, *175.*
Material income, 297.
Material outgo, 323.
Mechanical stimuli, 439.
Medulla, kelps, 48.
Medullosa, *182.*
Megaceros, 106.
Megasporangium, *134,* 135, *139, 172, 173, 174, 177, 261, 262, 263.*
Megaspore, *135,* 172, 196, 262.
Megasporocarp, *171, 172.*
Megasporophyll, 135, *197.*
Members, 297.
Membrane, cell wall, 306; cytoplasmic, 306; impermeable, 305; permeable, 305.
Mendel's law, 292.
Merismopedia, *6.*
Meristem, 133; primary, 419; secondary, 419.
Mesarch, 157.
Mesembryanthemum, origin of lateral root, *420.*
Mesocarpaceae, 38.
Mesophyll, 250.
Metabolism, 402; destructive, 403.
Metaxylem, 157, 241.
Micellae, 300.
Microcycas, 201.
Microorganisms, 409.

INDEX

Micropyle, 183, *261*.
Microsphaera, 75, 76.
Microsporangium, *134*, 135, *139*, 172, 173, *174*, 177, *184*, 189, 205, 220, 257, *258*, *259*.
Microspore, 135, *175*.
Microsporocarp, *171*, 172, 173, 174.
Microsporophyll, 135, *195*, 214, *220*, 257.
Middle layers, anthers, 257.
Mildews, 75, 76.
Mimosa, leaf, *452*.
Miscible, 303.
Monadelphous stamens, 255.
Monoblepharis, 64.
Monocotyledons, classification, 276; embryo, *273*, *274*, *275*; vascular system, 244, *245*, *246*.
Monosiphonous, algae, 45.
Moonwort, 149, *150*.
Morchella, *71*.
Morel, *71*.
Morphin, 415.
Morphogenic stimuli, 435.
Morphology, 1, 295.
Mosses, 110.
Mother cell, 127.
Motor organs, 451.
Movement, 417; amoeboid, 444; autonomic, 453; of cell organs, 450; ciliary, 445, 446; contact, 452, 454; excretory, 445; gravity, 455; growth, 457; leaf, 455, 456; nyctitropic, 456; paratonic, 454; photeolic, 455, 456; turgor, 451, 457.
Mucilage, blue-green algae, 6.
Mucor, *67*, *68*, *69*, 435.
Mucorales, 67.
Muscarin, 415.
Musci, 110.
Mushrooms, 87.
Mutation, 288.
Mutualism, 382.
Mycelium, 61.
Mycetozoa, 2.
Mycorhiza, 74, *382*, *383*.
Myriophyllum, stem section, *320*.
Myxobacteriaceae, 14.

Narcotin, 415.
Nastic movements, 431.
Nasties, 432.
Natural selection, 285.
Nectary, *339*.
Nemalion, *56*.
Neottia, mycorhiza, 383.
Nepenthes, leaf, *385*.
Nephrodium, sperm, *444*.
Nereocystis, *47*, *48*.
Nest fungi, 90.
Nicotiana, flower, *253*.

Nicotin, 415.
Nidulariales, 90.
Nitella, 42.
Nitrogen, source of, 378.
Nodes, 41, 145.
Nostoc, 7, *8*.
Notothylas, 106, *108*.
Nucellus, 183.
Nucleus, 6, *15*, 16, *297*.
Nutation, 423, *424*.
Nutrition, 356.
Nutritive mechanism, in ovule, 266.

Oedogonium, 27, *29*, *30*.
Oil receptacle, 340.
Oils, essential, 413.
Ontogeny, 295.
Oogonium, 27, *28*, *30*, *31*, *36*.
Oomycetes, 62.
Ooplasm, 66.
Oosphere, 17.
Oospore, 18.
Operculum, 113, *114*, 119, *120*.
Ophioglossales, 149; conclusions, 154.
Ophioglossum, 149; habit, *150*; sporangium, *152*, *153*.
Orchidales, 278.
Organ, 297.
Organized bodies, structures, 300.
Organogeny, flowers, 256.
Orthogenesis, 289.
Orthotropic organs, 459.
Orthotropous ovules, *261*.
Oscillatoria, 6, *7*.
Osmosis, 302, 305.
Osmotic pressure, 309.
Osmunda, sporangium, *156*; stele, *162*.
Osmundaceae, 155.
Outgo, material, 323.
Ovary, 260.
Ovule, 183; angiosperms, 260, *261*; gymnosperms, 196, *197*, *198*, 205, *206*, 209, 210, 213, *214*, 221, 222, 232, *233*, *234*.
Oxalic acid, 414.

Palisade, leaf, *250*, *251*, *319*.
Palmales, 277.
Palmella, 26.
Pandanales, 276.
Pandorina, *17*.
Panicum, coleoptile, *465*.
Panmixia, 291.
Pappus, 282.
Parallelotropic organs, 458, 460.
Paraphyses, *50*, *51*, 117.
Parasite, 61, 381; injury by, 383.
Parasitism, 381.
Paratonic movements, 454.

G

INDEX

Parmelia, 79.
Parthenogenesis, 40, 64, 169, 275.
Peach curl, 71.
Pecopteris, seeds, 183.
Pediastrum, 21, 22.
Pelargonium, capitate hairs, 337.
Pellia, thallus, 101.
Pellionia, starch grains, 389.
Penicillium, 74.
Pentacyclic flowers, 281.
Peony, flower, 252.
Perceptive region, 430, 463, 465, 477, 479.
Perianth, 252.
Periblem, 239, 240, 247.
Pericentral cell, 59, 60.
Pericycle, 241.
Periderm, 419.
Peridineae, 54.
Peridium, 90.
Perigyny, 255.
Perinium, 144, 147, 174, 175.
Periplasm, 66.
Perisperm, 270.
Perithecium, 76, 77, 78.
Peronospora, 67.
Peronosporales, 65.
Persistence, 457.
Petal, 252.
Petioles, sensitive, 472.
Peziza, 72.
Pezizales, 71.
Phaeophyceae, 44.
Phaeosporales, 45.
Phallales, 91.
Phanerogams, 180.
Phaseolus, in darkness, 437; leaf movements, 456.
Phellogen, 240, 419.
Phloem, 124, 345, 394.
Phosphorus, source of, 379.
Photeolic movements, 455, 456.
Photosynthesis, 363; process, 375; products, 373.
Phototaxy, 449.
Phototropism, 475.
Phycocyanin, 4.
Phycoerythrin, 55.
Phycomycetes, 62; conclusions, 69.
Phycophaein, 44.
Phycoxanthin, 44.
Phylloglossum, 131, 132.
Phyllosiphonic, 159.
Phylogeny, 295.
Physcia, 78.
Physiology, 295.
Phytophthora, 66.
Pileus, 87, 88, 89.
Pilobolus, 68, 333.

Pilularia, 176.
Pinaceae, 219.
Pine, archegonium, 223; embryo, 226; male gametophyte, 224; needle, 220; pollen, 221; pollen tube, 225; stem section, 219; strobili, 220, 221; wounded, 395.
Pistil, 253, 254, 260.
Pitcher plants, 385, 386.
Pith rays, 150.
Pitted vessels, 241.
Placenta, 260.
Plagiotropic organs, 458, 466, 478.
Plantaginales, 282.
Plasmodium, 2.
Plasmolysis, 309.
Plasmopara, 66.
Plectascales, 74.
Plerome, 239, 240, 247.
Pleurocarpae, 121.
Pleurococcus, 20, 21.
Plowrightia, 76.
Plum pockets, 71.
Poa, penetrated by fungus, 381.
Podocarpineae, 212.
Podocarpus, 212; microsporophylls, 214.
Poisons, 484.
Polarity, 440.
Pollen, 199; chamber, 183, 198, 210; chemotropism of, 474; sac, 260; tube, 201, 211, 216, 217, 225, 235, 268, 269.
Pollination, 268.
Pollinium, 259.
Polyembryony, 275.
Polyhedra, 23.
Polymorphism, rusts, 83.
Polypodiaceae, 156; antheridium, 167; sporangia, 162.
Polyporaceae, 88.
Polyporus, 88.
Polysiphonia, 58, 59, 60.
Polysiphonous, algae, 45.
Polystele, 157.
Polystichum, sporangium, 352.
Pore fungi, 88.
Porella, 103, 104, 105.
Porogamy, 269.
Portulaca, photeolic movements, 455.
Postelsia, habit, 48.
Potamogeton, escape of gas bubbles, 377.
Potato rot, 66.
Presentation time, 434, 461.
Pressure, atmospheric, 350; barometric, 329; diffusion, 304; root, 349.
Primary tubercle, Lycopodium, 127.
Primulales, 281.
Procarp, 56, 59, 60.
Proembryo, cycads, 200, 201, 202; Ginkgo,

INDEX

212; Torreya, *218*; Pinus, 225, *226*; Ephedra, *236*, *237*; angiosperms, 271, *272*, *273*.
Progeotropism, 460.
Promycelium, *83*.
Prosenchyma, 112.
Protective tissues, 318.
Protein enzymes, 401.
Proteins, 361, 391; synthesis of, 377.
Prothallial tubes, Tumboa, 235.
Prothallium, 165, *166*.
Protoascales, 70.
Protobasidiomycetes, 81.
Protococcales, 20; conclusions, 24.
Protodiscales, 71.
Protonema, 115, *116*.
Protoplast, 7, 297; work of, 298.
Protosiphon, 34.
Protostele, 125, 157, *159*.
Protoxylem, 157, 241.
Pseudopodium, slime molds, 2; mosses, *113*, *114*, 115.
Psilotales, 142.
Psilotum, 142, *143*.
Pteridophytes, 122.
Pteris, stem section, *161*.
Puccinia, *82*, *83*, *84*, 85.
Puffballs, 90.
Pulque, 334.
Pulvinus, 452.
Purslane, photoeolic movements, *455*.
Putrefaction, 355, 411.
Pycnidia, 83.
Pycnidiospores, 83.
Pyrenoid, 16, *39*, 40.
Pyrenomycetales, 75.
Pyronema, 72, *73*.

Quillworts, 138.

Radial bundles, 248, *249*.
Ramentum, 185.
Ranales, 279.
Ranunculus, nectar gland, *339*; root section, *249*.
Ray flowers, 282.
Reaction, mechanism, 431; modes, 428; time, 433.
Receptacle, flower, 253; Marchantia, 99.
Red algae, 54.
Regular flowers, 256.
Reproduction, 481.
Resins, 413.
Respiration, 423; aerobic and anaerobic, 404; products, 406; rôle of oxygen, 406.
Reversible action, 399.
Revolution, twiners, 468.

Rheotropism, 473.
Rhipsalis, chloroplasts, *376*.
Rhizopus, 67.
Rhodophyceae, 54.
Riccia, *93*, *94*, *95*, *96*, 97.
Ricciaceae, 93; conclusions, 96.
Ricciocarpus, 93.
Ricinus, endosperm cell, *392*; stem section, *242*, *346*.
Ringless ferns, 155.
Rivularia, 8, *9*.
Rockweed, 49.
Root, angiosperm, 247, *248*, *249*; branches, *248*; cap, *246*, *247*, *465*; diffusion from, 353; effect on soil, 315; hairs, 247, *248*, *312*; permeable regions, 311; "pressure," 336; pteridophytes, 122, 130, *131*, *137*, 141, *163*, *168*; system, 311; tip, *247*.
Roripa, rootcap, *465*.
Rosales, 280.
Rotation, clinostat, 462; twiner, 468.
Rubiales, 282.
Rusts, *82*, *83*, *84*, 85.

Saccharomycetes, 70.
Saccharose, 359.
Sac fungi, 70.
Sagittaria, embryo, *273*, *274*, *275*.
Salix, megasporangium, *262*.
Salts, and transpiration, 325; and waterproofing, 317.
Salvinia, *171*.
Salviniaceae, 171.
Sap pressure and turgor, 311.
Saprolegnia, *64*.
Saprolegniales, 63.
Saprophytes, 2, 61, 384.
Sargassum, 52, *53*.
Sarracenia, 386.
Scalariform vessels, 241, *244*.
Scale mosses, 101.
Scenedesmus, *21*.
Sceptridium, 149.
Schizaeaceae, 155.
Schizomycetes, 10.
Schizophyceae, 4.
Schizophytes, 4.
Scitaminales, 278.
Sclerodermales, 90.
Sclerotium, 2, 77.
Scouring rushes, 143.
Scytonema, *9*.
Secondary xylem, 241, 344, *345*.
Secretion, 332, 337; emission, 338.
Sedum, stoma, *320*.
Seeds, 180, *182*, *183*, *188*, *189*, 212, *232*; loss of, 355.
Seed plants, 180.

INDEX

Selaginella, 132; archegonium, *137*; embryo, *137*; female gametophyte, *136*; habit, *133*; sporangia, *134*; spores, *135*.
Selection, variable, 307.
Selective action, 307.
Sensitive plants, 429.
Sepal, 252.
Seta, 100, *101*, 103, *104*, 105, 113, *116*, 120.
Shoot, permeable regions of, 311.
Sieve plates, 242, 243.
Sieve vessels, 242, *243*; rôle, 394.
Silphium, fertilization, 260; male gametophyte, *267*; microsporangium, *258*.
Siphonales, 33; conclusions, 37.
Siphonostele, 133; amphiphloic, *157*, *160*; ectophloic, *157*, *162*.
Sleep movements, 455.
Soil, 312; capacity for water, 313; effect of roots, 315; water of, 313.
Solids, 302.
Solutes, 303; entry of, 316; natural, 303.
Solution, 300, 303.
Solvent, 303.
Soredia, 79.
Sorus, *156*, *163*, *165*.
Spadix, 277.
Spathe, 277.
Spectrum, absorption, 368, *369*.
Sperms, 17; thallophytes, *18*, *19*, *28*, *30*, *36*, *43*, *50*, *52*, 56; bryophytes, 92, 95, 102, 112, *117*; pteridophytes, 128, *129*, *135*, *140*, *148*, 167, *178*, *444*; gymnosperms, *199*, 201, 211.
Spermatium, red algae, 56; rusts, 83.
Spermatophytes, 180.
Spermatozoid, 17, 56.
Spermogonium, lichens, 79; rusts, *83*.
Sphacelaria, 46.
Sphaerella, *15*.
Sphaerocarpus, 105.
Sphaeroplea, 27, *28*.
Sphaerotheca, 75.
Sphagnales, 110; conclusions, 114.
Sphagnum, antheridia, *112*; archegonia, *113*; gametophyte, *111*; habit, *112*, *113*; leaf, *111*; sporophytes, *113*, *114*.
Sphenophyllales, 143.
Sphenophyllum, 143.
Spiral vessels, 241, *243*.
Spirillum, *11*.
Spongy region, leaf, *250*, *251*.
Sporangiophore, 143, 146, *333*.
Sporangium, 3; thallophytes, *3*, *27*, *45*, *58*, *59*, *67*, *68*; pteridophytes, *125*, *126*, 133, *134*, *139*, 142, 143, 144, *146*, 152, *153*, *156*, *157*, 160, *163*, *164*, *165*, *352*.
Spores, 3, 16, 62, 147.
Sporidia, *83*.

Sporocarp, 171, *172*, *173*, *174*, *176*, *177*.
Sporogonium, 95.
Sporophores, 62.
Sporophylls, 122.
Sporophyte, 32; thallophytes, 32, 60, 84; bryophytes, 92, 95, 97, 99, 100, *101*, 103, 104, 105, *108*, *109*, 113, 114, 115, 116, *118*, *119*, *120*; pteridophytes, 122, 132, 138, 143, 149, 156, 171, 176; gymnosperms, 181, 185, 191, 203, 207, 213, 220, 229.
Spirogyra, 39.
Sprout chains, yeast, 70, 71.
Squirting fungus, 68.
Stalk cell, 200.
Stamens, 183, *184*, 186, *187*, 195, 205, 208, 213, 214, 220, 221, *230*, *231*, 252, 253, 256, *257*.
Staminodia, 281.
Starch, 358, 375, 389.
Starch grain, *389*.
Statolith theory, 464.
Stegocarpae, 121.
Stele, 124, 239, 241.
Stem, angiosperms, 239.
Stemonitis, 3.
Sterigmata, 80, *89*.
Stigeoclonium, 26.
Stigma, 260.
Stigmatomyces, 78.
Stigonema, 10.
Stimulus, 426; chemical, 438; formative, 435; mechanical, 439; morphogenic, 435; tonic, 449.
Stink horns, 91.
Stipe, mushroom, 87.
Stomata, 109, 146, *250*, *251*, 319, *320*, 327; regulation of, 327.
Stomium, 164.
Stoneworts, 41.
Storage, 388.
Straightening, twiners, 469.
Strains, sexual, 68.
Streaming, 444, 451.
Strobilus, 122; pteridophytes, *124*, *132*, *133*, *144*; gymnosperms, *186*, *187*, *188*, *189*, *192*, *193*, *195*, *196*, *204*, *205*, *206*, *208*, *209*, *213*, *214*, *220*, *221*, *222*, *228*, *229*, *230*, *231*, *232*; theory of, 123.
Stroma, chloroplasts, 367; fungi, 76, 77.
Style, 260.
Substratum, fungi, 61.
Sugar, 390; cane, 359; fruit, 359; grape, 359.
Sulfur, source of, 379.
Summation, 432, 462.
Sundew, 387, 454.
Sunflower, nutation, *424*.
Suspensor, angiosperms, 271, *272*, *273*, *274*;

INDEX

gymnosperms, 202, 218, 236, 227, 237; Mucor, 68, 69; pteridophytes, 130, 131, 137.
Swarm spores, 16, 445.
Swelling, 300.
Swimming spores, 16.
Sympetalae, 239; classification, 280.
Sympetalous corolla, 255.
Sympetaly, 255.
Symphyogyna, 101.
Synangium, 161, 164.
Synanthales, 277.
Syncarpous pistils, 255.
Syncarpy, 255.
Synchytrium, 63.
Synsepalous calyx, 255.
Syringa, leaf gland, 338; leaf xylem, 343.

Tannins, 414.
Tapetum, 126, 153, 164, 174, 177, 257, 258, 259.
Tartaric acid, 414.
Taxaceae, 212.
Taxic movements, 431.
Taxies, 432, 446.
Taxineae, 212.
Taxodineae, 220.
Taxus, 213; microsporophyll, 214.
Telegraph plant, 453.
Teleutospore, 82, 83.
Temperature, and death, 483; and nastic curvatures, 443; and photosynthesis, 372; and transpiration, 330.
Tendrils, 469.
Tension of tissues, 425.
Terpenes, 413.
Testa, 183, 196, 205, 209, 213.
Tetanus, 432, 433.
Tetracyclic flowers, 281.
Tetraspores, 55, 59, 60.
Thallophytes, 1.
Thelephorales, 87.
Theobromin, 415.
Thermotropism, 479.
Thigmotropism, 469.
Thuja, archegonium complex, 222.
Tmesipteris, habit and sporangia, 142.
Toadstools, 87.
Tobacco, flower, 253.
Tolypothrix, 9.
Tone, 434.
Tooth fungi, 88.
Torreya, archegonium, 215; embryo, 218; female gametophyte, 216; fertilization, 217; male gametophyte, 217; microsporophyll, 214; strobilus, 213, 214.
Trabeculae, 130.
Tracheae, 241, 243, 342, 344, 345.

Tracheids, 150, 220, 241, 244, 342, 343.
Tradescantia, root tips, 247.
Translocation of food, 388; rhythmic, 396.
Transmission of stimuli, 430.
Transpiration, 321, 323; factors, 329; and growth, 326; and salts, 325.
Traumatropism, 472.
Tree ferns, 156.
Trehalase, 400.
Tremellales, 86.
Trichogyne, 56, 57, 80.
Trichomanes, sporangia, 156.
Triple fusion, 270.
Tropaeolum, nectary, 339.
Tropic movements, 431.
Tropisms, 432, 458.
True mosses, 115.
Truffles, 74.
Twiners, 467.
Tube cell, 199.
Tuberales, 74.
Tubiflorales, 282.
Tumboa, embryo, 236; female gametophyte, 234; "flowers," 230; habit, 229; strobilus, 229.
Turgidity, 308.
Turgor, 309; and growth, 310; movements, 451, 457; rigidity from, 310.

Ulothrix, 24, 25.
Ulva, 26.
Umbellales, 280.
Umbelliferae, 280.
Uncinula, 75, 76.
Uredinales, 82.
Uredo, 84.
Uredospore, 82.
Urostyla, movement of cilia, 446.
Use and disuse, 284.
Usnea, 79.
Ustilaginales, 81.

Vacuole, 297.
Vascular anatomy, Bennettitales, 185; Coniferales, 219; Cordaitales, 203; Cycadales, 192, 194; Cycadofilicales, 181, 182; Dicotyledons, 242, 245; Equisetum, 145; Filicales, 156, 159, 160, 161, 162; Ginkgo, 207; Gnetales, 229; Isoetes, 138; Lycopodium, 124, 125; Monocotyledons, 244, 245; Ophioglossales, 149; root, 247, 249; Selaginella, 133.
Vaucheria, 34, 35, 36.
Vegetative multiplication, algae, 6, 10; mosses, 116.
Velum, Isoetes, 139; mushrooms, 89.
Vicia, geotropic root curvature, 461.
Volva, mushrooms, 88.

INDEX

Volvocales, 15.
Volvox, 18, *19*.

Wastes, 412.
Water, ascent, 349; capillary ascent, 314; continuity, 301; and death, 483; entry, 316; exudation, 332; immigration, 308; influx, 325; loss, 331; migration into roots, 314; movement, 341; and plants, 299, 311; raw material, 366; relations, 301; soil, 313; solvent, 303.
Water ferns, 170.
Water molds, 63.
Water proofing, 317, 318.
Weber's law, 448.
Weismannism, 290.
Welwitschia, 228.
Wheat, aleurone grains, *392*.
Wheat rust, 82, *83*, *84*, 85.
White rust, *65*.
Witch brooms, 71.
Wood, heart and sap, 347.

Xanthophyll, 367.
Xenia, 271.
Xylaria, 77.
Xylem, 124, 241, 342, *343*, *344*, *345*; water path, 347.

Yeast, 70; fermentation, 410.

Zamia, embryo, *200*, *201*; habit, *193*; stamen, *195*; stem section, *194*; strobilus, *196*.
Zonal development, 254.
Zoospore, 16, *22*, *23*, *25*, *26*, *28*, *29*, *30*, *32*, *34*, *35*, 45.
Zygnema, 38, *40*.
Zygnemaceae, 38.
Zygomorphic flowers, 256.
Zygomycetes, 67.
Zygospore, 16, *17*, *22*, *23*, *25*, 38, *39*, *40*.
Zygote, 16.
Zymase, 410.

SCIENTIFIC MEMOIRS

Edited by JOSEPH S. AMES, Ph.D., Johns Hopkins University

THE FREE EXPANSION OF GASES. Memoirs by Gay-Lussac, Joule, and Joule and Thomson. Edited by Dr. J. S. Ames. $0.75.

PRISMATIC AND DIFFRACTION SPECTRA. Memoirs by Joseph von Fraunhofer. Edited by Dr. J. S. Ames. $0.60.

RÖNTGEN RAYS. Memoirs by Röntgen, Stokes, and J. J. Thomson. Edited by Dr. George F. Barker. $0.60.

THE MODERN THEORY OF SOLUTION. Memoirs by Pfeffer, Van't Hoff, Arrhenius, and Raoult. Edited by Dr. H. C. Jones. $1.00.

THE LAWS OF GASES. Memoirs by Boyle and Amagat. Edited by Dr. Carl Barus. $0.75.

THE SECOND LAW OF THERMODYNAMICS. Memoirs by Carnot, Clausius, and Thomson. Edited by Dr. W. F. Magie. $0.90.

THE FUNDAMENTAL LAWS OF ELECTROLYTIC CONDUCTION. Memoirs by Faraday, Hittorf, and Kohlrausch. Edited by Dr. H. M. Goodwin. $0.75.

THE EFFECTS OF A MAGNETIC FIELD ON RADIATION. Memoirs by Faraday, Kerr, and Zeeman. Edited by Dr. E. P. Lewis. $0.75.

THE LAWS OF GRAVITATION. Memoirs by Newton, Bouguer, and Cavendish. Edited by Dr. A. S. Mackenzie. $1.00.

THE WAVE THEORY OF LIGHT. Memoirs by Huygens, Young, and Fresnel. Edited by Dr. Henry Crew. $1.00.

THE DISCOVERY OF INDUCED ELECTRIC CURRENTS. Vol. I. Memoirs by Joseph Henry. Edited by Dr. J. S. Ames. $0.75.

THE DISCOVERY OF INDUCED ELECTRIC CURRENTS. Vol. II. Memoirs by Michael Faraday. Edited by Dr. J. S. Ames. $0.75.

THE FOUNDATIONS OF STEREO-CHEMISTRY. Memoirs by Pasteur, Le Bel, and Van't Hoff, together with selections from later memoirs by Wislicenus, and others. Edited by Dr. G. M. Richardson. $1.00.

THE EXPANSION OF GASES. Memoirs by Gay-Lussac and Regnault. Edited by Prof. W. W. Randall. $1.00.

RADIATION AND ABSORPTION. Memoirs by Prévost, Balfour Stewart, Kirchhoff and Kirchhoff and Bunsen. Edited by Dr. DeWitt B. Brace. $1.00.

AMERICAN BOOK COMPANY

INTRODUCTION TO POLITICAL SCIENCE

By JAMES WILFORD GARNER, Ph. D., Professor of Political Science, University of Illinois

$2.50

THIS systematic treatise on the science of government covers a wider range of topics on the nature, origin, organization, and functions of the state than is found in any other college textbook published in the English language. The unusually comprehensive treatment of the various topics is based on a wide reading of the best literature on the subject in English, German, French, and Italian, and the student has opportunity to profit by this research work through the bibliographies placed at the head of each chapter, as well as by means of many additional references in the footnotes.

¶ An introductory chapter is followed by chapters on the nature and essential elements of the state; on the various theories concerning the origin of the state; on the forms of the state; on the forms of government, including a discussion of the elements of strength and weakness of each; on sovereignty, its nature, its essential characteristics, and its abiding place in the state; on the functions and sphere of the state, including the various theories of state activity; and on the organization of the state. In addition there are chapters on constitutions, their nature, forms, and development; on the distribution of the powers of government; on the electorate; and on citizenship and nationality.

¶ Before stating his own conclusions the author gives an impartial discussion of the more important theories of the origin, nature, and functions of the state, and analyzes and criticises them in the light of the best scientific thought and practice. Thus the pupil becomes familiar with the history of the science as well as with its principles as recognized to-day.

AMERICAN BOOK COMPANY

EDUCATION IN THE UNITED STATES

Edited by NICHOLAS MURRAY BUTLER, President of Columbia University, in the City of New York

$2.50

THE frequently expressed need for a book giving a complete view of American education in outline is satisfactorily met in this volume entitled "Education in the United States."

¶ The volume consists of the twenty careful monographs, each written by an eminent specialist, on various phases of American education, which were originally planned as part of the American educational exhibit at the International Expositions held at Paris in 1900 and at St. Louis in 1904.

¶ The introduction by the editor sets forth the underlying principles governing American educational activity to the present time. Among the authors of the various monographs are: Commissioner Draper of the State of New York, the late Dr. William T. Harris, formerly Commissioner of Education of the United States, Dr. Elmer Ellsworth Brown, Dr. Harris's successor in the Commissionership, Professor Edward Delavan Perry of Columbia University, Professor Andrew F. West of Princeton University, President M. Carey Thomas of Bryn Mawr College, etc., etc.

¶ The subjects of the monographs include such important topics as Educational Organization and Administration, Training of Teachers, School Architecture and Hygiene, Professional Education, Education of Defectives, and Summer Schools and University Extension.

¶ For the benefit of teachers, reading circles, and classes in universities, colleges and normal schools, each monograph will be published separately at 20 cents and will be furnished in quantities at $15.00 per hundred (net).

AMERICAN BOOK COMPANY

ON METEOROLOGY

ELEMENTARY METEOROLOGY $1.50
By FRANK WALDO, Ph.D., late Junior Professor in the United States Signal Service

IN this book, embodying the latest phases of the science, and the most approved methods of teaching, the treatment, as far as practicable, is inductive. The fact that meteorology is largely an observational study is kept constantly in mind. The student is introduced to rational methods of investigation, and taught to observe weather conditions, to account intelligently for successive changes in the weather, and to make intelligent predictions for himself. Special chapters are devoted to the meteorology of the United States, in which the work of the Weather Bureau is clearly explained. The charts and illustrations are an important feature.

OBSERVATIONS AND EXERCISES ON THE WEATHER $0.30
By JAMES A. PRICE, A.M., Instructor in Physiography in High School, Fort Wayne, Ind.

THIS laboratory manual is intended to supplement the recitation work in physical geography and meteorology in secondary schools. It consists of a blank weather record covering forty days, to be filled in by the pupil from his own observations of the thermometer, barometer, hygrometer, weather gauge, clouds, winds, etc. Following these tables is a series of ingeniously devised exercises whereby the pupil, from the observation and study of his weather record, is led to deduce many of the general principles of meteorology. The instruments necessary for the observations are few and inexpensive.

AMERICAN BOOK COMPANY

AN ELEMENTARY TEXT-BOOK OF THEORETICAL MECHANICS

By GEORGE A. MERRILL, B.S., Principal of the California School of Mechanical Arts, and Director of the Wilmerding School of Industrial Arts, San Francisco

$1.50

MERRILL'S MECHANICS is intended for the upper classes in secondary schools, and for the two lower classes in college. Only a knowledge of elementary algebra, plane geometry, and plane trigonometry is required for a thorough comprehension of the work.

¶ By presenting only the most important principles and methods, the book overcomes many of the difficulties now encountered by students in collegiate courses who take up the study of analytic mechanics, without previously having covered it in a more elementary form. It treats the subject without the use of the calculus, and consequently does not bewilder the beginner with much algebraic matter, which obscures the chief principles.

¶ The book is written from the standpoint of the student in the manner that experience has proved to be the one most easily grasped. Therefore, beyond a constant endeavor to abide by the fundamental precepts of teaching, no one method of presentation has been used to the exclusion of others. The few necessary experiments are suggested and outlined, but a more complete laboratory course can easily be supplied by the instructor.

¶ The explanation of each topic is followed by a few well-chosen examples to fix and apply the principles involved. A number of pages are devoted to the static treatment of force, with emphasis on the idea of action and reaction. Four-place tables of the natural trigonometric functions are included.

AMERICAN BOOK COMPANY

DESCRIPTIVE CATALOGUE OF HIGH SCHOOL AND COLLEGE TEXT-BOOKS

Published Complete and in Sections

WE issue a Catalogue of High School and College Text-Books, which we have tried to make as valuable and as useful to teachers as possible. In this catalogue are set forth briefly and clearly the scope and leading characteristics of each of our best text-books. In most cases there are also given testimonials from well-known teachers, which have been selected quite as much for their descriptive qualities as for their value as commendations.

¶ For the convenience of teachers this Catalogue is also published in separate sections treating of the various branches of study. These pamphlets are entitled: English, Mathematics, History and Political Science, Science, Modern Languages, Ancient Languages, and Philosophy and Education.

¶ In addition we have a single pamphlet devoted to Newest Books in every subject.

¶ Teachers seeking the newest and best books for their classes are invited to send for our Complete High School and College Catalogue, or for such sections as may be of greatest interest.

¶ Copies of our price lists, or of special circulars, in which these books are described at greater length than the space limitations of the catalogue permit, will be mailed to any address on request.

¶ All correspondence should be addressed to the nearest of the following offices of the company: New York, Cincinnati, Chicago, Boston, Atlanta, San Francisco.

AMERICAN BOOK COMPANY

To avoid fine, this book should be returned on
or before the date last stamped below

OCT 18

CPSIA information can be obtained
at www.ICGtesting.com
Printed in the USA
LVOW13s1824050818
586019LV00050B/178/P